DON'T CRY FOR ME, ARGENTINA

Despite all the adverse reaction to her presence in Buenos Aires, Madonna felt comfortable. On one occasion, a journalist from a local newspaper was allowed to watch one of her tango lessons. After it was over, the reporter approached her.

"Do you get the impression that this is a macho society?" the journalist asked.

Like a true ambassador of good will, Madonna answered without hesitating. "Women of Argentina are treated well because Eva Peron was the champion of women's rights, and that's something I can relate to."

"Eva Peron is often called a whore and an opportunist," the journalist challenged the star.

"Either she was called a saint or a prostitute," Madonna replied, "which is what I am called by everyone, because of my name and because I'm in touch with my own sexuality. It's the obvious way to put a woman down, to call her a whore and imply that she has no morals and no integrity and no talent. And God knows, I can relate to that, too."

Days later, when asked his impressions of Madonna, the journalist thought for a moment before saying, "She is fascinating because she is so self-involved. Everything is 'me' or 'I' or whatever she can 'relate to' based on her own life. In mind and soul, she embodies Eva Peron!"

BARBARA VICTOR

GODDESS

HarperEntertainment
An Imprint of HarperCollinsPublishers

HarperEntertainment
An Imprint of HarperCollins*Publishers*
10 East 53rd Street
New York, New York 10022-5299

Copyright © 2001 by Barbara Victor
Cover photo copyright © AP Photo/Jonas Ekstromer
ISBN: 0-06-103113-5

First HarperEntertainment paperback printing: August 2002
First Cliff Street Books hardcover printing: November 2001

HarperCollins®, HarperEntertainment™, ™, are trademarks of HarperCollins Publishers Inc.

Printed in the United States of America

Visit HarperEntertainment on the World Wide Web at
www.harpercollins.com

10 9 8 7 6 5 4 3 2 1

For Gérard

contents

acknowledgments

·····················

One of the more unpleasant aspects of writing an unauthorized star biography is getting up every morning for more than a year with the realization that the majority of the people you want and need to talk to will do everything in their power to avoid you. It is a daunting challenge from the onset, and if the author is fortunate enough to find a few brave friends, business associates, and colleagues of the subject who are willing to speak on record, the rewards are great. And, if those friends, associates, and relatives speak out of admiration and affection, it is possible for the author to write a balanced portrait of the star and an impartial account of her life. As it concerns *Goddess,* while the bruises on my forehead remain from butting up against stone walls, I was also fortunate to have talked to many extraordinary and important people in Madonna's life. Thanks to Tony and Joan Ciccone for their warmth and hospitality when I visited them at their vineyard. Thanks as well to Elsie Fortin, who left no doubt as to her loving feelings toward her most famous granddaughter. Thanks to Patrick Hernandez and Muriel Van Lieu, who received me at a difficult moment in their lives, immediately after the untimely death of Jean Van Lieu. Many of the people interviewed for this book, however, agreed to talk to me on the condition that I change their names or simply quote them without attribution, which, in these cases, I have done. My gratitude goes to everyone who was courageous and generous enough to spend time with me, those cited as well as those who asked to remain anonymous. In either case, their input, knowledge, and generosity are appreciated.

I am also grateful to Carol Dickey for her invaluable help in organizing all the source and bibliography material; Tom Freeman and Mary Troath for their research on both sides of the Atlantic; Jacques Blache for sharing his knowledge about the music business; Boris Hoffman for all his kindness; Chris Dickey for his understanding about certain hostage situations; John Baxter for his unique humor about films and their stars; Mike Nolan for making Bay City a fun place to visit; the gang at HarperCollins, most especially Marjorie Braman and Leslie Engel. For my friends who are my family—Barbara Gordon, Dmitri Nabokov, Charlotte Rampling, Robert Nathan, Jean Noel Tassez, Thierry Billand, Heather Keller, Patrick Wajsman, Howard Schreiber, Brigitte Jessen, John Michel, and Danièle Mazengarbe—you all know how much I appreciate and value you. Also, thanks to Roberto Cerea and Franck de Paolo for all their understanding. My deep gratitude goes to Dov Zaidman.

It is great having an editor who is smart *and* funny. I've been very lucky to have been able to work with Diane Reverand, my editor and my friend, who always "gets it" regardless of how inarticulate the words may sound. Thank you, Diane, for making everything seem so easy and for being so available and supportive. Thanks as well to Tom Wallace, who brought me back in so many ways. And, finally, to Gérard, who was solid throughout this project and who has finally admitted that he didn't lose a wife as much as he gained an office during all my long absences across the Atlantic.

It's hard letting go but it's even better moving on. . . .

author's note
·················

*I*n 1993 a French magazine in Paris asked me to do an article about Madonna in the aftermath of her book, *Sex,* and her album *Erotica,* both of which came out in the fall of 1992. My interest in her had been limited to reading the occasional magazine piece or listening to the random song on the car radio. As I began looking for an original angle to my story, I learned that Madonna had an impressive twentieth-century art collection that included several important paintings by Tamara de Lempicka and Frida Kahlo. Only when I saw photographs of those particular works did I find myself intrigued by Madonna.

What fascinated me about her art collection was that several of the paintings by de Lempicka and Kahlo were so strikingly similar to certain photographs that had been taken of the star during different phases of her career that she might almost have modeled for the artists. Not only did Madonna embody those images painted on canvas decades before—either in her various bondage poses or when she flirted with lesbianism—but the paintings recalled several of the images Madonna had adopted during her rise to fame. De Lempicka works, for instance, depict a woman who is liberated well before her time. In one autobiographical canvas, de Lempicka, wearing an art-deco racing helmet, is driving a sports car, her boyish allure similar to that of Madonna who poses with a whip in her video "Erotica." In another work entitled *Printemps,* de Lempicka is locked in an embrace with another woman, not unlike Madonna and a

girlfriend seen kissing in Madonna's book, *Sex.* In a work by
Frida Kahlo that hangs in Madonna's New York apartment,
the artist has painted herself wearing a metal corset with
protruding nails that is meant to support her damaged spine.
Similarly, Madonna poses in a Jean-Paul Gaultier corset
made of black rubber trimmed in lace.

Madonna and Frida Kahlo have other similarities in addition to the singer's ability to imitate some of Kahlo's poses
on her canvases. Both women attack their respective artistic
media in very literal ways. To convey sadness, the artist
paints herself crying; to show physical suffering, she paints
herself bleeding; and to portray death, she paints corpses.
Much like Madonna, who has little sense of metaphor in her
work and whose music and lyrics depict specific incidents in
her life, Kahlo's paintings are also autobiographical.
Kahlo's art graphically tells the story of her struggle with
childhood polio as well as her unhappy marriage to the celebrated artist Diego Rivera, who constantly deceived her.
Madonna's videos graphically project her erotic feelings
about Christ or her obsession about death. Madonna, like
Frida Kahlo, is one of the few artists who has managed to in-
corporate self-pity and her own sad memories into her work
so cleverly that the public interprets it as being privy to her
private life.

The question that occurred to me was whether Madonna's
choice of art was indicative of a pattern. Was her taste in literature, music, and film dependent on her ability to identify
with or to transform herself into the character or subject
found in certain creative works of those whom she admired?
And if so, how big a role did her lack of cultural objectivity
have in her own success?

Her conflicts with Catholicism have repeatedly appeared
in her songs, since the story she tells is always faintly or blatantly autobiographical. In her videos, the plot seems to reflect an incident in her life, while in her stage shows she has
often invested in a borrowed identity from a historical figure
or movie star. After all that she has accomplished and de-

spite her attempts to present herself as a sexually liberated woman with a formidable intellect, the melancholy memories of her difficult childhood remain a very present and emotional aspect of her personality. To overcome some of the trauma she endured as a child, she has used illusion to guarantee her own psychic survival and sheer guts to claw her way to the top. An autodidact, she is the ideal audience for self-help books, alternative medicine, ancient mystical teachings, and New Age philosophy. Twenty-two years after she left her hometown of Bay City, Michigan, Madonna remains steeped in her middle-class, Middle American background. Armed with new props and toys, she is a curious combination of the spiritually healed twenty-first-century feminist and the tormented Catholic girl of the 1950s, yet another variation of her basic Madonna/Whore complex.

For more than a century, it has been fashionable to define the route to success in the entertainment business as a combination of ambition, talent, opportunity, and dreams. For Madonna, that definition needs to be rewritten. Though she is indeed ambitious, talented, and has certainly seized every opportunity presented to her, she has never been a dreamer. Rather than dreams, Madonna has goals. Pragmatic, demanding, disciplined, and controlling, she perceives the world of make-believe through her own subjective vision much as she views the works of others based on the similarities to her own life. And yet, despite her genius for changing her image, transforming old ideas and used concepts to fit her own style, Madonna has never mastered the art of fantasy. Her originality is in her ability to convince her fans that the story she tells is autobiographical. By making herself accessible to her public, she enables them to identify with the words she sings or lyrics she writes and encourages them to follow her example—that if she has survived, so can they. There are staunch Madonna fans who believe that her music is indicative of her growth, that it speaks to several generations of both genders and all sexual persuasions. They are convinced that Madonna's music is a barometer of the changing times, from the 1980s to the present, and that her success is in her range of composition, her ability to move from style to style without losing her audience.

From 1984, when she first appeared on the music scene with *Madonna, The First Album,* a collection of innocent popular songs, lighthearted lyrics repeated over an endlessly repeating beat, until today, seventeen years later, when *Music* appeared, a combination of French electronica, influenced by such groups as Air and Daft Punk, and more soulful folk songs, she has proven that she can outlast and outsell the new wave of young performers. Madonna has said that when she started out there was more personal expression in pop music, that unlike today, it reflected less of an organic nature of the business. More than expression, Madonna relies on self-expression and her ability to understand the unspoken thoughts and desires of her fans. Throughout her music career, Madonna's lyrics have not only matched her mood, looks, and style, they have also allowed her public to become part of the new trends and tastes in popular songs by making sure they could identify with the words even more than the tunes. It was, therefore, no coincidence that she decided to collaborate with Mirwais Ahmadzai, a thirty-nine-year-old Frenchman of North African descent, who has tremendous experience in the world of disco-punk. Mirwais, who produced *Music,* is an unconventional musician who has managed to combine and save the folk-pop realm from the late 1970s with the drum and bass of the new wave of electronic music. With Madonna, Mirwais found that he had created a new form of electronic music. "The big problem for instrumental electronic music," Mirwais explains, "is that you could do great music, but if you want to transfer complex feelings, sometimes with three words you can communicate more than with three hours of electronica. I think in electronic music we have arrived at this stage where a lot of people like songs—we are not frightened by the song. Ten years ago, a lot of people that love rock or pop music wouldn't listen to an electronic song; they'd think it's awful or horrible. Today, it's everywhere in the culture, and a lot of people are ready to listen to this music. The problem now is the instrumental format is too constraining, too small. I wanted to communicate more complex feeling." By collaborating with Madonna, Mirwais found the perfect partner, a singer whose voice would not overpower the instrumental and whose lyrics were vast in their emotional spectrum, yet contained in their complexity and length of phrase.

Madonna sings about incest, bisexuality, religion, love, death, and motherhood and is at her best when she makes the world believe that there is no difference between the on-stage and offstage Madonna. The dilemma when Madonna's music is discussed, however, is that her songs depend on many people other than herself. Though she writes the words and the melody and often the chord sequences, the majority of her recordings are collaborations with other songwriters, which makes it difficult to identify what Madonna's contribution is as opposed to the others involved in any song. Her success is in her ability to move effortlessly, as she has done, from dance music to party music, from pop music to music that was clearly influenced by the 1960s to writing lyrics that dealt with her own very personal torments and tragedies. In 1989, with the release of *Erotica*, Madonna made the transition from a singles artist to one that also garnered a large share of the album market, just as in 1990, with her *Like a Prayer* album, she made the transition from objective lyricist and singer to a performer who guaranteed that every song was autobiographical.

In an article published in *Vanity Fair* in December 2000, the point was made that Madonna's singer-songwriting-producing abilities have never been given their proper due. In response, Madonna said, "I feel that I've been given respect in the world of music. Well, maybe not. I mean I don't know. I don't really pay attention. I gave up looking for respect from people a long time ago. You just have to do what you want to do."

If respect has eluded her, it is because she has always concentrated on style over content, which in itself is ironic since there has never been a more successful performer in the music business whose music has been the subject of so little review and analysis.

In 1993, Madonna was an established singing star and composer with more than 60 million albums sold throughout the world, thirty-nine single recordings released in the United States, all of which had made the *Billboard* Hot 100 Singles Chart. In fact, for the previous ten years, since 1984, with the exception of 1988 when she didn't release a new record, she had always placed in the Top 10 and had sixteen gold singles, the second highest for any female singer, trailing only Janet Jackson, who had eighteen.

She had also been branded by the press as everything from a teen pop sensation whose "career would be short-lived" to a pro-feminist, from an antifeminist to an exhibitionist to a heretical ex-Christian. In 1990, *Forbes* magazine had estimated her pretax income to be in excess of $39 million and her earnings since 1986 to be more than $800 million with a net worth conservatively estimated in 1994 to be over $250 million. She owned a nine-room apartment on Central Park West and homes in Miami and Beverly Hills. In 1992, along with Freddy DeMann, who had once managed Michael Jackson and who had been her manager since July 1983, Madonna launched her own record company, Maverick, which, after a slow beginning, eventually became the sole international distributor for over 100 million copies of her own albums. Shortly afterward, Madonna added two other divisions, Mad Guy Television and Mad Guy Films, to her corporate holdings. When she claimed that she "ran around like a chicken without a head," it was no exaggeration. She was very much involved in the management of the television and film companies along with Guy Oseary, a twenty-five-year-old Israeli native whom she hired because of his skills as a marketing expert. Her life was organized and meticulous, and her days were divided into segments of fifteen minutes to one hour, including two hours that were set aside every morning for personal calls to friends, managers, lawyers, and publicists. She had taken only three vacations in the past fifteen years, and even on vacation she scheduled her leisure activities to avoid becoming anxious.

It was not difficult to feel overwhelmed by Madonna. When I finally met her in 1993 to interview her for my article, my first concern was to create a complicity that could somehow be objective in its focus. Almost immediately an unspoken agreement developed between us: every question and answer was couched in cultural or literary terms. It was a game of sorts, and one that she clearly enjoyed playing. As a result, she discussed her feelings and memories in terms of those movies, books, or poems she had most identified with during different stages of her life.

As a child, she recalled that her favorite film had been *To Kill a Mockingbird,* less because she identified with the child in the movie, Scout, than because she saw similarities between her own father and Atticus Finch, the character portrayed by Gregory Peck. According to Madonna, Atticus Finch, like her father, was an ethical man who applied decent principles and sound good sense to everything he did. Both men were committed to justice, honesty, and were quick to come to the defense of the underdog. But perhaps the difference between the two men, a point that Madonna failed to mention, had the most profound effect upon her life. Atticus Finch's morality was founded on a folksy, small-town, good-neighbor mentality that made him an exception to the others in his environment. Her father's sense of right and wrong was steeped in the Catholic religion and his determination not to waver from the rules.

When Madonna was only five, her mother, at thirty-one, died of breast cancer. Her death became the central event in the singer's early childhood. Not only did she carry with her the trauma of her mother's death, but also her name, the implication of which is the Blessed Mother, the virgin mother of God. By using Catholic iconography, transgression, and prayer imagery, the singer even managed to transform the

Madonna from an asexual and passive figure into a woman with erotic potential, a theme that has recurred in the singer's work as fantasy as well as in her life as reality.

After her father remarried, Madonna made her first transformation into a mythical character. She became Cinderella. In what would become a pattern, she adapted the storybook figure to fit her own personality. Unlike Cinderella, Madonna rebelled. Unlike the mistreated stepchild, she had a big mouth. She answered back. She was disrespectful. "I didn't resent having to raise my brothers and sisters as much as I resented not having my mother," she explained.

When she entered college, Madonna first became aware of the poet Anne Sexton. After reading "Double Image," she drew a parallel between the poet's words and her mother's death from breast cancer.

> On the first of September she looked at me and said I
>   gave her cancer.
> They carved her sweet hills out and still I couldn't answer.

Madonna found that the words of Sexton's poem reflected her own sense of guilt over her mother's death. "My earliest memories of my mother," Madonna says, "is of someone who was kind and good, so I never understood why she was taken away so young. If my mother wasn't guilty of something, then I began to think that I must be guilty, and that it was my fault she died."

Madonna continued to compare her life with various works of literature. She recalled that after she arrived in New York on her twentieth birthday, seeking stardom, she discovered *The Bell Jar* by Sylvia Plath, in which the author described her own traumatic experiences as a new arrival there: "Look what can happen in this country, they'd say, a girl lives in some out of the way town for nineteen years . . . and ends up steering New York like her own private car. Only I wasn't steering anything, not even myself . . . I couldn't get myself to react. I felt very still and very empty; the way the eye of a tornado must feel, moving dully along in the middle of the surrounding hullabaloo."

Years later, after Madonna's marriage to Sean Penn ended in divorce, when her hope of re-creating her parents' happy, albeit brief, union had been dashed, she admitted that the film based on Michael Ondaatje's novel *The English Patient* had had a profound effect on her. She was especially moved by the scene in which the character played by Ralph Fiennes makes his way across a desert to get help for the woman he loves. "To be loved like that," Madonna said, "or to love someone that way . . ."

There is no doubt that the artistic works that have made the biggest impression on Madonna are the ones that address the five pivotal incidents in her life—the death of her mother, her father's remarriage, her quest for fame and fortune in New York, her own marriage and divorce, the birth of her two children, and above all, her ongoing dilemma as a woman in moral conflict.

After watching all of Madonna's films and videos, I found a distinct difference in her styles. When she is acting or singing in a production of her own creation, she draws from her own experiences, either real or imagined, as an inspiration for her many images, personae, and disguises. When she portrays a character someone else has created, she consistently relies on mimicry and on her ability to transform herself physically to resemble the character she is playing. Rather than questioning Madonna's lack of fantasy, I suddenly found myself wondering if her need to identify with every work of art or every fictional and nonfictional character she portrays reflects a highly developed pragmatism and not merely an overdeveloped sense of narcissism. Is it necessary for Madonna to make a total transformation in order to give her fans the best performance? And, if so, how does she become that other person? What are her sources of knowledge and energy? Does it come naturally or is it all carefully thought out in advance?

In 1996, I was in Buenos Aires for the city's annual book fair. During that trip, my fascination with Madonna became more focused, and I began to contemplate the notion of writing her biography. After a succession of box-office failures, she had won the role of Eva Perón in Alan Parker's film *Evita*. Coincidentally, I found myself in the Argentine capital at the same time as Madonna and the rest of the cast were on location to film several pivotal scenes from Eva Perón's life. Many of the people I met had met Madonna and even helped her as she set about to meticulously research the life and times of Evita. I was invited by a high-ranking political official to visit the Casa Rosada, where I met and interviewed President Carlos Menem. In another coincidence, I found myself there at the same time as the cast and crew were blocking out the scene in which Madonna, as Eva, sings "Don't Cry for Me Argentina," from the balcony of the presidential residence.

While other actors immerse themselves in a role, Madonna becomes a medium of sorts who channels the spirit of the person she portrays into her own body, taking on that person's identity more for herself than for her audience. What impressed me about her approach to this role was the research she had done to transform herself into a woman who she claimed was her "cosmic soul sister." According to the journalists, actors, politicians, and singers in Buenos Aires who helped her understand Evita, including several who had actually met and befriended the future first lady when she was a radio personality, Madonna watched countless newsreels from the 1950s so that she would be able to capture Evita's facial expressions and gestures. She found out what her favorite food was and ate the same. She pored over old photographs and summoned local seamstresses to re-create the same suits and dresses, borrowed similar pieces of jewelry until she had transformed herself physically into the woman who was still revered as an icon and a saint. Madonna even studied voice for six months before shooting began to improve her vocal range.

One evening at the end of my visit, a group of actors and writers invited me to a well-known tango parlor to see excerpts from the late Astor Piazzolla's *Maria de Buenos Aires*. A commotion at the door signaled the entrance of Madonna, surrounded by an entourage of trainers, assistants, and bodyguards. I found it impossible to be in Buenos Aires and not feel, as Madonna did, the undercurrent of mystery and gothic evil that permeates the city. It was just as impossible not to be aware of the spiritual presence of Eva Perón when I talked to those who had survived the political upheaval of the Dirty War in the 1970s during which a military junta imprisoned and murdered innocent dissidents. The Perón period of the fifties is almost always evoked either as a comparison, reference point, or definition of the soul of Argentina. Listening to the tango music that evening, my fascination with Eva Perón and my newfound curiosity about the actress who seemed to have channeled Evita's spirit and soul allowed me to approach her to talk about her impressions of the city as well as her role in the film. Obviously consumed by the character she was portraying, Madonna began comparing the similarities between her life and Evita's. She talked about Evita's death at thirty-three from inoperable ovarian cancer and about her own mother's death at almost the same age from inoperable breast cancer. Both she and Eva had lost a parent at an early age, suffered the same rejection from their peers and family, used a succession of lovers to achieve their goals, managed to escape from a small town and make their way to a big city where, against all odds, each had achieved international acclaim.

Many months later, I realized some other, more stunning similarities between the two women, traits that enabled me to understand Madonna better than I had before. Each woman encouraged people to dream by allowing them to witness firsthand how the more fortunate lived—poor girl makes good. Both exist in a space somewhere between fantasy and reality. Each woman stimulates desire without necessarily satisfying demand. And finally, perhaps the most relevant parallel between the two is that both, despite all the success and adoration, all the devotion and fame, longed to be recognized as a serious actress.

In 1999, when I began researching my book on Madonna, interviewing family members and friends of her mother's, her own friends, colleagues and business associates, as well as people who had worked with her, I realized the biographical facts were less revealing on their own than they were in the context of the events and the people who had most influenced her and contributed to her success. Not only has Madonna invented biographical details about her life, but most articles written about her repeat the same facts or offer contradictory information. Journalists have systematically made up stories to satisfy the public's prurient interest in the star.

Artists frequently draw from their personal experiences to express themselves in their art, although they tend to sanitize and edit out certain feelings and facts to make their paintings, books, and music palatable for public consumption. Madonna, unlike the vast majority, has exaggerated and sensationalized those experiences that have touched or traumatized her the most. She finds sitting down to be interviewed boring, and to amuse herself, she creates rumors that she ends up denying. Her attention span is short, her sense of discipline and tenacity are evident only when she is in movement, either dancing or singing or creating a sequence in one of her stage shows. Her efforts produce a sound or an image that gives her the incentive and confidence to keep on creating more sounds and images to be used in future performances.

In the nineteenth century, talent and originality were the ingredients that made a star. The impresario of the era was Phineas T. Barnum, a canny showman whose genius was in his instinctive ability not only to recognize talent but also to convince the public that he was merely responding to their demands and desires rather than setting the trends himself. We live in an era in which image rather than talent is crucial, and aberration rather than originality is vital to success. If any superstar of the last two decades has used image and projected aberration, it is Madonna. A self-invented chameleon who, like Barnum, knows which trends and tendencies will ultimately capture the public's attention, she has succeeded in recycling ideas and tailoring them to fit her many different images.

While rebellion against her father and the Catholic Church were once the modus vivendi that catapulted her to fame, her rebellion against herself or the different images she has created for herself is now her raison d'être. Fame to Madonna has become an old lover whose every word, gesture, and technique she knows by heart. Though there is comfort in that kind of familiarity, she seems anxious to offer the public a glimpse of yet another side of her personality. Just as she has orchestrated her career from the beginning by challenging some of the most fundamental issues—religion, God, sex, death, life, and birth—she is currently changing her message from sex to birth, from death to spiritual growth.

During the past few years, Madonna has re-created herself once again, and that change was never more evident than when she appeared on Rosie O'Donnell's show to promote her film *The Next Best Thing*. Madonna, the forty-something single mother of a four-year-old, about to become pregnant with the baby boy she would deliver on August 11, 2000, was dressed smartly in a black Issey Miyake ensemble, her golden hair flowing to her shoulders, her face lightly madeup, her demeanor more coy than carnal. At one point during the program, Rosie ran a tape of Madonna in 1984, one of her first videos in which she appeared wearing the "boy toy" belt. Dressed in crinolines, dozens of chains, charms, and crucifixes draped around her neck, many pierced earrings, white ankle socks and short black boots, Madonna cavorted and danced around the stage. When the clip ended, Madonna responded like an amazed parent who had watched the antics of an adolescent daughter. "What was I thinking?" she asked 20 million spectators. "I mean, can you believe that I used to tie a pair of old tights around my hair?"

The grown-up woman was asking her public to commiserate with her about her rebellious behavior. But then, we are her family, the people from whom she expects unconditional love, the fans who have witnessed her mature as she has passed through all the predictable adolescent stages of anger, frustration, and defiance until she has finally grown up to become a responsible mother. In fact, more than her fans or adoring public, we are all the mother who was taken from her when she was barely six.

In her evolution, Madonna decided to move to London and start a new phase of her life. Unmarried, still sensitive because of her first failure with Sean Penn, having outgrown the subservient male who is all too willing to service her, or in the case of Carlos Leon to impregnate her, determined to excel on another level and, above all, to have another child, Madonna developed a new set of professional priorities when it came to her music as well as personal tastes. Once again, her sense of reality and survivor instinct propelled her to make that decision. From a professional point of view, when she appeared on Rosie O'Donnell's show with Benjamin Bratt to promote *The Next Best Thing,* the reviews had already been abysmal. This time around, the critics had hurt her more deeply than with any of the other negative press she had received for her previously unsuccessful movie ventures. Painfully aware that she was not getting younger, either for motherhood or stardom, Madonna knew that the time had come to reinvent herself once again. One of her spiritual advisers, a lapsed Catholic priest from Los Angeles, described her state of mind. "Madonna believed that Europe revered and admired older women, and in fact, she was very aware that actresses like Catherine Deneuve, Charlotte Rampling, and Isabelle Adjani, for instance, were still considered beautiful and getting roles. She knew that at forty-something, she couldn't keep undressing and prancing around a stage, and she was very sensitive to the ridiculous image of the 'older-woman, younger-man syndrome.' " One of her new friends in London recalled a transatlantic telephone conversation with Madonna long before Guy Ritchie was in her life. Madonna tearfully confessed that it was getting "harder and harder to find a guy that she wanted to go out with and have a relationship with." The friend continued, "She said it was like high school, when she had this bad reputation before she even lost her virginity. In the States, she had this slutty, vulgar, bad-girl image that she couldn't shake, and because of it, the kind of men she wanted just didn't take her seriously."

Shortly after she arrived in London with her daughter, Lourdes, Madonna called a press conference during which she explained that she was a changed woman. She attributed her past rebellion to the trauma she had experienced after her mother's death. Having a child had made it possible to make peace with her past. Her intention was to fall in love and eventually have another baby.

Her meeting Guy Ritchie, the British movie director, their affair, the birth of their son, Rocco, and their marriage in Scotland are all part of Madonna's current incarnation as the proper English wife and mother. It is difficult to imagine that her new English accent, classic Prada wardrobe, Manolo Blahnik mules, and $10 million house in the trendy West End of London means that her life has become static.

From The Madonna to Cinderella, from Marilyn to Evita, from the small-town girl to the woman who captured the attention of millions to become an icon of the last two decades, it is unlikely that she won't surprise us again.

After Madonna finished filming *Evita* in Buenos Aires, a messenger from the Casa Rosada dropped off a package for her at her hotel. It was a gift from President Menem, Eva Perón's autobiography, entitled *La Razón de mi vida,* or *The Reason for My Life*. Enclosed was a note written in English and signed by the president, explaining that, for many years, the book had been compulsory reading in every grammar school and was, in fact, still considered as sacred as the Bible by many adults. If one particular phrase had captured people's imaginations, the note continued, it appeared at the end. "I will return," Evita had written, "and I will be millions."

Once again, Eva Perón's words reflected Madonna's sentiments.

GODDESS

part one

....

Don't Cry for Me Argentina

chapter one
....

On October 13, 1995, Madonna landed at Heathrow Airport aboard a late-night Concorde under an assumed name. She was in London to begin working on the most crucial phase of production for the film *Evita,* a role that would prove to be her greatest screen success and one which she had coveted for more than ten years.

Dressed in black with dark glasses covering her face, she walked hurriedly toward passport control. No advance publicity had signaled her arrival at Heathrow, and therefore no screaming public or photographers' flashing lights greeted her. Only one lonely fan with a throwaway Kodak camera waited politely at the baggage-claim area. Madonna allowed him to snap several shots before she continued briskly on her way.

Alan Parker, the director of *Evita* and most famous for his movie *Fame,* had summoned Madonna and her two leading men, Antonio Banderas, who was to play Che, and Jonathan Pryce, the British stage actor who would portray Juan Perón, to London to record the score for the film. The idea was that the three principal members of the cast would spend approximately four months recording different versions of the thirty-one songs, ranging from loud and dramatic to smaller and more restrained, before a single reel of film was shot. When they were finished, Parker would choose the rendition he liked best, and the one he would visualize when he was actually filming the corresponding scenes. It was an enormous challenge for Madonna since *Evita,* more than mere musical theater, was operatic in sound and style. She knew it would be the first time she would sing without benefit of extravagant sets, costumes, and seductive dance steps that detracted from the thin quality of her voice. In 1995, instead of embarking on a tour to promote her album *Bedtime Stories,* she studied voice with Joan Leder, one of the best coaches in the industry, for six months before production actually began. The end result was that Madonna not only mastered the complicated musical written by Andrew Lloyd Webber and Tim Rice, but also developed an upper register that she never knew she possessed. In fact, during the six months that she trained with Leder, Madonna wrote two songs, "One More Chance" and "You'll See," for her *Something to Remember* album. She was now utilizing techniques that she had learned during her voice lessons. While Alan Parker had complete confidence in his star, Andrew Lloyd Webber wondered if she would be willing to forget her star status and work to improve her voice. In her defense, Alan Parker said, "She was determined to sing it as Andrew had scored it. I was sure that she was going to knock people's socks off. In the end, I was right because she was quite incredible."

Curiously, Joan Leder found Madonna to be "surprisingly shy." "I work clients back-to-back," Leder explained, "and Madonna always felt that Patti LuPone, who had done the role on Broadway, or Roberta Flack, another one of my clients, always had their ear to the door."

Training her voice was not the only challenge Madonna faced when she arrived in London to record. Parker also expected her to grasp the emotions that went along with each song and conjure them up at will. On more than one occasion in the West End recording studios, she would dim the lights and burn candles to create an "ethereal" atmosphere in order to feel "Evita's pain, frustration, or joy." In the end, she exceeded even her own expectations, although she considered the whole experience "humbling." It was no secret that from the very beginning, either Patti LuPone or Elaine Paige had been Webber and Rice's first choice to portray Eva Perón.

If Madonna succeeded in mastering the part, Alan Parker also achieved as difficult an accomplishment when, on December 24, 1995, he finally closed the deal to bring *Evita* to the screen. Optioned by such international directors as Ken Russell, Franco Zeffirelli, Herb Ross, Richard Attenborough, Alan Pakula, Hector Babenco, Francis Ford Coppola, and Oliver Stone, *Evita* had lingered in development hell for more than fifteen years. Despite their different styles and visions of how they would film *Evita,* they had all considered Madonna the obvious choice to play the second-rate Argentine actress who had risen from obscurity and poverty to become an international political icon. They had not been able to convince the studios and producers to accept Madonna's demands concerning salary as well as her suggestions that the composer and lyricist write additional songs for her. Another problem they shared was their inability to secure permission from the Argentine government to film the movie on location in Buenos Aires. From the beginning of every negotiation, it had always been a question of money. The government of Argentina expected to be paid by the movie studio for their cooperation in blocking off streets and allowing unlimited access to the various buildings and monuments throughout the city. In each case, the demands of the government were considered unreasonable by the producers and studios.

Alan Parker had the most recognizable directorial style when it came to musicals, partly because of his experience with *Fame* and partly because he had begun his career making television commercials set to music. By the time he was at the helm, Andrew Lloyd Webber and Tim Rice considered Madonna to be a bad box-office risk. With the exception of her first screen venture in 1985 in *Desperately Seeking Susan,* she had had a string of bad films to her credit, including *Shanghai Surprise, Who's That Girl,* and probably the most embarrassing of all with a cringe factor off the charts, *Body of Evidence.* Typical of Madonna, who always wants the man who rejects her or that deal that eludes her, when she heard that the role was slipping out of her grasp, she became even more determined to play the former first lady of Argentina. In a desperate attempt to secure the role, she wrote Parker a letter and sent it along with her video "Take a Bow," which she claimed had been inspired by Eva Perón and the "way she dressed." The video, made in 1995, was filmed in sepia and filled with scenes of Latin iconography; a finger pierced by a needle, a drop of blood falling into a drink. Madonna is in the stands watching a bullfight. Wearing a 1940s outfit with a veil covering her face, she compares the process of dressing herself to the toreador being fitted into his tight brocade jacket and satin pants to appear in the ring. The clip cuts from Madonna in the stands to Madonna in bed, wearing only sexy underwear, and writhing in what appears to be a masturbatory frenzy.

"I remember sitting down and writing an impassioned letter to Alan Parker," Madonna recalls, "listing the reasons why I was the only one who could portray Eva." She told Parker that she felt a "supernatural drive to play the part." She concluded, "I can honestly say that I did not write this letter of my own free will. It was as if some other force drove my hand across the page." She ended the letter by saying that fortune-tellers had been predicting for years that she would one day play Eva Perón on the screen.

Within days, Parker called Madonna and arranged for her to audition for Andrew Lloyd Webber and Tim Rice. Although the composer and lyricist were pleasantly surprised by Madonna's physical resemblance to Evita, they used that point against her by expressing their concern that her level of celebrity might eclipse the personality of Eva Perón. "Could she be contained," Webber asked, "in such a controlled atmosphere as moviemaking? After all, there were budgets to consider and a time frame that allowed no room for star temperament or caprice." Andy Vajna, the producer on *Evita* when Robert Stigwood had the film, and the producer as well for Alan Parker, recalled that he was concerned because "here was this pop icon and we weren't sure what we were getting involved in." As a result, Vajna called Penny Marshall, who had directed Madonna in *A League of Their Own,* and asked how she was to work with. According to Vajna, Marshall told him, "You don't have to worry about anything."

When Webber and Rice were still not convinced, Alan Parker made the point that despite her previous track record, she was still one of the few female stars who could attract large crowds at the box office, and Hollywood musicals, with the exception of *Grease,* which had appeared in 1978, were almost always losing propositions. In the end, they relented, and Parker closed the deal. Madonna would star as Eva Perón for a fee of $1 million. Despite her sense of triumph, Madonna admitted to several close friends that she felt as if she was going into a project with all the "odds stacked against her." On one hand, she had faith that the part would finally catapult her to respectful stardom, while on the other, she felt that everyone was just waiting for her to fail. Only after she had finished recording and was at the stage when she had to lip-synch the songs while actually shooting the scenes did she discover, much to her delight, that the process was similar to making videos. Months later, when the film was finally finished, Madonna breathed a sigh of relief.

"I consider it an act of God that I got *Evita,*" she told Parker. What Madonna did not know at the time was that Alan Parker, like his predecessors, was having problems getting permission from the Argentine government to film certain key scenes on location. He knew that if he was forced to make the movie on a soundstage, he would fail to project the mystical undercurrent of evil that had pervaded Argentina during the Perónist era. Parker didn't tell Madonna she wasn't the only one who would consider it an act of God if the film ever got made.

To make his star feel at home and relaxed in her new environment, Alan Parker had arranged for Tim Rice, the lyricist for *Evita,* to shepherd Madonna around London and to introduce her to interesting people. It was an especially happy time for Tim Rice, not only because *Evita* was finally going into production, but also because Rice had four musicals running in theaters in Los Angeles: *Jesus Christ Superstar, Joseph and the Amazing Technicolor Dreamcoat, Chess Moves,* and *Beauty and the Beast.* Even more exciting for Rice, he was in the middle of a collaboration with Elton John for a Broadway production of *Aida.*

As arranged, Rice telephoned Madonna at noon the following day at her hotel and was surprised when his star informed him that for the moment she would not be venturing out in public. After unpacking her Jean-Paul Gaultier wardrobe, she had decided to transform herself into what she imagined was the typical British woman. To achieve that new image before she transformed herself once again into Eva Perón, she had called Gianni Versace in New York and asked him to design a somber tweed suit with a skirt that fell demurely to the knee for her "London incarnation." Until the suit arrived two days later, Madonna hid in her $3,000-a-night penthouse suite at Claridge's.

When Madonna finally received Tim Rice in her hotel suite, she found that they had something in common about their mutual interest in Evita. At the end of her first year of high school, Madonna had been listening to one of her favorite rock stations when the disc jockey had talked about a woman named Eva Perón. Madonna had been fascinated to learn that the wife of Juan Perón had survived poverty to become an inspiration to her country as well as a spiritual and religious icon to her people long after her death. Sitting with Rice in London, Madonna learned that he had also first heard about Evita by chance on the radio. According to Rice, he had been set to do *Jeeves* for the London stage (along with Andrew Lloyd Webber and Alan Ayckbourn, who provided the book and lyrics) when he happened to hear a program on his car radio about Eva Perón, "the poor girl from a shabby suburb of Buenos Aires who had climbed to the top of Argentine politics and society." It was then that the idea for *Evita* had begun to take form and Rice had set out to research the life and death of Eva Perón. In February 1974, Rice had made his first trip down to Buenos Aires to get a sense of the local color and atmosphere, which he would successfully re-create on the stage.

In London with the woman who would re-create the role on the screen, Rice, the consummate gentleman as well as the lyricist who was concerned about his score and his star, squired Madonna around town. Privately, he was convinced that when people knew she was eager to be asked to all the A-list parties and events, his baby-sitting job would be over. Unfortunately, the empty guest book she kept on the glass table in her penthouse suite was a sad indication of her failure to make new friends. She had come to conquer London, and despite her staid tweed suit, no one seemed to be clamoring for her. With pressure mounting to complete the arrangements for the musical score, Tim Rice became increasingly unavailable, and as he did, Madonna became increasingly lonely. With only three weeks left before she was to begin recording, she decided to summon Carlos Leon and her friend Ingrid Casares over to London.

In 1993, Madonna had been seeing her former husband, Sean Penn, Harvey Keitel, John Enos, a nightclub owner, and a minor pop star named Louie Louie. She had also been living with Ingrid Casares in her Hollywood home once owned by Bugsy Siegel, the character that her former boyfriend Warren Beatty had portrayed two years before in his film *Bugsy*. During the time she was with Casares, Madonna admitted to several close friends and even to an Italian journalist that she had finally "found true love at last." Coy about identifying her perfect lover, she was nonetheless seen kissing Casares in several Hollywood restaurants. By the time Casares arrived in London, her place in Madonna's life had settled into that of best friend, close confidante, and trusted business associate. Several years later, Madonna would invest in Liquid, a Miami nightclub, along with Casares and Chris Paciello, a Staten Island man, eventually linked to the Mafia and convicted of murder, who would ultimately end up in a witness protection program.

Carlos Leon, Cuban born and darkly handsome, first caught Madonna's eye at a party in New York in 1993, several years before they actually met and began a relationship. Dan Cortesi, who worked for Madonna from 1992 until 1997 as her advance security person, claims that he was the one who arranged the first formal meeting between the singer and the fitness trainer. Cortesi, forty-two years old, small, with dark curly hair and kinetic gestures and expressions, talked about his experiences working for the star during an interview in New York on June 16, 2001. According to Cortesi, Madonna asked him to find out when Leon jogged through Central Park and make it his business to be there with a message that she wanted to talk to him. "Madonna met Carlos several years before," Cortesi recalls, "but because of her schedule, she didn't hook up with him until 1994 when they were both in New York."

At the time, Carlos Leon worked at Crunch, a franchise of fitness training centers in Manhattan, and lived in his own apartment in the same building as his parents, at Broadway and Ninety-fifth Street, not far from Carmine's restaurant. "Madonna knew that I couldn't catch up to Carlos running because I was out of shape and Carlos has about 3 percent body fat, so she teased me and said that I should hop on one of those police carts if I had to, it didn't matter how I did it, but I had to find him in Central Park," Cortesi says.

Without the help of the police, Cortesi managed to catch up with Leon and give him the message that "a certain person would like to meet you later in the day at the merry-go-round in Central Park. . . . Carlos laughed," Cortesi continues, "but he knew exactly who that person was."

When Cortesi reported back to Madonna, he told her that the message had been delivered and that Carlos Leon would be waiting for her at the designated time at the prearranged place. "She came down to the park and the two of them sat by the merry-go-round alone," Cortesi maintains, "while I waited behind a bench. They talked and laughed and at the end of the meeting, Carlos left and I called the car to come and pick Madonna up to drive her back to her apartment on Central Park West. When she got in the car with me, she told me that she liked him and wanted to see him again."

Madonna invited Carlos to several parties, sports events, and show business functions. Not surprisingly, he was in awe of his new girlfriend and impressed by her world, but at the same time, he was intimidated to find himself mingling with people whose faces he had seen only on the screen or in the press. Despite having been thrown into a crowd that seemed slightly unreal to him, Carlos managed to maintain his equilibrium because he was extremely close to his family, who systematically reminded him that a relationship with an international star was to be viewed only as an ephemeral experience. At the same time, his mother was proud of her son and encouraged him to gain as much experience as he could that might further his aspirations as an actor.

It was no coincidence that Dan Cortesi felt an instant affinity with the young Cuban, since he also came from a modest family. Living in the Bronx and struggling to make a living, it didn't take Cortesi long to discover that both he and Carlos were a couple of poor kids with "street smarts and street morals" who were allowed in for a look at how the rich and famous lived. While Cortesi knew that there was nothing permanent when it came to either his job or a love affair with Madonna, he became genuinely fond of Carlos and eventually protective of him. Developing more than just a kinship for his boss's new love interest, Dan Cortesi felt that Leon understood, as he did, the inequities of life. "We were both poor boys, working kids, who were just waiting to make a score, surrounded by people who dropped enormous sums of money without batting an eye. But Carlos wasn't taken in by all that stuff," Cortesi relates. "Here was this kid, just a street kid, a trainer, and all of a sudden he was on the top of the world and he was scared. He used to come to me before an event and ask me who was going to be there, because basically he hated all those people who air-kissed each other." Cortesi laughs. "And he hated all those little sandwiches and hors d'oeuvres they served but basically he felt comfortable around Madonna. I think he fell in love with her that first day, when he left the merry-go-round."

The couple were together in New York for a brief few months before the relationship was put on hold once again when Madonna left for Los Angeles, and it wasn't until several months later when she finally returned to New York that it resumed on a much more intimate and serious level. There was something extremely kind and sensitive in the way Madonna treated Leon during the first year they were together. She anticipated and understood how uncomfortable he may have felt in her opulent nine-room apartment on Central Park West and Sixty-fourth Street and therefore came to his small flat further uptown to spend the evening. Without exception, she left in the morning before the sun came up, slipping into the car that Cortesi had waiting for her to take her back to her flat. According to Cortesi and what Madonna told him during their early-morning, predawn rides together, one of the things she found so comforting about spending the night at Carlos's was that it reminded her of the unpretentious atmosphere that she had left behind in Bay City so many years before. Perhaps it would have been more correct for Madonna to claim that she never really knew that kind of peace and quiet, since back in Bay City, she had been one of eight children, forced constantly to vie for the attention of her parents. Whether or not it became a game, stepping back into another world, Madonna apparently found it amusing and satisfying to spend time at her lover's apartment and fool the paparazzi that hounded her every time she went out in public. In fact, when Dan Cortesi once parked his beat-up old Pinto, a car that he calls a "skashabonga," in front of Madonna's Central Park apartment, Madonna was so intrigued with the wreck that she instructed Cortesi to drive her in it to the Ninety-fifth Street apartment instead of in the usual Lincoln Town Car. "When Liz Rosenberg, Madonna's manager, found out that we were riding around in my skashabonga," Cortesi laughs, "she was furious. Here's a woman who is aware of everything when it comes to Madonna every minute of the day and she was afraid that if we got into an accident in my car instead of in a car that had been leased by Maverick or Warner Brothers, the insurance wouldn't cover her and Madonna could be sued for millions."

Until Liz Rosenberg spoiled her fun, Madonna would love riding around in the Pinto with the garbage in the backseat, one windshield wiper, and a radio that worked only if it was slammed once to jostle it into sound.

From the moment Madonna returned to New York from Los Angeles and resumed her relationship with Carlos, Dan Cortesi was once again the person who carried messages between the couple and who drove her to Leon's apartment. "Madonna met Carlos's family about a week after she got back," Cortesi says. "The first time she went there, she brought along Rosanna Arquette, one of her best friends, to show the Leon family that she had nice friends, too."

According to Cortesi, one of Madonna's greatest pleasures was to sit around Maria and Armando's kitchen table and drink the rich Cuban espresso that Carlos's mother made. "One thing I really liked about the family," Cortesi continues, "is that they didn't blink, they took Madonna as just another person, a friend of their son, which made Madonna very comfortable."

While Maria Leon may have felt at ease around Madonna, she was less comfortable that her son was in love with a woman whose reputation preceded her, as far as her inability to make a commitment to one man and nurture a relationship that would last forever. Maria Leon made it very clear to Madonna that Carlos was her "baby," and her major concern was not Madonna's stardom but rather that she would treat her younger son properly so that he wouldn't end up hurt and disillusioned. "The mother told Madonna that her son was a very sensitive person," Cortesi says, "and she made it very clear that her first concern was that her baby wouldn't get hurt."

Madonna was attracted to Leon for all the obvious reasons but she was also touched by his innocence and sense of morality and the fact that he wanted to remain a simple person without any particular ambitions to further his own life or career. Yet, Madonna, hyperintuitive and forced to be aware of hidden meanings and unspoken goals even when it came to her closest confidants, was also someone who was attuned to the slightest change in a person based on a word, an expression, or a gesture. It was because of her highly developed sense of survival and her determination to protect herself that Madonna became wary of Carlos's motives. The incident that introduced a certain mistrust into the relationship occurred one night when Madonna asked Carlos a question and apparently got what she considered to be an unsatisfactory reply. "I remember we were together once," Cortesi recalls, "and Madonna asked Carlos, sort of in a joking way, so now that you're going out with me, what happens if you become a big star, will I have to kiss your ass?" According to Cortesi, Carlos Leon's reply put Madonna on her guard. "He told her not to worry, if he ever became a big star, she shouldn't worry about having to kiss his ass."

It was then, again according to Cortesi, that Madonna began enlisting him to follow Carlos and find out all there was to know about his activities when she wasn't around, whether or not he was setting up auditions for himself or if he was talking to photographers or journalists in an effort to further his own career. "Everyone knew he wanted to be an actor," Cortesi continues. "It was no secret, so it wasn't so much that Madonna was jealous of other women," Cortesi continues, "as it was that she just wanted to know everything he did or said to other people. In fact, if anyone was jealous during the relationship, it was Carlos."

Despite Madonna's sporadic misgivings about Carlos and the fact that he was often ill at ease around her friends, the relationship flourished. As the couple saw each other more frequently and it became obvious to everyone close to Madonna that she was becoming more involved and attached to Leon, those same people who had functioned as the singer's closest friends and business associates felt threatened by the Cuban trainer's influence on her. "Madonna had two weak spots back then," Cortesi claims, "having a baby and finding someone who would function as her mother and she viewed Liz Rosenberg as a mother figure."

Rosenberg, who is called the "validator" by the millions of members of Madonna's fan club and who is the woman in charge of every aspect of Madonna's personal and professional life, is about ten years older than the star, married to her second husband and the mother of three children: a son from a former marriage, a daughter from her current husband, and a second daughter whom she and her husband adopted. While there was certainly cause to assume that Madonna was in love with Leon, Liz Rosenberg need not have worried that her illustrious client and close friend was about to change her habits or relinquish her way of life for one that would exclude the coterie of people who surrounded and advised her. Even while Madonna and Carlos were at the height of their love affair, according to Cortesi, she still found time to send her advance security man out with other messages for other men. "One night after Carlos and Madonna went to a Knicks game," Cortesi reports, "she told me to take Carlos home and get in touch with Sam Cassals and bring him to her apartment." Cortesi laughs. "To avoid the paparazzi, I picked up Cassals in the skashabonga and brought him back to the Central Park West apartment. Madonna was obsessed with him."

If Carlos Leon was aware that Madonna was sporadically involved with other men, he was smart enough never to confront her. He made no secret of the fact, however, that Ingrid Casares's constant presence at Madonna's apartment annoyed him. There was one particular incident that upset Leon more than others and that happened during the Fashion

Music Awards in 1994 in New York at the Twenty-third Street Armory. On that evening, Ingrid as usual went along with Madonna and Carlos, as did Chris Paciello, Casares's business partner. When their chauffeured Mercedes pulled up in front of the armory, Liz Rosenberg met them and immediately arranged for Carlos to take his seat in the audience. It was a good thing she did, because within minutes after Carlos left, Sean Penn, accompanied by John Enos, was waiting backstage for Madonna. In the presence of the others, Sean hugged and kissed Madonna and informed her that he would be giving her the award for the most fashionable woman of the year. According to Dan Cortesi, Liz Rosenberg was beside herself with worry that the press or the paparazzi would manage to slip in unnoticed backstage and take photographs of Madonna and Sean with Ingrid and John Enos. Carlos, who was in the audience, was forced to sit quietly while he watched Madonna's former husband, Sean Penn, present the award to Madonna. Instead of going out after the event, Leon announced that he was tired and wanted to go home. "Afterwards," Cortesi maintains, "I drove Madonna to the St. Regis, where she met Sean in the bar. She told me she would call me when she was ready to leave. Two hours later, I picked her up. For some reason, Carlos sensed that she was with Sean because he called me while I was waiting for her and wanted to know why I was still on duty. His excuse for calling was to find out what time I would be picking him up to take him to the Cirque du Soleil with Madonna in the Village the next day."

Shortly before Madonna signed the contract to star as Evita in Alan Parker's film, the idea of having a baby with Carlos was paramount on her agenda. According to Cortesi, she consulted Dr. Stanley T. West, a reproductive endocrinologist who had offices on the Upper East Side and in lower Manhattan. "The first time Madonna went there, I took her to Dr. West's office uptown," Cortesi maintains. "Another time I picked Carlos up at his apartment and took him down to West's downtown office. He was carrying a small cup and at first I thought it was a urine specimen but he told me it was sperm. He didn't want to do what he had to do in the doctor's office and instead did it at home, which meant he only had a little over an hour to get the sperm to the office. One of the times that I took him when he was carrying a cup, Madonna was waiting for him at the doctor's office."

After Madonna signed the contract for *Evita,* she went to London regularly for voice lessons and Carlos visited her there several times. By the time she was preparing to record the score, before the actual shooting of the movie would begin, she had not yet gotten pregnant, although she and Carlos had been together for more than fourteen months. During Carlos's visits to Madonna, she had once again foisted Ingrid Casares on him. As far as Madonna was concerned, it was the perfect threesome, although she made it clear to Leon and Casares that though they would be welcome for the three consecutive weekends, she wanted them out of London during the week. Her reason was strictly professional, she explained, since she needed time alone to concentrate and prepare herself emotionally for her part.

Each weekend the routine was basically the same. While Carlos Leon and Madonna spent hours together in the star's suite or in the hotel gym, Casares spent most of her time on the phone, trying to wrangle invitations to various high-profile parties. Not surprisingly, she had less success than Tim Rice. When she bundled her friends back to the States, Madonna's social life got more active. On several occasions, she would enlist her publicist to arrange dinners with certain English actors or rock stars who appealed to her. Hugh Grant accepted a dinner invitation only to back out at the last minute and stand her up without any explanation. Another arranged date that didn't work out was with the sexy but bizarre rock singer Henry Rollins. Then Madonna decided that the actor Rufus Sewell was even more attractive. Sewell, one of the few men she pursued without an intermediary, was starring in the British theater production of *Rat in the Skull* at the Duke of York theater. Slipping into the audience just before curtain, Madonna went backstage during intermission to invite Sewell to dinner at Le Caprice, a well-known London bistro. Sewell accepted Madonna's invitation, although before dessert was served, he ducked out to meet his regular girlfriend. Later the actor offered an explanation for his sudden departure by saying that he had always been extremely uncomfortable with people like Madonna and with all the other beautiful people because he mistrusted their intentions. According to Sewell, he never got over the fact that he was a chubby teen. With Sewell out of the picture, Madonna set her sights on Antonio Banderas, who immediately summoned his new wife, Melanie Griffith, to London. Apparently, Griffith thought that Madonna presented enough of a threat that she rearranged her schedule and remained on location with Banderas in England, Argentina, and Hungary.

Madonna had better luck with Tim Willocks, a British writer whom she met at a dinner in her honor at the home of Julie Baumgold, the wife of the editor of *Esquire* magazine. Willocks, a psychiatrist by training and a lapsed Catholic, was the author of *Green River Rising,* a book that was being favorably compared to *Silence of the Lambs.* Willocks made the mistake of talking to the press. His mother even made statements about how optimistic she was that the relationship between her son and the pop star would endure. Not surprisingly, Madonna soon tired of him, although she kept in touch after the affair was over. She expressed interest in optioning his book for a movie to play Juliet Devlin, the only female character.

Madonna's preoccupation with her social life ended when the time came to settle down to work. From that point on, there were no more late-night dinners with randy Englishmen, no more Marlboro Lights or the occasional martini, and no more weekend visits with friends she imported from the States. The tweed suit went back into the closet, and Madonna began her transformation into Evita.

chapter two
....

During the four grueling weeks that the principal members of the *Evita* cast were working on the score, Alan Parker still hadn't received permission from Carlos Menem, the president of Argentina, to film certain key scenes on location in Buenos Aires. But if time was running out for the director, the timing could not have been worse for President Menem.

The summer heat usually slowed down the Buenos Aires press. In November and December 1995, however, it had little effect on the collective hysteria that gripped the city. Several ambitious journalists had written a series of articles about the president's extramarital affairs, sexual escapades, and political blunders. The latest story to capture public attention was that Carlos Menem had forcibly evicted his naked wife from the Casa Rosada after her lawyers had served him with divorce papers. Even more damaging were reports about Menem's· alleged involvement in a narco-dollar scandal that implicated his sister and brother-in-law in laundering Colombian drug money through Argentine banks and pocketing a large commission for their trouble. Immediately following that story was yet another revelation. One of Menem's closest advisers had allegedly been selling twenty-five tons of contaminated milk to supermarkets throughout the country, resulting in the deaths of dozens of babies and elderly people.

Though the Argentines always enjoyed a good scandal, the real reason for the attacks on Menem during those lazy summer months was that inflation was at its highest point in a decade with unemployment levels reaching double digits. Given the general political and economic climate throughout Argentina, and the fact that the people had not yet recovered from the humiliating defeat the country had suffered at the hands of the British during the Falklands War, the last thing Menem wanted was to be pressured by a British director who intended to descend upon the Argentine capital with an English film crew to make a movie about a woman whom the people still considered to be a national treasure. Despite all the promises that Alan Parker had made about how his film would portray Evita in a favorable light, the Argentine president feared it would be the same as the stage productions. As usual, Eva Perón would be seen as a woman who had slept her way to the top of Argentine society and, once there, had looted the coffers of the poor to further her own narcissistic desires. Even if he was inclined to take a chance, when news of the project had been leaked in the Argentine press, the anti-Madonna sentiment was so violent that Menem was afraid to antagonize his constituents further, particularly Evita's most ardent supporters. The hysteria concerning Eva Perón was not a new phenomenon. In the two years following her death, the Vatican had received more than forty thousand letters attesting to various "miracles" that she had performed during her life and urging the pope to declare her a saint. Tomas Eloy Martínez, the Argentine writer, recalled in his best-seller, *Santa Evita,* that in the villages near where he'd grown up people still believed that Evita was an emissary of God, and local peasants continued to see her face in the clouds.

On the day that Madonna was scheduled to record the title song, "Don't Cry for Me Argentina," in the West End studios, the Evita hysteria in Buenos Aires reached an emotional peak. Clara Marin, one of Evita's former secretaries, threatened the star in front of a group of reporters gathered at a protest site near the Casa Rosada. "We want Madonna dead or alive," Marin screamed through a bullhorn. "If she comes here to [Argentina], then I will kill her. . . . Evita is our mother, our flag, our motherland." That evening, the front-page headline in the country's leading newspaper, *Clarín*, read, "Evita Lives! Madonna, Out!"

In response, the following day, Carlos Menem appeared on television. "I am very aware," he said to the millions of viewers, "that the Argentines who still hold Evita as a martyr and saint would not tolerate someone like Madonna portraying her on the screen, a woman who is the embodiment of vulgarity." Within days, all the local newspapers carried a front-page story that an Argentine actor who was also a close friend of the president's intended to make a rival version of *Evita,* starring Andrea del Boca, a soap opera star.

At the end of December 1995, after spending a morose Christmas in London, Alan Parker finally received an official response from Carlos Menem. The president wrote that he was having "great difficulty" with the fact that Eva Perón would be portrayed by a woman who had recently published a "vulgar and pornographic book entitled *Sex."* That evening Parker summoned his cast and crew together to announce that he was almost ready to call off the trip down to Argentina.

"Even now," he told the group, "this project continues to stumble upon obstacle upon obstacle. If it's ever finished, it will be a miracle."

The reaction of the company was a mixture of outrage and disappointment, with the exception of Madonna, who seemed completely unfazed by the news. Quite calmly, she told Parker that whatever he decided, she still intended to go down to Buenos Aires to meet as many people as she could who had known Evita, either from her days as a radio actress or after she had married Juan Perón. More than just interviewing people, she also intended to record her personal experiences and observations in a diary, which would eventually be published in the November 1996 issue of *Vanity Fair.* Madonna was convinced that the key to playing the character with more depth and insight, giving her pathos, softness, and vulnerability, was to retrace her life in Buenos Aires. She believed that Eva Perón, like her, was more fragile than anyone suspected, and someone who had carried around throughout her life a great deal of private pain and suffering from her impoverished past.

Parker was impressed. In fact, he was even more impressed when Madonna suggested that while she was in Buenos Aires, she could act as a kind of goodwill ambassador to convince President Menem that the film would be a tribute to the former first lady, a movie that would ultimately make the country proud. Without hesitating, Parker agreed, although privately he told the others that he held little hope that his star would succeed.

On January 20, 1996, Madonna arrived in Buenos Aires, accompanied by her assistant, Caresse Henry-Norman. Within minutes of entering the arrival building, she realized just how daunting her mission would be. Protesters, held back by a cordon of policemen, were carrying placards and signs. The message was clear. Madonna was not welcome in Buenos Aires. Outside where the star's chauffeur-driven Mercedes limousine was waiting to take her to her hotel, there were more protesters burning her in effigy. The scene was eerily similar to the countless newsreels she had screened that showed Eva Perón as the target of ugly demonstrations in which she, too, had been burned in effigy. Instead of becoming discouraged, from the moment Madonna stepped onto Argentine soil, she became more certain than ever that her destiny was somehow mystically and permanently linked to Evita's.

The Plaza Hotel on Florida Street in downtown Buenos Aires is famous for playing host to visiting royalty and heads of state. The decor is very French, and Madonna's suite in the hotel was decorated in Napoleon III style with overstuffed sofas, heavy furniture trimmed in gold leaf, velvet draperies, and massive crystal chandeliers. Upon her arrival, she found a message from one of President Menem's closest advisers, assuring her that he was arranging a meeting with the Argentine leader. In the meantime, while she was waiting for an appointment, he encouraged her to tour the city and learn as much as she could about Evita. What Madonna never knew was that all along the question was never *if* the Argentine government would give permission, but rather *how much* it would cost the producers of *Evita* to persuade them to agree. By then, the government realized that their previous demands had been too ambitious. They were prepared to come to an agreement that everyone would finally consider reasonable.

On January 21, her second day in Buenos Aires, Madonna received her first visitor. Tuco Paz, an Argentine diplomat for more than forty years, had known Eva Perón personally from the beginning of her political rise when she was only twenty-nine. Paz told Madonna that he had always found Eva to be shy and attributed her aggressive reputation to the fact that she talked only about politics, which was her greatest passion. One story Paz recounted particularly touched Madonna's romantic soul. Juan Perón would coach Eva in public speaking by sitting in a chair with his back to her while he picked a series of subjects at random. In a test of Eva's ability to respond quickly to journalists and political adversaries, she had to learn to speak on any topic without preparation or rehearsal. Madonna compared the loving way that a busy man like Juan Perón would bother to educate his wife with the concern that her ex-husband had demonstrated toward her when they had starred together in *Shanghai Surprise*. She recalled how Sean Penn would stop the action in the middle of a scene and take her aside to tell her how to play it more effectively. "I never felt more loved than when Sean took time to teach me how to be better." At the end of his visit, Paz told Madonna that Evita's favorite meal was pan-fried breaded veal with a fried egg on top, french-fried

GODDESS 25

potatoes, and a beer. For the next week, Madonna made that her daily fare.

Madonna may have been slow to grasp the political nuances that had catapulted Eva Perón into the people's hearts, but her timing and sense of drama was flawless when it came to transforming herself into Evita. One of the songs she had recorded in London described Eva Perón's own transformation into a glamorous and sophisticated first lady. The song is "Rainbow High," and as Eva is preparing for her "Rainbow" tour of Europe, she sings "Eyes, Face, Hair, Image," while choosing her wardrobe, furiously rifling through jewels and clothes. "Christian Dior–me," Madonna/Eva sings as she rejects a hat and tries on another. Juan Perón had come up with the idea of the trip, using his wife as an ambassador of goodwill to charm European leaders, to change the perception of his political regime as a pariah government. When Madonna recorded the song, she immediately compared it to one of her best video performances, "Vogue"—"Don't just stand there, let's just do it/Strike a pose—there's nothing to it."

"Vogue," filmed in 1990 in black and white with art-deco sets by Shep Pettibone, is one of the most stylish early Madonna clips. The feeling is 1930s chic derivative of the photographs that Horst P. Horst shot for *Vogue* and of his later movie portraits. In the opening montage there is a glimpse of a de Lempicka painting as well as a number of specific imitations or homages to Horst, for example, a girl photographed from the back sitting on a bed, wearing a laced corset. Madonna makes a series of transitions, from a stern figure in a man's black suit dancing with chorus boys in similar outfits to several carefully lit and posed close-ups in which she appears as Marlene Dietrich, Carole Lombard, and Rita Hayworth, all of whom are referred to in the lyrics.

It did not escape Madonna that both she and Evita used

props, clothes, makeup, sophisticated hairstyles, and jewels to entice and attract the masses. For both women, it was an example of their intoxication with fame and fortune.

More lyrics from "Rainbow High" describe how Evita justified spending so much money on clothes and jewels when her people were poor and unemployed. She claimed that she dressed up not only for the image of Argentina but also to entertain the people and make them forget their dreary lives. "They need their escape and so do I," she sings. How similar to Madonna's philosophy that when she cavorts onstage in suggestive outfits, singing sexually explicit lyrics, she is doing it for her fans, offering them an escape from the drudgery and rules of parents, school, and church.

Rather than descending upon Buenos Aires as a replica of the woman she would portray in the film, Madonna affected the change gradually to give the impression that as she walked around the city, she mysteriously manifested the physical traits of the former first lady. Several days after she arrived, she combed her hair into a neat chignon tied at the nape of her neck. A few days later, she began wearing brown contact lenses and a porcelain bite plate to cover the gap between her two front teeth. The lenses made her dizzy while the porcelain fill-in got in the way of her tongue, interfering with her enunciation. It took several days before she finally got used to them.

By the end of the first week in Buenos Aires, Madonna continued to change into Evita. She wore only art-deco jewelry, small clip-on earrings, large brooches, and an antique Tiffany watch surrounded by marquisettes on a thin black fabric band, an exact copy of the watch that Juan Perón had given Eva on her twenty-eighth birthday. The look was almost complete. One evening, two beauticians from the hotel beauty salon were summoned to the star's suite. While one waxed and tweezed her heavy brows into a pencil-thin arch; the other clipped her nails short and painted them a deep red to match her lipstick.

Arrangements were made for Madonna to have two permanent bodyguards who would work eight-hour shifts to accompany her around Buenos Aires. A section of the regular Buenos Aires police force that provided security for visiting heads of state and other high-profile personalities took charge of Madonna's security as well. Each morning, her personal bodyguards, along with Caresse Henry-Norman, her assistant, would sit down and work out Madonna's schedule, which, when it was firm and complete, they would hand over to a representative of the special security force. Before Madonna appeared anywhere in Buenos Aires, the police would already be waiting for her, barricades would be in place, and several undercover agents would be mingling with the crowd.

When Madonna's transformation into Evita was almost complete and she appeared in public for the first time, wearing seamed stockings, stiletto heels, and a vintage 1940s suit nipped at the waist with a straight skirt that fell almost to midcalf, she was literally surrounded on four sides by burly policemen in civilian clothes. The security force expected the worst, not only because she was Madonna, but also because she had successfully made the transition into Eva Perón. The first day she set out to explore Buenos Aires, Madonna wore a black veil that covered the upper part of her face and carried a tape recorder and a small notepad. Everywhere Madonna went, the reaction was predictable. People gasped, astounded at how much the actress looked like their beloved Evita. Her fans pushed and shoved to get as close to her as possible, some of them intent on tearing a piece of fabric from her suit as a souvenir, while others actually tried to kiss her hands. Curiously, her detractors were much better behaved and their anti-Madonna demonstrations were organized and contained in specific areas of the city. The biggest problem that the security had was not the crowds but rather the paparazzi, who had their own sources to inform them where Madonna would be in advance and enough experience to hide until she arrived, when they would pounce on her and take photographs.

In addition to her bodyguards and the police who protected her, Madonna was always accompanied by a young history student, who also acted as her translator. She found the most appealing part of the city to be an area along the Riachuelo Canal called La Boca, where sheet-metal houses were surrounded by old-fashioned New Orleans–style wraparound porches, painted in primary colors, with birdcages hanging over the doors. Originally made famous in the late nineteenth century when Genovese sailors roamed the docks, La Boca had become a landmark because of its massive street murals. The well-known Argentine artist Benito Quinquela had painted dark, stooped figures scurrying like ants set against the florid background of the canal. Madonna not only fell in love with the offbeat area but also with Quinquela's works and was disappointed that he did not paint on canvas. Transporting an entire wall was too difficult a task even for Madonna!

In La Boca, Madonna had her first religious experience in a small church along the canal. Venturing inside, she watched a procession of local residents walking slowly up the aisle. Several of the men carried a life-size statue of Jesus Christ high above their shoulders. Madonna was mesmerized by the figure of Christ, which had heavy chains and medals hanging over the chest and deep gashes, bloody wounds, and other lurid stigmata graphically painted on the plaster body. It was an image that could have been used in Madonna's controversial video "Like a Prayer." This was another sign that Madonna was destined to portray Eva Perón. According to her student guide, Madonna reached into her purse and took out a turquoise rosary, a treasured gift from her maternal grandmother, and began to pray. Following the procession out to the street, she stood quietly as it made its way along the colorful canal. Turning to her guide, she said, "I just had an uncontrollable urge to thank God for allowing me to see Buenos Aires and learn about the woman who gave so much love to her people. I'm convinced that

President Menem will give us permission to film *Evita* here."

Despite all the adverse reaction to her presence in Buenos Aires, Madonna felt comfortable with the attitude that the Argentines had toward Catholicism. She also related to the sense of mysticism that was so prevalent throughout the country, as well as to the people's genuine belief in astrology. From the most sophisticated upper-class salons to the most poverty-stricken barrios, from laborer to doctor, from high-ranking military leaders to the president himself, almost everyone carried icons, good-luck charms, religious medals, crystals, or worry beads to ward off evil spirits. Business appointments, romantic rendezvous, and professional and political decisions were made based on favorable indications by astrologers. Even the words to the tango music had mystical innuendo, both violent and dramatic in its meaning. Partners would be chosen according to the compatibility of their sun or moon signs. Madonna spent a great deal of time learning the tango, not only because she was first and foremost a dancer, but also because Evita had been a dance-hall girl in a tango parlor before going on to become a calendar model, radio star, and celebrity. In fact, the path that Evita had chosen nourished Madonna's superficial notion that she had taken similar steps toward stardom.

On one occasion, a journalist from a local Buenos Aires newspaper was allowed to watch one of her tango lessons. After it was over, the reporter asked Madonna if she understood the words. "You can kill my wife, kill my woman, but don't touch my mother or sister," he translated before asking if she didn't think they were misogynistic.

"Men danced the tango together while waiting for their turn in the brothels," Madonna replied, repeating what she had read in one of her tour books. "So, you know, guys say things when they're together and acting macho that they don't necessarily mean."

"Do you get the impression that this is a macho society?" the journalist pressed.

Like a true ambassador of goodwill, Madonna answered without hesitating, "Women in Argentina are treated well because Eva Perón was the champion of women's rights, and that's something I can relate to."

"Eva Perón is often called a whore and an opportunist," the journalist challenged the star.

"Either she was called a saint or a prostitute," Madonna replied, "which is what I'm called by everyone, because of my name and because I'm in touch with my own sexuality. It's the obvious way to put a woman down, to call her a whore and imply that she has no morals and no integrity and no talent. And God knows, I can relate to that, too."

Days later, when asked his impressions of Madonna, the journalist thought for a moment before saying, "She is fascinating because she is so self-involved. Everything is 'me' or 'I' or whatever she can 'relate to' based on her own life. In mind and soul, she embodies Eva Perón!"

chapter three

· · · · · · · · · · · · · · · · ·

*T*hough Madonna was confident about her creative ability to master the role of Eva Perón and felt at ease with the religious, mystical, and astrological symbolism in Buenos Aires, she had difficulty grasping the fundamental differences between Argentina and other Spanish-speaking countries. Based on her penchant for Puerto Rican and Cuban lovers and her instinctive gravitation toward anything that was Latin, she thought that she understood the mentality and culture of the Argentine people. For Madonna, Argentina was like any other country with strong Spanish roots where life is somehow more relaxed and love is seen as raw sexual fantasy. Madonna didn't understand that despite the similarity of language, Argentina is a country steeped in European culture, a blend of puritanism and sophistication. In fact, the ongoing joke around BA, or Buenos Aires, is that a *porteño,* or a native of Buenos Aires, is someone who "dressed French, talked Italian, and thought British." Her inability to grasp the cultural disparities was a result of her ignorance of certain historical facts that had made a large segment of the population so violently opposed to Juan and Eva Perón. At that time, Buenos Aires was a class-conscious society where social and political acceptance depended on one's being a member of one of the ten top families. The former first lady came from the lower class, the illegitimate and often neglected child of an impoverished servant and a married man. Not surprisingly, she had spent her entire life striving to be accepted by Argentine society. Madonna, the middle-class girl from Middle America, set out to shock the establishment. If Madonna passed herself off as the "poor girl made good," Evita obliterated the seedy side of her early life. Some lyrics and phrases in the film conjure up images of the life and times of Madonna, or more precisely, the hardships she has invented for her public. Both she and Evita understood how to seduce and overwhelm their public to win international acclaim and approval.

According to a well-known writer in Buenos Aires, once Juan and Eva Perón broke down those social boundaries that had created an ever-increasing gap between the rich and the poor, they set a new standard of acceptability in which anyone could succeed. "I explained to Madonna," the writer said, "that because of their climb to the top, they became an enemy of the aristocracy."

The writer was amazed when Madonna interpreted the lesson as further proof that she and Evita were heroes of the downtrodden. She was delighted that two people from the "wrong side of the tracks" had "made good" and gone on to take over the country. "She absolutely identified with Eva Perón," the writer goes on, "because she considered that she had also succeeded against the same odds." As they were about to part, Madonna thanked the writer for "making things so clear" and left him with the following words: "What you're really saying is that the Argentine people found out that all you had to be was bigger, bolder, and smarter than the rest to get to the top." In America, perhaps. In Argentina, never!

Marikena Monti is an Argentine singer who is often compared to Edith Piaf. She also met Madonna and recalls a conversation they had that left her with the impression that the star had become so obsessed by Evita that she refused to see the subtext of the city, which still included an awareness of a black period in the country's history. "I tried to explain that we do hideous things to each other here in Argentina," Monti begins. "We sleep with each other's husbands and wives, kill each other's children, and it's business as usual.

And, I tried to tell her within the context of the Perón era and, later on, the tragedy of the Dirty War, when thousands of Argentines simply disappeared. I also tried to explain my pessimism about the economy and the future of the arts under Menem's regime."

According to Monti, she told Madonna that there had once been an important intellectual movement in Buenos Aires, when she would sing about issues and humanity. "With the situation in the country today," Monti continues, "I told her it was hard for me to sing about the privatization of the phone company." Madonna's response was predictable when she replied, "I sing about sex, and that's always in style whether it's private or public."

Andrés di Tella is an Argentine filmmaker who had won an award, the equivalent of an American Emmy, for his film about left-wing Peronism. At the time Madonna was in Buenos Aires, di Tella was making a film about the early days of Argentine radio and television. "While I was filming my documentary," di Tella explained, "the people I spoke to in radio who knew Evita went on about how wonderful she was. The minute I turned off the camera, they revealed horrible details about her. People were terrified of saying anything against her. Even now, no one wants to speak ill of her in public, so she can't be dealt with as a human being. Unfortunately, Madonna will just keep the myth alive."

If Madonna was perceived by some to be the incarnation of religious blasphemy and sexual abandon, many intellectuals believed that Buenos Aires had a past that rivaled her own in terms of immorality. Alicia Sternberg, a well-known feminist writer, was one of those who stood up for Madonna. In several press interviews concerning Carlos Menem's refusal to allow Madonna to sing "Don't Cry for Me Argentina" on the balcony of the Casa Rosada, she accused the president of hypocrisy, since he had recently pardoned the leader of the military junta who had organized the Dirty War in the 1970s.

"How bad is Madonna compared to that monster General

Videla," Sternberg asked, "who now jogs freely around the streets of Buenos Aires?"

Elsa Osario, another outspoken journalist and writer whose screen credits include *The Tango Lesson* and *There Are No Men Left,* directed by Alberto Fischerman, also came to Madonna's defense or, more accurately, used the debate to further criticize President Menem. "With his pardon of the generals and his whitewash of everything that happened during that period in our country's history," Osario claimed, "the president gives society permission to forget. People develop antibodies to defend themselves until the whole country suffers from amnesia."

One of the most erudite and cultured women in Buenos Aires claimed that Madonna, thrust into a strange and foreign environment, simply had little or no frame of reference to keep up her end of a conversation.

"Most of the people who came to my parties," she explained, "were international, rich, and not particularly impressed with anyone. I felt sorry for Madonna, because she was obviously in way over her head and painfully aware that she was limited. Most of the time, she nodded and pretended to understand and that was fine, but when she asked a question or decided to express an opinion, it was off the subject, irrelevant, banal, and embarrassing for everyone. It seemed as if the only time she felt comfortable was when she discussed sex or the impact that Eva Perón had on the country from a sensual point of view."

The same woman recalls how shocked Madonna was when she saw that Argentines kissed friends and even strangers upon meeting them instead of shaking hands. "She told me she was afraid of catching germs and not being able to perform." The woman laughed. "And yet, during a dinner party I gave to welcome her to our country, she slipped into one of the bedrooms and was caught necking with one of the most notorious playboys in Buenos Aires!" As she was leaving with the man in question, Madonna asked her hostess whether his claim of being close to President Menem was true.

José Camaro, a close friend of Carlos Menem's, was on leave from a diplomatic post in Europe and was visiting Buenos Aires at the same time that Madonna was on her mission of goodwill. President Menem took advantage of the coincidence by instructing his friend to find out what Madonna's impressions were of Buenos Aires and of Eva Perón. Camaro was delighted to oblige, not only because he was loyal to Menem, but also because it would give him the opportunity to meet the woman whom he considered to be his sexual equal. Tall and dark with a dramatic shock of white hair, Camaro was a minor literary figure in Argentina and had written a roman à clef that had angered many of his closest friends and political colleagues. Camaro was the butt of jokes around European publishing circles since he made a point of telling everybody that, back home, people considered him to be the "Marcel Proust of Argentina."

In addition to his literary pretensions, Camaro had also acquired quite a reputation for himself as the typical Latin lover. According to several attractive and very married European hostesses who had succumbed to his charms, after the lovemaking was over, he would play an air guitar and serenade them with melodious tango songs. One former mistress who was treated to a medley of his make-believe strumming and passionate singing said of his postcoital behavior, "He was a parody of the Latin lover. In fact, after I saw *Evita*, it occurred to me that he could have played the part of that second-rate tango singer in the film better than the actor." She was referring, of course, to the part of Maguldi, the man who served as the young Eva Perón's ticket out of the small-town barrio where she was born, played by Jimmy Nail in the film.

Long after Madonna left Argentina and the film was already in theaters throughout the world, Camaro wrote a novella in which he described in lurid detail one torrid night that his protagonist, a man considered to be the best lover in the world, shared with an American movie star, a woman who was reputed to be the high priestess of sensuality. Although the names and places were changed, the book was never published.

Buenos Aires was a candy store stocked with her perfect physical type, the dusky, taut, romantic Latin lover who could dance the tango and talk about Eva Perón, one of the positive aspects of her visit.

Several days after Madonna had transformed herself into Eva Perón, Camaro arrived at her hotel suite for lunch. Approaching the star and kissing her hand, he took a step back and clutched his heart. The resemblance to Eva Perón was astounding. He couldn't believe his eyes. It was as if she were there in the flesh, alive and breathing. For him, he confessed, time had stopped. Madonna couldn't have been more flattered. Seated opposite her in the large living room of the suite, Camaro repeated, in case she had forgotten, that he was "working on the president" to allow the film to be shot on location in Buenos Aires. "You must be patient," he said.

"How patient?" Madonna asked.

"We may have to spend a few weeks together," he said suggestively.

This time, in response, Madonna sat forward on the sofa and looked directly into his eyes. "Look, José," she said evenly, "I want to have a good time while I'm here. I like Buenos Aires, and you look like someone who could make life interesting. But I didn't come all the way down to this godforsaken place to go back to England and record *Evita* on a soundstage."

Confident in his ability to seduce any woman in the world and very aware that he had what she wanted, a direct line to Carlos Menem, Camaro did not seem troubled by Madonna's ultimatum. Instead, he suggested that an interesting afternoon outing for the star would be a visit to the cemetery

where Eva Perón was buried. From the moment Madonna
arrived in Buenos Aires, she had been trying to organize a
visit to La Recoleta, the famous cemetery in the heart of the
city. The press had been hounding her to the extent that
every excursion involved elaborate plans that included a decoy car and roundabout routes. Madonna decided her assistant, Caresse Henry-Norman, would ride in the star's usual
car, wearing a scarf and sunglasses, while Madonna would
actually be lying on the floor of Camaro's car, leaving the
hotel thirty minutes earlier. The idea was that the press
would follow Caresse Henry-Norman as she made her way
to the cemetery while Madonna would already have arrived,
free to spend a few solitary minutes at Evita's tomb. With
José Camaro at the wheel, they set out for La Recoleta
undisturbed by motorcycles or screeching cars filled with
paparazzi. When they arrived, Madonna claimed that she
had "stepped into another world."

The cemetery, an unusual community of dead people, is a
collection of miniature Gothic-style marble mansions, each
one more ornate than the next, decorated with statues, religious paintings, and photographs of their departed occupants. Every year thousands of people from all over the
world visit the Duarte mausoleum where Evita is buried,
more than come to pay homage to Marilyn Monroe in West-
wood Memorial Park or to Edith Piaf's grave at Père
Lachaise in Paris. As Madonna approached the pink marble
mausoleum of the Duarte family, wild cats scurried in between the alleyways, whimpering or howling as they
searched for food.

Camaro read the words out loud that were etched in the
marble: Rest in Peace. The irony was that it had taken nearly
two decades after her death for the former first lady to actually rest in peace, since her body went missing for all those
years before it was finally found in Spain and returned to
Buenos Aires. Madonna listened with rapt attention as Camaro explained that a lot of people had lost their lives over
that incident. Sadly, he added, it was all over now, the mass

hysteria, demagoguery, and with it, perhaps, the glamour that had all but disappeared with that tumultuous era in Argentine history.

As Madonna bent down to place a bouquet of violets at the entrance of the mausoleum, she noticed another epitaph etched in stone: Don't Cry for Me Argentina. "That must bring a flicker of memory," she said wistfully, "or maybe even a tear."

While Madonna was wandering around the Gothic ruins of La Recoleta, Caresse Henry-Norman, as planned, was seated in the back of the star's car. On the way to the cemetery, two teenagers who had been hired by several paparazzi threw themselves in front of the decoy car, forcing it to come to a screeching halt. The hope was that "Madonna" would jump out to see if anyone had been injured, whereupon the photographers would be able to take their daily quota of pictures. Everything went as planned except that when Madonna's assistant jumped out of the car, the paparazzi realized that they had been fooled. Madonna had successfully eluded them. They were furious. By then, a crowd had gathered. While the press yelled insults at Caresse, the bystanders began pushing and shoving to get closer to the car. Finally, the chauffeur somehow managed to get the terrified woman bundled into the backseat so he could head to the safety of the hotel. They never made it. En route, they were stopped by the police and charged with leaving the scene of a hit-and-run accident. Within minutes, Caresse and the driver were in custody and on their way to jail. Several hours later, after Madonna was already back at the hotel, she learned through one of her bodyguards what had happened. Fortunately, he had contacts within the police department and was able to arrange things so that the pair were released. Madonna was outraged that the security detail of the regular police force who were in charge of keeping her and her entourage safe had made such a potentially life-threatening mistake. In response to a furious phone call that she made to the minister of police, two officials arrived at the hotel. In her diary that appeared in *Vanity Fair*, Madonna described her meeting with the two officials. "We discussed Peronism," she wrote, "and of course Evita and how her enemies were divided into two camps, the aristocracy and the Communists."

After several more minutes of abstract political discussion, one of the men explained to Madonna that while he was not a Peronist, he nonetheless admired Evita for what she done for the country. "And then," Madonna recounted in her diary, "he said the most amazing thing. He said that people were angry with Evita in her day for the same reason they are angry with me today, because we are both women with power."

For Madonna, it was just another sign that both she and Eva Perón were victims of men who could deal with powerful women only by discrediting them. As Madonna became more familiar with Eva Perón's effect on men, she even concluded that the lyrics and music as well as the story line in Parker's film wrongly portrayed her as a whore who had slept her way to the top. At one point, in one of their weekly phone conversations, she even suggested to Parker that "the implication in the musical was a male chauvinist point of view and absolutely ludicrous." Parker didn't bother to argue. He had more serious concerns than worrying about his star's analysis of Evita's character.

When Madonna turned on the television that evening, there were images of Eva Perón ministering to the poor during her political heyday, juxtaposed with clips of Madonna in some of her more raunchy videos. Hugo Rodríguez Cananilla of the Eva Perón Foundation, one of the most vocal opponents of Alan Parker's *Evita* and of Madonna in particular, had come up with the idea to draw those negative visual comparisons.

Furious, Madonna called the leading newspaper and told them she wanted to make a statement. Consuela Stamos, a young reporter who was fluent in English, took the call. Madonna began by saying that the reaction of the Argentine people had "hurt her deeply." "Form your opinions after you have seen the movie," she said. "I am full of admiration for her. She came from nothing and ended up with enormous influence over the country."

Stamos took everything down and then asked Madonna why she thought it would be a good idea for President Menem to allow the film to be shot on location in Buenos Aires. "For one thing," Madonna replied, "it would stimulate the economy." Gathering momentum, she asked rhetorically, "Why do you think I can't sleep at night? Because all my fans are in the street screaming for me. What do they care about not sleeping? They're unemployed so they don't have to get up in the morning."

Stamos feigned sympathy. "Look, with all the unemployment," the star continued, "the people should be grateful that a big movie company comes to Buenos Aires and offers hundreds of them jobs as extras. It's more than they have now, thirty dollars a day plus lunch." On that note, the interview was over.

When Madonna had calmed down and thought about what she had said, she summoned her bodyguard, a gentle blond giant of German extraction named Hans. One of the more amusing scenes around Buenos Aires was Hans scurrying after Madonna as she went sight-seeing or shopped, holding her small Evita box handbag daintily between his enormous hands. Madonna now wanted Hans to contact the newspaper and, in Spanish, prevail upon the reporter not to print the piece. "Explain that I was stressed-out and exhausted," she pleaded.

It was too late. The following day, *Clarín* published an exclusive three-paragraph interview with the star that did little to further her cause in Buenos Aires.

The next day another member of the Eva Perón Foundation issued a statement to the press: ". . . the wife of the former Argentinian leader should not be played by a woman named after the mother of Christ who has appeared in rock concerts in skimpy outfits, singing of lust." That evening, Madonna fired her bodyguard.

Despite all Madonna's efforts to seduce the people of Argentina, negative opinion only escalated. Marta Rivadera, a deputy in Congress from Menem's hometown province of La Rioja, went so far as to propose a decree declaring Madonna and Alan Parker personae non grata. The next time Madonna spoke to Parker, she referred to the phrase used by Rivadera, saying that it was just another way of calling them "dirty rotten scum." One wonders if Parker had ever heard that expression translated from the Latin in quite that way.

chapter four

······················

Still with no firm appointment with the president, Madonna was rightfully apprehensive when, on February 1, she met Alan Parker and Antonio Banderas at the airport in Buenos Aires. Parker had decided he would make the trip anyway to save time if things worked out, and to check out locations as well as to see if he could do anything to make things happen. As planned, Madonna whisked the director and costar directly to a cocktail party at a foreign embassy. There, they received a message from one of the president's aides that Menem would meet Madonna on February 7.

For the next week, she read everything that she could find in English about Menem. One of the things that impressed her was that he fashioned himself "a man of the people," a passionate yet vulnerable leader who believed that he was the quintessential example of what he called the New World "caudillo," a first-generation Argentine who had made a success of himself. It was yet another mystical sign. She saw amazing similarities between Carlos Menem and her own father. While the Argentinian president's family had immigrated from Syria without money or family contacts, Silvio "Tony" Ciccone was a first-generation American of Italian descent whose parents had sailed from Europe to America without any resources. Like Menem, Tony Ciccone had succeeded far beyond the dreams of his immigrant parents.

The day of the meeting finally arrived. Dinner with the president was to take place on a remote island in the middle of the El Tigre River, accessible only by helicopter or boat.

This was the house at which he conducted high-level political meetings. The arrangements to get Madonna to the island were straight out of a James Bond movie. Two secret
service agents in charge of delivering her to Menem brought
her down the servants' elevator of the hotel and smuggled
her out through the kitchen and into an unmarked government car. Instructed to lie on the floor of the backseat until
they had cleared the busy downtown area, she was finally allowed to sit up only when the car was speeding down the
highway. When they arrived at a small military airport on the
outskirts of the city, they were waved through the gates and
directed onto the tarmac. There, the car stopped near a helicopter, rotary blades whirring in the soft summer breeze.
Without a word, the star followed her two minders out of the
car and aboard the craft.

After a trip lasting forty minutes, most of it over water,
Madonna discerned from the window of the helicopter a
small patch of earth in the middle of El Tigre on which were
clusters of pine trees. As the helicopter began its descent,
she noticed a small concrete landing pad right in the middle
of an expansive manicured lawn. Approaching its mark,
swaying slowly in the breeze, the helicopter set down four
minutes later and approximately ten meters from a sprawl-
ing stone house, trimmed in white, with flowers lining the
large bay windows on the first floor. After one of the secret
service agents jumped from the craft, a uniformed guard
rolled a staircase up to the door of the helicopter and
Madonna, holding tightly to the arm of the other official, ex-
ited. The noise was deafening. Madonna, dressed in a long
evening gown and mink wrap, was hunched over against the
wind that whipped around her. Walking quickly away from
the craft and barely daring to look around, she followed her
minders into the house.

Paintings of somebody's ancestors, surely not Menem's,
adorned the walls of the marble foyer under which were two
dark mahogany buffets on either wall. An enormous crystal
chandelier, each crystal arm holding a candle, bathed the

entrance in a soft, flickering light. A small, dark-haired woman, stern and austere in her dress and demeanor, greeted Madonna formally. The star immediately felt intimidated, as if she were already being judged based on her reputation. In reality, the woman, who would serve as the translator, was herself overwhelmed and nervous in anticipation of meeting someone she would later describe as "notorious." Her first impression of Madonna, she would also relate after the visit, was shock at the "uncanny" resemblance that the star had to Eva Perón. Without any further conversation, the interpreter gestured toward a set of French doors, mirrored on one side with dark wood on the other, and indicated that Madonna should follow her into the dining room. More wood paneling covered the walls, and a long, rectangular table stood in the center of the room, on which was an exquisite arrangement of blue and white flowers, the colors of Menem's Peronist Party, set on an embroidered, pale blue tablecloth. Three place settings had several crystal glasses at each, with rows of silver forks and knives on either side of gold-trimmed plates.

For several days prior to the meeting, Carlos Menem had been recovering from his third hair-transplant procedure. With his orange-hewed skin from years of using cheap tanning lotion, he resembled a seedy lothario more than a venerable head of state. Nonetheless, Carlos Menem had gone to great lengths to make sure that the evening would be memorable. One of his close aides recalled that *el presidente* was "more nervous than when he had received the pope." Yet, despite any trepidation he might have had, Menem, not unlike his illustrious guest, used sex as the most efficient way to communicate and control. Famous for his well-planned seduction scenes, when he wasn't actively courting a female minister, secretary, or movie star, he created an atmosphere of sexual innuendo that was designed to destabilize his visitors.

Madonna wasn't feeling very well either. From the time she had arrived in the Argentine capital, she had been suffering from a lack of sleep as well as lingering stomach problems and nausea that she attributed to a diet different from her usual fare of vegetables and grains. Despite her physical problems, she looked stunning, a tribute to her doppelgänger. She was determined to succeed at what she considered to be the most important sale of her life. Aware that her reputation was more Fanny Hill than Harold Hill, the supersalesman from the 1960s musical comedy *The Music Man,* Madonna was determined to emulate the latter and downplay the former.

The president made his entrance into the dining room. If anyone had forgotten to tell Madonna that the head of the Argentine government measured only five feet two inches tall, she concealed her surprise. After shaking her hand and glancing over her body from head to toe, he said in Spanish, "There are serious problems today in Argentina, and I feel a duty to my people to protect the memory of our sainted Evita."

Despite her nervousness, Madonna rushed to respond: "I understand completely, because I have the same kind of responsibility to my fans." She hesitated only for a moment after she noticed a bewildered expression cross Menem's face. "You see, like Evita, my public loves me, because they can relate to my beginnings. I, too, come from nothing, and like Evita, I also had my heart broken at a young age when my mother died."

The comparison was not one that the president was prepared to draw, that of a woman revered as a martyr with a performer who had consistently denigrated the Catholic Church by displaying her every sexual fantasy. Smiling his typically enigmatic smile, Menem did not respond. Instead, he gestured to the table, indicating that dinner was served, but not before he gently brushed Madonna's cheek with his forefinger.

Throughout the meal, Carlos Menem maintained relentless eye contact with Madonna, glancing away only once when he focused on her bra strap, which had slipped out of her dress. As they ate the first course, Madonna considered it her God-given responsibility to fill the heavy silence. She began explaining how close she felt to Evita, how connected to her she was in so many ways. As the translator spoke rapidly in Spanish, the president nodded, encouraging Madonna to go on. She recounted the story of her own life and the death of her mother when she was only a child, a loss that had made her determined, like Eva Perón, never to need anyone else ever again. To her credit, Madonna probably knew more details about Eva Perón's life than Menem.

"Evita is the poor girl who made good, just like me," Madonna went on. "She came to Buenos Aires at fifteen to make a career in the movies. I came to New York at seventeen to make a career in music, and both of us had love affairs with men who helped us achieve our goals."

Menem listened intently, his eyes boring into hers.

As uniformed butlers cleared the table for the next course, Madonna gathered momentum. She told the president how dedicated she was to keeping Evita's memory unspoiled, how she felt as one with the woman, how she could relate to her suffering from adverse public opinion and unfounded rumors, how committed she felt about the project, unlike anything else she had ever done. Menem continued to listen in silence, his eyes never leaving hers.

Finally, as she neared the end of what was a monologue, she said in summation, "The bottom line is that we both achieved our objectives for ourselves and for others. Evita elevated the working class and the poor by offering them jobs and equal opportunity, while I gave women the courage to liberate themselves sexually."

After dinner, Madonna asked the president if he would listen to a tape of her singing "Don't Cry for Me Argentina." Menem was delighted. In the living room, seated on an overstuffed sofa upholstered in a blue-and-white flower motif, the president listened as Madonna's voice filled the room. When the song ended, Menem stood and walked over to Madonna. He took her face in his hands and kissed her gently on each check, then held her at arm's length and touched the tip of her nose. *"Suerte, niña!"* he said quietly.

As he turned to leave, he paused. Reaching into his pocket, he pressed a small icon into Madonna's palm. It was an ebony African charm, a good-luck piece, he explained in halting English, carved in the image of the god of fertility. Without another word, he walked solemnly out of the room.

The audience was over. Without further delay, the two secret service men were at her side. She was rushed out of the living room and through the foyer to the landing pad on the front lawn. The blades of the helicopter were already turning in preparation for an immediate departure.

Several days later, Alan Parker received word that President Menem had granted him access to several government buildings that were key to the story, including the Casa Rosada, the official presidential residence where Eva Perón had addressed throngs of her admirers from the balcony. Parker was thrilled. *Evita* would be filmed in eighty-two chaotic days in three different countries—Argentina, England, and Hungary—for a cost of $60 million.

The girl from Bay City, Michigan, had succeeded in her mission.

part two

....

Who's That Girl?

chapter five

· · · · · · · · · · · · · · · · ·

*A*s the story, which has now become a myth, goes, Madonna arrived at La Guardia Airport in New York City from Detroit's Metro Airport on August 16, 1978, her twentieth birthday. It was her first time out of Michigan, and the only time in her life she had ever taken an airplane. Wearing a winter coat on that sweltering August day and carrying one small suitcase and a teddy bear, with only $35 in her pocket, she told the cabdriver to "drop me off in the middle of everything." Armed with optimism, nerve, and a burning desire to be "more famous than God," she found herself in the middle of Times Square with nowhere to live, no friends or family to turn to, and no job.

Even then, her attitude was that if she wasn't prepared to be hurt and even die for what she wanted, she should give up, go back home, and meld into the oblivion of Middle America. *Failure* was not in her lexicon. From the moment she had been old enough to recognize her ambition, she had wanted out of her small Michigan hometown where God and wall-to-wall carpeting had dominated her middle-class existence. More than anything else, Madonna needed to prove to anyone who doubted her resolve to succeed that her decision to go out on her own was not capricious but rather proof of her strength and determination.

The irony was that the girl with such outward bravado who intimidated her classmates, fought with her sisters and brothers, and defied her father and stepmother was actually a sensitive and fragile person. Whenever she felt attacked, threatened, or frightened, she would get horrible stomach cramps and throw up. Alone in a strange and intimidating city, that was exactly how she felt. After several hours of walking back and forth on the same pavement, not daring to leave her suitcase unattended, Madonna finally got up the nerve to ask someone to direct her to the nearest YWCA. At least she knew she had enough money to pay for a room for one night. Years later, Madonna would forget the name of the man who was her first New York benefactor.

When Lionel Bishop met Madonna in the middle of Times Square, he lived in Manhattan Towers, a partially city-subsidized monster of a building that takes up the entire square block between Forty-second and Forty-third Streets on Tenth Avenue. The people who lived there were mostly in show business, from chorus kids to established performers like Theodore Bikel, Gower Champion, and Gwen Verdon, as well as welfare families and disabled elderly. At thirty-three, Bishop was an established dancer, although when he met Madonna, he was just recovering from an injured knee. To make ends meet, he was waiting tables at Curtain Up, a trendy restaurant that occupied the ground floor of Manhattan Towers. After he recovered, Bishop danced in the chorus of a number of Broadway shows including *Evita* from 1979, when it opened at the Broadway Theatre on September 25, until it closed in 1991. "When I saw Madonna that day in the middle of Times Square," Bishop begins, "I was coming back from Actors Equity where I picked up a check. Because of my injury, I was walking with a cane and probably still limping. She approached me. Asked if I knew where she could rent a cheap room and then plowed right ahead asking a million questions about New York. There was just something about her. She was adorable and really ballsy."

Bishop describes himself as somewhat shy and enough of a typical New Yorker not to open up to a total stranger. "She piqued my curiosity," he continues, "and I found myself asking her what she was doing in New York, where she came from, you know, all the questions that I usually could care less about knowing. Don't ask me why, but when she told me she had just arrived and wanted to be a dancer, I invited her to stay with me." Bishop laughs. "She was desperate, but before she took me up on my offer, she looked at me really hard for a moment or two and suddenly blurted out, 'You're gay, aren't you?'" Bishop laughs. "It would have probably been more relevant had she asked me if I was a serial killer."

For the next two weeks, Lionel Bishop shared his one-bedroom apartment with Madonna. Though Madonna was grateful for a roof over her head, she had no intention of staying there indefinitely. She was anxious to get out on her own, and she wasted no time in finding a job and another place to live. "One day, she came home and announced that she was moving out," Bishop explains. "She had found this hellhole on Fourth Street in the East Village and a job at the counter at Dunkin' Donuts on West Fifty-seventh Street." Bishop remembers that she started work the following day and moved out about a week later, taking all her worldly possessions with her. Since she didn't have a telephone, she promised to call and keep in touch, to let him know how she was doing. He never heard from her again. "About two months later, I wandered into that Dunkin' Donuts," Bishop recalls, "hoping to see her, but she wasn't working there anymore." He shrugs. "The next time I saw her was on television in her video 'Material Girl.'"

Twenty years after her arrival in New York, Madonna remains steeped in her middle-class, Middle American background.

In her most recent British incarnation, she lives in a lavish $10 million town house in London's West End with her English husband, the director Guy Ritchie, and their son, Rocco, along with her daughter, Lourdes, from a prior relationship, a long way from the modest house in Bay City. It is there, in that small central Michigan town, approximately 110 miles from Detroit, where she and her late mother were born and where her maternal grandmother still lives, that she learned to transform all her anguish and anger after the

death of her mother into the determination to succeed even
far beyond her own imagination.

In the spring of 1986, Madonna appeared on NBC's *Today*
show hosted by Jane Pauley. At the time, Madonna was at
the height of her musical success, having just put out her album *True Blue,* the title chosen as a tribute to her husband,
Sean Penn. Her single "Papa Don't Preach" was number one
on the music charts and became the subject of debate on
teenage pregnancy among feminists and politicians. Though
Madonna had predicted that the song would be taken the
wrong way, she had no idea that her lyrics would be interpreted by some conservatives as a stand against abortion. As
usual, Madonna had stirred up controversy. Pauley asked
Madonna where she came from, to which Madonna replied,
"I come from a stinky little town near Detroit." Not surprisingly, her remark caused an outpouring of indignation
among local community leaders and private citizens in the
Detroit area, who called newspapers, radio talk shows, and
television stations to voice their displeasure.

Madonna made no attempt to apologize until more than a
year later, on August 7, 1987, when she appeared at the Silverdome in Detroit during her Who's That Girl world tour.
There, in front of forty-two thousand people, including family, friends, and many local political officials, she offered an
explanation. "I said Bay City stinks," Madonna said somewhat awkwardly to the audience, "but all I meant to say is
Bay City smells. I didn't mean the people of Bay City stink.
The Dow Chemical plant was right near my grandma's
house so I should know." In fact, when Madonna was growing up, not only was the Dow Chemical plant spewing pol-
luted fumes, but a beet refinery and sugar plant was also in
town. Between the two, it was a "stinky little town." She
then proceeded to sing her next song, aptly entitled "Causing a Commotion," but the damage was already done.

Timothy Sullivan, then mayor of Bay City, is a roly-poly

politician whose vocal stand against abortion contradicted his claim that he was "Bay City's champion of women's rights." After the concert, he announced that he was taking back his offer to give Madonna the key to the city. According to Elsie Fortin, the star's maternal grandmother, despite his purported outrage Sullivan called her at home at least "seven or eight times a day" for months to persuade her to convince Madonna to give a concert that would benefit the town. The idea was that the singer would transform the city into a rock-and-roll shrine and do for Bay City what Elvis had done for Tupelo, Mississippi.

From the turn of the century until 1960, Bay City was important for its lumber and shipyards. During those boom years, Midwest lumber barons settled there and built Georgian- and Victorian-style mansions that still stand today. In 1952, the first presidential yacht was designed and built in Bay City for the newly elected Republican president, Dwight David Eisenhower. In 1960, the craft was shipped back to be refitted and refurbished under the direction of Joseph Kennedy, who had purchased it for his son John F. Kennedy, rechristening it the *HoneyFitz*.

For almost two decades, from 1960 until 1978, Bay City slipped back into oblivion and was once again just another small Midwestern town in the heartland of the automotive industry, where the winters were brutal, the summers sweltering, and the annual income for an average family of four was $15,000.

In 1978, Bay City was back in the news when a rock group composed of four Scotsmen named themselves the Bay City Rollers. Considered to be Britain's first "boy band," the group was famous for their short tartan trousers and simplistic songs such as "Sha La La" and "Shang-a-Lang." The truth was that the four crooners had never been to Bay City, but while looking for a catchy name, one of the four had thrown a dart on a map that landed there. Only when Madonna emerged on the music scene in 1984 was Bay City legitimately represented by a young woman whom the local journalists would call "Bay City's queen of sensuous funk."

For all the change that has occurred in the world since the end of the last world war, Bay City remains frozen in a 1950s time capsule. The atmosphere around town and the mentality of the residents reflect the mores and values found in the television programs of that era. Those were the days when sitcom mothers were wise and forgiving, saving their men from their stubborn blunders without making them feel like complete fools. In Bay City 2001, the men who frequent the diners or luncheonettes still call waitresses "honey" and often pat them affectionately on their well-padded backsides as they go off to place their orders. Rather than taking offense, the attitude of the women remains "boys will be boys." They seem less concerned about what is politically correct and more content that they are in charge of the house and the children as well as the finances. Most of the men are on a weekly allowance.

The streets are wide with oak trees that cast shadows on small wood-frame and fieldstone houses, most of which are built in typical Cape Cod saltbox style. In the more affluent areas, wings have been added to the existing structures, although even in the upscale neighborhoods there are still detached garages that open and close with a key, or carports made of aluminum siding. The lumber barons are long gone, and their grand homes have mostly been turned into garden apartments or boardinghouses.

The small front lawns on the west side of town, considered to be more fashionable, have pink flamingos or statues of jockeys placed along the uneven rows of cobblestones leading to quaint covered porches. There are few streetlamps, and the only light comes from ersatz brass lanterns hanging from wood beams next to strips of flypaper on the porches. During the Christmas season, the atmosphere is festive with flickering colored lights that encircle the houses and store-bought fake snow that is sprayed on the windows, while plastic Santas and reindeer appear on many of the rooftops.

Each section of the small city is so self-contained and closed, with its own grocery stores, cemetery, bingo parlor, and bowling league, that people from one side of town can spend their entire life in Bay City without ever venturing outside a four-block radius either to shop or to socialize. And yet, regardless of which side of town people come from, they are considered newcomers if their family history does not go back as far as the end of the Second World War. Another indication of what constitutes the elite around Bay City has less to do with financial or social standing than it does with ethnic background, which in turn determines which Catholic church they belong to. Of all the different groups in Bay City, including German, Polish, Italian, and Irish, the French are considered the most select, and the French Catholic church is held in the highest esteem.

When Madonna became famous, one of the stories she told about herself was that she had grown up in a predominantly black neighborhood. The truth is that the majority of the residents in Rochester Hills, where she lived after her mother died and her father remarried, were middle-class whites. The basis for her claim stems from the fact that when Madonna visited her grandmother, she was aware that being Italian in Bay City was comparable to being black in Rochester Hills. On the one hand, it was a deliberate act of rebellion for Madonna to consider herself to be Italian like her father, rather than French like her mother's family. On the other hand, she felt an enormous warmth and closeness to the Italian Catholics in Bay City. She loved their old-world habits, the heavy Gothic furniture in their homes, their passion, and their love of music that they blasted from their record players and radios through the open windows even during the chilly winter months. Madonna found the old women, widows and spinsters, to be loving and kind, accessible and almost mystical, dressed in all black right down to their heavy, opaque stockings and lace-up shoes. She enjoyed watching the men play boccie together every evening after work in the city's main square. The Italian approach to religion also intrigued Madonna. With the exception of the old women, people only went to church to marry, baptize their children, and be buried. The French Catholics were more like the Irish. They went to mass every morning and were joyless in their unwavering faith.

There were other explanations for that invented biographical history. One is that Madonna's first two hits were played primarily on black radio stations. It wasn't until her third hit, which was also her first big-budget video, "Borderline," that her public as well as the executives at the record company actually met her and realized that she was white.

Yet another reason is that years after Madonna left Pontiac and Rochester Hills, when her family still lived there, in the early 1980s, there were occasional race riots, looting, and police brutality. Whenever a black family moved into the neighborhood, two white families moved out. It never occurred to the Ciccone family to leave. More than a social statement, it was a pragmatic decision. Joan Ciccone, Madonna's stepmother, had already made a name for herself as the owner of a reputable day-care center, which was housed in a new wing of the family home. Relocating would have meant that she would have had to start all over again in another neighborhood where the same ethnic changes would eventually have been made anyway. Selling their house and finding another they could afford was unrealistic since real estate prices in the community had gone way down.

Wandering around Bay City and talking to the people, it is obvious that local shopkeepers and merchants are very up-to-date when it comes to their most famous citizen. It is interesting to hear what they remember most about Madonna. Carl Jacobson, for instance, the former president of the Bay City Library Board, admits that when he thinks about Madonna, his first thought is *Sex,* the book, he is quick to add. Jacobson recalls that at the time *Sex* appeared in October 1992, the Library Board decided not to buy it. "If anyone requested it," Jacobson explains, "library staffers would try to locate it. After all, what's garbage to one person is prime rib to another."

Devoted Madonna fans in Bay City were almost unanimously unimpressed by *Sex*. They saw it less as vulgar than as "crass commercialism." One woman explains, "Madonna made the mistake of making her fantasies too visible by taking them from the abstract to the printed page. There's something less appealing about a static image than when Madonna moves and plays and mocks and grimaces, something more ironic and less hard-core about her videos than an actual book. One of the biggest faults with *Sex* was that it failed to capture Madonna's sense of irony and, instead, was perceived by some as 'hard-core,' and by others as merely childish."

Another resident of Bay City who still buys all Madonna's videos and music recalls her reaction when *Sex* appeared. "I was in my formative years when Madonna sprang onto the music scene, and to me, she represented someone who wasn't afraid of her own sexuality and not afraid to flaunt it. You know, as a young girl, you're taught to suppress that side of you. I guess she represented a new beginning, a reclaiming of your own sexuality and using it on your own terms. That's when I really admired her. When *Sex* came out, it should have been written *$ex,* because *$ex* sells, and that's what it was all about. The book had nothing to do with us, with the girls and women who were just learning how to express ourselves, thanks to Madonna. We weren't interested in all those kinky things. We were just beginning to get it together with normal guy/girl sex, or with trying to find out if we liked sex with guys or with women. Madonna went too far too soon for us."

A male fan believes that Madonna is "slightly off when it comes to sensuality." He says, "Maybe because she doesn't understand that sensual is not necessarily based on pornography."

Other Bay City residents like Frank Whalen and Ron Vodlers remember when the singer appeared nude in *Penthouse* and *Playboy* magazines. Whalen, then the manager of the 7-Eleven store in Bay City, was inundated with phone calls from people who wanted to reserve copies, while Vodlers, who managed Unkle Milty's Party Store, recalls how he sold "five *Penthouses* and six *Playboys* in the first day," when usually only five or six are sold in a week. It isn't surprising since, at the time, *Playboy* printed 5.9 million copies, 350,000 more than its normal run, while *Penthouse* shipped 5.2 million instead of the usual 4.9 million.

Despite Madonna's more obvious exploits, the majority of people in Bay City are less interested in her sexual escapades or her controversial songs and videos about the Catholic Church than they are about the comments she made on the *Today* show some fifteen years earlier. While the average Bay City resident may not have a sufficiently raised consciousness, he certainly has a long memory and a healthy appreciation for a local girl who made good.

On the wall of St. Joseph's Church, the oldest Catholic church in the Saginaw Valley, a sign reads, "Some people strengthen the society just by being the kind of people they are." On the opposite wall of the church, facing the Eucharist chapel, is a list of parishioners according to the year that they joined, including a small cross next to the names of those who have since died. The longest list is that of the Fortin family, who were one of the first in the city to join the congregation, between the years 1949 and 1950. Next to the names of all the members, someone has written on the stone wall in black Magic Marker, "God loves Madonna."

chapter six
••••••••••••••••••

*E*lsie Fortin, Madonna's maternal grandmother, is now eighty-nine years old and considered the matriarch of the family. Born in Standish, Michigan, a tiny hamlet about thirty miles to the north, Mrs. Fortin moved to Bay City in 1932 when she married one of its natives, an ambitious businessman who was more than fifteen years her senior. For the twenty-five years that they were together, until Williard Fortin's death in 1957 at sixty-one years old, they were a devoted couple who were looked upon as an example that hard work and deep religious faith brought rewards not only in heaven but also on earth.

Shortly after their marriage, the newlyweds moved into an unassuming bungalow at 87 State Park in an area of Bay City known as Bangor Township. There, within the first ten years of their union, Elsie Fortin produced eight children: six boys—Dale, the firstborn, Michael or Mickey, David, Gary, Earl, and Carl—and two daughters, Marilyn and Elsie Fortin's firstborn daughter, Madonna Louise. The family was devoutly Catholic, and Williard had a reputation as one of the rising stars in the Bay City business community. His first job was with the H. Hirschfield and Sons Scrap Metal Company, where he worked his way up the corporate ranks until he left to join Derocher's Construction Company as an executive vice president. As a result, the Fortin children had everything that any middle-class family could buy back in those prewar years. They were the first family to have a washer and dryer, and Elsie took great pride that her brood never wore hand-me-downs. Every Sunday, she would parade them to church in brand-new store-bought outfits. By 1947, through wise investments in the stock market, Williard Fortin had made enough money to move his family to a better neighborhood and into a bigger house. The property that he chose, 1204 Smith Street, was in an area of town known as The Banks and had once belonged to one of the lumber barons. It had a half acre in the back, bordered by woods, and a quarter of an acre in the front. Instead of moving into the house, Williard decided to tear it down and build in its place a ranch house with all the modern conveniences of that postwar era. Designing the house himself to fit the needs of his large family, he built five bedrooms so that only two children shared a room, a large eat-in kitchen where the family could share casual dinners, a master suite, living room, dining room, a sunroom for his wife's collection of plants, and a finished basement.

For all the years they were married, Williard Fortin controlled the family's finances and never thought to explain to his wife how to handle things when he was no longer around. Elsie Fortin was so sheltered and protected by her husband that throughout the years they were together, she was unaware of her husband's assets and barely knew how to write a check. When Williard died in 1957, he left his forty-six-year-old widow unprepared to manage the family's finances. Because of a series of bad investments. Elsie Fortin found herself unsure financially. In 1975, at sixty-four years old, when life should have been easy for the widow, she was forced to sell the Smith Street house and move into a small two-story structure at 404 North Dean Street. It was an easy sell, and the new owners, Jerry and Grace Trojan, who bought the property for $42,000, were thrilled. "The house was like a mansion to me," Grace Trojan says. "The rooms were huge and there were lots of unique details and little features, like under-the-cupboard recessed lighting in the kitchen and lights that came on in the closets when you opened the doors."

When the Trojans relocated to New Mexico in 1977, they sold the property for $52,000 to the Przygockis family, who lived there for the next nineteen years. "When Madonna became popular," Mrs. Przygockis recalls, "people were constantly coming to the door to get a tour of the house and to take photographs. They came from as far away as Japan and Germany." During the time that the Przygockises lived there, Robin Leach featured the house on his television program *Lifestyles of the Rich and Famous* when he did a segment on Madonna. In 1996, the house was sold for $115,000 to Michelle Campau, who turned it into a senior citizens' residence.

For more than a quarter of a century, despite her famous granddaughter's many offers to relocate her to a more luxurious home, Elsie Fortin has lived alone in that small but impeccably tidy two-story house on Dean Street. Much to her dismay, she can't stop the monthly checks that have automatically been transferred by her granddaughter into her Bay City bank account for the past fifteen years. "I try not to spend it," Mrs. Fortin says, "so when I die, everything will go to my grandchildren."

In the carpeted living room with a view on a small but equally tidy backyard, several statues of the Madonna are on a black-brick fireplace, and a white ceramic Madonna hangs on the wall to the right of the kitchen. There is a curious absence of any family photographs, most notably of her famous granddaughter. According to Mrs. Fortin, when they were on display in the living room, they would invariably disappear along with certain people who came to visit. "It happened a few times," Mrs. Fortin explains, "so I just decided to keep all the family photos hidden away. I look at them when I'm alone and then put them back in their boxes."

The living room is set up for convenience rather than style. A recliner chair upholstered in brown tweed is next to a table on which is a sturdy telephone with several lines and a hold button and an amplifier built into the receiver. On the opposite wall is a state-of-the-art flat-screen television with a VHS, both gifts from her granddaughter.

One of Mrs. Fortin's great pleasures is listening to Madonna's music and watching her videos and concerts. "When they play," Mrs. Fortin says, "it's hard to believe she's my granddaughter. I've got to give her a lot of credit. She really came up the hard way."

On the subject of some of the contents of those videos and concerts, Mrs. Fortin admits that she finds the sexy image hard to cope with. "I have always prayed," she says, "that her antics would not mar her beautiful name." On the other hand, Elsie Fortin claims that the idea of her granddaughter as the personification of sex is more a "marketing ploy," and not a reflection of her true personality. "I think she purposely wants that bad-girl image. She gives that impression, but I never felt she was like that."

The 1988 Buick that sits inside Elsie Fortin's unattached garage is rarely used. In the spring of 2000, the most famous grandmother in Michigan had a second hip replacement and no longer drives. When she needs to go shopping or to the local hospital for physical therapy or to church where she attends mass every morning at seven, she is always accompanied. Although most of her thirty-three grandchildren are scattered throughout the United States, from Colorado to California, from Nevada to New York, and currently as far away as London, Mrs. Fortin's five surviving children are all in the area. Her youngest son, Carl, makes the trip from his home in Detroit to Bay City twice a month to spend the weekend, while his son, Andrew, the only grandchild who actually lives in Bay City, helps with the household errands. Another of Mrs. Fortin's sons, Earl, lives across town and chauffeurs her around, and two more sons, David and Mickey, and the only surviving daughter, Marilyn, all alternate having their mother visit them on holidays and weekends. Until several years ago, Mrs. Fortin spent a great deal of time with her cousin and closest friend, Carolyn Davis, who lived directly across the street. In June 2000, Carolyn Davis died.

These days, the octogenarian can be found sitting on her front porch and chatting with neighbors, who regularly stop by to see how she is. The local townspeople refer to her simply as "Grandma," less for the distinction of having such a famous granddaughter than because she has always functioned as the grandmotherly sage of the neighborhood. Whenever anyone has a problem, whether it is marital discord or rebellious children, Elsie Fortin is the one whom people come to for counsel, and she offers it with her typical common good sense.

Tracey Horne is a large woman with short, curly hair and glasses who not only went to high school with Madonna in Rochester Hills, but currently lives across the street from Elsie Fortin. Leaning against a 1966 silver Eldorado Cadillac that sits in her driveway, parked near a brand-new sport utility vehicle and an oversize camper that looks like a motel on wheels, Horne describes the last time she saw the singer. It was in 1990 when Madonna came to visit her grandmother.

"A big limousine pulled up in front of Grandma's house," she begins, "and naturally all the kids, including mine, went running toward it, because they never saw a car that big in their lives. The kids were really excited, and when Madonna got out, everyone started to talk to her and ask her for autographs. It really burned me up, because she had this big bodyguard who shoved the kids out of the way." Horne pauses and finally decides to say what is on her mind: "Hell, this is my neighborhood and that big monster had no business pushing the kids around or stopping me from going over to Grandma's house. I'm always over there, more than Madonna, so that really turned me off." Horne thinks for a minute. "If you ask me, the only thing that changed after

Madonna became famous was the money. If there's one thing that sticks in my mind about her when we were kids, it's that she always acted like a star."

During all the years that Madonna spent in Bay City with her maternal grandmother during vacations and weekends, she came to understand that while the entire Fortin family was well liked and respected, it was her mother, Madonna Louise, who was remembered with the greatest affection and looked upon almost as a saint. Invariably, people would tell Madonna what an unusually beautiful girl her mother had been, a young woman whose disposition fit her name. For as long as Madonna could remember, they had also told her how she was her mother's perfect clone, an exact replica of the woman who had died so tragically and so young. As Madonna got older, the comments about her mother were more painful. Rumors spread that the Fortin girl had died so young because her Italian husband had made her pregnant so many times in so few years that her strength and resistance had been irreparably depleted. For the young Madonna that was painful to hear.

One of the women in charge of the office at St. Joseph's went to high school with Madonna's late mother, and according to her, all the boys were at one time or another "besotted" with the elder Fortin girl. "She was the most popular girl in school," she recalls, "which is strange, because she was never part of the crowd. She was always considered different, sort of above the rest of us. There was a saintly or untouchable quality about her." Another of Madonna Fortin's classmates was Jim Brennan, who recently organized a multiclass reunion at St. Joseph's in July 2000, in honor of the church's 150th anniversary, which fell on March 18, 2000. He remembers Madonna's mother as someone who never got into trouble and never made an enemy. "Madonna was definitely not one of the crowd," Brennan says, "and yet no one ever teased her or picked on her for being different. We

were all kind of in awe of her." One local resident who dated
Madonna is a much-loved merchant known around Bay City
as "Mr. Wine." Roy "Jay" Crete, now a balding man in his
sixties with an effusive laugh and gregarious nature, has a
package store where he sells everything from jawbreakers to
local wines from north Michigan vineyards. He remembers
Madonna's mother fondly and claims that she was his first
"real date" in high school. "A whole band of us walked to
school every day together," he says, "and as we approached
St. Joseph's, we would pick up kids along the way until
about twenty of us would arrive at school at the same time.
Madonna was Madonna, and she was perfect for her name.
She was sweet, beautiful, kind, and lovely."

Another local who claims to have been briefly engaged to
Madonna Fortin has other recollections of the young
woman. "I wouldn't call her a saint," the former fiancé
maintains, "because we did all the usual things that young
couples do. But I would say that she had an aura about her
that was sort of like a movie star, like she was above everybody else without being snobby or anything. I wouldn't call
her saintly, because she laughed at off-color jokes and liked
to dance, but she was very mature for her age and very wom-
anly and extremely dignified for someone so young." Their
plans for a future together didn't work out. "When you're a
kid and you live in a small town, you always imagine that
your first girlfriend will end up being your wife and the
mother of your children. That's how I felt about Madonna.
At the time, I remember really believing that this was it for
me and that we would spend our lives together right here in
Bay City."

Those who knew Madonna all agree that her idea of femininity was to act helpless and not particularly knowing. According to those same friends, she was much shrewder and
smarter than she let on. Not only did she have a quick mind,
but she could fix anything from a car to an electric outlet.
What she loved to do most was to dance and sing, and many
of her old friends all thought that she would eventually end

up onstage. One close girlfriend describes the room that
Madonna shared with her sister, Marilyn. "The one thing I
remember is the dressing table she had with a flowered skirt
and all the makeup and beauty lotions that Madonna collected. She loved to dress up and experiment with makeup."
Madonna's former fiancé also recalls how her greatest
pleasure was always looking different, changing her hair,
dressing to fit an occasion or holiday by wearing all green
on St. Patrick's Day or little "Christmas tree earrings" for
Christmas mass. "Sometimes we had these theme dances at
school, and when it was Latin, Madonna would fix herself
up as a flamenco dancer," he says. "She had a lot of imagination."

For Madonna, beauty meant everlasting happiness, and
growing up meant falling in love, getting married, and having lots of children. She had no particular professional ambitions, although she worked briefly after finishing a local
junior college. "She was the type of girl who hid her problems," the former beau explains. "She never complained,
and she didn't like anyone who did. Life was for living and
having fun." On the surface, Madonna Louise Fortin was the
ultimate good Catholic girl, who never considered crossing
the line and causing her parents or priest to think poorly of
her. "She was regal, in a sense," the former boyfriend continues, "and extremely well behaved and polite. She didn't
say much, but she was a great listener."

Underneath the surface, Madonna knew exactly how to be
irresistible and at the same time unattainable. She knew
what she wanted, and she recognized her attributes as realis-
tically as she knew her weaknesses.

There are many similarities between Madonna and her
late mother, especially when it comes to love. They shared
the same optimism and a romantic belief in everlasting happiness that would cost the younger Madonna anguish after a
series of broken relationships and the older Madonna guilt
when she defied her family only one time in her life—for the
sake of love. There are also fundamental differences be-

tween mother and daughter. While Madonna senior thought of herself as Cinderella in the sense that if she could just get to the ball, she would be noticed and win the handsome prince, her daughter thought of herself as Cinderella the victim of the wicked stepmother. Contrary to her mother, who longed for the handsome stranger on the white horse to carry her off, from the time that her father remarried and she was forced to care for her younger siblings, Madonna made up her mind that she was the only one who could change her destiny. Though Madonna Louise Fortin, the adored older daughter of caring parents, never had any emotional trauma to mar her childhood, her namesake and daughter lost her mother when she was only five. Madonna didn't just believe that the world owed her some sort of recompense because she was a motherless child, but that God Himself owed her an explanation for taking her parent away. As a result, Madonna had no qualms about standing up for herself and fighting for her place in the family. It was less because of a lack of modesty than that instinct made her believe she was smarter than her stepmother, and she used that intelligence to survive and to thrive. In a moment of quiet reflection, Tony Ciccone admits that his oldest daughter has the same perseverance as his parents had when they uprooted their family to start a new life in America.

chapter seven
....

*I*n 1988, an Italian-American sculptor, Walter Pugni, created a thirteen-foot statue of Madonna clad in a small bikini and affecting a sensual, bent-over pose that she has used many times onstage. He offered the statue to Pacentro, a small Italian village near Rome, in the Abruzzi region of Italy, on the condition that the local officials place it prominently in the center of the town square. Initially, the townspeople, including some of Madonna's surviving relatives, signed a petition rejecting Pugni's offer. Acting more out of pragmatism than emotion, Raphaele Santini, the mayor of Pacentro, launched a campaign to change their minds. Santini imagined that the statue would attract hordes of tourists. While the townspeople were reconsidering their decision, Mayor Santini was contacted by Bay City commissioner Thomas E. Bock, who informed him that if Pacentro didn't want the statue as an homage to Madonna's *paternal* grandparents, Bay City would be honored to have it in tribute to her *maternal* grandparents. As calculating as Mayor Santini was about the Pugni Madonna, so was Commissioner Bock, who imagined that it would bring tourists from all over the world to Bay City. Bay City residents, unlike the citizens of Pacentro, were in favor of the statue, and in fact, Bock had even chosen the site where it would stand. He intended to put Pugni's Madonna on one side of the entrance to the Sage Library where a statue of General Black Jack Pershing already stood. In the end, the citizens of Pacentro relented, and the statue was accepted and placed in the middle of the Piazza

San Marcelo, in a direct line with the altar of the San Marcelo Church and right beneath the window of the mayor's office in Pacentro's city hall. Though that was the end of the odyssey concerning the bikini-clad Madonna, officials in both Pacentro and Bay City have been trying, from 1988 until today, to gain support to link the cities as "twins." So far, officials in Michigan and local potentates in the Abruzzi region of Italy have refused the request.

In 1928, Gaetano Ciccone, a laborer from Pacentro, along with his wife, Michelina, and their five sons, sailed from Italy for America. Their youngest son, Silvio, whom everybody called Tony and whose older brothers would later nickname Sucho after they came back from Korea, was the only child born after the family arrived, on June 1, 1931.

At the time the Ciccone family sailed across the Atlantic Ocean, Pacentro was one of the most beautiful fifteenth-century Italian cities, with impressive landscapes and structures made of ancient white marble. Religious monuments, statues, and such famous churches as the Santa Maria Maggiore, San Marcello, and the Immacolata still stand and bear evidence to the important religious influence that the small city once enjoyed. For the Ciccone family, Pacentro was a city where the surrounding peaks and bad winters presented the constant threat of being cut off from the rest of the world. The winters were bitter cold, food and warm clothing were scarce, and work for Gaetano was a day's donkey ride away over dangerous mountain roads. Today, Pacentro is one of the most important manufacturing centers for winter sports equipment and is the site of some of the most impressive and beautiful ski resorts in Italy. Tourists from all over Europe flock to several of the more famous mountain peaks, which include Mount Corvo, Pizzo Interme, Corno Grande, Mount San Franco, Mount Ienca, Pizzo di Camarda, and Mount Pratello.

* * *

Tony Ciccone, at seventy, looks younger than his years. Still vigorous and attractive, he is tall, muscular, and slightly bow-legged with bushy eyebrows and thinning hair that is slowly turning gray. The expression in his green-blue eyes is both receptive and suspicious, and even with his easy smile and impeccable manners, he projects a wariness about what he has come to believe is the superficiality of the world around him. As the father of an international and controversial star, he is forever forced into the unpleasant position of questioning the true motives of friends and casual acquaintances and tends to assume the worst, which, he claims, leaves no room for disappointments. Over the years, he has been the victim of cunning paparazzi who have gained access to his house using a number of different disguises and ruses.

His relationship with Joan, his second wife of more than thirty years, is tender and leads people to speculate that his quick temper has calmed and that he has mellowed over time. Recently, while Tony and Joan rode their tractors around their vineyard property in northern Michigan, picking up twigs and pieces of fallen trees, Joan drove into a hanging branch, barely missing her eye and leaving a nasty mark on her cheek. Several minutes later, when Tony saw his wife coming out of the kitchen, holding an ice pack against her face, his reaction was a combination of humor and concern. "My wife is an urban orchid," he explained, smiling. "Nature is her natural enemy."

Before Tony retired more than eight years ago from his job as an optics and design engineer with Chrysler, he had already decided to fulfill his lifelong dream to become a vintner. At first, he wanted to buy property in northern California, near the Napa Valley area, since it was tried-and-tested wine country and also because four of his children lived out there. When he discovered the price per acre as well as the cost of labor, he changed his mind and began looking in northern Michigan. Contrary to several articles in local Michigan newspapers, Madonna never invested any money in her father's vineyard property. A proud man, Tony has consistently refused to accept the luxury cars and other expensive gifts that his daughter has had delivered on birthdays and Christmas. Throughout his life, he has lived within his means and instilled that ethic in his children, insisting that they spend only on essentials.

In 1995, Tony and Joan Ciccone bought fifty acres of vineyard property in Suttons Bay in northern Michigan with a panoramic view of Grand Traverse Bay and the rolling hills of the Leelanau Peninsula. Situated near the northern Michigan resort town of Traverse City, an area that is also the summer residence of some of Chicago's wealthiest families, the land cost the Ciccones approximately $40,000 an acre plus an additional $20,000 more per acre to cultivate it and make it suitable to yield grapes. Ironically, Tony and Joan used to camp out in the area when the children were small when Traverse City was famous for its cherry orchards. Back then, it was a mecca for the beer and T-shirt crowd and not the rich and famous. In the past few years, the region has been built up and gentrified, although, despite its trendy restaurants, luxurious summer homes, and the dozen or so vineyard properties that were in existence when the Ciccones moved in, Traverse City remains a small town. With the exception of the annual summer music festival at Interlochen, there is no cultural activity, which the second Mrs. Ciccone finds depressing. In fact, the only way she agreed to be transplanted from the city to a remote vineyard was if her husband agreed that she could travel downstate to Taylor, Michigan, twice a month to visit her widowed mother, several close girlfriends, and her biological daughter, Jennifer, who teaches school in the area. "Making the trip to Detroit or Taylor is my cultural and emotional fix," Joan says. "Every three weeks or so, I go back to visit and shop and see an opera or a concert."

When the time comes to harvest the grapes, Joan and Tony have plenty of company. Her brothers as well as some of their children along with several of the couple's seven grandchildren all make the trip to Suttons Bay to help out.

Though this is his first attempt to market wine made from homegrown grapes, when they lived in Rochester Hills, Tony Ciccone had a small vineyard where he cultivated California grapes that produced enough wine for the family. The house in Rochester Hills where Madonna and her siblings grew up remains unsold. From time to time, Melanie, Tony's youngest daughter with his first wife, goes there to prune and tidy up the vines. Tony believes, as his father did, that wine should remain natural and totally dependent on the earth without any artificial ingredients added to enhance either the quality of the grapes or the wine's taste or color. "I grew up loving wine and with a basic knowledge that nature is responsible for a good wine," he explains. In tribute to his parents, printed on every brochure for the Ciccone Vineyard are the following words: "Tony and his five brothers are forever grateful for their parents' love of wine and their sacrifices."

Operating a vineyard has proven to be a full-time job, although it takes approximately three years before it bears any grapes. The Ciccones have planted rosetto, cabernet, and merlot grapes as well as Pinot Grigio, chardonnay, and cabernet fond. For the first time last season, they submitted four of their wines at an international taster guild in Grand Rapids, Michigan. For the four wines entered, the Ciccones won four medals. Without any hesitation, Joan admits that she is proud of her husband's accomplishment, although somewhat surprised that he has done so well with the vineyard in so short a time. "Tony even designed the labels," Joan says. "He took photographs of the actual grapes on the vines with a digital camera and had them reproduced for the bottles. The only regret I have is that he should have started this when he retired eight years ago instead of waiting so long." Despite the brutal winter climate, construction delays, hard work, and nature's three-year time frame for producing grapes, neither Joan nor Tony regrets their decision. As far as they are concerned, producing wine is a wonderful way to spend the rest of their lives.

Every year, Tony and Joan visit Pacentro to keep in touch with his surviving relatives. In 1985, on their first trip, Tony made a point of preparing the Italian branch of the family for what they might eventually hear about his oldest daughter. When Madonna arrived in Turin in September 1987 for her Who's That Girl concert, at the local sports stadium for sixty-five thousand people, Amelia Vitucci, a second cousin, traveled from Pacentro to meet her famous relative. After the concert, Vitucci took her family backstage. At the end of the visit, she gave Madonna a framed map of Pacentro, which is on display in the Ciccones' living room. Many of the older relatives were too weak to make the pilgrimage to Turin, although Madonna's eighty-two-year-old great-aunt, Bambina De Guilio, sent a note with Vitucci, which said that she regretted not being able to see her famous niece to "hug and kiss her." More than a decade later, during a meeting with Mrs. De Guilio at her home in Pacentro, the elderly woman had a somewhat different opinion of her great-niece. "The girl is a singer," Signora De Guilio said tersely, "just a singer. In my time, we didn't behave like that." Wandering around Pacentro and talking to the residents, one hears what has become the prevailing sentiment about Madonna. One of the clients at a local bar in the center of Pacentro explains, "That girl sings, dances, and shows her thighs. Is it any wonder that her elderly aunt considered her a *malafemmina!*"

Since 1995 when they bought the vineyard property, Tony and Joan Ciccone's visits to Pacentro are also geared to learning more about the old techniques of wine growing in the Abruzzi region of Italy. "When he sets his mind to something," Joan says of her husband, "there is no stopping him. He has to learn everything so he can do it all perfectly!"

Apparently, Madonna not only inherited her father's blue-green eyes and heavy eyebrows, but also his determination from an early age to make something out of his life.

*   *   *

When Gaetano and Michelina Ciccone left Pacentro, their goal was to reach Pittsburgh, where rumor had it that jobs were available in the steel mills. Landing in New York, the family traveled to Pennsylvania and eventually settled in an overcrowded tenement in predominantly Italian Aliquippa, a steel-mill town, a suburb of Pittsburgh. It was a tough life, but they never complained. For them, America was a land of opportunity where there was always enough money to have a decent roof over their heads, to put food on the table, and to have warm clothes for the harsh Pittsburgh winters.

Although Gaetano and Michelina Ciccone died within months of each other in 1968, Madonna remembers her paternal grandparents as a very "present and important force throughout my childhood." She recalls, "They barely spoke English and I didn't speak Italian, but I have only loving memories of them and of very warm and noisy family reunions. If I had to compare my father's mother, Michelina, to my mother's mother, Elsie, I would say that one was the typical old-world Italian grandmother, while the other had views on life and love that were much more pragmatic." When Madonna was having violent arguments with Sean Penn, Elsie Fortin, her more pragmatic grandmother, called Madonna to advise her. "I told her that life is too short," Mrs. Fortin says with a slight smile, "and that she should do something about the situation and not prolong the agony."

Years later, Tony Ciccone would lament his father's decision to settle in Pennsylvania. "Given his love of wine and his ability to cultivate grapes," he says, "he should have kept right on going until he landed in California. Maybe life would have been different for them." Notwithstanding the harsh winters in Pittsburgh, and difficult conditions of the soil, Gaetano Ciccone still managed to cultivate a small vineyard in his Aliquippa backyard.

The Ciccones were only one of hundreds of immigrant families who had made the journey across the ocean in search of a better life and settled in that steel-mill town. They, unlike the other recent arrivals, held on to their old-world customs as a matter of pride and never made much effort to integrate themselves into their new surroundings or to learn English.

Perhaps because he was the youngest, born after his parents had already spent several years in America, Tony was the only child who was not forced to quit school to help support the family. From the time he was old enough to go to school, Tony was determined to make something of himself. He instinctively knew that the only way to rid himself of the stigma of poverty and to become integrated into society was to get a college degree. As Madonna explains, "My father wasn't ashamed of his parents, he just wanted better for his own children. He was the only one who had a college education, and the only one who aspired toward that typical upwardly mobile American way of life."

After graduating from high school, Tony Ciccone did odd jobs to get through college at Pennsylvania State University, where he majored in engineering. Just as rumor had it in Pacentro that the steel mills in Pittsburgh were hiring immigrant workers, rumor had it in the fifties that young men with degrees in engineering were being hired for higher than normal starting salaries in the automotive business in Detroit. After finishing university, Tony had no trouble finding work as an optics and design engineer in the car industry. His first job was in a missile and tank plant in Warren, Michigan, where he worked mostly on defense contracts that General Motors had with the government. With the compulsory draft still in effect, Tony, who was settled in his new job and for the first time in his life was confident about his future, was not anxious to be shipped overseas. His older brothers, all of whom had been drafted and served in the Korean War, suggested that he fulfill his military obligation by volunteering for the Air Force Reserve. It was a logical way for him to serve his country while studying more advanced techniques related to his chosen profession. Within days of signing up, Tony Ciccone was shipped off to Alaska and then to Texas. In Texas he became close friends with a fellow serviceman named Dale Fortin, who hailed from Bay City, Michigan. When Dale announced his intention to marry a local Texas girl and asked Tony to serve as his best man, the event forever changed the young Ciccone's life.

At the wedding in Dallas, Tony met his friend's younger sister, a beautiful dark-haired, dark-eyed girl with an angelic smile who had the unusual name of Madonna. It was love at first sight for Tony, who was devastated to learn that she was engaged to someone back home in Bay City. Despite his sister's commitment to another man, Dale Fortin convinced her to go out with Tony at least while they were all in Texas celebrating his marriage. For the entire week that Tony was on leave and Madonna was visiting, the couple spent almost every minute together. According to Elsie Fortin, when her daughter finally returned home, she began a correspondence with the young engineer she had met in Texas. "There was no doubt in my mind that Madonna was in love with Tony," Elsie Fortin recalls. "It didn't surprise me that Tony was madly in love with her. She was a beautiful girl. Everyone who knew her loved her. She could have had any boy she wanted."

From the very beginning, Elsie Fortin judged that there was a cultural chasm between the Ciccones and the Fortins. With the exception of the grandchildren that they eventually shared, she believed they had nothing in common. It didn't matter that the elder Ciccones had an innate knowledge of music and opera or had lived with nineteenth-century Italian painting and sculpture. Elsie Fortin had more practical ambitions for her daughter that did not include marriage to the son of penniless immigrants. Her idea of success was that Madonna would re-create the life that Williard had briefly given Elsie before he died—the split-level ranch with under-the-cupboard lighting in the kitchen. Fortunately for the young couple, Elsie Fortin was also wise enough to realize that the very things that she found unacceptable about Tony were exactly what her daughter found attractive.

For Madonna, Tony was someone between that prince on a white horse and a day laborer, the dusky immigrant on a scaffold who, despite the grime and dirt, carries centuries of culture and mystery within his soul. He was different from the boys in Bay City, someone who had obviously not had an easy life. She found his smoldering energy and sexuality exciting. A part of this kind, loving daughter was a woman who craved someone who made her feel alive, a man who was slightly on the edge and dangerous. Deep down, she had always fantasized about bringing an Italian home to her family in Bay City. Tony was ideal. He was a scrapper, a street fighter who had learned to turn his aggression into ambition and his anger into energy. He was someone who, despite his sense of humor and love of a good time, was focused on achieving professional and monetary success. As soon as he met Madonna, he knew that she was a big part of his dream.

She was the typical American girl who was secure enough to follow her husband anywhere necessary for him to advance in his career. She had no complexes or hesitation about fitting in or making new friends. Madonna Fortin was Tony Ciccone's ticket out of not belonging, his guarantee that he would never again be betrayed by a country that purported to welcome immigrants but that, in reality, made fun of them behind their backs. He loved her simplicity. Madonna, who died at thirty-one, before she achieved anything more than producing six children in six years, was the kind of woman who "hummed while she did the ironing." By the time they married, Tony was already an upwardly mobile first-generation American, determined to expunge all tradition out of his life. He wanted nothing that was old, nothing ethnic, nothing that wasn't 100 percent American. He wanted a wife who hummed while she ironed.

* * *

At the time that they met, Madonna Fortin had just finished a brief semester at a local junior college and was working as a technician for two Bay City radiologists, G. L. Heaelshaw and A. L. Ziliac. As was the custom back in the 1950s, dental and medical assistants were trained by the individual doctors who hired them and were not required to get a diploma at a technical school. Years later, when Madonna was searching for an explanation for her mother's breast cancer, she made it her business to locate the seven other women who had worked in that same office and had been exposed to daily doses of radiation. Madonna's inquiries revealed that none of the women, who all still lived in the Bay City area—Joan Behrman, Betty Vil, Kitty White, Marlene Alavie, Nina Dajet Suanton, Marian Harris, and Carol Rupp—had suffered any cancer. Six months after Madonna Fortin Ciccone died, her closest friend, Jane Fournier, who lived next door, also died of breast cancer.

In 1955, Madonna Louise Fortin and Silvio Tony Ciccone were married at the Visitation Church in Bay City, Michigan. Her sister, Marilyn, was her matron of honor, and her brother Dale, who had introduced the couple, was Tony's best man. Following the wedding, the young couple set out by car for Alexandria, Virginia, where Tony had been lent out by General Motors to work on another government defense project. On May 3, 1956, their first child, a boy they named Anthony, was born. When the baby was only three months old, Tony was recalled to Michigan, where he resumed his work at General Motors.

The Ciccones settled in a small brick bungalow at 443 Thors Street in the suburb of Pontiac, twenty miles northwest of Detroit. There, on August 9, 1957, their second child, Martin, was born. Four more children followed in quick succession: Madonna, born on August 16, 1958, followed by Paula barely a year later, then Christopher in 1960, and then Melanie in 1962. Tragedy struck when Melanie was barely six months old. During a routine gynecological examination, the doctor discovered a lump in Madonna's breast. After more invasive examinations, it was diagnosed as breast cancer. Back then, the disease was an unspeakable horror with little or no chance of a cure. Madonna's doctors advised her to begin radiation therapy right away, although they warned her that the treatment would seriously affect her ability to care for her newborn. Still nursing and with five small children and a husband who depended on her, Madonna decided to postpone treatment until she could wean the baby and make sure that the others would be properly cared for. Despite the torment that Tony went through and the realization there was little chance that his wife would survive, he, along with their priest, supported his wife's decision. The doctors viewed their patient's decision as a self-imposed death sentence. On several occasions, they warned the couple that given the normal increase of hormone activity while a new mother is nursing, the disease would advance more rapidly. The doctor's battle was useless since the family priest had more influence on their patient than they did. Two months after the initial diagnosis, Madonna finally agreed to begin chemotherapy. By then, it was too late.

Tony Ciccone experienced a series of devastating emotions that would forever mark his life as well as the lives of his six children. Madonna was the center of his life, the only woman he had ever loved, the person who shared his deep religious convictions and his sense of humor. For a man who was so determined to succeed in everything he did by sheer will, hard work, and deep religious faith, he was suddenly rendered impotent as he watched his wife slip away. Elsie Fortin, who could only endure the tragedy by means of her deep faith in God, tried her best to comfort her son-in-law and grandchildren, although she was physically and emotionally incapable of caring for them. Forced to hold down a full-time job, Tony Ciccone scattered the little ones with different relatives. Every evening after work, Tony would visit his wife in the hospital before making alternate visits to his children at various homes in the area.

Madonna spent approximately a year in Mercy Hospital in Bay City, wasting away and unable to withstand the painful chemotherapy, which the doctors eventually stopped, since it was doing more harm than good. From time to time, she would come home only to find that she was too weak to care for her husband and children. One of the most frequently reported stories was that little Madonna had supposedly once hit her mother on the back in frustration when the ailing woman was too sick to play with her. When Madonna saw her mother's tears, she understood that her lethargy was not for lack of love but rather strength. From that moment on, Madonna understood that her mother's enormous emotional strength and faith had kept her from wallowing in the tragedy of her situation. "My mother gave me an incredible lesson in life," Madonna explains, "about how to put things in perspective and how to prioritize those things which are life-threatening, serious, or just annoying."

Friends and family members who were around during those bleak days maintain that Madonna thrived in a way that she hadn't when she was well. "She had a mission," one friend remembers, "and she seemed determined that either she would beat it or she would maintain her dignity. She saw it as a challenge." Another friend recalls that the cancer only made Madonna more religious and accepting of what she considered to be "God's will." "There was never ever a moment when she got angry or said that God was unfair," the friend says. "If anything, Madonna took it as a sign that her children were special and resilient or God wouldn't have given them this obstacle to surmount."

Even after she lost all her hair and was reduced to helpless gestures and often disjointed words, she made a pretense at charm and good humor, valiantly carrying on as if nothing were wrong. On one occasion when she was at home with neighborhood visitors, they all watched the children scrambling around the floor, playing and laughing. With tears in her eyes, she turned to her guests and said, "We make beautiful babies, don't we? At least no one can ever take that away from me."

On her last visit home, before she was transported back to the hospital for the final stay, she insisted that someone pack all her cosmetics in a small train case along with a camera. Once back in her hospital bed, she asked the nurse to watch carefully while she applied her makeup. When the nurse asked her why she was "fussing" like that, Madonna answered, "I want you to take a picture of me so the undertakers will know how to make me up for my funeral."

On November 22, 1963, as the country mourned the assassination of President John Kennedy, the Ciccone family sat in vigil at Madonna's deathbed at Mercy Hospital. On the morning of November 30, 1963, the doctors advised the family that the situation had become critical. Miraculously, on the last day of her life, when her husband and mother were visiting, Madonna rallied. Sitting up in bed and laughing with her family, she suddenly announced that she had a craving for a hamburger. Tony and Elsie were delighted by her transformation and actually believed that she was going into some kind of remission. Unfortunately, they told the children that their mother seemed to be getting better.

That night when she went to bed, little Madonna had a vision in which her mother was well and had actually come into her room to tuck her in and kiss her good-night. Years later when Madonna was reminded of that incident, she would say that, deep down, she knew that her mother was dying. "I think children are a lot smarter about death than adults think they are," she said.

In the early-morning hours of December 1, 1963, with her husband at her side, holding her hand, Madonna Louise Fortin Ciccone slipped into a coma. Several hours later, she was dead.

When little Madonna awoke that morning, she wandered into the kitchen and found her grandmother, aunts, and uncles all sitting around the kitchen table weeping. Her first reaction was bewilderment. Why were they so upset when her mother had recovered? There had been no miracle, Madonna was told. Her mother was with God in heaven. As she was passed around from relative to relative to be hugged and comforted, she started to argue until her words became heart-wrenching screams. They were lying, the little girl cried, they were wrong, her mother was fine! Wriggling out of their embraces, she raced around the house, searching for her mother, slamming doors, looking under beds. It was all a game, she thought fleetingly, or maybe another dream, a nightmare. Eventually, she collapsed from exhaustion, feeling completely alone, lost, and confused and, for a long time afterward, never really able to grasp that her mother was no longer there. "Martin and Anthony suffered a lot, I think," one relative recalled, "because as boys, they were taught to keep their emotions in check. They held everything inside, and it doesn't surprise me that Martin had the biggest problems with alcohol." According to the same uncle, Melanie, Paula, and Christopher, who were too little to understand the implications of their mother's death, all accepted the notion that their mother was safely in heaven. "That made them feel better," he continues, "although Christopher wasn't buying that kind of happy ending." All the relatives agree that Christopher had always been an extremely sensitive child, prone to tears and generally fearful. "He had a deep fear of being alone," a teacher from Christopher's elementary school recalls. "I don't think he was as close to his mother the way Madonna was, but he was generally fearful after she died that there would be no one to take care of him."

According to her other relatives, Madonna was always the smartest and most verbal of all the children and also the one who was the closest to her mother. "It really turned her life around," they all agree. "Of all the kids, she was the one who resented her father getting married again. I don't think she ever got over that. In a way that was almost as traumatic for her as her mother's death." Unlike Christopher, who feared for his own survival, Madonna made up her mind that she didn't need anyone to care for her. From then on, she became her own parent.

The death of their mother produced a ferocious anger within all the Ciccone children with the exception of the baby, Melanie, that came out in different ways. Madonna responded to the loss with a fury that was fueled by her resolve never to let anything hurt her ever again. Forced to function as a child much older than her years, Madonna took on the household tasks and acted as a surrogate mother to her younger siblings.

chapter eight

....

*M*adonna's rise to stardom was swift. Only five years elapsed from the time she arrived in New York in 1978 to the moment when she appeared on the international music scene in 1984, wearing a transparent wedding dress and singing "Like a Virgin." After Madonna became a star, she implied that as she'd clawed her way up the ladder to success, she had been so poor that she often went hungry. "I worked my ass off to get where I am today," she has said, "and even ate out of garbage cans to survive." When she first arrived in New York, though she certainly struggled, worked at menial jobs, and squatted in an abandoned music studio on the Lower East Side, the choice was hers. She may not have grown up in a culturally sophisticated environment where good taste was inherent and price no object, but she was far from materially deprived. She dropped out of college to go to New York against her father's wishes, with the understanding that he would not subsidize her. Contrary to her claims, her determination to succeed and her fight to survive have nothing to do with the typical Mildred Pierce syndrome about never being poor or hungry again, and everything to do with the promise that she had made to herself never to depend on anyone for anything ever again. Even then, there is a contradiction. During those tough early years, she always managed to find someone who either believed in her talent, was intrigued by her charm, or attracted to her sensuality and who was willing to pick up the bills until she became rich and famous.

Years later when she was lobbying for the movie role, she was even more convinced that she had been "born to play" Evita when she equated her struggle for stardom with that of the former Argentine first lady. Madonna believed that she, like Eva Perón, had suffered the same rejection from her peers and family, had used a succession of lovers to achieve her goals, and had finally managed to get out of a small town and into a big city without any money or promise of a job. In fact, in that pleading letter that Madonna wrote to Alan Parker, she cited the similarities between herself and Eva Perón. "Both of us evoke passionate sentiments from the people. Both of us are either loved or hated, perceived either as a saint or an opportunistic whore who relied on self-invention and publicity to achieve international acclaim." In closing, she wrote, "It is my destiny to play her. I have a strange affinity for Latin culture, in my music, friends, the relationships I have, food and art."

When Madonna finally landed the part, Alan Parker was clever enough to create two scenes that, subliminally at least, created the impression that Madonna and Eva had endured similar traumas in their lives.

One of the opening scenes of the film is a funeral procession in a rural Argentine town. The atmosphere is dark and dreary as the mourners make their way slowly toward a small church where the deceased is laid out in his coffin. The camera captures a child on the periphery of the crowd, dressed in tatters and clutching a pathetic bouquet of flowers. Suddenly, she breaks away from her mother and siblings and rushes toward the church. The implication is clear. The child and her family are not welcome at this funeral, although the emotion and the determination of the little girl makes it apparent that she knows the dead man and wants desperately to reach his coffin. Once inside the church, she flings herself over the body, smothering it with kisses and crying, "Papa!" As the crowd pulls her away, there are cries of "bastard child," and the audience understands that she is the illegitimate daughter of a man who was a respected local potentate whose friends and legal family are gathered to mourn him.

To Parker's credit, what makes this scene so wrenching, produces an outpouring of sympathy for the little girl, and sets the mood for the rest of the film is that the child bears an uncanny resemblance to a young Madonna with her dark hair and eyebrows, heart-shaped face, and scrappy determination.

The young actress who played Evita as a child, Marie Lujan Hidalgo, had an inordinately close relationship with the star during the making of the movie, sharing a "mutual and instant connection" to one another. "When we first met," Hidalgo says, "Madonna wanted to know all about me and my family, whether I had a good relationship with my parents, how I became an actress, what my life was like. People told me that she had a completely different personality around me than around the other cast members." Hidalgo also sensed that Madonna was so immersed in her role that she instinctively comforted Hidalgo for the loss of her father, as if those events had really taken place in Hildalgo's life. "Madonna really believed that she was Evita and had lost her father, so she really believed that it was me, that child, who had suffered that loss."

Drawing upon the physical resemblance between Madonna as a child and the child actress portraying Evita was not the only technique that Parker used to create the impression that his star and the character she portrayed were one and the same. Using a child actress who resembled Madonna more than she resembled Eva Perón validated the premise that both were considered outsiders, children from the "wrong side of the tracks" who were on the periphery of society. The reality was, however, much different, both for Madonna and Evita.

While Eva Perón was illegitimate by birth, she and her three sisters and one brother not only carried the name of their father, Juan Duarte, a well-to-do landowner, but also enjoyed a close relationship with him. For the fifteen years that he was with Evita's mother, until he died in a car accident in 1920, Duarte divided his time between his legal wife and three daughters and his illegitimate family. However, after his death, all support stopped. In the end, the only legacy that Duarte left his second family was the right to carry his name. From that point on, life was difficult for Eva, who never forgot how she was forced to work as a maid, along with her mother and sisters, in the homes of the local rich people. This was Eva Perón's first exposure to the disparity between the upper and lower classes in Argentina, an experience that was supposed to have provided the incentive for her to do everything in her power to elevate the workers.

Madonna, after the loss of her mother, was never excluded by society and, in fact, was given preferential treatment by a large and loving extended family as well as by the nuns who taught her. All through elementary school, as Madonna progressed from grade to grade, her teachers would write on their evaluation sheets, "Be patient. Mother died."

Alan Parker also draws subtle comparisons between Madonna's life and that of Eva Perón in one of the last scenes in the film. Of all the transformations that Madonna makes in the movie to become Evita, the most touching and believable is in the deathbed scene, when the dying first lady of Argentina refuses to believe, or refuses to admit to her husband, that at thirty-three years old her body has failed her. The torment and the anguish that Madonna projects as a dying Evita, the tears and the willful denial that she is, indeed, loosing the battle to inoperable ovarian cancer, is one of the few times where the actress reaches deep within herself to become the character, rather than relying on mere physical resemblance to Eva Perón. It is a remarkable on-screen moment as Madonna conjures up memories and feelings and puts herself into her mother's skin as she loses the battle at thirty-one to cancer. Once again, the reality for both dying women was quite different.

In Parker's *Evita*, a grief-stricken Juan Perón, played by Jonathan Pryce, finally blurts out what both he and his wife have avoided putting into words: "You're dying, Evita." In the film, Juan Perón's devotion to his wife during the last weeks of her life is heart-wrenching. The real Juan Perón, however, found it repulsive to enter his wife's room as he equated the odors and sounds that surrounded her with impending death, which he found intolerable and revolting to his senses. When Madonna went to Buenos Aires to research Evita's life, she also learned that Perón actually forbid the doctors to give her painkillers. Always the politician, he was thinking ahead and didn't want to ruin the quality of Evita's skin when she would be on display in the capitol's rotunda.

For many years after her mother's death, Madonna was under the impression that her father uttered similar words, forcing his wife to face that she was dying. When Madonna's mother was on her deathbed at Mercy Hospital in Bay City and had a sudden craving for a hamburger, her husband and mother imagined a miracle or at least a temporary respite from the cancer. According to what Elsie Fortin told people at the time, it was her daughter who dashed any hope the family might have had when she sat straight up in her bed and said quite matter-of-factly, "I'm dying, and I want to see my children for the last time."

In August 1989, when Madonna turned thirty-one, the age of her mother when she died, it was a turning point in her life and in her career. While others might have had a sudden awareness that they had arrived at the same age as their deceased parent, Madonna had a different awareness. For her, the natural course of life was out of sync. She found herself suddenly too old to be her mother's daughter and her mother forever too young to be the grandmother to the children the singer hoped to have someday. That was the year that she dedicated her album *Like a Prayer* to her mother with the words, "This album is for my mother who taught me how to pray." The songs are more autobiographical than ever before and are considered by many to be her best. Coproduced and cowritten by Madonna with Patrick Leonard, Stephen Bray, and Prince, *Like a Prayer* not only addresses such issues as love, loss, death of a parent, and rebellion, but is also one of the best examples of Madonna's musical ability to maintain a consistent tone and dance beat while experimenting with different style tunes and sophisticated piano ballads. There is something for everyone in that album, and as she has said, she "offers up an image that can be either misconstrued or embraced by all sides of the religious, political, or social spectrum." In fact, *Like a Prayer* could have been written in response to a questionnaire sent out by Madonna to a cross-section of teenage girls and women. Not only did Madonna insert her own anguish into the lyrics, but each subject of every song is instantly recognizable to her public as all the cuts touch on emotional dilemmas and traumas to which everyone could relate, even if they have not had the same experiences. Rather than just changing her image, Madonna sings each song with different intonations and expressions. In "Oh Father," there is a tear in her voice when she confesses to her father how she had felt unloved as a child after her mother's death. In "Keep It Together," she sings about the importance of family, while "Cherish," an optimistic fifties love song, and "Till Death Do Us Part" tell the story of her failed marriage to Sean Penn. The most touching song, however, is "Promise to Try."

Madonna is realistic enough to realize the tendency to give someone who is gone attributes he or she never possessed. "I have to be careful sometimes," Madonna has said, "because when someone dies and the years go by, you tend to make them into something they're not." "Promise to Try" is both a moving homage to her mother as well as a plea that she makes to herself to stop grieving. It is about letting go, about Madonna yearning to have a mother and, at the same time, forcing herself to accept that she is gone forever, about Madonna's struggle between the reality and the fantasy of her memories.

"Don't let memory play games with your mind / she's a faded smile frozen in time," she sings.

Madonna admits that she often talks to her mother even if

she will never know if she hears her or not. According to the star, she tells her things that a "girl can only say to her mother. Private things."

From that point in her professional life, Madonna transformed the stage into her private confessional. Through her music, she has not only come to terms with her own demons but has also created an unusual intimacy with her fans.

Christmas 1963 was a season for mourning for the Fortin and Ciccone families. During those first few weeks after Madonna died, Elsie Fortin was inconsolable. It was inconceivable to her that God had taken her vibrant daughter at a time when her six small children needed her so much. Ten years earlier, Elsie had buried her son Gary, who also died of cancer. With every ounce of strength that she had left, Mrs. Fortin prayed that she would not lose the faith that had sustained her throughout her life. It was a difficult task, and on many occasions, she confessed to her priest that she was not certain she would resist. Her faith would be tested yet again, when almost three years to the day after her daughter died, her oldest son, Dale, who had introduced Madonna and Tony at his Texas wedding, would die of cancer as well. These three of Elsie Fortin's children are all buried at the Calvary Cemetery in Bay City.

In 1968, when Rose Kennedy buried her fourth child, Robert Kennedy, people around Bay City began comparing Elsie Fortin to the matriarch of the Kennedy clan.

After her mother died, Madonna's close relationship with her grandmother was based on her obsession to know everything about her mother. Elsie Fortin recalls how she and her granddaughter would spend hours together with Madonna posing countless questions. "I would try and answer them as best I could," Mrs. Fortin said. "The last thing I wanted was to give my granddaughter the slightest misinformation or wrong impression about my daughter." Though it was extremely painful to constantly conjure up images of her late daughter, it did make the child she had lost seem always present. "Madonna has her mother's mouth and nose," Mrs. Fortin maintains, "and her mother's smile, her mother's bone structure, petite and delicate. She also moves the way her mother did, and as she matures, her facial expressions become so much like her mother's that it's like a part of my daughter is always with me." Elsie Fortin also insists that Madonna's musical talent comes from her mother: "My daughter loved to sing and dance, and I can still see the two of them dancing and singing along with records or the radio. Whenever little Madonna did something on her own, her mother would applaud and encourage her to continue."

According to Elsie Fortin, her daughter imparted a sense of unconditional love to all her children, but especially to her oldest girl and namesake, with whom she was the closest. "There were times when I would tell her that she was too involved with Madonna," Mrs. Fortin insists, "because I felt the other kids were excluded." If Madonna was indeed the favorite child, her mother was nonetheless patient and nurturing to all the children. Rather than disciplining them when they misbehaved, she would hug and kiss them. "She once told me that she felt she had so little time with them as kids," Elsie Fortin claims, "that she didn't want to waste one minute being angry or seeing her kids cry."

Throughout the years, Madonna has said that her mother's death gave her the impetus to succeed in life. Melanie Klein, the eminent child psychologist, believed that the quality of love and care that a child gets from her mother rather than her father during the first crucial five and a half years of life molds her character and her sense of self-worth. Klein's theory of the "good breast" and "bad breast" describes how a mother can treat each of her own children differently, nurturing one while ignoring or deprecating another, and how the child who was given the "good breast" naturally has a much more highly developed sense of self-confidence.

Not all motherless or cherished children go on to great success in life. An actress who worked with Madonna on *The Next Best Thing* is less generous when she quotes Somerset Maugham: "Madonna is in the 'front rank of the second-rate.' Her mother may have given her the confidence that contributes to star quality, but she certainly didn't give her that other important ingredient—talent!"

Obviously, talent, discipline, luck, and timing count as much as or more than parental love. But Madonna had something else. After her mother died, she responded by taking charge of her own destiny. Later on, she became her own stage mother, the parent she had never had who pushed her to achieve in ways that her mother might never have done. If her mother had lived, perhaps Madonna would have become complacent rather than ambitious.

chapter nine
··················

*I*n her book *The Psycho-Analysis of Children,* Melanie Klein writes that "the importance which the girl's mother image has for her as a 'helping' figure and the strength of her attachment to her mother are very great. . . . She needs good things to protect her against the bad ones and to establish a certain equilibrium inside her. In her fantasy her mother's body is therefore a kind of storehouse which contains the means of satisfying all her desires and of allaying all her fears."

Klein also writes of the importance for a child to develop another figure in his life in addition to his parents to give support against the outside world. "Other persons," Klein says, "such as a kindly nurse or brother or sister or grandparent or an aunt or uncle can, in certain circumstances, take over the role of the 'good mother' or the 'good father.' "

As Madonna approached puberty, the scars that remained from the loss of her mother manifested themselves in ways that confused her and made her feel guilty. Claude Delay Tubiana is a prominent French psychiatrist who is an expert in the field of the sexual development in children and the author of *Chanel Solitaire,* an intimate portrait of Coco Chanel. Dr. Tubiana was an intimate friend of the famous designer and recounts the secret heartache, traumas, and tragedies that she encountered throughout her life and that she overcame to become a star in the world of Parisian haute couture. Not unlike Madonna, Coco Chanel had many influential lovers who helped her achieve her enormous success, and she also had a difficult childhood. As a psychiatrist and writer, Dr. Tubiana draws certain similarities between the two women. "A young girl's relationship to her mother," Dr. Tubiana explains, "is never exclusive and is bound up with Oedipus impulses. Her anxiety and sense of guilt in relation to her mother also affect the course of those Oedipus impulses. If a girl is frightened of her mother or, in the case of Madonna, loses her mother before the age of thirteen, she is deprived of something very basic as it concerns her attachment to her father, something is fundamentally affected by the quality and the length of time she is attached to her mother. In Madonna's case, the normal course of development was interrupted prematurely, which not only played havoc with her natural oedipal instincts but also her eventual sexual development."

Under ordinary circumstances, a young girl's healthy oedipal relationship with her father grows out of a powerful and drawn-out connection to her mother. In Madonna's case, that relationship ended prematurely when her mother died. As Madonna got older, she was aware that her father had suddenly adopted a more careful and measured response to her seductive ploys and feminine wiles. The behavior that Tony had once thought adorable when Madonna was a toddler and a little girl he suddenly considered inappropriate. On more than one occasion, when his oldest daughter crawled on his lap or wandered into his bed in the middle of the night, he was embarrassed and uncomfortable. As a result, he became stricter, cooler, and more distant with Madonna than with the other girls.

Many people who have worked closely with Madonna confirm that she responds well to stress and stays balanced "in the center of a hurricane." When John Schlesinger directed her in *The Next Best Thing,* he was amazed that despite her lack of acting experience, she never doubted for an instant that she had mastered her part. The film was difficult even for a consummate professional, Schlesinger adds, and was one of the "worst experiences" in his life for a number of reasons. From the beginning, he had problems because the producers were reluctant to address the issue of a gay man becoming a parent (the theme of the film) and were constantly calling for rewrites of the script.

In the film, Madonna plays Abbey, an unmarried yoga instructor with no love prospects on the horizon who is very aware that her biological clock is running down. After a drunken one-night stand with her best friend, a gay gardener played by Rupert Everett, Abbey gets pregnant. "Madonna has a highly developed and elaborate defense mechanism against criticism and loss," John Schlesinger says. "As someone who grew up in an extremely loving home, I can only imagine that Madonna's mother must have given her a phenomenal combination of nature and nurture for her to have such self-esteem. She is indomitable. Whatever her failings as an actress, it's difficult for a director to ignore that attitude she has of 'I am the center of the universe.' Madonna projects the kind of energy that makes a star."

On the surface, Madonna appears to be bulletproof. She has the unusual ability, especially for a performer, never to get paralyzed by her failures. Instead, she is propelled forward by every bad review and negative article that is written about her. "I think I have a motor inside of me," she says, "that makes me never go down. I feel it pulling at me, and sometimes it's stronger than at other times. But no matter what happens, working is the one thing that makes me fight all those demons inside of myself."

According to a close friend and business partner, Madonna has been extremely hurt by criticism and bad reviews. "She has always said that people assume because she's rich and famous," the woman says, "that all that nasty stuff that's written about her is just part of the price she has to pay. When she feels that she has done something really good, whether it's a video or a film, and the critics massacre her efforts, I have seen her really upset and crying. The only thing that gets her up and active again is her discipline that she will beat the depression. She always minimizes her problems by comparing them to what happened to her mother. I give her a lot of credit."

By giving her favorite daughter such exceptional nurturing and unconditional love, Madonna Fortin Ciccone is also responsible for Madonna's belief that there are no limits to her capabilities. According to Schlesinger, during the shooting of the first half of the film, Madonna would constantly question his efforts to direct her. "Her determination to manage the film set cost her in terms of her performance," Schlesinger says. "For the first few weeks, she would constantly tell me that she didn't understand what I was trying to say to her or to get her to do. At the time, I knew I had to try and find a means of communicating with her, because I couldn't just treat her as one would a consummate professional actor. What I tried was to not have too much premeditation when it came to directing her, because I thought that things would happen naturally. Unfortunately, she turned out to be a famous performer who has made it based on a certain artificiality and connotation. In the end, I blame myself, because I was the director and unfortunately I made the mistake of believing that her talent in the realm of music and video would carry her as an actress. But what was most incredible was that because of her powerful belief in herself, she almost convinced me."

Rupert Everett is more indulgent about Madonna's performance in *The Next Best Thing*. "Her main problem is that her 'Madonnaness' overpowered any acting talent she may have," Everett says. "By that I mean, the art of being Madonna, the persona that her fans depend on for always giving them the best performance, never holding anything back or disappointing them, but always giving them the sheer shock they expect from her performances, often gets in the way of her talent. The fact is that she didn't challenge us enough in the right way obviously, because she didn't have the experience to know what should be changed. For instance, being good in a film has a lot to do with having a good role. If the actor is supposed to light a cigarette and set fire to her hair, it's a great scene no matter how you act it. But if someone cuts the part about setting fire to her hair and all the actor does is light a cigarette, then no matter how well you do it, it's just another cigarette being lit. Basically, the powers that ruled were afraid of making Madonna unsympathetic and quirky, which was hard luck on her. Had they left the scenes the way they were written, she would have come across as funny and eccentric. In the end, we failed her, all of us, because we left her with a role that was bland and forced her to act in a film that didn't give her a lot of scope."

Madonna's eighty-nine-year-old maternal grandmother, Elsie Fortin, says of her granddaughter, "I think she has difficulty acting in some of her movies, because when she's not playing herself, her fans have trouble relating to her."

During one of her conversations with her grandmother when Madonna was a child, she learned that when her mother found out she was pregnant with her, she wanted the same doctor who had delivered her twenty-six years earlier to deliver her third baby. It would be the only pregnancy for which Madonna Fortin Ciccone would travel the eighty miles by car from her home in Pontiac, Michigan, to Bay City. Not surprisingly, little Madonna interpreted that revelation as further proof that she had been the favorite child. She relished hearing how her mother had waited out the last few weeks of her pregnancy at Elsie Fortin's house, where she slept in her girlhood bed covered by the identical blue-and-white lace quilt that she had used throughout her adolescence. On August 16, 1958, Elsie Fortin took her daughter to Mercy Hospital in Bay City, where Dr. Abraham H. Jacoby, the same man who had delivered all of Elsie Fortin's eight children at his home at 2202 Ninth Street, delivered Tony and Madonna Ciccone's firstborn daughter. One of Madonna's deepest regrets was that Dr. Jacoby, who was already sixty-two years old when she was born, was long gone when she was old enough to talk to him.

Elsie Fortin also told her granddaughter that she had been the one who had persuaded her daughter to baptize the baby Madonna, which at the time went against the wishes of Tony Ciccone. It was an unusual request, since French Catholics never call a child after a living relative, especially a parent. Still, Mrs. Fortin insisted that tradition be broken, since she had always had a frightening premonition that her daughter would not live long enough to have "old bones." In some odd way that the eighty-nine-year-old woman still finds difficult to explain, she had had a sense that her granddaughter was destined to become something special. "When little Madonna was born," she recalls, "I had a sense of some finality that I could never explain, but because I am a very religious person, I knew if my feelings proved right, at least the name would live on if she gave it to the baby."

Madonna found that story to be almost mystical, yet one more sign of a divine connection between herself and her deceased parent.

After her mother died and her father remarried, Madonna felt unloved and alienated from her father. The motherless child who was once the favorite was forced to accept another woman as a mother figure. In reaction to the betrayal Madonna felt, she developed an uncanny sense of survival that stayed with her throughout her life. More than just learning how to survive, Madonna learned how to thrive. As a little girl, she knew to limit her tantrums so that, when she had one, it would make an impression, and people would sit up and pay attention. Whenever she found herself in a situation she could neither understand nor change, she was clever enough to fade into the background. More than any other asset that she possesses, Madonna has mastered the art of control so that her acting passive and humble in an environment she has not conquered is as effective a method as humiliating and terrifying her coworkers or catching them off guard in those situations when she is in charge.

On the occasion of the English premiere of *Evita*, Madonna's good friend Sting gave a party in her honor at The Ivy, a chic London restaurant. The guests were all important figures in the world of British cinema, stage, and rock and roll. Madonna was the most glittering star of the moment, who deserved all the accolades that were coming her way for her performance in the film. Instead of reveling in her success, Madonna arrived late, dressed in nondescript black slacks and a white T-shirt, her face scrubbed clean and her blond hair pulled back in a ponytail. While the guests milled around, waiting for her to appear, she slipped unnoticed into the restaurant and sat quietly at a corner table in the dimly lit bar. One well-known actress recalls her amazement when she finally noticed her. "Everybody was wondering where she was," the actress recalls with amusement, "and suddenly I turned around and there she was. Sting rushed up to her and hugged her, and then everybody gathered around, raising glasses and applauding." The actress laughs. "When we asked her why she didn't let us know she had arrived, she said, in this timid little voice, that she didn't want to disturb us, because we looked as if we were having so much fun. Can you believe it? The party was for her, and there she was, hiding in the corner like a child."

Another guest that evening at the *Evita* party was an American director who had worked with Madonna on another film. He viewed that "humble act," as he called it, as typical of what Madonna does when she feels intimidated. "Don't be fooled," he says, "she isn't comfortable around real actors, because she is deathly afraid of being discovered as a fraud. There's a little bit of that and a little bit of putting on that invisible act to get attention."

Madonna's sense of survival and her instinctive ability to use control in different ways on a film set also enable her to learn from other actors' mistakes. One of her close friends, who brought her daughter, Lourdes, to visit her on the set of

The Next Best Thing every day, said of her acting technique, "Madonna considers it like high school. She watches and waits like a good Catholic schoolgirl. When one of the others gets chewed out by the director for doing something wrong, she knows never to do what they did. She's the Goody Two-shoes on a set, which, of course, she learned when she was forced to protect herself after her father remarried and her stepmother constantly picked on her."

On every set of each film Madonna has made, regardless of the quality of the script, the talent of her costars, or the sensitivity of the director, she has always been given high marks for her behavior. During the shoot, she is a diva on the defensive. After a film is finished, and the reviews aren't good, her excuse has frequently been that when she acts in someone else's film, based on someone else's characters, and speaks words from someone else's script, when that "someone else" is in control of the production, it is doomed to fail. "I suppose I'm not very good at sitting around and waiting for someone to give me orders," she has said. "I've been unlucky with my films because it's difficult for me to be a brushstroke in someone else's painting."

On a subconscious level, her obsession with death, the realization that she couldn't prevent the demise of her mother, accounts for her need to control the only aspect of her life that she can: her career and the people who work for her.

There is a very different Madonna when it comes to her music and videos. On those occasions, she has said, "I'm not going to make a record and not show up for the vocals or do a video and have nothing to say about the script." When Madonna first launched her own label, Maverick, it was less to create another lucrative financial corporation than it was to guarantee her success as a singer. From the beginning, she understood that for any artist, after a record is cut, a book is written, or a painting is finished, the amount of promotion and ultimate success of the product is up to the record company, publisher, or gallery. Madonna wasn't taking any chances by putting her career in the hands of people who wouldn't care as much about her work as she did. Nile Rodgers, one of her most frequent record producers, explains it by saying, "That arrogance bit is all about how she sticks to her guns, that's all. It's that attitude that comes from growing up in a huge family, you know, always having to fight and yell for things like time in the bathroom."

Alek Keshishian is the director of "On the Road," "Behind the Scenes," and "In Bed With Madonna," as well as the Blond Ambition tour. More significantly, he is the person who came up with the idea of filming the Blond Ambition tour from behind the scenes, which was eventually released as the documentary *Truth or Dare*. When Keshishian was a second-year student at Harvard, he began directing Harvard's Experimental Theater, which he continued to do until he graduated. During that time, he created a pop opera of Emily Brontë's *Wuthering Heights,* which included recordings by Billy Idol, Sting, Kate Bush, and Madonna. The source of his inspiration was Madonna. Kate Bush's music represents "Cathy," until she marries "Linton," when her music becomes Madonna's. The production was so popular that Keshishian was given permission not only to use it as the subject of his doctoral thesis, but also to stage it at the American Repertory Theater. At the time, his agent, who was at Creative Artists Agency, was so impressed by the result that he arranged for a tape of the pop opera to be shown to Madonna. Impressed as well, she invited Keshishian, along with a crew, to come to Japan in March 1990, where she was currently on her Blond Ambition tour, to film her performance, as well as unrehearsed material, which could eventually be used in a television special. After Keshishian showed some footage to Madonna, he suggested that it could be used instead as a documentary. To persuade her, he pointed out that documentaries are often made of feature-length movies, but never of a rock star on tour. She agreed, and in the end, Alek Keshishian shot more than 150 hours of film, following Madonna on her tour throughout Europe and North America.

If Keshishian had made a video of the behind-the-scenes preparation of any one of Ms. Ciccone's movies, the arrogance and self-indulgence that she displayed in *Truth or Dare* would be glaringly absent. Instead, her public would get a chance to see a humble Madonna who was always on time, cooperative, hardworking, and generous.

Underneath the brash facade and often arrogant demeanor still lurks the motherless child, unsure of her place in the family and no longer the recipient of unconditional parental love.

After her mother's death, Madonna went through a period during which she felt invisible. She had the impression that people couldn't see her, that she had ceased to exist, since the one person who had given her unlimited attention was gone. One of the most difficult realities for her to accept was that her mother, the most important person in her life, would never know her after the age of five. That loss remains the motivating force for her ambition, her need to prove that she exists through the attention and accolades and even negative criticism that she receives from her public. If Madonna has anything in common with Eva Perón, it's not that each lost a parent at a young age, but rather that each woman, notwithstanding her many accomplishments, had an insatiable craving to achieve stardom or be acknowledged in every area of life. Despite the millions that Madonna has made and the millions of people Evita seduced, even after her death, each longed to be recognized as a serious actress. Yet, while the two women are similar in their need to be noticed and appreciated, there are also very different in how they captured the attention of their adoring public. Evita's public was entranced by the drama that the first lady projected. Her every speech and appearance was tantamount to an ongoing film, a welcome diversion to the reality of the dreary lives that the

Argentine people endured. They knew who Eva Duarte was before she became Mrs. Juan Perón and were aware that her new incarnation as a grande dame was nothing less than a brilliant performance. Politics in the Perón era was theater, with plots and subplots that provided entertainment and at the same time made the people participants in their own destiny. Though the majority knew that Evita's life story had been fabricated and exaggerated, they didn't care. Madonna's public, on the other hand, needs to believe that she is opening up her soul to them, that they are privy to her innermost secrets. If Madonna could act, she wouldn't be Madonna. If her fans didn't believe that all her lyrics were based on personal experiences and that every plot of each video was autobiographical, they would regard her as just another performer. In both cases, the public created the myths of Madonna and of Evita based on what they needed to be entertained. Living vicariously through movie stars and politicians was the only way that people could bear the horrendous poverty that was part of everyday life in Argentina in the late 1940s and early 1950s. In the United States, from the 1980s until now, voyeurism, confessional television, the breaking down of the barriers of our celebrities' private lives, unauthorized biographies, intimate details of the sexual behavior of our politicians, are the best ways to capture the public's attention. The need to know in America as opposed to the need to believe in Argentina accounts for the differences between what Evita and Madonna each gave to her audience to achieve stardom.

Elsie Fortin remembers Madonna as a "very pretty and very independent little girl," and that "she craved attention and she usually got it. She was so appealing and so determined that it was hard not to give in to her."

Other relatives from Bay City remember a photogenic little girl who liked to be taken to the Bay City State Park and Tony's Amusement Park, where she dared to go on the most dangerous rides, but only if her relatives promised to "watch." According to her uncle Earl, she was a "born performer" and instinctively played "to the crowd." According to another uncle, she "came to life" in a crowded elevator or on a bus when she knew strangers were listening to her conversation. "That's when the lights went on," the uncle says, "and she suddenly got adorable, asking all these precocious questions that everyone would laugh at or compliment her on how bright she was." Madonna came out of her difficult childhood with a mania for organization and detail. Her obsession with her mother's death and that she could do nothing to prevent it accounts for her need to control every aspect of her career.

Don Davis, who played a coach in Penny Marshall's film *A League of Their Own,* remembers how impressed he was by Madonna's work ethic when she showed up on the set with her own personal baseball coach. "She worked harder than anyone else," Davis says, "until she understood the game and learned how to hit. She absolutely immersed herself in her role." During the filming, Madonna met Rosie O'Donnell, the actress and talk-show host, who also had a supporting role in the movie. The two women became immediate friends. At the time, rumors were that the basis of their closeness was sexual. The truth is that when Madonna discovered that O'Donnell had lost her own mother to breast cancer when she was ten, an instant and deep empathy developed between them. "When you lose a parent so young," O'Donnell says, "you become literally starved for memories. Madonna and I talked about our mothers all the time, and it helped a lot. It makes us both feel that our mothers were still with us, and Madonna and I shared that."

chapter ten

•••••••••••••••••••

*G*iven the lifelong obsession she has had with her mother, it is not surprising that Madonna's ideal woman became forever captured in the typical American housewife of the 1950s that her mother personified. While her mother's sense of fulfillment was founded in her relationship with her husband and God, both of which typified the 1950s woman, Madonna added another dimension, a harder edge that was more sexual than flirtatious.

Throughout her career, during each of her incarnations, from the "material girl" to Marilyn, from Dita the Dominatrix to the Russian peasant with the gold-capped front tooth, to a variety of her on-screen and onstage roles where she has been everything from a missionary *(Shanghai Surprise)* to a woman who uses her body as a lethal weapon *(Body of Evidence)*, from a spunky, low-class, heart-of-gold baseball player *(League of Their Own)* to a mousy secretary in David Mamet's *Speed-the-Plow,* from a gun moll in *Dick Tracy* to *Evita,* and finally to Madonna's current real-life mutation as the first nursing mother to turn the breast pump into a fashion accessory, sex is the most blatant component of her images. More than just to shock, Madonna has addressed the issue of female sexuality, a subject that somehow got lost in the shuffle when women were fighting for other areas of equal rights.

If Madonna has made any major contribution to feminism, she has given voice to those women who have been ignored and excluded by the mainstream movement. She is the patron saint of the trailer-park feminist. By validating those women who are dissatisfied with who they are, how they live, and with whom, women who are not struggling for professional or academic equality, but rather just trying to live without brutality and harassment, women in trailer parks, tract houses, bungalows, and subsidized apartments, women who frequent malls, dress in Kmart fashions, or who follow recipes on the back of cereal boxes, Madonna has paid homage to her mother by immortalizing the typical 1950s American housewife.

Pat McPherson is a feminist writer who cowrote a paper along with Michelle Fine, a professor of women's studies at City University of New York (CUNY), entitled "Hungry for an Us: Adolescent Girls and Adult Women Negotiating Territories of Race, Gender, Class, and Difference." McPherson's main area of expertise is the critical analysis of heterosexuality in the movies, and she is currently at work on a book that covers the subject from the 1930s until today. According to her, Madonna offers the homebound housewife an outlet to stretch her imagination and feel empowered. "I have always assumed," McPherson says, "that white women are Madonna's major audience, women who have come of age, who are not career women but mostly blue- or pink-collar, working middle-class women. Madonna proved that she could reach those women who were excluded by academic feminists, and in fact, when Madonna reached the apex of her popularity, it was at a time when academic feminism was at its most vocal and strongest. She offered another way to be a feminist for those women who came from blue-collar homes, who were neither intellectuals nor interested in abstract theories."

A friend and neighbor of Madonna Fortin Ciccone's remembers that the young wife and mother "always put on makeup and combed her hair before Tony came home." She says, "Sometimes I'd watch the kids so Madonna could pull herself together for him. It was a ritual. She was the picture-perfect wife, waiting at the door, surrounded by her kids, who were bathed and clean for their good-night kiss with their dad. She never had any problem about making the transition from mother to wife. She used to tell me that when she went to bed, she always wore a sexy nightgown and would never let her husband see her with pin curls in her hair like the rest of us." She pauses. "Maybe that's why Madonna and Tony had a great sex life, at least that's what she told me."

Elsie Fortin confirms that her daughter and son-in-law had a wonderful marriage. "They were always very warm and loving in front of the children," she says. "My son-in-law was proud of the way my daughter looked and kept the house and children. He never expected that she would go out and earn a living."

Another woman who knew the Ciccones and still lives in Pontiac, in the same neighborhood where Madonna and Tony Ciccone lived, remembers that Madonna was "hooked" on magazines that offered the average housewife advice on how to be more attractive, sexy, and seductive for her mate. "It was like we lived on another planet back then," she says, "when women weren't afraid to be subservient to their men and lived just to please them. I remember one article that Madonna and I read together about how to tell if your husband was having an affair. Madonna said that even without reading it, she knew that Tony would never stray. When I asked her how she could be so sure, she told me that she knew how to be a lady in the living room and a whore in the bedroom."

Several people who knew Madonna when she was preparing for her role in *Desperately Seeking Susan* remember how she watched reruns of situation comedies from the 1950s. "She studied them for hours," one old friend claims, "looking for something she could take and make her own, a gesture, a style of clothes, an expression. It was not so much her character that she needed to understand but rather Roberta, the part that Rosanna Arquette played, which was actually her alter ego."

In *Desperately Seeking Susan,* Rosanna Arquette portrayed an unfulfilled and frustrated housewife who looks for ways to escape from her humdrum life. Another movie that addressed a similar subject was Frank Perry's 1970 film, *Diary of a Mad Housewife,* starring Carrie Snodgress. Perry's film portrays a bored housewife, married to an insufferable social-climbing husband, who takes a lover only to find that her marital problems are not solved. Susan Seidelman, the director of *Desperately Seeking Susan,* created a more complicated, almost Shakespearean scenario that connected the two main female characters on a much deeper level. Rather than simply taking a lover, Arquette's character lives vicariously through Susan, the young street urchin that Madonna portrays. The emotions of the relationship between Arquette and Madonna in the film surpass those of the eventual affair between Arquette and the man she takes as her lover, played by Aidan Quinn. Madonna is perceived as a savior of the trapped middle-class wife. She not only offers her permission to be a little less conventional as a heterosexual but also offers the possibility to be a little bisexual as well.

Watching the reruns of the 1950s situation comedies, Madonna realized that every female character fell into two distinct categories. She was either idealized as the comic side of the typical housewife, as in *I Love Lucy,* or as the wholesome side, as in *Father Knows Best* or *Leave It to Beaver.* What was missing was the erotic potential that these women possessed. In *Desperately Seeking Susan,* the combination of a subtle script and Madonna's clever interpretation of the role sent out the message that women can act out their fantasies without necessarily changing or jeopardizing their social situation. This theme would appear in her music and videos and would turn Madonna into a symbol of hope for the typical homebound woman. Another friend who knew Madonna when she was researching the role says,

"Eventually, Rosanna's character became what Madonna's mother might have been if she had lived. It sounds bizarre, but it was something Madonna hit upon when she was making the movie and it just stayed with her."

For Madonna, a liberated woman has power without sacrificing her femininity and has sexual pleasure without paying a price. She has made a concerted effort, in her music and videos, to dispel the myth that, for women, sex is synonymous with love. "The biggest mistake that the feminists made," Madonna has said, "was that they felt they had to dress like men and behave like men to get anywhere. They were convinced that in order to be respected and be in control they had to act like men. Women always had the power, they just never understood that you can be just as powerful being feminine." Madonna has also said that she prefers men who are "in touch with their feminine side." "They are the strongest men," she has stated, "in the same way that my father was in love with my mother and desired her but wasn't afraid to show his emotions. He didn't consider it a weakness to be sensitive to my mother's needs."

The video "Express Yourself" is another example of Madonna's belief that feminism is nothing more than freedom of choice for women. In the video, Madonna is seen chained to a bed, a scene that provoked criticism by Andrea Dworkin, one of the most vocal and militant antipornography feminists. In response, Madonna claimed that she was not only in full artistic control but also paid out of her own pocket to produce the video. The atmosphere in the video is surrealistic, inspired by Fritz Lang's 1926 film, *Metropolis*. It tells the story of a lonely sophisticated woman who, despite her money and success, is not happy. In one sequence in a parody of female domination, she imagines herself as a queen who reigns over fifty men who work in abysmal conditions. If there is any message to be sent about deplorable working conditions for the lower class or women's liberation at the expense of men, Madonna ignores it and, instead, inserts a sexual slant. The female character in "Express

Yourself" invites one of her blue-collar employees to her penthouse. As the pair begin romping around her satin sheets, there are fleeting images of S&M with Madonna wearing a black rubber dress. Coproduced by Steven Bray, who also cowrote the song with Madonna, the video sends out the message that nothing can ever go wrong during an S&M romp if the participants are in total control. "I think the world would be a better place," Madonna has said, "if people just let go of their inhibitions."

Life in Madonna's world guarantees pleasure without pain. Life on the street, however, is quite different.

Onstage or off, dressed in seductive costumes, Madonna is protected by bodyguards, burglar alarms, high walls, and a staff that isolates and protects her. "There is simply too much negativity in the world today," Madonna has said, "to waste time on superficial appearances. All I'm trying to do is give the average or ordinary person some relief from that viewpoint or that reality." Unlike her teenage fans, Madonna can dress and behave as she pleases without risk of being raped, hassled, or humiliated. Unlike her adult fans, as a public figure worth approximately $500 million, she has unlimited choices when it comes to love, motherhood, marriage, and divorce. While Madonna can act as she pleases in a protected and controlled environment, the average girl or woman who imitates her has many more risks.

Madonna's video "Papa Don't Preach" is another performance that is steeped in controversy as well as in double meaning. Costarring Danny Aiello as the irate father, the story is about his daughter, played by Madonna, who wants his blessing when she announces that she is pregnant and intends to have her baby. The most obvious controversy is that Madonna advocated single motherhood, teenage sex, and promiscuity; others saw the message as a stand against abortion. Anita Harris, a visiting professor at the City University of New York, on leave from the University of Auckland in New Zealand, whose field is the sexuality of adolescent girls, believes that the video was dangerously unrealistic for the average teenage girl. "Madonna never bothered to caution all the unmarried teenage girls that the character she played in 'Papa Don't Preach' was not exactly realistic," Harris explains. "After all, most young girls can't come to their fathers to ask for their blessing or to ensure that they will have security and some semblance of a normal life if they choose to keep their baby. Nor did Madonna point out that in most cases unmarried teenage girls can't rely on their boyfriends to stick around and presumably offer marriage." Harris goes on to say that the problem she often has with Madonna is that she sends out the message that dressing and acting in a provocative way is part of women's liberation. "If Madonna does that and gets away with it," Harris maintains, "it doesn't necessarily mean that other girls can do the same thing and be accepted and acceptable. If you're a fourteen-year-old and you walk down the street in your town dressed like Madonna, you put yourself at risk. If you aren't raped or assaulted, you would certainly get a reputation. The point is that you don't have the same kind of freedom as a Madonna, who can do those things within the safe confines of her life. The girls I talk to would like to be able to walk down the street and wear what they want without being the object of sexual predators. They also want the right to have sex or not and not be hassled by men, but unfortunately that isn't the case."

Madonna has always had a much different view of reality when it comes to female sexuality and pornography. "Generally, I don't think pornography degrades women," she has said, "since the women doing it want to do it. No one is holding a gun to their heads."

Madonna often forgets that material deprivation and drug addiction are other kinds of guns held to a woman's head.

In many of Madonna's other erotic videos, rather than watching a man toiling away at intercourse while women function as props or vessels for male pleasure, she has omitted the sole male partner and in his place used a succession of men or women, whom she, the protagonist, ultimately discards. By simulating masturbation, she also offers her female audience a new take on an old feminist message: a woman needs a man the way a fish needs a bicycle.

However, Michelle Fine, the CUNY professor, believes that young women are often unaware of female sexual pleasure. The message that Madonna sends is often lost on them. "I sit in on a lot of sex-education classes," Fine explains, "and it strikes me that male desire is automatically woven in since all you have to do is talk about reproduction and you have his orgasm and his ejaculation. Her desire is never considered, which makes the discourse about female sexuality all about victimization, danger, or morality, but never about pleasure."

"Like a Virgin" is an example of how Madonna plays with words and double meanings. In the video, she never actually says that she is a virgin in the most obvious meaning of the word, but rather alludes to being a virgin in the emotional and romantic sense. The boy she is singing about has managed to reach that secret place in her head and heart that she has never surrendered to anyone else. "Burning Up," another video that purports to address female sexual independence, shows Madonna pleading with her boyfriend to treat her as an equal. But when he decides to let her drive his car, he suddenly disappears and Madonna ends up in the driver's seat. In "Borderline," yet another example of a video that supposedly empowers women, Madonna is discovered by a fashion photographer while she is break-dancing with her Latin boyfriend. When she embarks on a new career, the boyfriend is resentful and jealous of her newfound independence. There is a double message, however, when the character Madonna portrays suddenly realizes how superficial her life is as a superstar model and how much more meaningful true love and a good relationship can be. She drops the photographer and her career and runs back to her lover, who has apparently also realized where he has failed her. They are reunited in a pool hall where we see him patiently teaching Madonna how to play pool, giving her the respect and attention she deserves. In fact, throughout her show at Radio City Music Hall in 1985, where she performed these songs along with others, she seemed to be talking to the girls in the audience more than the boys. As Madonna touched herself and moved seductively around the stage, the message she sent was that a woman doesn't need a man to enjoy her own body.

Madonna is not the only female icon of the middle-class woman nor is she the first. Back in time, Mae West was everything that any good girl or average woman was taught *not* to be. She was brazen, sexually aggressive, independent, and original. "Every man I meet," West once said, "wants to protect me. I can't figure out what from . . ." Her rebellion found its way into the hearts of her fans as she represented the antithesis of the Hollywood star. Her power was in her strength, and her strength was in her sexuality. She broke rules and never had to pay a price, at least on-screen. She demanded pleasure and yet never made excuses for her needs. Like Madonna, Mae West walked a fine line between what was allowed and what was forbidden, forcing people to think about those so-called moral restrictions that society places on women.

Today, there are Roseanne Barr and Martha Stewart, two women who have also liberated the middle-class woman, although each addresses very different aspects of middle-class life. Madonna, unlike Barr or Stewart, does not talk about the daily realities of a woman, wife, or mother. Rather, she reaches the same audience by offering the possibility that women, unlike the sitcom wives and mothers of the 1950s, have an erotic potential.

While Roseanne is seen as a survivor, an example of hope for those women who have been diminished or abused by their parents or humiliated and abandoned by their men, Martha turned the drudgery of housewifery into an art form. Roseanne gets under the beds and behind the furniture, addressing the unspeakable such as family violence and bad sex, an example of the latter being when she said about her soon-to-be ex-husband, Tom Arnold, "What he lacks in size, he makes up for in speed." Martha is the high priestess of the produce department, proving once and for all that Truman Capote was wrong when he said that the only difference between the rich and the poor is that the rich have better vegetables.

Roseanne commiserates with women on their sad lot in life while sending out the message that because women are superior to men, they should rebel. Realistic enough to know that she is the exception rather than the rule, Roseanne captures her public by acknowledging that even if they never reach the stardom and success that she has, they nonetheless share a big secret—that men are laughable. One of Roseanne's most biting lines was to a group of militant lesbians who had criticized her for not addressing that segment of the women's movement. "I don't know why lesbians hate men so much," Roseanne said. "They don't have to sleep with them."

Martha, on the other hand, arrived on the scene when housekeeping was fraught with both resentment and longing. Her audience started with the women who relied on television commercials to tell them which product cleaned the best, and along the way, she picked up that generation of women who were too embarrassed to admit that they also wanted impeccable homes as well as the ability to prepare gourmet meals. Martha showed those women that they could have it all, including the professional success, as well as a pride in homemaking that had been denied them for two generations. If Roseanne is a self-proclaimed "domestic goddess," coining the phrase as a more palatable description of "housewife," and Martha is the high priestess of produce, Madonna is purely and simply a goddess. She is the modern version of Diana or Artemis with the torch in her right hand, the protector of virgins as well as the goddess of the heart and the hunt at the same time that she is

Aphrodite, the goddess of love, the more passive and traditionally feminine deity.

In a more contemporary version of feminism, Madonna is Dietrich or Harlow as easily as she is Marilyn or Carole Lombard. In fact, in the 1970s, Madonna would have been the ideal Marabel Morgan woman who wraps herself in Saran Wrap, a chilled martini in her hand, when she greets her husband at the door. In the 1990s, when Madonna's book, *Sex,* appeared, the public was introduced to Dita, the fantasy woman who crossed gender barriers while assuring her public that a little sadomasochistic play was harmless fun. Whether Madonna is holding a martini or a whip, the impression she gives is that she is playing a role less for her partner's pleasure than for her own. And yet, because she changes images as readily as she changes her own opinion, she also provokes contradictory reactions. In some segments of society, some believe she is a good example for priests to take vows of celibacy and withdraw into their monkish intellectual world to escape the temptations of the flesh and the devil. *Rolling Stone* honored Madonna six times on their cover less for her artistic accomplishments than for her unparalleled capacity to liberate her fans' most erotic fantasies. Patrick Leonard, an old friend and constant collaborator, claims that what sets Madonna apart from other performers is that she has "shown that she can reflect her own life and sexuality in her art by making sure that her music isn't something that is held at arm's length."

Like any heroine in an ongoing soap opera, Madonna sends her fans the comforting message that she has the same desires, fears, insecurities, and conflicts as they do. More than just drawing parallels between herself and her public, Madonna encourages them the way her mother nurtured her. She offers herself as an example that anything is possible and that any ordinary girl who works hard can get lucky and become a star. As the opening credits roll in her video "Like a Virgin," Madonna's singsong voice, imitating a heavy New York accent, explains away her fame by saying, "I went to

Noo Yawk, I din know anybody, I wanted to dance, I wanted to sing, I wanted to make people happy, I wanted to be famous. I wanted everybody to love me, I wanted to be a star, I worked very hard and my dreams came true." That message is one of the most important components of her success, because she transcends the usually distant fan/star relationship, replacing it with one that assures them, *I am you, you are me, if I can do it, so can you.*

Several events that occurred during Madonna's early childhood continue to have a profound effect on her. When Madonna was five, her mother took a photograph of her wearing her wedding dress. The picture of the little girl enveloped in the folds of white taffeta would become a harbinger of her inner turmoil and determination to replace her mother in her father's eyes. After her mother's death, Madonna kept the photo next to her bed. For years, it traveled everywhere with her and would haunt her as a symbol of loss, not only of her mother but of her father as well.

When she was four years old, Madonna had trouble sleeping and got into the habit of wandering into her parents' bedroom and crawling into their bed between them. "My father was always against my coming into their bed," Madonna recalls, "but my mother was always for it." One of the strongest physical sensations that remained from those nocturnal visits was of cuddling up against her mother's red silk nightgown. For Madonna, the softness of the fabric and the vague smell of her mother's perfume would become a synthesis of the ideal woman.

Shortly after her mother died, when she was barely six, Madonna remembers having a "sexual awakening." She had a sense that she had an absolute authority over her own body. "As a child I was always flirtatious," Madonna has said. "I was one of those little girls who crawled on everybody's lap. I flirted with everyone, my uncles, my grandfather, my father, everybody. I was aware of my female charm.

I knew I had something powerful, although I didn't know what to do with it. I was just very aware of it." From then on, Madonna considered herself the primary woman in her father's life, and for months after her mother's death she would continue to wander into his room at night and try to crawl into his bed.

During one sequence in the *Truth or Dare* documentary, while Madonna is engaged in risqué "girl talk" with the comedian Sandra Bernhard, she tells her how she couldn't sleep at night when she was little. "I used to climb into my father's bed," Madonna joked, "and after he fucked me, I went right to sleep."

Melanie Klein writes in *The Psycho-Analysis of Children* that the "cause of her [the young girl's] attachment to her father [is] being fundamentally affected by her attachment to her mother. Freud also points out that the one is built upon the other and that many women repeat their relation to their mother in their relation to men." Klein also states that "how far she [the young girl] will be able to maintain her feminine position and in that position evolve a wish for a kindly father-image, also depends very greatly upon her sense of guilt towards her mother and father. Furthermore, certain events, such as the illness or death of one of her parents . . . can assist in strengthening in her either the one sexual position or the other, according to the way in which they affect her sense of guilt."

While Madonna's response to Bernhard was flip, the normal attachment that Madonna felt for her mother as the "possessor of the nourishing breast," the natural parent who would protect her against anxiety and harm, was taken from her prematurely when her mother died. In response, Madonna expected her father to provide the same nurturing that she had gotten from her mother, and when he didn't or couldn't, especially after he remarried, her bitterness knew no bounds.

Madonna has always regretted that her father was not more open and communicative with her. It would have made it easier to explain her feelings instead of harboring such resentment. Even today, long after the fact and years since she has accepted that her father made a new life for himself, she still has difficulty with his inability to recognize her success. Madonna would like him to acknowledge that her need to succeed was based on what she had endured as a little girl. There is a charming naïveté about Tony Ciccone, a reticence to concede that his oldest daughter, much as he had done years before, has the same determination to turn adversity into success. Rather than appearing impressed by her, he projects a combination of awe, bewilderment, vague embarrassment, and only a hint of parental pride. Though he recognizes Madonna's celebrity, he is careful not to make it seem more important than the accomplishments of his other seven children. "All my children are struggling hard to make a niche for themselves, so I can't be more proud of one than the other. I don't measure success in terms of money," he explains. "Deep down, I consider that it was much more difficult for my parents to have made a life in America after they left Italy. That took a lot more determination and courage and another kind of talent!"

For the girl who feigned masturbation with a crucifix in her video "Like a Prayer" and simulated oral sex on a water bottle in her documentary *Truth or Dare,* Madonna nonetheless still needs her father's approval for everything she does. Her behavior is just as contradictory when she claims that her sense of "romanticism" and her concept of "true love" are defined by her father, including his purported belief that love and sex are inseparable and that making love is as sacred an act as taking Communion. "He is someone who believed that you shouldn't make love to someone until after you're married," Madonna said. "He stuck by those beliefs and that represented a very strong person to me."

While Madonna was not witness to her father's behavior prior to his marriage to her mother, she was well aware that after her mother's death, until he remarried, Tony Ciccone was devoted to his children and conducted his life not as a single man but rather as a single parent. Despite the ambiguity in her relationship with her father, Madonna is deeply attached to him. Shortly before her wedding to Guy Ritchie, she said about her father, "Things have been tough, and we've gone through bad periods when we didn't even speak, but I just love that man."

The caveat at the beginning of her book, *Sex,* is extremely telling. "I am an actress," she proclaimed, "and I took on the persona of Dita [the dominatrix heroine] only as a role which I could identify with and which I chose to portray to allow my fans to liberate their own sexual fantasies. Nothing in this book is true. I made it all up."

Despite Madonna's sexual bravado, it is not difficult to imagine that those words were written for one person only—her father.

chapter eleven

·················

After her mother's death on December 1, 1963, Madonna decided that because she had been her mother's favorite, carried her name, and resembled her more than any of the other children, she was the guardian of her mother's memory. As the oldest daughter and the child who had the most accurate recollection of her mother's brief life and protracted death, she designated herself "family historian."

In the months following Madonna Fortin Ciccone's death, the children continued to be shuttled to relatives and friends, although they would stay most often and for long periods of time with their maternal grandmother. "I had the children a lot during the summers after my daughter died," Mrs. Fortin explains. "In fact, the whole family would come and visit quite often." In addition to her daughter's six children, after her son Dale died, Mrs. Fortin took care of his seven children as well. "Thirteen of my grandchildren each lost a parent, so I felt it was my duty to give them all a sense of family, although I must admit," she adds, "that I was closest to Madonna." Carl Fortin, who, at the time, was a musician in a local nightclub band, agrees with his mother. "We were always a close family," he says, "but my sister's death brought us all closer together, because there were so many kids still growing up."

Throughout her life, Madonna has constantly expressed the desire to find out everything about her mother, and yet, according to Bay City residents who grew up with her, Madonna has never sought them out.

Wanda McPharlin was Madonna Fortin Ciccone's neighbor and best friend and the mother of Moira McPharlin, who was Madonna's best childhood friend when the families lived in the same neighborhood in Pontiac, Michigan. After her father remarried and the family moved from Pontiac to Rochester Hills, the two best friends didn't see each other as often but still remained close. When Madonna was in the tenth grade and Moira, who was two years older, graduated from high school, the friends lost touch completely. McPharlin left home and for several years heavily used drugs and alcohol and went "on the road" to work as a topless dancer. Not until many years later, when Madonna was a star and Moira McPharlin was in recovery, married, and the mother of four little boys and pregnant with her fifth child, were the two women reunited. Moira became part of rock-and-roll history when she went backstage in Detroit after Madonna's Blond Ambition concert and found herself one of the cast of characters in *Truth or Dare*. Though she got her fifteen minutes of fame on-camera, she had no idea how brutal that brief encounter would be.

Moira waits backstage for Madonna to appear. Alek Keshishian, recording everything with his handheld camera, follows Madonna, surrounded by her entourage as she makes her way toward her dressing room for the reunion with her childhood friend. On the way, Madonna explains how much she worshiped Moira, how Moira taught her how to "shave her legs and use a Tampax." Madonna's on-camera flip account is tame in comparison to her diva demeanor when the two women actually come face-to-face.

The camera is back on Moira, who hears Madonna approaching. Moira is nervous and obviously intimidated as the star appears. They hug and kiss. Moira asks if they could sit down and talk for a few minutes privately, to which Madonna replies that she doesn't have the time. Holding her pregnant belly, Moira asks Madonna if she ever got her letter several years back, asking her to be the godmother to her little boy Mario. Madonna replies that she received the letter long after it had been mailed. Moira, tears welling in her eyes, hastily explains that this pregnancy was an accident and, knowing that she only has a minute or two with the star, blurts out that she would like Madonna to be the unborn baby's godmother. "I want you to bless this child," Moira says hurriedly. "I want you to pray that it's a girl so I can name her Madonna." Madonna responds that she will have to think about it, a reasonable answer for someone who takes the role of godmother seriously. And yet, that brief exchange makes it painfully apparent that each woman views the meeting from opposing ends of the emotional spectrum. One imagines Moira McPharlin spending months trying to find the best way to broach the subject with her now famous friend, and finally when the moment comes and she actually gets to ask the question, her request is refused in an instant, and her dreams are dashed. Madonna, however, apparently uses the occasion to shock her public. The camera is jostled about during an uncomfortable silence that follows the brief conversation. Madonna turns to leave, still surrounded by her entourage, while Moira appears visibly crushed. The camera pans back to Moira, who suddenly gathers momentum and murmurs sotto voce, "Little shit!" This is a simple, unsophisticated woman who is no match for the star. The camera is now on Madonna, who turns back and looks at Moira for an instant. Again Moira is in the camera's sights, vague expression of hope in her eyes, until Madonna says cheerfully to no one in particular but to everyone who happens to be standing around, "Did you know that Moira was the first girl I ever finger-fucked?" Clearly mortified, McPharlin tries to make light of her surprise distinction in the singer's life. "We never did that, Madonna!" McPharlin protests. Madonna laughs. "I remember getting in bed naked with you," she says before turning to her squad of admirers and adding, "I distinctly remember seeing Moira's bush in my face." Moira shakes her head, desperately trying to recover. "Oh, yeah?" She looks helplessly at the others. "See what a combination of alcohol and drugs can do? You lose a lot of stuff like that."

Madonna has been photographed sprawled across her mother's grave. She has written songs about her, created videos where gruesome images of death and dying figure prominently in the story line. She has given interviews about her feelings of loss and rejection and has declared on numerous occasions that the death of her mother contributed to her quest for fame. However, she has never shared a major part of her grief. Only with her maternal grandmother has she talked intimately about her mother, evoked memories and asked questions about the woman who disappeared from her life when she wasn't yet six. In response to a tragedy or a trauma, some people will replay the event while others will block it out. Madonna has managed to do both.

After several months of shuttling the children between relatives, Tony Ciccone realized that he couldn't continue to keep the family separated. He decided to hire a housekeeper to manage his brood while he tried to carry on some semblance of a normal life. Predictably, he went through a succession of women who were unable to cope with children who were so unwilling to accept a stranger as an authority figure. One woman who lasted longer than most, a total of three weeks, and who had been recommended by the parish housekeeper at the Visitation Catholic Church in Bay City, remembers that a "sadness hung over the house like a pall." Rita Cavanagh elaborates, "It was a house without joy, and even though there was noise and children and chaos, it wasn't a happy home. The thing that stays with me is the sadness in that man's eyes when he walked through the door at night. It was almost painful for him to pick up those kids, because it must have reminded him so much of their poor mother." Mrs. Cavanagh claims that she left not so much because the children overwhelmed her, but because she found herself depressed. "No matter what I did, I just couldn't heal that big hurt they all had. Those kids broke my heart."

In the spring of 1966, Tony Ciccone hired a pretty, petite, blond, blue-eyed twenty-three-year-old woman. Joan Gustafson went to work as a housekeeper to earn enough money to start a day-care center. One of her oldest friends, who still lives in her hometown of Taylor, Michigan, has another opinion about why Joan Gustafson decided to marry into a ready-made family of six. Joan, who was the only daughter in a family with limited education and financial resources, always wanted to move to the "big city" and marry a successful man. "Detroit was the big city to Joan," her friend says, "and when she decided to get a job as a housekeeper in a suburb of Detroit, she was hoping it would be a home where there was no woman. She didn't want anyone telling her what to do. Joan wanted to run the show. She used to tell people that she wanted to save enough money to start a day-care center."

Given Tony Ciccone's sense of propriety, his courtship of the young woman who was twelve years his junior lasted only several months before the couple married. According to Joan's friend, Joan was instantly attracted to the single father of six, who did not seem particularly interested in or aware of the feelings he evoked in the young housekeeper. "She was very perceptive," the friend explains. "She sensed right away that he was conflicted. We had many conversations when Joanie told me that while he mourned his wife, he was still a man who had needs."

Initially, Joan arrived at the Ciccone home in the morning and left after dinner. One evening, Tony arrived later than usual because of a blinding snowstorm. He suggested that Joan stay overnight instead of risking a dangerous drive back home. "It was a natural transition," the friend maintains. "He needed someone to talk to and probably more, and one thing led to another . . ."

After the marriage, the transition from caretaker to step-mother was clear when she moved in to become the woman of the house who shared her husband's bed. While there was no ambiguity about their relationship, the transition was brutal for all the children, but especially for Madonna. The relationship between Madonna and her father became increasingly strained. "After my mother died," Madonna said, "I became fearless. There was nothing more precious that I could lose, so I became blunt." That fearlessness and bluntness, unfortunately, occurred at the same time that Tony expected Madonna to treat his new wife with respect.

A neighbor once told Tony Ciccone that he had the "good fortune to have married two saints." According to the neighbor, Joan Ciccone was a paragon of patience and understanding. Another friend says, "When I first met Joan, she was only twenty-three. It was inconceivable that this pretty, bright young girl would take on six children as her own. At the time, my own daughter was not much younger than Joan, and at one point I remember the two became kind of friendly. My daughter told me that Joan didn't think twice about it. She just knew that it was her destiny to be the mother to these children, and nothing about it seemed to faze her." During a recent interview, Joan made it clear that when she decided to marry Tony, it was not only because she had fallen in love with him, but also because she had fallen in love with his children. Several of the Ciccone children, however, take issue with that statement. "I'll never understand why she married Dad," a Ciccone daughter says. "She was really young, and to take on six bratty kids was tough enough for us but also for her. She was cute and could have married a young guy and started her own family. It was always a mystery why she chose Dad."

Immediately after becoming Mrs. Ciccone, Joan, who is both compulsively organized and hopelessly scattered, decided that it would take a "will of iron" to control the children. Whatever her method, it was not an enviable task for anyone, and especially not for a twenty-three-year-old. To compensate for her age and that she was small and looked so young, Joan ran the household like an army drill sergeant, a style that did nothing to ingratiate her in the hearts of her stepchildren. She assigned chores to each child according to his or her age and abilities. Madonna, the oldest girl, was automatically expected to help her new stepmother care for the younger children. "I think I resented it more after my mother died," Madonna has said, "since I felt that all my adolescence was spent taking care of babies, changing diapers and baby-sitting when all my friends were out playing. I think that's when I really thought about getting away from all that."

According to several neighborhood people who knew the family during those years and whose children went to school with the Ciccone children, Joan was a "nightmare of accusation," someone who collected lists of grievances and injustices when it came to her stepchildren that she would pull out and exact payment for at any moment. One woman recalls that her attitude toward Madonna was especially harsh. "I used to watch Joan bringing the children to school, and sometimes we carpooled together with the other mothers in the neighborhood. There were times when I actually felt sorry for Madonna, because Joan would systematically make her sit in the back of the car, or she would buy treats for all the kids and not give any to Madonna. There was always a reason, like Madonna had disobeyed or misbehaved or sassed her, but she was the one who was always being punished."

Madonna would never show how she felt even if she had been unfairly accused or picked on. Instead, she would stare arrogantly at Joan as if to challenge her for more. The relationship between the two became a test of wills, which almost always ended with Madonna as the winner. "Joan would go absolutely nuts," the same friend recalls. "The more she kept piling it on, the more Madonna just refused to snap. It was really terrible, and after a while I began to feel sorry for Joan because she looked like an idiot in front of a child, the way she would reel out of control. Madonna was obviously stronger and more stubborn."

Despite all the trouble that Madonna gave her, Joan does not hide her admiration for the child who became the most successful. When Joan Ciccone offers a tour of the vineyard, the first stop is her living room, where she guides her guest to the baby grand piano that sits in the middle of the floor. It is covered with an array of family photographs. The most prominent are of Madonna: Madonna and Lourdes, Madonna and Carlos Leon, the father of Lourdes, Madonna with Joan, Madonna with Sean Penn, Madonna with Warren Beatty, Madonna with the entire family, Lourdes on her own. During that same interview at the Ciccone vineyard, Joan is admittedly thrilled to visit Madonna in New York, Los Angeles, Miami, or London, where she and her husband stay at one of the singer's lavish homes. Joan, however, like Tony, categorically denies that they ever accepted any expensive gifts or borrowed money to buy the vineyard. In fact, when Tony and Joan went to London for Madonna's wedding to Guy Ritchie, they decided to visit a château in the Bordeaux region of France before going back to Michigan. Reservations were arranged and made by the Starr Travel Agency in Montreal. When asked if he wanted a deluxe or superior room, both of which came to under $100 per night, Tony opted for the cheaper accommodations.

Whatever Joan's failings as a stepmother, Tony appreciated that he had a partner who took over all the physical responsibilities of the home. Despite his determination to distance himself from his cultural roots, his attitude toward his wife and daughters was that of a typical Italian Catholic male. Not only did he expect his wife to care for him, but he also expected his daughters to wait on him as well. "It was a little bit like he was the king in the house," Madonna has said.

When it came to his sons, he didn't tolerate laziness and

tried to instill in them the same work ethic he had learned from his own father. He expected them to do the "heavy work" around the house and yard. He made no distinction between his children as it concerned their ability to "express themselves properly" and insisted that they not only use good grammar but also make sure that when they offered an opinion, they knew what they were talking about. He had no patience for "I think" or "I'm not sure" and would consistently send a child from the dinner table to look up a word in the dictionary or check the meaning of something in the encyclopedia if he or she faltered during a discussion. One family friend recalls that Joan often had a difficult time following Tony's example. When the kids got older, she would often be the target of their ridicule. "When their father wasn't around," the friend says, "they would purposely ask Joan to spell something, and she would inevitably spell it wrong. Later on, when Tony checked their homework and came across a misspelled word, they would tell him that Joan was the one who told them how to spell it. Naturally, all hell broke loose. Most of the time, Tony blamed the kids for not going directly to the dictionary, although there were occasions when he got mad at Joan." Another friend maintains that Tony was not the ideal mate: "He had a short temper and would really lay into his kids verbally if they annoyed him. But he would also yell at Joan if she was sloppy or said something that he considered dumb."

Another family friend and former neighbor compares the two women who were Tony Ciccone's wives. The friend claims that the differences between them reflect how Tony had changed over the years. When Tony and Madonna married, they were optimistic and inexperienced. Their relationship was based not only on building a life, moving to a new city, far from the Fortin family, and starting their own family, but also on their mutual discovery of sex. Each child was a source of enormous pleasure to them and proof of their love for one another.

Joan Ciccone obviously had a more difficult time. She had married a man whose view of life was no longer optimistic. He had deep scars that would never heal. Though he loved his children, he had even looked upon them as a burden during the three years he was forced to care for them alone. When he married Joan, he not only expected her to care for the children, but also to make up for all he had endured as a single parent. In a way, they had struck a deal. In return for the organization that she brought to the family, which allowed Tony to concentrate on his job, he would provide the upper-middle-class suburban life that she craved. During the years following the marriage, Tony advanced rapidly at General Motors, and Joan added a wing onto the house that eventually became her day-care center.

Joan learned quickly that Tony expected a drink waiting when he walked in the door, dinner on the table, and the kids quiet. According to one of the children, the television screen had to be wiped clean of dust or greasy fingerprints when he sat down to watch the nightly news, and "God help any one of us if we made any noise." The Ciccone offspring recalls, "Joan had her hands full." After the broadcast ended, he would question his children, the youngest first, to hear about their day. "Every evening," a son recalls, "we were expected to tell him one thing we learned, either in school or at church."

A daughter has the distinct memory of a home that was run with as much precision as the trains ran in Italy under Mussolini. "Everything happened on time, and there were no deviations. If we were late for dinner, Joan would take away the dessert. If we got one of our outfits dirty that we wore to church, we had to wear it like that the following week. There was a mutual love of order that they both had that went beyond any kind of affection or emotion, at least that's the impression I had." Another Ciccone child recalls with amusement that every Sunday after church, her father and Joan would retire to their bedroom, only to reappear about an hour later to have lunch with the family. "We assumed it was their once-a-week lovemaking session," she says.

Madonna's memory of her mother's house was one of constant disorder with toys and clothes strewn everywhere, babies crying, and not much discipline. With six small children, the first Mrs. Ciccone spent less time worrying about order and more time running after her toddlers. While Joan's conventional style was a direct affront to Madonna's determination to be different, it was also proof that Joan had successfully replaced her stepdaughter's role as surrogate mother. Joan Ciccone still recalls the moments when she literally wanted to run away, when Madonna and her siblings drove her to tears. Those were the times when she was comforted by her friends rather than by her husband. "Tony had too much on his mind," she says. "The last thing he needed when he came home at night was my complaining about the children. Fortunately, I had very good girlfriends who had children about the same ages as mine. They would tell me that their own biological children were just as impossible, which made me feel that I wasn't a total failure as a mother."

As the only daughter growing up in a lower-middle-class, strict Lutheran home where there were few luxuries, little time for frivolity, and an unwavering work ethic, Joan had been given the same household chores and responsibilities that she eventually thrust upon her stepdaughter Madonna. That she was the most appealing and original of all the children, the one with the most talent and personality, made Madonna's life more difficult. Even more unlucky for Madonna was that everyone constantly told Joan how Madonna was the "spitting image of her mother."

Joan tried to get pregnant from the moment she and Tony married, and much to her disappointment, it took almost two years before she did. When she finally was expecting a child, the impending birth was a victory in more ways than one. Finally, she would be on an equal basis with her predecessor, the legitimate heir to the deceased queen.

chapter twelve
....

*M*adonna always felt she was a victim of her stepmother's sense of Lutheran duty that made her such a meticulous and exacting parent. Her idea of being a good mother meant having strict rules about cleanliness, organization, a balanced diet, regular bowel movements, and bedtimes. Another friend who knew the Ciccone family well during the years that the children were growing up believes that Joan was basically a decent and responsible person. "Unfortunately," he explains, "everything went by the book. She was a black-and-white person, which meant that if the kids behaved, they were happy. If they acted out, they were spoiled. There was never any room in Joan's mind for them to have bad memories or traumas or psychological problems. As far as she was concerned, they had everything. She cooked, cleaned, sewed their clothes, and signed their report cards. They lived in a pretty house and had enough food. In her mind, they wanted for nothing."

When Madonna approached adolescence, Joan decided it was time to tell her the facts of life. As usual, her style was matter-of-fact. She began the discussion without warning while she and Madonna were doing the dishes one evening. Madonna was less uncomfortable with the contents of the lecture than she was with Joan's approach to the subject. There was no talk about love or foreplay, emotions or hormones, that would be the basis for more discussion about adolescent sex. The words she used could have been found

in the directions that came with an Erector set, they were so
devoid of any human feeling.

Joan's sense of order when it came to dressing her brood
was as direct and regimented as everything else she did. She
bought bolts of fabric on sale at the local sewing store and,
with her sewing machine, made the same dress for
Madonna, Paula, and Melanie, and later on for Jennifer, her
own daughter. Forced to wear exactly the same clothes as
her siblings was perhaps more painful to Madonna than
having to care for them. It didn't help her budding sense of
individuality that she was required to wear the drab
Catholic school uniform every day. Determined to be different and despite the meager choice of clothes, she would
rebel by wearing two different-colored socks and floppy
bows in her hair. She would also wear red or green underwear and hang upside down on the jungle gym so everyone
would notice. Later on in high school, when she briefly
joined the cheerleading squad, Madonna would do cart-
wheels wearing either no underwear or transparent lace
panties. Madonna's refusal to look like the others challenged Joan's imagination. Eventually, she came up with
the idea of buying everything for the kids in red, white, and
blue so that when Madonna asserted herself, at least everything would match.

Although Tony was not particularly adept at expressing
emotions or handing out compliments, when it came to vent-
ing his anger, there were no double messages or hidden
meanings. In contrast, Joan had a penchant for elusive patterns of address, which left all the children with a sense of
frustration and impotence. Years after she had already become a star, Madonna once commented that all her siblings,
in one way or another, were "basket cases" who had been
demoralized by Joan's litany of "You're not living up to your
potential" or "You're doomed to be a failure." Unlike the
others, Madonna turned that daily criticism into a compul-
sion to be the best and to realize her every potential. She

could bear anything as long as she knew that she was one day closer to escaping her home and family.

Paula, the sister closest in age to Madonna, was often the recipient of Joan's remarks—for example, "I wish I had a pretty daughter." Paula suffered the most under Joan's constant harangue, basically because she always felt that she was less attractive, dynamic, and talented than her older sister. For all the years that they were growing up, Paula lived in Madonna's shadow. Madonna was prettier. Madonna had bigger breasts. Madonna sang and danced better. Madonna made the cheerleading squad. Madonna got the good grades. As an adult, Paula lived in New York for a while and tried to become a model. Briefly represented by the Ferrari Agency, her hopes were eventually dashed when the agency dropped her because she was too short for runway work and not photogenic enough for print. As her sister became more and more successful, Paula became more disturbed. There was an ugly moment in a powder room in Malibu at the wedding of Madonna and Sean Penn when Paula stood at the sink and wept. "I was supposed to be the famous one," she cried in the presence of two startled guests. "That was supposed to be me marrying a movie star, me making albums and starring in movies, me, not Madonna!"

Martin, the second-oldest child, escaped into alcohol, as did Joan's own son, Mario, who had a moderate success as a male model for a while. He was an American version of a Fabio cover boy with his long blond hair, blue eyes, and muscles. His brushes with the law, and his use of cocaine, which also ravaged his looks, raised questions about Joan as the superior Ciccone mother. Melanie, the youngest of Madonna and Tony's children, was the best adjusted. Only five when her father remarried, Melanie accepted Joan as her mother more readily than the others. The relationship between Melanie and Madonna was also close as the little girl brought out Madonna's maternal instinct. The physical resemblance between the two sisters is startling, although Melanie is more delicate and fine-featured, the less glamorous and more pious version of their mother. Madonna was matron of honor when her sister married exactly ten years after Madonna married Sean Penn. When the couple decided to move from Michigan to California, Madonna got Melanie a job in the publicity department at Warner Brothers Records. At thirty-eight, Melanie Ciccone Henry is still married to the same man and lives in Los Angeles. She was the only sister who was invited to Madonna's wedding in Scotland to Guy Ritchie.

Madonna has always had a special relationship with her younger brother Christopher. When they were little, she often protected him from his older siblings or schoolmates, who teased him because he wasn't interested in sports or in girls. In fact, Chris's artistic nature is the basis for the close relationship, both professionally and personally, that still exists between them today. For a time in the 1970s, Chris was one of Madonna's backup dancers when she started performing club dates in New York. "I stopped," Christopher Ciccone explains, "when she started touring." Their collaboration took on a different form when Chris designed and decorated Madonna's houses, including her Central Park West apartment in New York. He has also directed music videos for Tony Bennett and Dolly Parton, among others, and is perhaps best known for designing and directing his sister's Girlie Show and Blond Ambition tours.

At forty years old, Chris Ciccone is a successful designer and decorator and, until recently, owned a trendy gourmet French/Chinese restaurant in New York. In the spring of 2000, the restaurant burned down. Recently, he launched a line of furniture for the upscale firm of Bernhardt that, in his description, is "simple and classic." He is also trying to interest Hollywood in an original screenplay about a female bullfighter. He envisages Penélope Cruz and Sigourney Weaver in the lead roles.

When Madonna was little, she always sensed that Joan wasn't interested in understanding her. She felt that though Joan always attended to her physical needs, there was never any thought to her inner problems. Joan's simplistic approach to child-rearing frustrated and depressed Madonna. According to a former neighbor and friend of Madonna Fortin Ciccone's, she once visited the family in Rochester Hills and remembers that Joan made several subtle comparisons between her prowess as a mother and that of her predecessor. "She said something like, 'God knows how these kids would have grown up if I wasn't their mother. At least I'm organized and have my feet on the ground so they get a good dose of reality.'" The former neighbor admits that Joan was left on her own a great deal, especially when the children got older and their father worked longer hours. "When she needed him the most," she continues, "Tony not only had more responsibility at work, but the commute from the office was long. Often, he got home after the kids were already in bed. She really raised those kids as a single parent, which is kind of ironic."

Tony was completely involved when it came to the children's schoolwork. He expected good grades and would reward them with a quarter and later fifty cents for every A on a report card. Madonna usually collected the most money, which was yet another source of contention between her and her siblings. They resented her not so much because she had surpassed them at school, but because they were convinced that she was their father's favorite. In response, Tony Ciccone always insisted that Madonna got straight A's because she has an IQ of over 140 and not to gain his affection. "I should know how I felt," Madonna argues, "and I know I would have done anything to be his favorite."

The truth was that while Tony was pleased with her work at school, he was extremely displeased with her relationship with his wife: "The good grades didn't make me feel any better about their constant fighting." In fact, Tony maintains that because of all the trouble she caused, Madonna was far from being his favorite child: "Actually, when the kids were small, Madonna gave me more trouble than the others. Years later, after Madonna became 'Madonna,' I continued to be equally interested in all my children's careers, problems, and progress and probably was closer to the others because I saw them more often."

Joan and Tony insisted that they never had any report that the children were discipline problems in school. When it came to their behavior, they were never rewarded for being good but were punished for being bad, although Tony and Joan did not have the same concept of how to punish them. "There was never any difference between my sons and daughters. I knew the boys would grow up, get a job, and support a family," Tony Ciccone explains. "If anything, I was more apt to encourage my daughters to think about having a profession, and I was prepared to offer them the same advantages of college and training as their brothers, but with the understanding that there would be the same consequences for them if they didn't obey or do well in school."

On more than one occasion, when the future rock star answered back or was stubborn, she was not spared Joan's temper. On the way to church, when Madonna voiced her usual complaint about having to wear the same dress as her sisters, Joan hauled off and slapped her. When her nose bled all over the dress, Joan was forced to turn the car around and go home. Ironically, Madonna's main complaint was not that she was treated more harshly than her sisters, but that there was a double standard in the house in favor of the boys. From the time she was old enough to express herself, she was a "freethinker" in a home and in a church where doctrine was the law. The unspoken understanding was that girls had to be protected and restricted more than boys, because girls could get pregnant. By the time she was ten years old, Madonna already had her period. According to a classmate, she would come to school once a month with a bulky plastic package filled with sanitary napkins. One of the teachers in Madonna's elementary school remembers how embarrassed the little girl was when she was unprepared for her period, which had arrived several days early. When the teacher dismissed the class for recess, Madonna remained in her seat.

Approaching her desk, the teacher asked if she wasn't feeling well. "I remember how she just looked at me with those big, beautiful, blue eyes filled with tears." The teacher smiles slightly. "I understood immediately that there was a problem, and she was terribly embarrassed. We wrapped my sweater around her, and somehow we made it to the teachers' lounge, where I gave her what she needed. She was absolutely mortified, and I remember thinking that this was a child in a woman's body."

The same year that she got her period, Madonna also started getting interested in the opposite sex. Her favorite game was chasing the boys after school in the playground. While her brothers were allowed to roughhouse without being accused of breaking the rules of the Catholic Church, Madonna was expected to "play" like a lady. The reaction of the nuns and her father was the same. They all told Madonna that good Catholic girls didn't behave like that. On her own, Madonna decided that confessing her sins to a priest as an intermediary instead of going directly to God made as little sense as not being allowed to wear jeans to church. When Madonna would ask her father why she couldn't love God as much wearing pants, for example, or why she couldn't play the same games as her brothers, he always had a stock reply: "Because I said so."

Sister Mary Connolly taught Madonna at St. Andrew's parochial school in Rochester Hills. One of her strongest recollections is that Madonna was always concerned about her father's reaction to bad reports about her. "She was always terrified that her father would find out that she had misbehaved. But it wasn't so much that she was afraid of him as she was upset that he would be disappointed in her or think less of her."

According to a close friend of the family's, Tony Ciccone had "little time to deal with a rebel within the ranks of eight children and a new wife." One of the most telling comments that Madonna has made about her relationship with her father was when she said, "As a child, sometimes I wondered who I was worshiping, God or my father." This conflict would appear and reappear in her songs and videos. One of her teachers in junior high school, the first secular school she attended, said, "The thing that made it hard for Madonna, as for any girl who comes from a strict Catholic family, is that she is brought up to keep a lid on everything sexual and emotional. So where's all this energy going to go? In Madonna's case, it came out in her work."

chapter thirteen
····················

*I*n 1968 when Madonna was ten years old, Joan gave birth to a daughter, Jennifer, followed by a son, Mario, who was born in 1969. "Things just kept getting worse," Madonna explains. "For the three years after my mother died, my father was alone, and I clung to him. It was like now you're mine and you're not going anywhere. Like all young girls, I was in love with my father and I didn't want to lose him. At first, right after he got remarried and I stopped being the mother or the woman of the house, it was bad enough. But when Joan had her own children, that's when I really made up my mind that no one was going to break my heart again. I was determined to stand on my own and be my own person and not belong to anyone."

The age difference between Jennifer and Madonna made it difficult for the two to be close as children, although several family friends claim that Jennifer is similar in character to Madonna. She is a perfectionist, a tireless worker, and very much her own person. Of all the Ciccone sisters, Jennifer, because of her age and her personality, has never resented Madonna's fame. Given the absence of conflict, it is a mystery why Jennifer wasn't invited to Madonna's wedding to Guy Ritchie. "Martin was in rehab," one friend concludes, "so he couldn't come, and there was no love lost between Anthony and Paula and Madonna, but Jennifer? Why she wasn't invited or didn't show, that's a mystery!"

Anthony, the oldest Ciccone child, is currently forty-four years old and has been struggling to become an actor and a dancer. Named after his father and the one who looks most like him, Anthony was the son that his father could depend on to behave after his mother died, and he lived with a succession of relatives. Along with Madonna, Anthony was also expected to watch the others when a housekeeper was late or didn't show up. According to another family friend, Anthony functioned as a "child in an adult's skin." The same friend explains, "Tony always considered Anthony as his 'little man,' and that's what he'd call him. So right from the beginning, the kid never had an adult he could go to with his own problems. He kept everything inside and tried real hard to be the grown-up and take care of the other kids."

As a boy, Martin, who is only eighteen months younger than Anthony, was close to him, although their relationship became strained during high school when Martin was heavily involved with alcohol. He was married at eighteen and then divorced, and his first child and the Ciccones' first grandchild, a daughter named Adrien, is currently a student at Cornell University. Throughout the years, Madonna has always considered Martin the "loose cannon" of the group and has made no secret that she disapproves of his lack of discipline and his disloyalty. For long periods of time she has refused to speak to him because she has suspected that he has leaked stories about her to the press.

Shortly after Joan's second child was born in 1969, she decided, with Tony's encouragement, to adopt his six children. It would be the most heart-wrenching moment for Madonna since the death of her mother, as well as for Elsie Fortin, who took it as the final separation between her daughter and her daughter's children. Not surprisingly, the only child to whom Elsie expressed those feelings was Madonna. Years later, Elsie Fortin would say that had Joan and Tony Ciccone waited until the children were older to proceed with the adoption, she wasn't convinced that all six would have given their consent.

Tony Ciccone felt that the decision to allow Joan to adopt the children was natural and expected. "Joan was a wonderful mother and felt absolutely no difference between my kids and our kids. It just seemed like the most logical culmination to the whole process of our marriage."

According to Joan, adopting the children was not done when there was "an ex-wife somewhere competing for the kids' affections . . . it wasn't a question of custody or divorce. This was simply a matter of the heart. I felt like their mother, and I wanted to believe they felt that I was their mother, so why not make it legal?"

As a close friend of Joan's explained it, "It wasn't so much a legal thing as it was symbolic for Joan that she was the one and only Mrs. Ciccone, and the kids were hers. She didn't want any history or baggage to interfere with her place as the woman of the house. That was the most important thing for her."

When Anthony was thirteen, Martin, twelve, Madonna, eleven, Paula, ten, Christopher, nine, and Melanie, seven, the Ciccone family appeared in court to make the adoption official. Joan carried the infant, Mario, who was six months old, while Tony held Jennifer, who was not yet two. Anthony held tightly to Melanie's hand, while Martin, with an expression on his face that would eventually become his characteristic sulk, stood awkwardly next to Paula. Madonna and Christopher lingered behind the others. Anyone who observed the family that day as they stood in the courtroom might have noticed that the two younger children, both fair like their mother, were the only ones who seemed happy. The others all looked like lost waifs.

After the proceedings were over, Tony and Joan had a celebratory lunch at their house with several close family friends and neighbors. The atmosphere was anything but happy. At one point Tony was forced to separate Paula and Martin, who began fighting, banishing them from the table, while Anthony disappeared into his room with a violent stomachache. Melanie was the only child who seemed oblivious to the sense of loss the others were experiencing. If she had any negative feelings, they were directed at Jennifer, who had taken her place as the "baby girl" of the family. Years later, when Melanie was an adult, she would suffer enormous guilt when she finally learned the facts of her mother's illness and death. On the day of the adoption, Melanie spent the day cuddled against Joan, while Christopher sat like a "little soldier" at the table. One of the guests at the lunch recalls that Chris was the only child who kept his emotions to himself. "He was polite and quiet," the family friend says. "The only indication that he was upset happened that night when he crawled into Madonna's bed to sleep." As for Madonna, she was also quiet, although she threw everything up immediately following the meal.

While Joan always made an effort to treat all the children equally and Tony is the biological father of all eight, the couple's insensitivity to the six older children's feelings was based more on ignorance than malice. Neither parent understood that for the children, the adoption represented irrevocable confirmation that their mother was never coming back. The couple never considered that each child, according to his or her own level of maturity, spent childhood and early adulthood in mourning. What made it even harder for the kids was that they lived in a typically middle-class environment where any deviation from the conventional was grounds for exclusion. Madonna always felt that "losing" her mother had set her apart from her peers, as if somehow her carelessness had resulted in the loss of her parent.

Another close friend of the family's who also was present that day believes that it was up to Tony to have been more aware of the situation. "Joan was basically flaky," the friend says, "so he [Tony] shouldn't have expected her to be sensitive to the memory of his late wife. In a way, I can't blame her. She came into this guy's life when he had nothing except trouble and responsibility, and she lightened everything up. In her mind, he should have been happy, and he was, but on the other hand, he should have realized how the kids felt, especially the older ones."

On the promise of anonymity, one of the Ciccone children talks about a nightmare that occurred for years after their mother's death. "I kept seeing my mother trying to get into the house, except every time she tried a door, Joan would lock it, and then she'd try another door, but Joan was already there, locking that one, too. In my dream, we were all racing around the house in different directions. My mother would try one door, and Joan would lock it, and I would be right behind her unlocking it, but by then, my mother was at another door, and we all just kept going around and around . . ."

When Madonna was eleven, the family moved from Pontiac to the more affluent suburb of Rochester Hills, where Joan was finally able to put her own personality into the family house. The result produced yet another rift between stepmother and stepdaughter. Madonna was embarrassed when she brought friends home to a house that was decorated in what she considered to be a boring style of muted colors and safe patterns, a decor that was similar to the display-window perfection found in the department stores in downtown Detroit. Madonna's rebellion took a different form. She daydreamed about being poor and living in a home where the furniture was threadbare. Instead, she was condemned to live with Early American–style reproductions and matching lamps that sat on matching end tables that matched the coffee table, all demonstrating her stepmother's lack of originality. Joan also chose several original oils done by local Michigan artists and posters of some of the more famous works of Manet and Monet, as well as posters for the children's rooms. In keeping with her matching mania, she made sure that the colors of the paintings or posters blended with the upholstery and carpeting with no thought that the children might want to express their own tastes or experiment with color. Eventually, Joan developed certain special touches that she learned at a variety of craft classes she took. The kids called her "artsy-craftsy Joansy" behind her back. Handwoven baskets filled with potpourri were everywhere around the house, and for a while, on every available radiator, there were flowers in various stages of drying that were generously sprayed with inexpensive perfume. Invariably Madonna would make a point of throwing open the windows even in the middle of winter to get rid of the smell.

A neighbor recalls one example of Joan's mania for perfection. The neighbor was visiting when Madonna cracked open one of the walnuts that were permanently on display in a dish on the living-room coffee table. She was immediately sent to her room without supper. In Joan's defense, regardless of what she did or didn't do—and she would certainly have been criticized had she not tried to make the house comfortable—she would never gain her stepchildren's approval or gratitude.

As Joan became more interested in decorating, she spent more and more time in the antique stores in the Michigan countryside or at various antique fairs. Her most treasured acquisition was a nineteenth-century spinning wheel, which Madonna and Christopher, the most aesthetic of the children, thought was ridiculous. As adults, they found it amusing that Joan constantly referred to it as an antique, since the same spinning wheel was in almost every home in Rochester Hills.

Currently, the Ciccone house on the vineyard property in northern Michigan is arranged with the same kind of display-window perfection. The spinning wheel is still prominently displayed in one corner of the living room. The only deviation from Joan's sense of order and determination to be recognized as the one and only mistress of the manor is a photograph that sits on the piano in the center of the living room. Among the pictures of children and grandchildren and several wedding photos is a picture of Madonna and Tony with their six children. The walnuts in a dish on the coffee table are now ceramic.

* * *

By the time she entered Rochester Hills Junior High,
Madonna had more freedom than ever before. She had
classes with boys and didn't have to wear a uniform. Though
the other girls her age were permitted to wear light lipstick
for special occasions, Madonna was not. Tight skirts and
sweaters were taboo as well, and she was constantly admon-
ished about looking "haughty and arrogant." "Lower your
eyes and look humble," her parents would tell her when she
was reprimanded. Tony also made it clear that "idle time was
the devil's workplace," and going to school every day was
not enough. "You always had to be doing something produc-
tive," Madonna recalls, "like schoolwork or housework or
prayer, never just sitting around and never having too much
leisure time. You always had to be challenging your mind or
body." In keeping with that philosophy, Tony imposed new
rules for her as well as for her two older brothers. He decided that his three older children would study a musical instrument, more to instill in them a further sense of discipline
and accomplishment than to nurture any hidden talent they
might have had. All three opted for piano lessons, although
before long Madonna began a campaign to persuade her father to let her substitute ballet for music. Tony was not prepared to make an exception for one child, but he was getting
weary, as was Joan, of the constant battle they were forced
to wage to get her to practice. Madonna's excuse was that
she hated learning "other people's music." He finally relented and allowed her to study ballet, but only after she
pointed out that she could take dance classes as part of the
cultural program at Rochester Hills Junior High. From her
first lesson, her teachers thought that she had talent and that
dance was a good way for her to express herself. Rather than
encouraging her gift, Joan made it clear that Madonna could
only continue the lessons month-to-month, depending on
her behavior at home and at school. Every month Joan made
a calendar, and at the end of each day, Madonna was either

awarded a commendation or a demerit. More than five demerits a month meant that ballet classes were suspended until she had thirty days in a row of good behavior. Madonna was so determined to continue dancing that she learned not to react when her brothers picked on her or when Paula, who was increasingly resentful, baited her. Madonna was blossoming into a graceful young woman with a body that naturally attracted boys, while Paula remained the family "jock," boyish and flat-chested and considered a pal by the opposite sex. One of the often-told anecdotes is that once Paula, Anthony, and Martin hung Madonna by her blouse to the clothesline. According to a neighbor, when Joan found her there, she didn't rush to cut her down but enjoyed the joke with the others while Madonna dangled helplessly.

Madonna was completely involved with her dancing lessons, but another side to her had little to do with her dedication to ballet or her enjoyment of classical music. According to Moira McPharlin and several other girlfriends from that period, Madonna still behaved like any normal teenager. She enjoyed popular music, especially the Monkees, and loved the usual teen magazines like *Seventeen* and *Glamour*. Ever the rebel, when Madonna was finally in a secular school where catechism was not part of the daily academic routine, she actually looked forward to mass on Sunday. In fact, the comfort she derived from the ritual and discipline would stay with her throughout her life.

Anyone who has worked with her knows that the enterprise known as "Madonna" never goes on holiday. It is a twenty-four-hour-a-day, 365-day-a-year business that is open to any and all new ideas and talent, revivals, scripts, music, videos, and any other creative and innovative project that comes along. Madonna has made it a policy to give anyone a chance if she believes in that person's talent and commitment and, above all, recognizes a willingness to work night and day to achieve a goal. Even when she is not working on a project, she finds it difficult to settle down and sleep. Once she is on tour or making a film, she trains as if for a marathon, making sure she cuts down on her socializing to get her rest. She has often said that if she wants to "feel good," she sleeps six hours a night; if she wants to "look good," she sleeps seven; and if she wants to "feel ecstatic," she sleeps eight. In addition to the tireless work ethic that she learned from the Church, she has always appreciated the sense of family that the priests and nuns instilled in her. Even after she left home and was estranged from her siblings and father, they remained important to her.

When Madonna was fourteen years old, she was confirmed and, by tradition, reaffirmed her faith in the Church. She chose the name Veronica as her confirmation name after the woman who gave Jesus her veil to wipe his brow as he carried the cross to Golgotha. As a child, Madonna thought the gesture was dramatic. As she got older and reread the passage, she decided that she, like Veronica, was a passionate person who relied on instinct to survive. Veronica stepped away from the crowd to reach out and comfort a condemned man who had been rendered powerless. Madonna also took risks that ultimately changed her life. "When I chose Veronica as my confirmation name," she says, "it was the beginning of my own awareness that I was different than other people. Just like Veronica had the nerve to step forward to comfort Jesus, when I got successful, I dared to step forward and expose my most private fantasies, which gave my fans the courage to be different."

Though the mystery and gothic aura of the church intrigued her and she found the moral aspect of Catholicism appealing, her connection to religion and her relationship with her father became increasingly confused. According to one of the nuns who taught Madonna and who took a special interest in her when she was a teenager, the Church and her father became inseparable. Both were so firmly entrenched in her daily life that every action was weighed against a reaction, either from her priest or the nuns who taught her or by her father, who expected her behavior to be beyond reproach at home.

One nun, a small woman as round as she is high, with bright blue eyes and a ruddy complexion, recently retired after having taught at St. Andrew's parochial school for thirty-five years. She is convinced that Madonna's "sexual rebellion," after she became a star, was less against the Church than it was against her father. "In Catholicism," the nun explains, "we teach the children to strive for perfection, and as a result, we are all asking the Lord to forgive us and cleanse our soul so that we can serve Him better." At one point Madonna confided in the nun that she was always getting in trouble with her father and constantly asking him to forgive her. "She asked me to explain to her what the difference was between God and her father," the nun says, smiling slightly. "An interesting question for a little girl . . ."

Years later, after that same little girl became an international star, she would address that dilemma in many of her most controversial hits. For instance, when Madonna sings "Oh Father" in her video "Like a Prayer," she is hunched over a pew in church and choking out lyrics, the gist of which left many fans wondering whom she is singing to, God or her father: ". . . you never wanted to hurt me, why am I running away? Maybe someday when I look back, I'll be able to say somebody hurt you, too . . . you can't hurt me now, I got away from you. I never thought I could . . ."

Madonna always felt that the nuns were the only ones who deeply cared about her after her mother's death. In an effort to show her gratitude and affection, at one point she announced that when she grew up, she would either be a movie star or a nun. For Madonna, it was a completely rational choice since nuns, despite their vows of chastity and modesty, represented the epitome of cloistered sexuality. A nun was the bride of Christ, and Christ was the ultimate erotic man. That declaration was perhaps the first inkling of what would be her obsessive contradiction between sex and religion, abstinence and sensuality, the Madonna and the whore.

After all, what better example of this conflict than to transform the image of her name from an asexual and passive figure to the ultimate sexualized and liberated woman?

When several of the nuns told Madonna that before a girl can take her vows, she has to be modest and uninterested in the opposite sex, Madonna decided that she was perhaps better suited for stardom. As it turned out, she proved that show business and religion are not mutually exclusive.

chapter fourteen

· · · · · · · · · · · · · · · · · ·

*M*other Dolores belongs to the cloistered order of nuns at the Regina Laudis Convent in Bethlehem, Connecticut, and is one of the few women of the veil who have been in show business. Before Mother Dolores entered Regina Laudis more than thirty-five years ago, she was Dolores Hart, the movie actress who is best remembered for her costarring movie roles in the 1950s with Elvis Presley. Although her sensual looks have faded and her hourglass figure is hidden beneath her flowing habit, even at sixty-five, with her face devoid of makeup and framed by a wimple, she is still breathtakingly beautiful. "It isn't surprising that she considered becoming either a nun or a movie star," Mother Dolores explains. "For Madonna and for many other children, a nun is like a movie star. She is dressed in costume and presides over a classroom or a stage. She is mysterious and yet open, remote and at the same time accessible to discuss anything and everything with her young charges. For many Catholic children, nuns are the embodiment of beauty and goodness. As a small child, Madonna was able to see the drama in the Church."

According to Mother Dolores, it was clear from the beginning that Madonna was not meant to take her vows. "Most people erroneously believe that giving up a secular life to become a nun is filled with torment and misery," Mother Dolores continues. "That is simply not true. When I decided to leave Hollywood and enter a convent, I was so sure that was where I belonged that never for an instant did I think about what I would be giving up, whether it was sex or makeup or the movies or all the glamorous things that had been part of my life. I understood from the beginning that it was God calling me to serve Him. If Madonna was meant to take her vows, she would have had no doubt that that was her destiny." Mother Dolores smiles. "You know, there are many different ways to serve God, and Madonna is making many people aware of the Catholic Church and all its teachings who might not have been aware if she didn't exist. She reaches so many young people who have conflicts with the teachings of the Church that her approach to Catholicism isn't necessarily negative. Madonna addresses issues in a way that her fans can understand that she has the same dilemmas that they have which correspond to the difficulty of living in today's world."

More than any other video, "Oh Father" is an example of the traumas that have touched Madonna the most profoundly: the heartfelt torment when she decides to forgive her father for betraying her, the touching memory of her mother's death, and her irrepressible sense of travesty. In a brief scene in "Oh Father," a priest covers a body with a sheet that becomes a field of snow with Madonna sitting in the middle, obviously symbolizing the death of Madonna's mother. In the video, as the family makes the trip with the body from the funeral parlor to the cemetery, a billboard appears on the side of the road advertising Coca-Cola. The irony of course is that Coke is Pepsi's major competition, and the controversial video "Like a Prayer" was the basis for the Pepsi commercial subtitled "Make a Wish." In the five-minute video, set in a church, Madonna is surrounded by religious imagery, including stigmata, burning crosses, an all-black choir, and a statue of a black saint that comes to life when she kisses its feet. The story line also sends a moral message that could have been based on *Mississippi Burning,* a film that came out at about the same time as the video. In "Like a Prayer," Madonna witnesses the stabbing of a white woman by a gang and the subsequent arrest of an innocent black man (the black saint who becomes a living man after his feet are kissed) for the young woman's murder. After several minutes of singing and dancing in a field of burning crosses, Madonna decides to report to the police what she has witnessed in an effort to free the black man. Given the clip's religious, racial, and musical messages mixed in with saints turning into sexual human beings, it is not surprising that Pepsi decided to distance itself from the highly controversial subject matter. Madonna always believed that the executives at Pepsi were less put off by the sacrilegious elements of the video than by the fact that the company was not receiving enough of a plug in the commercial to warrant a boycott of the soft drink by a shocked public. In the end, Pepsi decided to walk away from a signed deal, which cost them Madonna's $5 million fee.

It wasn't the first time that a work of art steeped in Catholic iconography resulted in an adverse public reaction. In the 1970s in England, James Kirkoff, who wrote the words to the Stephen Sondheim musical *Into the Woods,* also wrote a poem called "The Love Who Dare Not Speak Its Name." As a gay man, Kirkoff told the story, drawn from his own fantasies, about a Roman centurion who, while guarding the crucified Christ, becomes sexually aroused. It was not unlike Madonna's portrayal of her own erotic feelings, in "Like a Prayer," for the crucified Christ. At the time, Mary Whitehouse, who is still living and continues to head an organization bent on "cleaning up" the contents of television programs, successfully brought a case against Kirkoff for blasphemy. The eventual public outrage against Whitehouse and the court's reversal of the decision to censure Kirkoff mirrored the numerous letters that Madonna and even the Pepsi company received concerning the latter's decision to pull the commercial. The general feelings expressed by fans and Pepsi consumers indicated how much they appreciated the video's message and how they wished they could have found a way to "sort out their own problems when it came to certain aspects of their religion." In response, Madonna made the following statement: "The video's message was a social statement in defense of an interracial relationship and an idea I had to promote that kind of joyousness in church."

Father Gary Siebert has been the assistant pastor at Holy Cross Church in the heart of Times Square in Manhattan for the past five years. A Jesuit, he has had a varied career as a dancer in a company directed by a disciple of Martha Graham, a professor at John Jay Criminal College, a media consultant for Robert MacNeil of the *MacNeil/Lehrer NewsHour,* and also as the priest who tended to Martha Graham spiritually at the end of her life. An attractive and articulate man whose views on the Catholic Church are outspoken and controversial, Father Gary's positive opinion of Madonna goes back long before he learned that the doyenne of dance admired the singer and before he was aware that Graham identified with Madonna's approach to the Catholic Church. "Martha, like Madonna, loved the drama in the Catholic Church, and one of her first compositions was about the Madonna. Even more relevant is that Martha always danced to the floor, which she often said was symbolic of the way Catholics drop to their knees to worship. She loved the fact that Madonna always played to the floor, whether she was writhing around or simulating prayer and sex."

Father Gary Siebert understands how the public could relate to Madonna's message of fear and oppressiveness in Catholicism, its passion and discipline and obsession with guilt. "What's sexier than a naked man on a cross?" he asks rhetorically. "Why shouldn't everyone, not just Madonna, love the crucifix? There you have the near-perfect fantasy, a naked, utterly passive guy who's not going anywhere. He is literally nailed. 'Like a Prayer' should be required viewing in every Catholic church. The truth is that the Church can't expect people to worship that image without taking at least a smidgen of it into their personal life. Growing up in that kind of strict and unforgiving atmosphere both at home and at school where the smallest act of defiance is considered a sin accounts for Madonna's obsession with women as either virgins or whores. Madonna is expressing the same ambivalent state of heart, mind, and soul as any other confused Italian Catholic in America. The difference is that Madonna tapped into the conflict that every human being has whether they are Catholic or not, and that is that every one of us constantly suffers from varying degrees of guilt about believing or not believing, feeling sexual pleasure, or just by being alive and having a good time when millions of others we see on the news or read about are suffering and dying."

Father Gary believes that from the time she was a little girl, Madonna somehow understood that there was little difference within the Church between art and life. "She grasped the drama in the teachings of the nuns at Catholic school," he explains, "beginning with baptism. When you immerse a baby in water, you're playing like you're drowning a baby, life to resurrection. In fact, all the sacraments are borderline experiences, to die with Christ and rise to a new life. Think about the final scene in *Godfather I* when there's a baptism going on at the same time as a series of brutal Mafia murders."

Rather than denigrating the Church, Father Gary believes that in all of Madonna's performances, she celebrates life, which, by definition, includes religion, God, sex, death, and birth. "These are all conditions and experiences that every human being not only can identify with in the abstract but also lives with on a daily basis. Madonna accepts the fact that life is ambiguous, which is the strong point for the Church's sacramental life."

While Madonna has been criticized for her explicit sexual fantasies concerning the crucifixion, Father Gary maintains it is only because the current Catholic hierarchy is so out of touch with reality that those in power simply "don't get it" and are most often offended by the "form rather than the content." Father Gary explains, "The church has become powerless, and when you render a ritualistic system impotent, it becomes violent, which explains the Church's approach to gay people and to women. And by that I mean that their approach is quite ruthless and uncompromising because they have to protect what has become a very unpopular position."

Profoundly influenced by the Church and by her own disharmony with her religion, Madonna's music and videos have reflected the decadence that was prevalent during the nineteenth century when many works of art and literature depicted sadomasochistic portrayals of the crucifixion. By using baroque iconography to challenge some of the most revered symbols, Madonna has joined the ranks of those artists who personify Catholic defiance. She, like so many writers and artists, has interpreted the rituals of the Church and the graphic images of the crucifixion to represent a sexual act. Unlike the other artists who have responded to the erotic image of Christ according to their own sexual proclivities and preferences, she has always played with the sexuality of the crucifixion from both sides of the erotic spectrum—homosexual and heterosexual.

William Burroughs, the author of *Naked Lunch,* addressed the fantasy of execution and ejaculation, the hanged man who releases sperm at the moment of death. In a collection of essays entitled *Don Antonio,* Somerset Maugham writes about the painter El Greco. Based on the painter's style in depicting crucified figures and their suffering—the naked, penetrated man on display—Maugham assumes that he was homosexual and used the crucifixion to paint his own gay sexual fantasies. Oscar Wilde, who was raised in the Irish Catholic Church, eroticized the figure of John the Baptist, the immediate precursor to Christ, in his play *Salomé.* The more holy the figure, the more tempting it is to drag that character down to the carnal level of human sin. Wilde has Salomé dance for King Herod, who, as a reward, offers her anything she wants. The object of her desire is the head of John the Baptist, about which she has fantasized, conjuring up images of his "white skin" and of "biting his lips until they bleed."

Paul Gambacinni, an American who lives in London, where he is known as Mr. Rock and Roll, has a popular radio program on the BBC. He believes that Madonna's attitude toward the Catholic Church is not only brave but extremely intelligent. "Having been raised Catholic," Gambacinni says, "when I first saw 'Like a Prayer,' I understood immediately that it was a sincere attempt on her part to work out her feelings in the same way that Scorsese tried to do in *The Last Temptation of Christ*. Both artists are extremely unusual and daring when they address issues that are so very deep and personal through popular entertainment."

Gambacinni maintains that when Madonna uses Catholic iconography in her art, she is not being gratuitous or frivolous nor is she conjuring up those images solely to cause a sensation. "I am convinced," Gambacinni said, "that for Madonna, it is a genuine attempt to work out contradictory heartfelt feelings. As a Catholic, I see Madonna as someone who is trying to say that part of this whole Catholic thing is nonsense but it means so much to me."

The problem, according to Gambacinni, is the subtext within Catholicism that the Church refuses to address and which Madonna has defined in "Like a Prayer," when she explains the erotic feelings she has for the crucified Christ. "When I first saw it," Gambacinni says, "I thought, how brave, how fantastic that she could express what we knew all along, that the Church forces us from the time we are children to worship the form of a nearly naked and brutalized man. The Catholic Church refuses to admit that the image in itself is pornographic. You are made to worship the consequence of violence, human hopelessness, and near nudity. I remember my most tender feelings as a teenager when I was still in the Church would be for male friends who had been injured. Compassion poured out of me, the well opened because this was my religious training. I had been taught to anoint the crucified Christ."

In his opinion, out of one hundred people who have been brought up in an intense Catholic environment, several at least will interpret the crucified image of Christ as having sadomasochistic and erotic undertones. "It's inevitable," Gambacinni says, "when children are confronted by that overpowering figure, because it's physically huge in the Church, it's obvious that there's going to be some kind of deviant response. Especially since children have their First Communion at the age that Saint Thomas Aquinas said, 'Give me a child until he is seven . . .' "

It is unlikely that Madonna consciously set out to imitate those other tortured Catholic artists but instead genuinely responded to the same stimuli within the Church as they did.

J. K. Huysmans is another example of a major nineteenth-century figure of literary decadence. In his book *À rebours,* translated as *Against the Grain,* he writes about Gilles de Rais, Joan of Arc's military commander, who was both a hero as well as a devil worshiper and monster who slaughtered innocent people. Cynically, Huysmans makes the point that if a person is sufficiently educated, even if he has led a life of total debauchery and evil, he knows enough to repent on his deathbed. De Rais does exactly that, and as a result, the torturer goes to heaven.

In "Act of Contrition," for which she was accused of being a "devil worshiper" and criticized by the hierarchy of the Catholic Church for dealing with such a sacred subject with irony and humor, Madonna addresses the issue of remorse. By flipping over the tape of "Like a Prayer" so that she can recite over it, she attempts to intone the Catholic Act of Contrition. It comes to a comic and abrupt end when Madonna repeats, "I resolve. I reserve. I have a reservation. What do you mean it's not in the computer!!!" And in "Sanctuary" from her album *Bedtime Stories,* she enigmatically sings, using religious phrasing, "Whoever speaks to me in the right voice, Him will I follow."

"There is really no difference between life and art in the Church," Father Gary Siebert says. "Go back to the twelfth century and think about the Spaniards and then think about Madonna and her videos, and you'll see how most of the Spanish statues are all pornographic, even if they have a halo. Almost all of them depict some form of sado-masochism at the same time that the priests preached celibacy."

One of the best examples of Madonna's typical struggle with good and evil and her attempt to make peace with her mother's death is seen in her video "Bad Girl." It is one of her best works artistically, and yet one of her least success-ful, perhaps because it was made for her *Erotica* album, which sparked such negative controversy throughout the world. The chorus of the song, "Bad Girl . . . drunk by six . . . kissing someone else's lips . . . smoked too many cigarettes today . . . I'm not happy when I act this way."

"Bad Girl" is about a woman named Louise Oriole (Louise is Madonna's middle name, and Oriole is the name of a street where she lived as a child), who, despite all her power and success, is unhappy about the way she lives and acts, but can't help herself since all she has known since she was "six" was how to be "bad." The age is significant since Madonna was eight months short of six when her mother died. Highly derivative of the film *Looking for Mr. Goodbar,* starring Diane Keaton as the uptight Catholic girl by day who goes from bar to bar by night in search of a one-night stand, *Bad Girl,* aka Louise Oriole, does the same thing. "Bad Girl" tells the story of a woman filled with pain who rarely likes to look in the mirror because all she sees is sad-ness. In "Bad Girl," Louise has a guardian angel who watches over her, although he does nothing to stop her self-destructive acts. We understand that he wants her to "learn the hard way." The fate of the woman in *Mr. Goodbar* is a horrific final scene in her own bed when a man she has picked up and brought home murders her during sex. In "Bad Girl," Madonna/Louise picks up the most ominous man in a bar and takes him home, but not before her guardian angel kisses her in what symbolizes the "kiss of a death." Her fate is sealed. At the same moment that the audience realizes that the angel knows she is about to die, Madonna/Louise realizes it as well. Rather than resist, she is happy, finally at peace that she doesn't have to live the way she has lived since she was six.

Both "Bad Girl" and "Oh Father" are Madonna's attempts to make peace with her pain. In the former, the character's monsters or traumas are self-inflicted, whether because of her lack of discipline or her promiscuity. In contrast, the implication in "Oh Father" is that her suffering was brought on by her father's "abuse" when he remarried and replaced Madonna as the woman/wife/caretaker in his life after his wife died.

The "Erotica" video, made in 1992, imitates the murky lighting of amateur film and video by including the unsteadiness of a handheld camera. Within the stylistic imitations, the material itself is absolutely accurate, evoking pornographic iconography from the 1920s and combining it with erotic images taken from mainstream design. Madonna appears as an androgynous cabaret performer in a 1930s Nazi-era Berlin club, similar to how Joel Grey portrayed his character in the film and Broadway production of *Cabaret*. She has slicked-back hair and carries a toy monkey with a painted mask recalling those created by Wladyslas Benda for the Ziegfeld Follies and for photographers like Edward Steichen, who used those images in fashion magazines in the 1930s. In the video are also brief shots from what might be a gay New York club from the 1980s, the Anvil or the Mine Shaft, with a biker fetishist sitting under a sign saying "New York Strap and Paddle." There are also shots of Madonna with a dog whip in the throes of some S&M act, crawling sex slaves attached to the leash of a dominatrix, and a lesbian couple, similar to Man Ray's pictures of Nusch Éluard and Meret Oppenheim, while other poses are right out of a Helmut Newton photograph. The video ends with a shot of a nude Madonna hitching a ride on a Hollywood street. The only problem is that one has difficulty remembering the song, but that hardly matters.

chapter fifteen
....

After graduating from junior high school in 1972, Madonna spent the summer before she entered high school at Elsie Fortin's house in Bay City, accompanied by Moira McPharlin. At the time, one of Madonna's uncles, Carl, had formed his own rock band and was only too happy to take his fourteen-year-old niece, who looked years older, around town. Dressed in tight jeans and T-shirts with her face covered with too much makeup, Madonna tried cigarettes and cocktails that summer and behaved like a vamp. Throughout the visit, Elsie Fortin was serene about Madonna's provocative image and convinced that, deep down, her granddaughter was a decent girl who was just going through the normal stages of adolescent rebellion. "I wasn't worried," Mrs. Fortin says. "I believed times had changed since my own daughter was a teenager, and it just seemed so obvious that Madonna was letting off steam. Her stepmother and father were too strict with the kids back home."

Madonna may have dressed and acted provocatively, but Elsie Fortin was not wrong when she judged her granddaughter to be far more responsible than the image she projected. Madonna already had a highly developed sense of survival and a need to be in control. Drugs were not the way to achieve what she wanted—fame, money, international acclaim—and clearly not the way to get out of Rochester Hills.

* * *

If Madonna expected her stepmother and father to indulge her newly acquired grown-up, sexy look as her grandmother had, she was disappointed. When she returned from vacation, Joan told her that she looked like a "slut," and Tony forbade her to wear makeup and revealing clothes. The relationship with her siblings became increasingly tense; Paula and Martin sided with their parents and, on one occasion, cut up all of Madonna's halter tops and dungarees. According to a source close to Martin, he was embarrassed because his friends would make suggestive remarks about his sister. That same source claims that for Martin, Madonna was not a star when they were kids growing up. She was just his kid sister.

Another friend of Madonna's recalls that she had one of the worst reputations in school. According to the former classmate, Madonna seemed to relish it and did nothing to dispel any of the rumors. In fact, Madonna has admitted that she always had a sensuality that boys "misunderstood," and that made girls "wary" of being seen in her company. "The girls didn't want to hang out with me because I had this reputation," Madonna explains, "and the boys didn't want to go out with me because they were embarrassed to be seen with the so-called slut of the school. It was so dumb because I was called slut when I was still a virgin."

Camille Paglia, the feminist writer and academic, has always admired Madonna more as a feminist than as a performer. "In the 1950s," Paglia explains, "girls had to be virgins. In the 1960s, pressure was on girls and women to put out. Madonna's greatest contribution to the feminist movement was to challenge that message by telling women and girls that they could say *no* and still keep the guys interested."

Just as Madonna became the patron saint of the trailer-park feminist, she is also the poster girl for the high school coed with the bad reputation, the so-called class slut who has gotten her bad name only because she acts and dresses to titillate and tantalize. "I've been called a tramp, a harlot, a slut," Madonna has said, "the kind of girl that always ends up in the backseat of a car. If people can't get past that superficial level of what I'm about, too bad for them!" And yet, as connected as she is to her teenage fans, she has always rejected the idea that she is a role model. "It's their choice to imitate me and not my duty to bring them up," Madonna has said. "My only responsibility is to be true to myself and to promote a life-affirming point of view."

When she first entered high school, Madonna kept company with the local bikers. On a dare, she attended mass naked underneath a long coat. Her choice of friends and her rebellious behavior did nothing to help her reputation around school. In reality, Madonna was surprisingly careful about having a sexual relationship and was one of the few girls who made it clear to everyone that she was never going to be forced into doing things that she didn't want to do. If *failure* was not in her lexicon, neither was *peer pressure*. In France there's a line of bodysuits called Anti-Flirt, an accurate name since they snap shut at the crotch, providing fabric barriers against advanced foreplay. When Madonna was a girl, she went to the usual parties along with her friends but always wore a turtlenecked bodysuit to protect her virginity.

Cal Townsend, who once had dreams of joining the Hell's Angels and who currently owns a hardware store near Detroit, where he is also a member of the Rotary and Kiwanis Clubs, remembers Madonna from her "wild days" in high school. "She was always very theatrical," Townsend says, "and a tease. I think our crowd, the bikers, were the only guys who really knew that she wasn't fast, because we all tried to get somewhere with her and failed. The preppy kids were too dumb to realize that she was all talk. They judged her on her behavior, which was kind of wild, but basically, she was a good girl who was scared of her dad."

While other girls dreamed of movie stars and rock-and-roll heartthrobs, Madonna was already a complex young teenager who found herself deeply touched by what she described as the "courage and determination" of Eva Perón, whom she had heard about on the radio during her freshman year of high school. Her Argentine idol had once been a young girl much like herself who preferred to be alone than with a group of teenagers, to concentrate on her goal of getting out of her hometown and reaching Buenos Aires, where she was determined to make a name for herself. One of the facts that intrigued Madonna about Eva Perón was that in October 1933 she was given a small part in a school play, an emotional patriotic melodrama, that would serve as her inspiration to become an actress and leave the poverty of her hometown of Junín.

Consumed by Eva's story, one night at the dinner table Madonna began describing Evita for her family. Tony immediately encouraged his daughter to go to the library and study the political climate in Argentina that accounted for the rise of Juan Perón along with his wife. To her credit she listened to him and scoured the library for every book that would give her more insight into Evita and life in Argentina during the 1940s and 1950s. Her determination to learn about things that interested her was typical of her attitude to study everything until she knew it perfectly. And yet, when she dropped out of university after her first year and decided to go to New York to become a star, she ignored her father's pleas to continue studying dance and drama in an academic setting. His concern was that she was not ready and was only setting herself up for failure and disappointment. Madonna argued that the only way to know if she had what it took to become a star meant risking defeat.

In 1973, Madonna decided that the best way out of Rochester Hills was to become an actress. When she found out that her school didn't have a drama club, she created one, naming it The Thespians, and eventually had leading roles in several of its more successful productions, including *Godspell, My Fair Lady,* and *The Wizard of Oz.*

Madonna was resolute about not letting friction with her parents and siblings at home interfere with her progress at school. Although she has admitted on several occasions that she had problems with self-doubt and self-loathing, what saved her from the all-too-usual fate of a teenager with a self-destructive streak was her determination to overcome anything in her character that she considered a weakness. Drugs were never an option. When her brother Martin became involved with alcohol, she made no secret of her disapproval. Over the years, she would pay for his many stays at rehabilitation centers throughout the United States.

Madonna joined the cheerleading squad, the French Club, sang in the choir, and followed all the current rock stars. Living in a suburb of Detroit where the Motown sound was the major musical influence, her favorite singers were Stevie Wonder, the Supremes, Marvin Gaye, and the Jackson 5. The Motown sound eventually influenced Madonna when she gravitated toward all those "innocent little pop songs" in the early 1980s in New York and rejected anything that was heavy metal or soul.

Just as he had insisted that the older children study a musical instrument in junior high school, Tony Ciccone insisted that they find after-school jobs. He also made it clear that he expected them to donate a percentage of their time or their salary to charity. Madonna volunteered her time to an organization called Help A Kid, where children from underprivileged and one-parent homes could have a one-on-one relationship with a teenager. Always more comfortable around children, Madonna was one of the most popular counselors and always in great demand. She could be counted on to give advice and affection to children who were left mostly to fend for themselves. During the summer holidays, she continued working with children as a paid lifeguard at the smart Avon Hills Swim Club in Rochester Hills. To earn money, her brothers had paper routes or packed groceries in the local supermarket, while Paula and Melanie did baby-sitting and waited tables. Madonna found a job as a salesclerk at a stationery store. According to the man who hired her, she was organized, responsible, and meticulous when it came to classifying his paper stock, and she flirted with the customers. "She was real pretty and the guys loved to kid around with her," he says, "which didn't hurt business."

When a job became available in a dress boutique, Madonna took that. Another salesgirl in the store who is now a wife and mother in Rochester Hills remembers that the singer had a knack for imitating the customers. "She always had an attitude with the customers," she says. "She didn't like picking up the clothes from the dressing room and hanging them up, so we ended up doing it for her, but only because she used to make us laugh all the time. Behind their backs, she would walk like the customers, and after they left, she would go into an act, catching every gesture and expression they used. It was hysterical, and we had a hard time controlling ourselves." The woman also remembers that Madonna got along better with the men who came in the shop with their wives and girlfriends. "Sometimes the guys would pay too much attention to her, and we'd lose a sale. Actually, that was one of the reasons why she got fired."

As the school year drew to a close and with it the dance program, Madonna decided that she had learned all she could in an nonprofessional setting. She wanted to find a school that would challenge her and put her in competition with students who were better than she. By then, Joan and Tony saw that she was committed to her classes and making progress, so that when Madonna broached the subject of going to a private dancing school, they agreed. Through one of her teachers, Madonna learned about a girl who was reputed to be a serious ballet student. From the moment they met, Madonna found herself instantly attracted to the aspiring ballerina.

Kathy was slight, small-boned, and graceful with dark hair pulled tightly back in a bun at the nape of her neck. She was different, a quiet girl who had a goal that was not part of the usual high school curriculum. It wasn't the first time in her school career that Madonna had found herself attracted to someone who was not part of the crowd. She had always rejected the usual band of hippies, the boys with long hair who smoked dope. The rock-and-roll crowd, even the ones who had formed their own band, didn't inspire her either, since they spent most of their time drunk on beer instead of playing or composing original music and sounds. As for the jocks and the cheerleaders, while Madonna found them appealing for a while, she eventually gave them up when she realized that her cheerleading girlfriends weren't interested in anything except boys and sports. Instead, Madonna remained on the periphery of the "in" groups and was mostly friendly with those students whom the others considered to be nerds, boys who were physics majors or girls reputed to be bookworms rather than bombshells.

From the moment Madonna met the aspiring ballerina, the two girls became inseparable to the exclusion of everyone else.

From that point on, dance would play a pivotal part in Madonna's destiny. In high school, her passion for dance was responsible for her attraction to Kathy, who became her first lesbian lover. The affair would last through high school, during the year that Madonna spent at the University of Michigan, and later, when she moved to New York. Kathy made regular visits to New York and shared Madonna's apartment on the Upper West Side of Manhattan.

chapter sixteen

....

*K*athy is forty-two years old today. Married to her second husband and the mother of two teenage children, she is slim and attractive with dark, short hair. Kathy has long since abandoned any notion of becoming a dancer. Before she married, she worked for a while as a model and in public relations. Her affair with Madonna lasted between the ages of fifteen and twenty-one. According to Kathy, it was "a complete and total love affair that was not just based on sex." They were best friends as well as lovers.

Seated in her comfortable living room, Kathy reminisces about her relationship with the star. "In the beginning," she says, "we told ourselves that we were experimenting and practicing so that when we actually kissed a boy, we wouldn't be so inexperienced." Kathy smiles. "Believe me, we had no idea what sex was all about and certainly no idea what lesbian sex was all about. We learned. I remember Madonna bought a lesbian magazine, and we would read about all the different positions and places where a woman was sensitive, and we just experimented. There was no aggressor in our relationship."

Despite the intensity of their relationship, Kathy claims that neither she nor Madonna ever considered themselves lesbians. Madonna's philosophy was that there was no such thing as homosexual or heterosexual, and she unknowingly quoted Truman Capote when she would say that either a person is "sexed or not." "When I came to New York to visit Madonna," Kathy continues, "we used to talk about how we felt a lot and how we were both surprised that we were so turned on by each other."

Adam Alter, one of Madonna's benefactors when she first arrived in New York, who owned Gotham Music and groomed Madonna to become a recording star, said Madonna was a sexy, brash, talented young girl. "Was I attracted to her?" Alter asks rhetorically. "Everyone was, men and women, but nothing ever happened between us, because I wanted to keep our relationship professional."

Later on in her career, as Madonna brought lesbian sexuality into the mainstream, she offered an unrealistic image that all lesbians are beautiful, successful, and feminine. According to Adam Alter, his partner, the woman who would briefly become Madonna's manager, Camille Barbone, was admittedly bisexual and let her feelings for Madonna get in the way of their professional relationship. Barbone, a small, wiry woman with short-cropped hair and glasses, came from a middle-class family in Queens, the daughter of a policeman. When their association was over and Madonna went on to become a star, Barbone claimed it was Madonna who had tried to seduce her.

In 1987, Kathy was married to her first husband and Madonna was already a star. She remembers that her former lover sent her a book written by Shere Hite entitled *Women and Love: A Cultural Revolution in Progress: The Hite Report.* "There was a section in the book on gay women which said everything in a much more intellectual way that Madonna had said years before." That book caused Kathy's first divorce. "When I showed it to my husband at the time," Kathy recalls, "I decided to tell him all about my relationship with Madonna. He just freaked out. To be honest, the marriage wasn't all that great, but that really did it. Things just got worse and worse until we eventually split."

Madonna's passion for Kathy when they were teenagers did nothing to get in the way of her determination to become a star. In fact, through her lover she eventually found the kind of ballet school that she knew she needed. Shortly after they met, Kathy introduced Madonna to the Rochester School of Ballet, where she was studying, and to the man who would prove to be the most influential person in Madonna's young life and career: Christopher Flynn.

When Madonna met Christopher Flynn, he was forty-two and she was fifteen. The meeting and the age difference conjured up more similarities between Madonna and Eva Perón.

After the death of her father, life did not improve for Eva Duarte, especially after her mother found another "father" for her brood when her daughter was only ten years old. The Duarte children, along with their mother and new stepfather, moved from the dismal town of Los Toldos to the equally depressing town of Junín, the sole attraction of which was a movie theater. As an adolescent in Junín, Eva kept mostly to herself. As the youngest and unmarried daughter, she was expected to help her mother run the boardinghouse that the family bought to support themselves. In 1933, when Eva was fifteen, she went to see a tango singer appearing onstage at the movie theater. A weak and narcissistic parody of a Latin lover, Agustín Maguldi was forty-two years old with an inflated opinion of his talent and his charm. When he finished his performance and returned to his dressing room, he found the teenager waiting for him. They became lovers, and the next evening Eva was riding in his car on her way to Buenos Aires.

Christopher Flynn, an attractive man, had studied in New York at Ballet Arts under Vladimir Dokoudovski. Although Flynn was dedicated and devoted to classical dance and had excellent training, he did not fare well in the competitive ballet world. Flynn had the perseverance but not the strength necessary to lift the ballerinas above his shoulders or to endure a rigorous two-hour performance.

Kathy and Madonna were both fifteen, but Madonna was

way behind her friend in terms of years of practice and the quality of her prior lessons. Her determination to succeed and her discipline not only enabled her to catch up but also impressed Flynn and created a relationship between them that went beyond that of teacher and pupil. Almost immediately, he sensed something unusual about Madonna, and from the moment Madonna entered Christopher Flynn's life, both she and he claimed that their "world had changed."

According to a close friend of the teacher's, Flynn felt that Madonna had enormous potential. "Chris told me from the beginning," Flynn's friend says, "that he could sense that Madonna was just hungering for information and knowledge. It was obvious to him that she possessed an innate intelligence that had never been exploited. He knew without ever meeting her family that Madonna lacked any cultural or intellectual background, and yet he was certain that all she needed was someone to take her under his wing."

In addition to teaching her movement and dance, Flynn gave Madonna self-confidence. He told her she was beautiful, interesting, and had a magnetic personality. Flynn was the first artistic person she knew, someone with whom she could be free and who appreciated that she was different without attributing her uniqueness to a behavior problem. It would be the first time in Madonna's young life that someone in a position of authority didn't consider her a rebel because she made a point of not following the usual fads. Instead, Flynn encouraged what he considered to be her "artistic eccentricity."

In return, Madonna considered Flynn to be her primary teacher. She played Monroe to his Miller, Bacall to his Bogart, Hellman to his Hammett, eagerly soaking up everything that he offered, his show business experience as well as his cultural knowledge. She adored him, calling him "my mentor, my father, my imaginative lover, my brother, everything because he understood me." As for being her "imaginary lover," that would change briefly after Flynn followed Madonna to the University of Michigan in Ann Arbor, where he arranged to have a visiting professorship in the dance department for a semester. Long after he died, she would tell people that Flynn "took this hunk of unmolded clay and made it into a very definite style and shape . . . from that point on," Madonna insists, "I was able to refine myself."

As their relationship intensified, Flynn began taking Madonna into Detroit on weekends, where he introduced her to the world of museums, concerts, operas, art galleries, and fashion. He also took his star pupil to a variety of gay clubs and bars in Detroit, broadening her horizons into an exotic and sophisticated new world. The club scene in Detroit, before the AIDS virus made its deadly impact, was the meeting place for one-night stands or long-term affairs. At fifteen, Madonna was completely uninhibited and had no qualms about getting up and imitating dance steps. Everyone who met her liked her, not just because she had talent, but because she was so original. In fact, the music, movement, and attitude of the gay crowd would serve as the inspiration for some of her more risqué dance numbers and for her eventual androgynous style. With Flynn as her guide, she would wander around and watch the various couples off in corners or on velvet sofas making love. "Chris taught her to believe in herself," Kathy explains, "which gave her the courage to dress and look so original. I think he also gave her the guts to include bisexuality in her act, although he used to tell us that not all gay women are lipstick lesbians." Kathy recalls that Christopher Flynn taught Madonna that if she wasn't as talented or ambitious as she was, she'd be a gross monstrosity. "After a while," Kathy continues, "she was completely oblivious to what kids thought about her. She used to say that she didn't care about anyone's opinion who didn't help her get ahead. It was a good lesson in life for both of us."

Flynn also taught Madonna to be more sensitive to the frailties and weaknesses of her brothers. He made her conscious of the feminine side of the male and the masculine side of the female. When Madonna's brother Christopher began coming to her dance classes, and Flynn had a chance to observe the boy, he realized why the others perceived him as "different." Flynn decided to tell Madonna that her brother was gay and that she should be aware of how difficult it was for him to assert his sexuality as a teenager living in a small Midwestern town, the son of a staunch Catholic father. Years later, Madonna talked about her brother's homosexuality during an interview that she gave to the *Advocate,* a gay magazine, in 1991. Christopher Ciccone was indignant. He accused Madonna of "outing" him. "It wasn't her business," he said at the time. "I was not happy about that—not because I have a problem with it, and it certainly wasn't anything I ever hid, but because I don't talk about the people I know, and I expect the same from them."

Tony Ciccone's reaction to his son's homosexuality was predictable, although years later he would say that he had not been shocked. After Madonna and Christopher made peace following the appearance of the article in the gay publication, they used to joke that after having watched his daughter feign masturbation with a crucifix in front of millions, finding out that he had a gay son must have been almost anticlimactic for their father. "Nothing less than a relief," said the brother and sister, laughing.

Not only did Christopher Flynn encourage Madonna's originality, but he also saw to it that she never forgot her goal to become a dancer. According to one of Flynn's friends at the time, "Chris knew she had a crucial ingredient that even those who possessed more talent didn't have—a kind of fearlessness that was unusual for a girl so young."

According to Elsie Fortin, Madonna's grandmother, one of the most meaningful comments about her granddaughter was made by Christopher Flynn. "He made more sense than anybody else," Mrs. Fortin recalls. "He once said that all the articles about my granddaughter are deceptive because they make her out to be this kook who says things off the top of her head, when in reality, she is the most intelligent and hardworking student he ever had. She never missed a class. Come hell or high water, Madonna was always there."

Under Flynn's tutelage, Madonna gradually became aware that she was different from other girls her age, although she still didn't understand what that meant or how it could be harnessed and defined. "Madonna always told me that she felt overwhelmed by how passionate her feelings were," Kathy says. "Her biggest complaint was that people didn't understand her, especially when she was young. There would be many occasions when she'd realize that she had just alienated someone and scared them away, a boy or a friend or whomever. She used to ask me what to do because their reactions to her were confusing. Either she'd get more arrogant and say, 'I don't need you,' or she'd get upset and cry."

Christopher Flynn was one of the first people Madonna met who made no secret of his homosexuality. Eventually, Madonna confided in Flynn about her relationship with Kathy. One of his former lovers, who watched Flynn suffer and eventually die from AIDS in 1990, recalls that Madonna and Flynn formed a duo that was focused and disciplined but also offbeat and unconventional. Kathy believes that Madonna began getting along better with her family when she finally made up her mind that her "emotional agenda was elsewhere."

"She just decided that she wasn't emotionally involved with them because her affections and priorities were focused on other things and other people," Kathy explains. "She didn't get hurt or angry anymore, or at least she learned how to control her outbursts and instead directed all her energy on improving herself. Between Chris and her dancing lessons and our relationship, which was still very, very private, Madonna found something that she excelled in, that was hers, a talent that she owned, and friends who became her family."

As things seemed to be falling into place for Madonna, she began to question her own sexuality. After Madonna met Kathy, she spent almost all of her time with her and in dance class when she wasn't in school, to the exclusion of anything else. Madonna had all but abandoned her old friends to spend her free time with Kathy when, at the end of her junior year of high school, she suddenly needed to know she could reenter their world. Perhaps she wanted to prove her own thesis, that someone was neither homosexual nor heterosexual but merely sexual.

In May 1976, Madonna decided that it was time to lose her virginity. Russell Long, who currently runs his own construction firm in the Detroit area, recalls how surprised he was when Madonna began making sexual overtures to him. To this day, he is convinced that her decision to seduce him was less a matter of youthful passion or physical attraction than that he was one of the few boys who had never manifested much interest in her. Curiously, Long's analysis of what made him attractive to Madonna would be shared by many other men in the singer's life who have claimed that she was usually attracted to the most unwilling target of her affections. After he succumbed, she would predictably discard him and go on to a new conquest.

Long, who was a year older than Madonna, was good-looking in the style of the Marlboro man with rugged all-American good looks, long hair, and an easy smile. A superb athlete and attractive to the girls, he nonetheless had a minimum of sexual experience. His affair with Madonna lasted only several weeks, and their sexual encounters took place in the backseat of his father's car. Almost apologetically, Long admits to having limited memories of Madonna. Twenty-five years after the fact, what he does recall is that she was definitely the aggressor with a sexual personality that was more determined than sensual. "Having sex with Madonna," Long says, "was more of an accomplishment for her than it was anywhere near making love."

When rumors began to spread that Long and Madonna

were having an affair, she did nothing to dispel them and, instead, encouraged them as a matter of pride. "She was her best PR person back then," Long says, laughing. "I would be the one denying stuff, and she would just blurt out that everything people heard was true!" Not surprisingly, Kathy was hurt by Madonna's affair with Long and had several serious discussions with her during which she threatened to end their liaison. Eventually, Kathy decided that it wasn't worth breaking up over.

"Madonna told me that she intended to sleep with Russell before they even started dating," Kathy says. "At the time, I was really hurt and angry, but we never stopped seeing each other." She shrugs. "It was just something she felt she had to do, and I guess I understood it. There was a lot of pressure on both of us, and Madonna reacted in her way, while I reacted in mine. There was never any question that I would go out and find some guy to date just because Madonna did."

As it turned out, Kathy had nothing to fear. After the affair ended with Russell Long and until she graduated high school, Madonna's romantic interest remained focused solely on Kathy.

It has never really been clear why Flynn decided to entrust his dancing school in Rochester Hills to several assistants and take a visiting professorship at Ann Arbor. Several of Flynn's friends swear that it was purely coincidental that he was offered the post at the same time as Madonna was preparing to enter her freshman year there. Others claim that he lobbied to get the job because he was determined to guide Madonna's career. Joachim Navarro, one friend who studied with Flynn at Ballet Arts in New York, maintains that Chris was so sure that Madonna was destined to be a star that he didn't want anyone teaching her technique that she would eventually have to unlearn. "There's no doubt in my mind," Navarro states, "that Chris went to Michigan to hover over her, and he would have stayed on if Madonna hadn't decided to pack it in and leave for New York."

Seducing Flynn, according to one of the teacher's close friends, was not only unnecessary as far as cementing what was already an intense and close relationship between them, but an unfortunate example of Madonna's need to introduce sex into every friendship or partnership as the final proof of commitment and intimacy. The affair between Madonna and Flynn lasted only several days. When it ended, neither ever referred to it again.

chapter seventeen
....

At the end of her senior year of high school and at Flynn's urging, Madonna applied for a dance scholarship at the University of Michigan School of Music. After graduating a semester early, in the spring of 1976, she found out that she had been accepted as a scholarship student in Ann Arbor for the following September. Though she was thrilled to be leaving home, Madonna was suddenly apprehensive about committing herself to the time it would take to become a ballerina. She was in a hurry to make it. Ballet training took years of hard work and discipline.

When she arrived in Ann Arbor that September, Christopher Flynn was already there. The day she walked into her first ballet class, he was also there to offer moral support. Dancers are usually stick-thin and dressed in pink tights and black leotards with their hair tied back in chignons. Madonna looked like an escapee from a girlie show in Times Square. Her hair was cropped short in punk fashion and dyed blond with thick black roots, and she wore footless tights topped off by layers of cutoff T-shirts held together with safety pins. One of her teachers remembers a girl with natural talent but limited technique in classical dance, who nonetheless had amazing agility, rhythm, and grace. "When I first saw her dance, I thought immediately that she could be a wonderful jazz or modern dancer," the teacher says, "and I told her that at one point, but she apparently didn't want to change in midstream."

The turning point in Madonna's dancing career came several months later when Pearl Lang, a distinguished American dancer, choreographer, and teacher, was invited to Ann Arbor as a visiting professor. Miss Lang also had the distinction of having been a solo dancer with the Martha Graham dance company and the only person to whom the legendary dancer had entrusted seven of her own roles. In 1952, Lang formed her own dance company, which still exists today and for which she has created fifty-nine dance works. The initial meeting between Madonna and Pearl Lang in 1976 at Ann Arbor would be the first of several, ultimately resulting in Madonna's performing in one of Lang's dance companies. Today, Pearl Lang is eighty years old and still beautiful with all the gestures and grace of a dancer. She continues to be a force in the dance world and does all the choreography for her company. She is married to the stage and screen actor Joseph Wiseman, who is most famous for his role as Dr. No in the first James Bond movie. Lang remembers the "waiflike creature with the unusual name and fearless disposition."

"A beautiful girl and a beautiful dancer named Christine Dugan, who graduated from the dance department at Ann Arbor, was a student of mine at the studio in New York that I opened with Alvin Ailey," Miss Lang begins. "As it happened, Christine's father was a professor of Chinese at the University of Michigan, and through him, the head of the department contacted me to come there as their artist in residence and choreographer for their graduate dance program. I was in residence at Ann Arbor for one year, but because of my professional commitments in New York, I set down several conditions."

Lang promised she would be in Ann Arbor at least six times during the year as well as for the final performance in May, but she refused to spend the entire year in Michigan. "I arranged for Christine Dugan to take my place and teach when I was away," she explains.

Madonna, an undergraduate at the time, never got the opportunity to take a class with Pearl Lang, although she came regularly to audit, always accompanied by Flynn. Not until the end of the year, after Madonna watched the May recital, did she make up her mind that one day she would dance for Pearl Lang.

When Christopher Flynn first arrived in Ann Arbor in 1976, he was living in a motel off-campus while he was waiting for an apartment to become available. One evening, Madonna visited Flynn in his motel room and confessed how attracted she was to him, how she adored him, and how much she wanted to make love to him. According to another friend of Flynn's, it was only three months after the brief affair ended that Flynn was diagnosed with thrush, a viral infection that is often one of the opportunistic diseases that appears as a result of HIV.

Flynn's friend is still visibly moved when he recalls the dance teacher's account of the events that evening in his motel room. "He seemed genuinely amazed that someone who was so clearly gay and never had any doubts about his sexual preferences could be turned on by a woman, especially by someone who was almost like a sister or a niece. In the weeks before he died, he talked a lot about Madonna, and I think he felt proud that they had an affair. Actually, when I think about it, he was prouder that it didn't interfere with their friendship. They remained close to the very end. We used to get fed up with Chris bragging how he actually got it up for her, but I guess it just proved that she was really something special. Even at eighteen, Madonna had a sensuality that went beyond gender."

That first year at Ann Arbor was a lonely time for Madonna, who spent most of the time alone in her room, reading and studying. As she had done for most of her life, she relied on herself more than on her professors. College was a place to grow and to learn as much as she could by her own instincts and keen observation. Gradually, she discovered Ernest Hemingway and F. Scott Fitzgerald, as well as the German writer Rainer Maria Rilke, whom she was delighted to learn had been a lover of Marlene Dietrich's. She devoured James Agee and Charles Bukowski, whom she found funny and raunchy for the way he always "put himself down." She read James Joyce, J. D. Salinger, D. H. Lawrence, Thomas Mann, Françoise Sagan, and Marguerite Duras. She also enjoyed Milan Kundera, Jack Kerouac, and Kurt Vonnegut. When she wasn't alone in her room reading, Madonna would go to the library and listen to the works of Vivaldi, Bach, Pachelbel, and Handel's *Water Music*. Eventually, baroque music became her favorite because she liked the "feminine" quality in the compositions.

Under Christopher Flynn's guidance, Madonna also developed an interest in art and, through her teacher, discovered Corot, James Brown, and Francesco Clemente. Although young and unsophisticated, her taste was already developing to the extent that she decided on her own that she liked only certain periods of Picasso. Rejecting modernism, cubism, and postmodernism, she was intrigued by Keith Haring, whose art interested her less than his ability to capitalize on his paintings the way rock stars promoted their records. Another artist she admired both for his style and accessibility to the public was Jean-Michel Basquiat, who would become her lover when she moved to New York. Reckless, extravagant, and generous, Basquiat gave Madonna a great number of his canvases. When she aborted his baby in the fall of 1979, he took back everything except for one small painting, which she still owns today and which hangs in the guest bathroom in her New York apartment.

Madonna had old-fashioned tastes in music. Her favorite artists were Ella Fitzgerald, Sarah Vaughan, vintage Sinatra, and Sam Cooke, and she admired the current hits by Joe Williams and B. B. King, Chaka Khan, and Aretha Franklin. Chrissie Hynde, who sang with the Pretenders in the seventies and eighties, would serve as her inspiration, and Debbie

Harry, from the rock group Blondie, would be a singer whom Madonna would admire long after she became famous.

One evening, Chris Flynn suggested that she accompany him to a local bar near the university called the Blue Frogge. Concerned that his favorite student was spending too much time alone, Flynn decided that it would be easier to talk to her and find out how she was feeling about her studies and her dancing courses in a more relaxed atmosphere.

Steve Bray is intelligent, talented, and attractive, an African-American who back then played drums with a local rock-and-blues group that had club dates in the Ann Arbor area. To earn money to survive, Bray waited tables at the Blue Frogge, where Madonna met him. Four years older than Madonna, Bray became her lover and would remain her on-again, off-again lover for the rest of the school year. Occasionally, Madonna would even accompany Bray on his club dates, which were usually in the lounges of local motels or small chain restaurants like Howard Johnson. During her relationship with Bray, Kathy was still very much a part of her life, and when Kathy visited, Madonna would disappear and spend the weekend alone with her. During the weekends when Madonna was with Steve Bray, they would often head over to Christopher Flynn's off-campus apartment to discuss their respective dreams in the world of music and dance. Eventually, Madonna turned those abstract discussions into very real plans, and she began expressing doubts about remaining in school. According to Steve Bray, Flynn encouraged her, telling her that if she didn't take that step, she would never know if she had what it took to become a star.

When Flynn learned that the American Dance Festival, under the direction of Pearl Lang, had moved from Connecticut College to Duke University, he could finally offer Madonna a concrete suggestion as an alternative to school. After researching the project, he learned that Lang was scheduled to hold auditions that summer after the school year was over. She intended to choose twenty promising dancers, not only as students, but as potential new members for one of her dance companies. When Flynn told Madonna what he had learned, she didn't hesitate. Not only did Flynn arrange for her to live in a Duke dormitory on-campus, but he also loaned her the bus fare for the trip from Detroit to Durham. When she arrived at Duke University and was settled, she finally mustered up the courage to call her father to tell him what she had done. It would be the first of several rifts between father and daughter. Tony Ciccone made it clear that she was on her own, financially and emotionally.

Steve Bray was a realist as well as an artist, someone who understood that both he and Madonna would do anything to further their careers. Though he was unhappy that Madonna had left, he was smart enough to realize that if he had tried to control her, he would have lost her forever. He also understood that he couldn't help Madonna the way Flynn could since he had no connections in the world of dance. Bray knew that his girlfriend had talent, incredible energy, and sex appeal, but much to his disappointment, she had never expressed any interest in singing or songwriting. "If you can use the term *star quality*," Bray said, "then that's exactly what Madonna had, even at eighteen. She was absolutely irresistible!"

It wouldn't be the only time that Madonna left a lover behind to further her career, although she has consistently denied that she has discarded people during her climb to the top, a claim that is shared by Bray. "Her boyfriends got as much or more from her as she got from them."

Instead of being permanently discarded, Bray was merely temporarily misplaced. Perhaps Madonna put it best when she said, "You can't succeed unless you move on, and you can't take the whole world with you."

Bray, a talented musician and songwriter, still collaborates with Madonna. In 1980, he showed up in New York and joined the band that she had put together with Dan Gilroy, her then boyfriend, which they called the Breakfast

Club. At Bray's urging, they abandoned hard rock and started composing and playing music that was more disco. She abandoned Bray after she got her first big break with Seymour Stein and Sire Records, when she used the talents of Reggie Lucas, a Warner Brothers producer, for her first album, *Madonna/The First Album*. She called upon Bray again, though, and used his songwriting skills to help her with her second album, *Like a Virgin*. Their friendship and artistic collaboration would endure for many years.

In June 1976, Pearl Lang was in residence at Duke University, and auditions had already begun when Madonna arrived. "Six of us sat a long table," Miss Lang begins, "where we could judge the dancers' performances and choose the ones we felt were the most promising." Twenty-five years later, Pearl Lang still remembers the "skinny, dark-haired girl" who was, in her words, "an absolutely beautiful dancer." From where she was sitting, Lang couldn't see the girl's face, but she knew that she wanted her to be one of the twenty students to stay at Duke and to study with her. At the end of the audition, Madonna was one of the twenty dancers who were chosen. Suddenly, as everyone was preparing to leave, the same skinny girl with dark hair walked briskly up to the judges' table.

"She was really brassy," Lang says, smiling at the memory. "I recognized her right away as the same girl who had danced so spectacularly during the audition. She walked right up to me and told me that she came from Michigan and that she had once watched Pearl Lang dance there and give classes when she was artist in residence at Ann Arbor. Then, she looked right at me and said that the only way she would take that scholarship was if she could study with Pearl Lang." Again Lang smiles. "I told her that I was Pearl Lang and that she could study with me for the summer."

There have been several different versions of that story, one of which was told by someone who claims to have been one of the dancers who auditioned with Madonna. According to the dancer, Madonna knew in advance who Pearl Lang was and only pretended not to know in an effort to impress her. Lang disagrees. "She was honestly embarrassed when I told her who I was. She blushed, and she didn't know what to say. Frankly, she didn't have to go through an act. She already had been chosen as one of the twenty, so what was the point?"

Madonna spent six weeks at Duke University, taking classes every day with Pearl Lang. "She studied advanced technique," Lang recalls, "and she worked with me in my repertory class. She was marvelous, and I put her in a rondel by Carl Philipp Emanuel Bach which was very fast. She performed it beautifully."

Lang recalls that one Saturday, after her enormous success onstage, Madonna walked into class with a sweater that was torn down the back and that had only one shoulder. "It was held together by a big safety pin," Lang says. "I immediately told her to change because I was worried that when the male dancer lifted her, that pin could take out his eye." Lang pauses. "But that was Madonna, she was always doing something to catch your eye, to get attention." When she reprimanded her, Lang remembers Madonna's reply. "She told me that she couldn't help herself, because she lost her mother when she was very young and was used to doing crazy things to get attention." Lang shrugs. "What could I say after that?"

The following Monday, Madonna marched into class, slightly less disheveled, and asked to talk to Lang privately. "She came right to the point," Lang says, "and asked me if I might need anyone in my New York company. I told her that there was a possibility, but I knew she had no money. I pointed out that first she had to go back to Michigan before she could take off again for New York. I asked her how she was going to manage to get there, find a place to live, and have enough money to eat. Her answer was typically

Madonna when she told me not to worry about it, that she
would work it out."

After the summer session ended at Duke University, Pearl
Lang went back to New York, where, along with Alvin Ailey, she was the artistic director at the American Dance Center. In August 1978, the day after she arrived in New York,
while Lang was teaching, Madonna appeared in the studio
and announced, "Here I am. I made it!"

"Well, I suppose somewhere in the back of my mind, I
never doubted it for a minute," Lang admits, "although I was
a little surprised to see her. That year, we were commis-
sioned to do a series of Sephardic songs and a Vivaldi
composition called *Piece of Grass.* I also had to choose a
second cast for *I Never Saw Another Butterfly,* based on several poems written by children who had been interned and
killed in Terezenstad concentration camp in Prague during
the war. I needed someone who looked hungry and painfully
thin. Madonna was perfect. I put her into the part and she
was beautiful, absolutely perfect, and she toured with me
that year and then spent two weeks at the Public Theater doing the piece with Joseph Papp."

According to Pearl Lang, when Madonna was on tour
with her company, she kept very much to herself. "She was a
strange girl," Lang recalls, "very private and not at all eager
to become friends with any of the other dancers. I remember
that she used to make a point of calling long distance on
Sunday, when the rates were cheaper. She would have a
handful of change and sit cross-legged on a chair, the receiver cradled between her chin and shoulder. I always pre-
sumed she called her friends or her family, but I never asked
her, and she never volunteered any information about her
personal life away from the troupe."

Life imitates art. After the tour ended, Miss Lang became
increasingly concerned that Madonna was undernourished

and had no visible means to support herself. According to Lang, she got in touch with a friend who was the manager of the Russian Tea Room, a restaurant right next door to Carnegie Hall on West Fifty-seventh Street. "My friend hired her to check coats," Lang explains, "so at least I knew that they fed the staff one meal a day, so she wasn't going to starve to death."

At the end of the summer, Lang's company needed a place to rehearse. Since Martha Graham was not going to be using her studio, she offered it to Lang. "And that's the reason for the discrepancy that Madonna danced for Martha Graham," Pearl Lang begins. "Madonna never danced for Martha, and the only time she ever saw her was once or twice when we first took over the studio to rehearse, and Martha wandered in to check that everything was in order. She may have met her later on, when she was already famous, but back then, I was her mentor."

Pearl Lang had always chosen several promising dancers in her various companies and classes and worked with them more closely than the others. Madonna was one of those students Lang considered to have the talent to become a great dancer. "You know, certain dancers remain in my head," she explains, "and every time I see a particular ballet or movement I automatically think of one of those dancers who worked with me. Madonna had the most gorgeous back, and I will always remember her dancing in *La Rosa en Flores,* which is a girl's dance. I see her doing it all the time whenever I want to revive it. She just automatically comes into my head."

Several months later, Madonna walked into class and once again asked to speak to Pearl Lang privately. According to Lang, Madonna told her that the classes were beginning to hurt her back and that studying to become a dancer was much harder than she had ever imagined. "Of course it's hard, I told her," Lang says, "but so what? No one ever said that dancing was easy!" The next day Madonna didn't show up for class. Before long, she was coming in infrequently.

Several weeks later, Madonna announced that she had decided to give up dancing. She was going to become a rock singer.

"Later on I learned that a boyfriend from Michigan, a drummer, had arrived in New York and they were working together," Miss Lang explains, and sighs. "So, with all that promise, she gave up dancing." To this day, Lang still believes that Madonna could have been a great dancer. "The problem with her from the beginning was that she was never willing to see a discipline through to the end, at least one like dance that took enormous stamina."

The next time that Pearl Lang saw Madonna was on the screen when she was starring in *Evita*. "She was wonderful," she says, "really marvelous. If she had to give up dancing, this was the role that came naturally to her. It convinced me that she had enormous innate talent." Lang pauses. "There's no doubt that Madonna is Eva Perón!"

part three

....

Lucky Star

chapter eighteen

••••••••••••••••••

Nothing is riskier than going off alone to a strange city to make it as a performer. It was an astounding enterprise for a twenty-year-old girl who relied more on her charm than her talent and less on her training than on her wits. E. B. White once wrote that "no one should come to New York to live unless he is willing to be lucky." But Madonna had more than luck. She had relentless energy and determination.

When she arrived in New York in 1978, Madonna was not even sure that she wanted to become a dancer. "When I was a little girl, the first thing I wanted to be was a movie star," Madonna has said, "and then I wanted to be a singer. Then I got into dancing more and started concentrating on that. By the time I landed in New York, I knew I needed one particular skill to make it, and I had to arm myself since I didn't know anyone and had never been there before. All I knew for sure was that once the public knew I existed, I wouldn't have any problems." When Pearl Lang said that Madonna didn't have the discipline to become a dancer, she was wrong. What Madonna lacked was the patience to limit herself to one particular area of show business. In her mind, talent was an acquired trait. She was open to whatever medium claimed her first.

From the moment she arrived in New York, she found herself surrounded by talented young hopefuls who were poised on the edge of greatness as well as hopeless dreamers who were poised on the edge of oblivion. There were no future has-beens in her entourage. The people she met either

made it and died, like so many in the Andy Warhol crowd, or
never made it at all, or in the case of some, reached their creative peaks when Madonna knew them only to retreat into
academia. Whether they had talent or not, Madonna listened
to everything they had to say. Her mind was a computer. She
memorized the names and numbers they offered, registered
the advice, tips, and trends that struck her as worthwhile, and
discarded those that seemed worthless. Some of the people
who knew Madonna when she was struggling say that she
inhaled everything around her, sucked everyone dry until
she was satisfied that there was nothing left to take, before
she moved on. She had no qualms about insinuating herself
into a conversation whether or not she knew the people involved. She had the charming bravado of a child and the
modesty of a stripper.

Others who met Madonna in the late 1970s and early
1980s would accuse her of disloyalty, of breaking promises,
leaving debts owed for everything from studio time to dental
work. Others would argue that there was no place for sentiment if she was going to get where she wanted to be. Above
all, she was a businesswoman. She had a product to sell.
That it happened to be herself—a product called Madonna—
didn't make her any less efficient. Surviving from day to
day, hand to mouth, from audition to menial job, often took
precedence over the values she had learned back home. Although she was basically honest, she bent the rules of friendship, extracting favors, breaking promises, and disregarding
people's feelings. She dumped her managers and mentors
without the slightest hesitation when she realized that their
promises of stardom were based more on psychobabble and
self-help jargon than on firm appointments for an audition
or concrete leads for a day job that made it easier to survive.
Madonna may have disregarded her friends' feelings or discarded the lovers who passed in and out of her bed, but she
rarely lied. As far as she was concerned, it took too much
energy to make up devious stories for the sake of being polite or to waste her time lying to make herself seem more

important. Every minute was spent on achieving what she wanted—stardom.

Young, sensual, and adventurous during those difficult years in New York, Madonna had sex when she felt like it, although she always insisted that she never slept with anyone to get ahead. If she did happen to make love with people who were in a position to help, it was a happy bonus.

When she began to form her professional image of uninhibited sexuality, she drew almost entirely from her personal experiences. If her mother went to her grave without imparting the mystery of her life to her five-year-old daughter, Madonna was determined to give the world the plot and motivation of her own life. This is one star who never had to make a comeback because she was never gone. When she felt her time was waning and she had nothing new to offer her public, she branched out or pulled inward, made a movie, got pregnant, used her publicity apparatus to focus on her sexual preference of the month whether it was Sandra or Sean, Ingrid or Rosie, Carlos or Warren.

Even as a novice in a New York filled with the hip and the savvy, she knew that the secret of rock and roll was no longer about staying young forever, about dreams and heroes. It was about staying a step ahead of the trends, mixing them up with the social drift, tapping into what girls need to feel secure, boys need to fantasize, men need to dream, and women need to remember. Most of all, Madonna's music and onstage persona was a recipe about how to feel good without feeling guilty.

Sometimes, feeling good caused other consequences that had nothing to do with guilt.

After Madonna moved out of Lionel Bishop's apartment in Manhattan Towers, she went to live in a dismal studio at 242 East Fourth Street in the heart of the East Village, one of the most drug-infested areas of the city. Every day on her way back from work at Dunkin' Donuts on West Fifty-seventh

Street, she was terrified of getting raped or mugged when she walked from the subway to her apartment. Some time during the first week that she was living in that East Fourth Street tenement, Madonna attracted the attention of a band of young Hispanic teenagers. Dressed in her unusual, provocative style, she had a childish sexuality that appealed to everyone regardless of age or gender. As she headed from the subway to her apartment, the band of boys followed her, whistling, making clucking noises, and shouting suggestive Spanish words. Turning around only when she had reached the safety of her building, her gaze settled on the tallest boy in the group. Darkly handsome with long hair, the sinewy adolescent with high, wide cheekbones and an odd hint of silver in his eyes stared back at her without flinching. The attraction between the fifteen-year-old with the sexual maturity of an experienced Latin lover and the twenty-year-old girl from Bay City, an interloper in that solidly Spanish neighborhood, was palpable. After several moments, Madonna turned back around and walked slowly through the door and upstairs to her apartment. At ten o'clock that night, there was a knock on her door. If she didn't sense who was there, it was extremely imprudent for her to have opened the door without hesitating. The boy had waited until his parents were asleep before he slipped out of his apartment to "take a chance." Armed with two Percodans and a gram of coke, the new chic drug that was in all the trendy bars and nightclubs, he entered Madonna's apartment. What happened between them was instantaneous, although Madonna made it clear that she wasn't interested in any of his ice-breaking tokens of friendship. According to the boy, who is now married and the father of a little girl, Madonna was willing to take risks, but only if she knew she would garner the rewards. "I brought the drugs because I thought she was into that kind of stuff, but she wasn't. She didn't need anything to turn her on." He pauses. "Except me."

The repercussions were predictable. Word of the teenager's success with the offbeat young woman spread throughout the neighborhood, until his parents, the owners of a local bodega, found out what everyone else already knew. The couple had a more severe view of the relationship than their neighbors, yet were smart enough to realize that had they forbid their son from seeing Madonna, they might as well have tried to stop him from breathing. They took the only logical alternative. They confronted Madonna and threatened to turn her over to the police for impairing the morals of a minor if she didn't get out of the neighborhood.

Years later, Madonna would see the irony in the situation when her audience, mostly adolescents, would be the ones who made her concerts sold-out successes. Ten thousand bodies would breathe in unison, sitting on the edge of their seats as Madonna gave them an evening's entertainment that promised to fulfill their fantasies. She was ageless when it came to the adoration of her fans, even if she was already well into her twenties and thirties by the time she was selling out throughout the world. From that first night on East Fourth Street, when the affair began, her teenage lover would tell everyone that Madonna was ageless.

Several days after the scandal became neighborhood fodder, Madonna was at Dunkin' Donuts when one of her coworkers, another recent émigré from the Midwest, casually announced that she was looking for a roommate. It seemed that one of the people who was sharing her apartment on Morningside Drive on the Upper West Side was leaving to get married. The offer could not have come at a better time. Without even asking how much or any other relevant details concerning the apartment, Madonna jumped at the chance to rent a room. Less than a week later, she once again gathered up all her worldly possessions and took the bus from the Lower East Side to her new home on the Upper West Side.

In late 1979, Pearl Lang invited Madonna to a party at her Central Park West apartment where the guest list was the usual New York eclectic gathering of established performers and those who were still waiting tables while they waited for their big break. Dressed in her usual tattered punk garb, Madonna wandered around the room, catching fragments of erudite conversation that was right out of a Woody Allen movie. At twenty-one, she was high on her own ambition and hadn't yet developed any complexes about what she didn't know. Her curiosity and guilelessness charmed the cynical and the jaded, while her tough facade intimidated the gullible and insecure. In her naïveté, she also didn't yet understand that creativity, ambition, and a healthy libido were considered threatening traits for a woman to possess. At Lang's party, Madonna met a young artist and musician named Norris Burroughs. The meeting would be serendipitous. More than just becoming her lover, he would eventually introduce her to Dan Gilroy, a musician and songwriter who would teach her how to play the guitar and encourage her to compose her own music.

Burroughs had heard about the party through one of the regulars at the now defunct restaurant and nightclub Max's Kansas City. According to him, Madonna stuck out in the crowd of bohemian artists, established art-gallery owners, and New York intellectuals. "She was wearing an old sweater with ragged sleeves, and she put her fingers through the holes as we talked," he says. "She had the most incredible eyes and lips, although what completely mesmerized me was the way her whole body spoke when she moved or talked. It was uncanny how she lapsed in and out of various accents, depending upon the cadence of speech of the person she was talking to. I must admit she didn't sound like someone who came from Detroit."

Burroughs recalls that she had an endearing quality about her that was a combination of tough and vulnerable. "It was interesting because at the time she didn't seem very vain at all. She was colorful and very savvy and street smart for someone who had just arrived in New York. Almost immediately, she told me that she wanted to be a dancer and that she was living like a gypsy. She really didn't know anyone in New York, but instead of being terrified in a strange city, she was aggressive and determined to make it."

Rail-thin with an angular jaw, ramrod posture, short-cropped hair, and pea-green eyes, Norris Burroughs was born in July 1952, the year of the dragon according to the Chinese calendar and a Cancer in astrological terms, both references that he immediately describes as, for him, they are pivotal to his existence. "If you correlate Western astrology with Chinese astrology," he says intently, "a Cancer born in the year of the dragon actually lives in the castles he builds in the air. I'm ruled by muses and inspiration. I'm interested in knowing things and absorbing things and then incorporating them into my work, and I expect people to take the time to read into those meanings to understand what I'm trying to say. Ideally, when you're right on and hitting a bull's-eye, there's no separation between an artist and his art."

If Madonna considered Christopher Flynn to be the first artist whom she met, she judged Norris Burroughs to be the first intellectual.

Burroughs, whose mother is a descendant from a *Mayflower* family and whose father was an African-American Shakespearean actor, was born in Harlem. When he was five, his family moved to the north Bronx. After graduating from the High School of Music and Art, where he studied painting, illustrating, and design, he briefly attended the Parsons School in New York. In retrospect, he believes that while Madonna was sexually attracted to him, she was also aware that he was a source of artistic energy for her.

"There's no doubt that we were immediately attracted to each other," he begins. "She used to say to me, 'Get your gorgeous Brando body over here . . .' Basically, Madonna was attracted to anybody who was sensual and who understood sensuality. She felt an instant kinship with eccentric or bohemian artists. In the late seventies in New York, there was a romantic, liberal artist environment where the heroes of the moment were the Beatles, the Stones, Janis Joplin, and Jimi Hendrix. I felt comfortable in that element because I already had that kind of romantic sensibility from my family."

When Madonna met Burroughs, he was on the edge of the underground avant-garde art scene and worked with another avant-garde artist by the name of Spin, who was a close friend of Andy Warhol's. Spin and Burroughs had a store in Greenwich Village called the Tee Shirt Gallery, at which they created custom-made T-shirts for their customers, airbrushing and hand-painting fantasies or personal messages on command. According to Burroughs, Spin had done several impressive designs with Peter Max and Salvador Dalí, as well as with Warhol.

"The whole idea was to create one-of-a-kind T-shirts," Burroughs explains. "I'm really interested in knowing things and absorbing things and then incorporating them into my work. Basically, I'm a storyteller. When I do a piece of work or a painting, it has a subject and a theme, and obviously an artist wants his work to be seen, which is why I hooked up with Spin."

On the night that they met, Madonna went home with Burroughs to his small flat on St. Marks Place in the East Village. Several weeks into the affair, he moved to Sixty-first Street and First Avenue. "We always met at my place," Norris recalls, "mainly because I lived alone and she always had several roommates. We'd spend days and nights together, and then she'd disappear for weeks before she'd call me and we'd get together and have these intense lovemaking sessions that lasted for days."

When the couple ventured out, neither had much money. They often went to Riverside Church in that section of Harlem called Sugar Hill. "She loved anything Greco-Roman," Norris recalls, "anything that had old-world beauty." According to Burroughs, her fascination for the Gothic and the baroque had less to do with religious connotation than it did with the mystery and ritual she found so appealing. "She used to talk about her Italian Catholic background and how she loved the theatrics of the Catholic Church. She also claimed that being Catholic had given her a moral core, and it was very apparent as I got to know her better that she responded well to stress and stayed balanced in the center of a hurricane."

Burroughs remembers that Madonna talked about her mother's death and admitted that it was because of all that she had gone through as a child that she had developed an "elaborate defense mechanism" against loss. He has never been surprised by her success, like Christopher Flynn and Steve Bray, and to a great extent attributes it to her charisma. "I don't think I ever met anyone who believed in herself more than Madonna did. For her, life was all about primal instincts and passion. After she made it, a lot of people used to say that she wasn't that talented or that good-looking, and I would always say that when you meet her or see her close up, it's all about her energy and charisma."

Despite all her appeal and charm, Burroughs also remembers a young woman who was completely uncompromising when it came to getting her own way. "When she wanted to do something and we didn't see eye to eye, she would get this sort of look on her face that said that she was going to do what she wanted no matter what I thought."

During one of their disagreements, Burroughs told Madonna that his guitar teacher had remarked that he was petulant. "She smiled when she heard that and said that people always used the word *petulant* to describe her, which wasn't really negative or obnoxious but more like a charming spoiled brat."

Contrary to many stories that Norris Burroughs claims were circulated after 1984, when "Material Girl" appeared and Madonna began her ascent to superstardom, he maintains that he was not the "only man to have dumped the star," but after spending three or four months together, he decided to let her go. "I always had a lot of admiration for her will, so we didn't spend a lot of time butting heads. Basically she was a good person, which is why I never felt used or abused by her. She never treated me badly." After the relationship ended, because both were clever enough to realize that they were too self-involved for compromise to make a love affair work, they remained friends for a while.

One night remains vivid in Burroughs's memory, an evening of lovemaking that was extremely sensual and sweet. "It was a romantic moment where we were really connected. I can't remember actual details," he says, "but we just blended." The last time that Norris Burroughs saw Madonna was in 1982, when she was performing at the Ritz, a downtown club on Fourth Avenue and Eleventh Street. "She was just starting to break, and I think she had just signed with Sire Records and cut a couple of tracks that ended up on twelve-inch." Though the meeting was brief, Burroughs has the impression that she was happy to see him, mainly because she evoked her own memory of that tender and connected evening they had spent making love. "I never saw her again, because I didn't feel comfortable about keeping in touch. I was afraid she'd think that I wanted something, so I preferred to hang on to the memory of the time we spent together when we were both struggling."

Despite the intensity of their physical relationship and Burroughs's great admiration for Madonna, he never took her seriously as a girlfriend. "I didn't think it was possible for two single-minded and self-centered people to be an item," he explains. "I was never possessive with her because I sensed that she was more serious about her career and her goal to be famous. Given the type of person that she was, I found it difficult to downplay that type of energy, that indomitable 'I am the center of the universe' kind of energy that sustained her."

In 1989, things seemed to break for Norris Burroughs. At the time, a music craze that became an underground cult sound called house music was spreading across England and France. Margaret Thatcher, then the British prime minister, had banned it as "immoral" and "sexually suggestive." Burroughs had a band he had appropriately named Craze that

played only house music, which, because it never really
caught on in the United States, forced him to go overseas.

"It actually started as underground club dance music in
Chicago," Burroughs explains, "and then got really popular
in Europe. We had a hit record in England and in France, just
about the time that Margaret Thatcher banned it. I remember
going to Paris and being treated really well and then coming
back to New York and being nobody. That was another reason I never tried to get in touch with Madonna again, because I realized how illusionary fame is and how it doesn't
really matter what you have to say, even if it's interesting
and important, as long as you're famous."

Norris Burroughs admits that his one chance at stardom
lasted the proverbial fifteen minutes. He is convinced the
reason Madonna never faltered is because she's a "goddess."
"Goddesses make mistakes," Burroughs says, "but they go
on. I believe that to the extent that I believe in life energy.
What separates a god from a mortal? Why does Madonna
have a divine spark that lifts her above the average person?
Because people embody ideas and energy, and because we
make people out of myths. She's like Jim Morrison, who
was ripped apart by women but kept renewing himself every
year until his death. Madonna continues to renew herself
and has survived to become a myth."

In the same way that Christopher Flynn sensed an innate
sensibility in Madonna, Burroughs also saw a woman who,
while not having been grounded in the classics, had managed to develop her own intellectual tastes. "She was very
into the Hemingway book *A Moveable Feast*," Burroughs
says, "and loved anything that romanticized the artists' life
in Paris. She read everything she could on F. Scott Fitzgerald
and Zelda, Picasso, Françoise Gilot, Gertrude Stein. She just
loved the idea of being an artist or a dancer, a bohemian ex-
patriate." According to Burroughs, she also identified with
James Dean, whose mother had died when he was a young
child. "She thought he was beautiful and magnetic," Burroughs claims, "and she was generally attracted to that flash-

in-the-pan star, like Dean or Jim Morrison, the Roman candle that explodes across the sky and then burns out."

Burroughs always felt that Madonna was a case study in what makes a star. "When our affair ended," he says, "I sort of thought I would catch up with her later."

"Later" for the couple never happened.

chapter nineteen

....

*M*adonna's new apartment on Morningside Drive was typical of the prewar buildings in that area of Manhattan. The large and airy rooms included two bedrooms, a living room with a wood-burning fireplace, beamed ceilings, and a kitchen with enough space for a small table. She was ecstatic. Her new living conditions would not last more than several months, but while she was there, it would be the first time since leaving home and moving out of her dorm at the University of Michigan that she felt secure. Upgrading her standard of living brought an additional problem. Even if she worked every day as a counter girl, earning $50 a day for eight hours, most of which she spent on her feet, she simply wasn't making enough money to pay the rent, eat, and have change left over for carfare. Even if she managed to work overtime to make ends meet or took on a second night job, there wouldn't be enough hours in the day for her to go out on auditions or take dance lessons. The solution came to her once again through Christopher Flynn. During a phone conversation with her former teacher, he reminded her that when she had been at the University of Michigan she had posed nude for the students in the art department. At the time, she claimed that not only was it easy work and no problem for her to get undressed in front of a roomful of strangers, but that she could earn more money in an hour than she could in a week doing menial jobs. "I basically spaced out," she said, "and thought about a million things other than I was stark naked while a bunch of people sketched me." Posing nude in New York brought an even higher hourly rate, and Madonna calculated that she could earn more money in an *hour* working for a photographer or an art teacher than she could working all *day* as a waitress. Within days, Madonna found work posing nude for several photographers through word of mouth around the struggling community of would-be actors and singers.

Her first job was with Bill Stone, a photographer whose work had been published in *Life* and *Esquire* magazines. Best known for his sepia portraits of nudes whom he posed in the style of Botticelli and Modigliani, Stone intended to use Madonna in a setting that was reminiscent of Matisse. Instead, much to his amazement, he found that his new model had her own very definite ideas about how she wanted to be portrayed. The result was a series of photographs in which Madonna appeared both androgynous and feminine, a combination of a feline dancer and a 1950s sex symbol. Everyone who saw them agreed that she brought out both the sensual and paternal instincts in men and the sensual and maternal instincts in women.

The next photographer who hired Madonna was Martin Schreiber, who, in 1980, was teaching a photography course at the New School in Manhattan. His concept was to make nudes more accessible and acceptable to the general public during what he considered to be a puritanical artistic period in the late 1970s and 1980s. "I wanted to make people less uptight about their bodies," Schreiber explained, "or at least that was my intention."

In February 1980, his advanced students turned their cameras on a beautiful and unconventional model who had answered an ad in a Village newsletter. Her name, she said, was Madonna, and she had to be paid in cash because she didn't have a bank account. Schreiber, whose books include *Bodyscapes* and *Last of a Breed,* was admittedly very taken with his new subject. "She was much skinnier years ago," he recalls, "and there was something special about her, that's for sure. I think she's quite beautiful now, but she had a different kind of beauty back then."

Her attitude was also extremely unusual for a model, since she was completely relaxed and uninhibited. Before the session began, Madonna, draped in a white sheet, wandered over to chat with some of the students who milled around, drinking coffee. She told them that she had come to New York to study dance, but had decided that she wanted to be a singer. One of the photography students recalls his first impression of the future star: "She struck me as someone who had tremendous inner resources, and yet, there was something otherworldly about her. She had absolutely no idea how the real world worked. I suppose I'd say that she was a complete contradiction. One side of her personality was this incredibly sexy young woman, and the other side was this cash register. She just knew she was worth something and wasn't going to let anyone get away with not paying for her talent."

For the two days in February that Madonna posed in the unheated studio, she seemed as undisturbed by the freezing temperature as by the fact that some of the students studied her less from an aesthetic viewpoint than a sexual one. One aspiring photographer recalls a brief conversation with Madonna during which she explained that she had never earned more money in her life than she was getting from Martin Schreiber. "I had the distinct impression," the photographer says, "that she didn't know where her next meal was coming from, and yet, she knew without any doubt that as long as she was prepared to suffer, she would eventually make it. As a Catholic myself, I understood that whole suffering and reward system."

Martin Schreiber's style was to photograph the bodies of his subjects and rarely the faces. In Madonna's case, he made an exception, and the result was a series of nude studies that were much more intimate than any he had ever done before. Schreiber managed to catch her exactly as she was at the time, raw, brazen, and yet vulnerable, touching in her naïveté and naked ambition. The collection, eventually entitled *The Last of the Madonna Nudes,* depicts Madonna as a guileless, hungry, painfully thin young girl, posing perhaps for her rent or perhaps for the disturbing effect she would have on those who studied the portraits. "I was fascinated by her face and bone structure," Schreiber admits, "maybe even more than I was with her body." The photographer and his model began having an affair, although Schreiber always had the feeling that Madonna was more interested in his connections and his ability to feed her a decent meal now and again than she was in him as a lover.

At the same time as she was posing for Martin Schreiber, she was also working at the Art Students League on West Fifty-seventh Street for Lee Friedlander, another well-known photographer who was making studies of anonymous nudes for art and photography classes. His shots eventually landed on the desk of editors at *Playboy* magazine long after Madonna became famous. The photographs of Madonna that were published in *Penthouse* had a more complicated history, and one that ended in litigation.

Two Texas photographers, Herman and Susan Kulkens, who claimed to have known Madonna from her college days in Ann Arbor, Michigan, also shot nude pictures of her before she became famous. At the time, they got a signed release from Madonna in return for a small sum of money that granted the couple rights to "sell or use the photos as they saw fit." In early June 1985, they sent twenty-two photos to Bob Guccione at *Penthouse* magazine, although they claimed that they had not made a concrete deal. When Guccione announced that he intended to run a seventeen-page, fully explicit nude-photo layout of Madonna in an upcoming issue, the couple sued to bar publication as well as for $2 million in damages. The case was heard in the Manhattan federal court before U.S. district judge John Keenan. In his defense, Guccione claimed that on June 21, as agreed, he had sent the Kulkenses a deposit of $25,000 along with a letter, confirming the agreement. According to their affidavit, the Kulkenses returned the check uncashed. In response, Guccione, claiming that he had a binding agreement with the Kulkenses, published the photographs in *Penthouse*.

Madonna's reaction to the nudes that appeared in *Penthouse* after she became famous explains a great deal about her.

A year before the Madonna nudes were published, *Penthouse* had published nude photographs of Vanessa Williams, who had just been crowned Miss America. The compromising pictures cost the beauty queen her throne and embarrassment, just as Marilyn Monroe had been shattered by the "girlie calendar" that had emerged on the market after she became a star. Madonna has often said that she is blackmailproof, that she has never done anything to be ashamed of. The difference between how Williams and Monroe reacted to the release of nude photographs and how Madonna reacted tells a great deal about the latter's character. While the former Miss America and Marilyn Monroe both pleaded for sympathy from their adoring fans, Madonna was more concerned that she had neither artistic nor financial control over the photographs. Never for a moment did she regret having posed during those lean years in New York when she had no money for food or rent. At the time, *Penthouse* wrote that the "snap of her great magical garter was more powerful than a thousand ERAs barreling headlong down the vast sexless water slide of Judeo-Christianity."

Everything Madonna did in her career came out of her own life, her loneliness, the people who treated her badly, the ones who loved her and left her, her conflicts with religion. She never told her story as if it belonged to someone else, nor has she ever successfully sung a song made famous by another singer. She is too smart to put herself up for comparison. When others sing about the girl from the wrong side of the tracks, who meets the guy who transforms her and takes her away to live happily ever after, Madonna sings about her anger that a boyfriend or a parent tried to take advantage of her when she was down or tried to control her when she was without recourse. Her message has always been that she would rather die than have to depend on anyone else to survive.

True to character, Madonna has always made her own rules. The video "Material Girl" is an obvious parody of *Gentlemen Prefer Blondes*. Though Madonna made herself up to look like Marilyn Monroe, she insisted that aside from the blond hair and bombshell image, there was no similarity between the two. In the video "Material Girl," Madonna wore a replica of the dress worn by Marilyn Monroe in *Gentlemen Prefer Blondes*. The designer Bill Travilla, who also designed fashions for *Knots Landing* and *Dallas,* had created the original dress for Miss Monroe, but never got any credit or mention from Madonna. Paraphrasing her hit song, Travilla said, "Like a virgin, I've been knocked off for the very first time."

In the beginning, Madonna admitted that she enjoyed the comparison the public made between herself and Marilyn Monroe. "I saw it as a compliment," she said, "because she was extremely sexy and had blond hair and so on. Then it started to annoy me because nobody wants to be continuously compared to someone else."

After Madonna had discarded the Monroe image, she began to discuss the basic differences between herself and the star. "I think she really didn't know what she was getting herself into," Madonna said, "and simply made herself vulnerable. I feel a bond with that, because I've certainly felt vulnerable at times, and I've felt an invasion of privacy and all that, but I'm determined never to let it get me down. Marilyn was a victim, and I'm not."

Transforming herself into the Monroe character was another example of how Madonna made her own rules and even had her own interpretation of method acting. Since Monroe had once had an affair with John Fitzgerald Kennedy, Madonna made it her business, during her Monroe incarnation, to have a brief one-night affair and several weeks of intense phone sex with John Kennedy Jr. Even if Jacqueline Kennedy hadn't expressed her outrage about the brief fling, admonishing her son for his "lack of discrimination," it is improbable that the encounter would have developed into a relationship. One of Mrs. Onassis's former colleagues at Viking Books in New York City recalls how embarrassed the former first lady was. "I think that was the moment when she really began to wonder if her son would end up with the same inability as his father to have a lasting and faithful marriage. I don't think it was a question of Mrs. Onassis considering Madonna to be vulgar, as it was a fear that her son, like his grandfather and his father, had a penchant for Hollywood stars. This worried her more than anything, since she hoped he would eventually settle down with someone from their world."

Beginning a career of transforming herself, Madonna's first attempt to change her image happened during those early days in New York. This delicate-boned girl from nowhere, who still used hokey Midwest expressions, managed to create a fashion look that was an early version of poverty chic. Disguised as an urban bohemian, she had a flair for pulling together outfits that were a combination of baby-doll pink satin and lace and biker black leather and chains. Through Norris Burroughs and his connections with some of the people who were regular fixtures at Andy Warhol's Factory, a white, mirrored loft at 33 Union Square West in lower Manhattan, Madonna met Futura 2000, Fab Five Freddy, Keith Haring, the artist she had admired when she was at school in Michigan, and Jean-Michel Basquiat, with whom she would have a brief affair several years later.

On the surface, Madonna looked as if she fit right in with the sexually ambiguous, visually shocking, underground, homoerotic artistic world Warhol had created. And yet, despite Warhol's own humble beginnings in Pennsylvania, he never accepted Madonna as part of the crowd. She was different from the others, not because she came from a small town or had less talent, but because she had built-in boundaries that allowed her to survive. Or, perhaps because he sensed she had more talent than most of the others.

In 1983, Ed Steinberg, who produced Madonna's first video, "Everybody," ran into Madonna at a party at Mr. Chow's, a trendy Chinese restaurant on East Fifty-seventh Street. Tina Chow, the wife of the owner of the restaurant, was an old friend of Andy Warhol's and would ultimately become one of the early female victims of AIDS. Her death would make the public aware that the disease was not limited to drug addicts or gay men.

At the same party was Jean-Michel Basquiat, barely twenty-three years old and already a well-known artist whose paintings were fetching $10,000, bought by such collectors as Richard Gere and Paul Simon. Though Basquiat looked vaguely familiar to her, Madonna did not remember that she had met him during the days when she hung around Warhol's Union Square loft. Back then, his hair wasn't dyed blond, nor was it cut in a punk style. Her first impression of the artist from Brooklyn, the son of a Haitian father and Puerto Rican mother, was that he was exactly her physical type. Later on, after they talked, she would discover they had other things in common as well. Like Madonna, Basquiat had had a tumultuous relationship with his father and had left home at fifteen to find success as an artist. Also similar to Madonna, Basquiat had had no doubt, even when he was living on the streets of New York, that one day he would become famous. Their affair was brief and passionate. Not only was Madonna seeing several other men, but she was disapproving and unwilling to watch him sink deeper and deeper into his dependence on hard drugs. Two months after they met, Madonna aborted his baby, or at least that was what she told Basquiat. There were rumors that even Madonna wasn't certain who the father was. Some people thought it was Jellybean Benitez, the self-promoting songwriter, and disc jockey at the Fun House, while others believed it was Mark Kamins, the disc jockey at the Dance-teria. As one friend of Madonna's says, "Back then, there was no limit to the possibilities of whose baby she aborted."

Jean-Michel Basquiat believed the baby was his, and the abortion was something, according to one young woman who had known both of them briefly during the Warhol period, that the young artist never got over.

Kitty Romano, a bubbly and plump Italian American girl from Brooklyn who hung around the Factory in the hope that she would get a part in one of Warhol's underground movies, looks back on those times with nostalgia. She also remembers Madonna as "extremely funny with unbelievable energy, but someone who was hopelessly naive."

Romano, who, in the early Warhol days, never did anything more than clean up after his parties, wash his brushes, and pay the maid, seems disappointed even after so many years that the filmmaker and artist considered her too "ordinary for stardom." Romano smiles slightly. "I wasn't grotesquely fat enough to make it in his movies," she explains. "But I was reliable, and Andy was smart enough to keep me around because he knew he could trust me not to get drunk or stoned and lose the keys or forget to do something around the space."

For the two months that Romano was in Warhol's circle, she befriended Madonna. "She was so green," she continues, "and so young in many ways. Almost everyone, except Madonna, was doing drugs. She was definitely not into anything that was self-destructive."

In one area of her life Madonna was, if not self-destructive, then careless. After years of wearing heavy pierced earrings and of dyeing her hair blond, her lobes had ripped and her hair was beginning to fall out. With barely enough money to nourish herself, she eventually asked Kitty Romano if she knew anyone who could help her. According to Romano, she had a friend who worked at Bumble and Bumble, a hair salon on West Fifty-seventh Street, who gave Madonna treatments for a special price and even let her pay him off over six months. Romano also sent Madonna to her family doctor in Brooklyn, who sewed up the holes in her lobes and, when they were healed, repierced her ears.

Romano believes that Madonna was drawn to her because they were about the same age, relegated to the fringes of the Warhol group, and both had strict Italian Catholic fathers. "I invited her home to my parents one night for dinner, and the first thing my father asked Madonna was if her father knew where she was and what she was doing." If Madonna was taken aback by the question, she didn't show it. "She was very honest when she admitted that her father disapproved of what she was doing in New York," Romano recalls, "but then she laughed and said when she was a star, he would forgive her and understand why she had to do this."

In 1983, when Madonna and Basquiat became romantically involved, she would come crying to Romano when the artist would disappear for days. "She would go nuts," Romano says. "She was sure that he was seeing someone else, since he stopped calling." Romano shakes her head. "I don't think there was anyone else because, when he wasn't with Madonna, he was usually unconscious or on some kind of a trip. The irony was that Jean-Michel cared about Madonna as much as he could care for anybody in his state and actually tried to spare her from finding out about his problems. Of course, in the end, she knew, and that was one of the reasons for the breakup."

Ironically, when Warhol finally noticed Madonna, it was during her affair with Jean-Michel Basquiat, and for a while, she enjoyed the dubious status of being known as his girlfriend. At the time, Warhol insisted upon referring to her as the "girl that Basquiat was doing," or more often just "that girl with the bizarre name."

Five years after they met, in 1989, Jean-Michel Basquiat died of an overdose of heroin on the floor of his loft, or as Madonna described his death at the time, he did the "artist thing, filled with self-doubt and guilt about finally making it." She told friends and mourners at the time, "I don't get off on self-mutilation." When her friend Ingrid Casares was having a drug problem, Madonna refused to see her or speak to her until she got into a treatment program.

The rules Madonna lived by were simple, based on her own moral code. Unlike the masses of people who have watched her perform, Madonna can afford to give the impression that she has no limits. The reality is that her rebellion is closely linked to her sense of discipline, which is based on her need to control and succeed. Then as now, she gave herself permission to do whatever she liked as long as it didn't interfere with her ability to get up in the morning and go to work.

After Basquiat's death, the charm of the Warhol crowd held little interest for her. She felt stalked by death and abandonment and, to those who knew her only slightly, projected a kind of worldly fatigue. For those who knew her more intimately, she looked more like an exhausted child who had been staying up past her bedtime for too long. She was one of the lucky ones from that self-destructive era. When she eventually made it to stardom, if ambition and discipline got her there, self-preservation allowed her to stay there.

Years later, despite Warhol's not having nurtured her talent or taken any interest in her, Madonna still managed to take something from him and fashion it to fit her own style and image. *Truth or Dare,* her unrehearsed documentary, was a movie without a plot like the films that Warhol had made so well in the 1970s. Unlike the Warhol works of that era, however, which used the camera to pry and spy on the underbelly culture of the underground, making his viewers voyeurs under the guise of art, Madonna's so-called *cinéma réalité* gave new meaning to narcissism. When critics doubted that it was unrehearsed, a truthful video of a day in the life of a star, Madonna responded, "It's like when you go into a psychiatrist's office and you don't really tell them what you did, you lie, but even the lie you've chosen to tell is revealing."

Whatever her failings, Madonna rarely confused commercialism with art or pop culture with religion. She is not someone who has taken up the microphone for a variety of causes. When she has, it has always been because she has been personally touched by the issue. When she has given charity concerts for AIDS, she has spoken out on an intimate level, citing those she has loved and lost to the disease, rather than calling attention to an AIDS that ravages millions in Africa because international drug companies refuse to lower prices so the poor can also be saved. Even breast cancer remains a private issue that concerns only her mother's death from the disease and not a public cause in which she urges women with a genetic propensity to get regular mammograms.

Truth or Dare was a one-woman show in every aspect of its creative development to the final product, which starred only Madonna with a supporting cast of her peers, friends, family, and colleagues, who all played Costello to her Abbott. The film showed the performer at her most ungenerous, ungracious, and unkind, although several of the most surrealistic and comical moments happened when she made the mistake of transforming herself into an "artist" who stands up for what she calls her "artistic integrity." In equally dubious taste is that she risks religious blasphemy and offends the believers among her fans more than when she lusts after a black saint in her video "Like a Prayer."

With Alek Keshishian's handheld camera recording her every move, every evening before going onstage Madonna gathers her cast to lead them in prayer. In Detroit, we are drawn into a circle with Madonna, sucking on a cough drop, and her dancers holding hands, and she asks God to give her that "little something extra" since she is about to go onstage in her hometown. In Toronto, again armed with a cough drop instead of a rosary, Madonna asks God to see to it that the authorities don't stop her from doing her masturbation scene onstage. When the prayer ends in that particular city, we are treated to an embarrassing encounter between Madonna and

Freddy DeMann, her then manager, during which he tells her that two Toronto policemen are poised to arrest her if she doesn't cut some of the more risqué dance sequences out of her show. Refusing to sacrifice her art or bow to censorship, Madonna instructs him to make her position clear to the authorities. If they don't "back off," she adds, she is prepared to go off to jail. Obediently, DeMann meets the two potbellied law enforcement officers and engages them in a serious discussion of human rights and artistic freedom concerning whether Madonna intends to feign masturbation onstage despite the threat of being hauled off à la Lenny Bruce in the middle of her performance.

The scene is surrealistic because Madonna actually believes that her audience will buy the transformation of Madonna into artist and activist, willing to risk her freedom to stand behind her rights as an artist. After all, this was the twentieth century, when a performer can have oral sex with an Evian bottle, encourage two gay men to tongue-kiss on-camera, have a romp in bed with her entire *Truth or Dare* cast, or feign masturbation onstage. It is comical, because even the Toronto cops appear not to believe the situation they find themselves in. In fact, they seem very aware that their brief moment in the annals of the Madonna archives will be marvelous fodder for all their future New Year's Eve parties and summer barbecues.

In 1990 when the video "Justify My Love" came out and was banned on MTV, it was Madonna and not her director, Jean-Baptiste Mondino, who took full responsibility for its every note, movement, and sexual innuendo and nuance. Madonna was invited by reputable journalists to appear on a variety of interview programs to defend her work. Wearing a demure white blouse buttoned up to the neck, her hair pinned back in a librarian-style bun, Madonna went on ABC's *Nightline* with Forrest Sawyer to defend what she described once again as her "artistic freedom."

Madonna's most intelligent and realistic defense of her music was a comparison she made to the singer formerly

known as Prince. "All his songs talk blatantly about fucking
and nobody says anything. He's allowed, because he's a
man. Male rock stars flaunt it without having their music attacked. I thought about that, and I'd think, why aren't they
letting all this stand in the way of appreciating Prince's music?"

When Madonna appeared on Arsenio Hall's show and
talked about spanking as she used it in "Hanky Panky" from
the album *I'm Breathless,* which was inspired by the film
Dick Tracy, starring Madonna and Warren Beatty, Hall
claimed that finally "Madonna went too far." When Hall
asked Madonna if the song expressed her own feelings on
discipline, Madonna replied, "I don't like it really hard,
though. Just a little stinging, and it's good." The theme came
out of a line used in the film *Dick Tracy,* when Madonna,
playing Breathless Mahoney, extols the virtues of a good
spanking and says to Dick Tracy, portrayed by Warren
Beatty, "You don't know whether to hit me or kiss me." The
song also features the important line "My bottom hurts just
thinking about it."

The miracle of Madonna is that the scandal she creates has
always been for public consumption. Unlike her peers and
colleagues who have made it to stardom, she has never
risked drugs or asylums, trashed hotel rooms, bounced
checks, involved herself with a married partner, got caught
masturbating in a public place, or carried a concealed
weapon.

A prudent rebel, she has guaranteed her "wanna-bes" that
they could change their appearances without permanently
marring their looks. She has also assured their parents that
their children's transformation is an innocent moment, after
which they can revert back to themselves. Interpretation for
Madonna was always safer than definition. It gave her the
possibility to change her mind, her style, her tune, and her

image, which gave her fans the possibility not to commit themselves to any one fad.

On May 27, 1985, *Time* magazine did a cover story on Madonna, which was "a defense of teenagers who are caught up in the Madonna craze." *Time* pointed out that "these same young people who were Madonna fans could be out stealing hubcaps or doing drugs. At least onstage she exhibits a kind of asexual sexuality, mostly caught up in a style that is less revealing except for a naked midriff than it is a thumbing the nose at conventional fashion. The difference between Madonna and the other girl singers that emerged during the recording heyday of the middle 1980s is that she has never been a product of MTV or any other superficial media packagers as she has always exhibited too much personality and independence."

Madonna set other examples as well for her public.

Madonna never feared success. Defeat was her enemy, to be forced to go back where she'd come from, either literally or metaphorically. For a while when she first landed in New York, she refused to say the name of her hometown, as if by articulating it, something beyond her power would carry her back there against her will.

chapter twenty
· · · · · · · · · · · · · · · · ·

*S*everal months after Madonna and Norris Burroughs broke up, she bumped into him on the street. Back then, her life moved at such an incredibly fast pace with so many changes that if a day or a week passed, not to mention a month, it was impossible to know where she was living, or with whom. Since she had last seen Burroughs, Madonna had moved twice and was currently living in the Riverside Drive apartment of a Columbia University professor and his two teenage sons.

Every year, on May 1, Norris Burroughs, along with a musician friend of his named Dan Gilroy, a quirky, clean-cut Irishman, a cross between Art Carney and Jimmy Cagney who usually had a toothpick stuck in his mouth, had a "rites of spring party." Currently, Dan Gilroy writes music for commercials and lives in Texas with the actress Shelley Duvall.

"We'd borrow a loft," Burroughs explains, "and we'd celebrate spring, dance around and act wild." It was at the party that Madonna met Dan Gilroy, who was not particularly impressed with his friend's ex-girlfriend. Madonna judged Gilroy to be rude and pompous, while he thought that she was depressing and morose. As the evening wore on, they found themselves in a lively conversation about rock and roll and the general state of the music business. At the time, Dan, along with his brother, Ed, were living in an abandoned synagogue in Queens, which they also used as a studio to compose and record their music.

"We all used to go to the 'gogue' and hang out," Burroughs recalls, "and basically listen to Dan and Ed try and find new sounds, which they were hoping to record."

Dan Gilroy is credited with giving Madonna a guitar and encouraging her to experiment with different chords and sounds. "I heard the songs she wrote in the beginning," Burroughs continues, "and I even used to sing with her. They were basic bar chords and guitar, and while it's easy to write simple rock-and-roll songs if you can sing and play basic chords, she had something special." He smiles. "When she was with Dan, we still had a few kisses here and there, but mostly I would help her with her music."

Burroughs admits that he has never been a big fan of Madonna's singing or songwriting ability, but he can still understand why it became so popular: "It's infectious, the timing is good, and it's all about girl power, feminism, and young women's sexuality." He pauses. "Basically, it's all about her special kind of energy."

On September 25, 1979, the Broadway production of *Evita,* starring Patti LuPone, opened at the Broadway Theatre and instantly became the toast of New York. Through a friend who knew someone who worked at the theater, Madonna managed to get in after the curtain went up. She stood in the back, behind a pillar, and watched the play. Though she was lucid enough to know that she would never have the chance to play *Evita* on the New York stage, seeing Eva Perón's life acted out before her eyes was enough to convince her that one day she would achieve similar success and international recognition.

At the same time that the Broadway show opened, the British director Ken Russell was set to direct *Evita* for the screen. He immediately sought Julie Covington, who made the role famous on the London stage, to play Evita in his film. When Covington turned it down, Russell proposed the role to Barbra Streisand, who also turned the project down.

In a last effort to keep *Evita* alive, Russell offered the part to Liza Minnelli, who accepted it, only to learn that Russell was unable to get the financial backing he had been promised. At the time, Tim Rice, the lyricist, was lobbying for his good friend Elaine Paige to sing the title role on-screen as she had also made the role famous on the London stage. When Ken Russell argued with Rice, refusing to cast someone who resembled Princess Margaret in the title role, Russell did nothing to endear himself to the man who had considerable say in pushing the project forward.

Added to Russell's woes was that at this point in his career, after a series of overbloated and overblown films that were failures at the box office, including *Lisztomania* and *Tommy,* followed by such unimpressive bombs as *Altered States* and *China Blue,* he was considered a bad risk.

While Ken Russell was at a glitch in his career, which would result in his losing the movie project, Madonna was working with Dan Gilroy on her music. Years later, she once said, "How ironic that *Evita* was introduced to the American public at the same time that I was writing my first song."

By 1980, Madonna was concentrating mainly on her music. Dan Gilroy had become not only her primary romantic interest, but the person who, more than anyone else, encouraged her to practice on his synthesizer and to go out on as many auditions as she could, if for no other reason than to gather experience and to see what her competition was up to. One of those auditions was held in a cavernous rehearsal hall on Broadway. Two music producers from France, Jean Van Lieu and Jean-Claude Pellerin, were looking for a group of girls to sing backup for a French singer who had made an international name for himself with one disco tune called "Born to Be Alive," which had sold 25 million records throughout the world.

Patrick Hernandez, who is half Spanish and half Italian, is still referred to as The Myth throughout Europe because of the enormous success of that one hit record. A thoughtful and down-to-earth man, who never had any formal musical training, Hernandez, at fifty-two, lives quietly in the south of France with his family. Tall and stocky, with unkempt, graying hair, he still recalls the audition and remembers one hopeful who stood out in the crowd of more than fifteen hundred young women. Once again, Madonna was lucky. She could have auditioned for anybody, but instead fell upon an international star who also happened to be a decent human being. "At the time I met Madonna in New York," Hernandez says, "she was running after the best opportunity, anything that paid her something to survive." He shrugs. "And I'm a nice guy, I never exploited her. I only helped her."

In 1965, when Patrick Hernandez was sixteen years old, his parents sent him to a small seaside town near Canterbury in England to learn English. His father, who was a pharmacist, and his mother, an accountant, hoped that their only son would become an English teacher. Patrick always had a passion for music and grew up in a home where music was a regular part of his life. Every Sunday, his father, who played the banjo and mandolin, would organize musicales at their house. Without family or friends and living far from Paris, where he had had access to many different cultural diversions, Hernandez found there was nothing much to do in that dreary English town except study and listen to music. The Beatles had just become popular in England, although not yet on the Continent, and Hernandez, obsessed with their sound, decided to play, compose, and sing his own music. Like Madonna, he had never had any formal musical training and learned to play by instinct and by ear. Little by little, he taught himself drums, the keyboard, and bass and began to write his own music on the piano and the guitar. When he finished his studies, he returned to France and had a marginal success playing at weddings and parties with a series of small groups in the suburbs and provinces. In 1974 and 1975, he joined more prestigious and professional groups and even made several records that never sold. In 1977, he formed his own band called Paris Palace Hotel, or PPH,

which also had limited success. For a while his group was
the butt of jokes around Paris, often referred to as PPH, or
passera pas l'hiver, which in French means "won't last the
winter." After several years, when things still seemed not to
be breaking for the aspiring rock-and-roll singer, he decided
that he was too old to make a serious name for himself in
show business. Breaking up the band, he moved to a region
in France called the Périgord, where, along with a girlfriend,
he set about cultivating veal for the market.

Though Hernandez believed that stardom had eluded him
forever, he was still being represented by a brilliant Belgian
impresario and record producer by the name of Jean Van
Lieu. Van Lieu and his wife, Muriel, who would work with
him throughout his life, until his death in 2000 at sixty-one
from lung cancer, had both tried to convince Hernandez not
to give up on his group and abandon the music business. By
the time Jean Van Lieu called his client turned farmer in the
Périgord to announce that he had several interesting projects
for him, Hernandez was already getting bored with the
country, the veal, and the girlfriend.

Van Lieu pointed out that since Hernandez wasn't working for anyone and didn't have his own group, he might consider coming back to Paris and working for Van Lieu. "He
thought that maybe together we could come up with something that he could market," Hernandez explains. After several fruitless phone conversations, Van Lieu finally sent
Hernandez a telegram, asking him to come to Belgium. Hernandez left the Périgord and spent several months at the Van
Lieu home, marking the beginning of a lifelong relationship.

An innovative record producer, who had a reputation for
giving unknown artists a chance either to record their own
compositions or to have them recorded by well-known
singers, Van Lieu received music written by young com-
posers from all over Europe. His idea at the time was that
Hernandez would record several of the more promising
pieces, although as Hernandez explained during a recent interview in Paris, "In retrospect, if Jean made one error, it

was in thinking that I was solely a singer and not a composer." As it turned out, Patrick Hernandez was both.

During one of their recording sessions as they searched around for the "right sound," Hernandez asked Van Lieu if he would mind listening to a "little tune" that Hernandez had composed on his guitar and for which he had written the words in English. The name of the song was "Born to Be Alive."

According to Hernandez, he was inspired by a song written by Stephen Ball called "Born to Be Wild."

"It just came to me," Hernandez recalls. "I was sitting in a corner near my fireplace and just strumming the guitar when I thought about all the people who I knew who were alive but not really living. How they all went about their routine little lives, not daring to pack a guitar over their shoulders and travel the world, smoke hashish, meet new people, have new adventures."

The year was 1978 and disco had become the rage throughout the world because of the hit movie and album called *Saturday Night Fever*. Van Lieu immediately recognized that "Born to Be Alive" could become a hit, but only if it was adapted to the disco sound. The result was a major success for the Van Lieus and Patrick Hernandez, a recording that entered the *Guinness Book of World Records* as number three in the American Hit Parade for all-time greatest hits. Fortunately for Hernandez, Jean and Muriel Van Lieu, who owned the copyright, and Jean-Claude Pellerin, their partner, who owned the publishing rights, advised him to keep all the foreign rights for the song to be sold, dividing the profits three ways, on a country-by-country basis.

Muriel Van Lieu was eight months pregnant with her daughter when her husband put her in charge of the New York audition. With the help of her producers and a choreographer, she put ads in all the professional magazines and newspapers, calling for young men and women, dancers and singers, who would eventually be chosen as a backup group for an internationally famous singer. Tall, blond, and attractive, Muriel Van Lieu dresses in designer clothes and comes to Paris once a month from her home near the French/Belgian border to take care of copyright business and to shop. Along with her daughter, who is now twenty-one, she runs a discotheque, H_2O, which during an average weekend entertains more than four thousand people. Recently widowed, she remembers with absolute precision that time more than twenty-one years ago when she first met Madonna.

"Out of the fifteen hundred kids who showed up for the audition," Muriel Van Lieu begins, "we intended to keep thirty to tour with Patrick throughout the United States, and out of the thirty, we wanted to keep twenty to bring back with us to Europe for television shows there." With only four days to audition all the people who showed up, the idea was to choose a mixed racial group of male and female dancers and singers, some blond, others dark or brunet, a combination of short and tall, thin and voluptuous. Contrary to how most auditions were run and especially since there were so many people to see in so few days, Muriel Van Lieu insisted that she wanted to see one candidate at a time onstage, rather than viewing them in groups. "My choreographer asked each one to do free movement as well as a combination that he choreographed, and finally we wanted them to sing a song that they could choose," she explains. "In my head, I was looking for someone who had a distinctive look, kids who were different-looking, who stood out from the crowd. I understood a little English, but I had an interpreter with me. In the beginning, I didn't talk to the kids, because first I watched them perform, and then, if they were good, I wanted to talk to them to get an idea of their personality."

On the second day of the auditions, Madonna walked onto the cavernous stage.

"For the first three days, there were only three of us sitting in the audience—me, the choreographer, and my manager—judging the audition," she continues. "When Madonna

Madonna the Boy Toy

*(Photo by Robin Platzer/
Getty Images)*

Madonna performing

(Photo by Robin Platzer/Getty Images)

Madonna poses for
a photo in 1986.

*(Photo by G. De Keerle/
Getty Images)*

A dancer crawls
between Madonna's
legs during a concert,
May 4, 1990,
in Houston, Texas.

*(Photo by Paul Howell/
Getty Images)*

With brother Christopher at the *Vanity Fair* Oscar party at Morton's, Los Angeles, March 23, 1998

(Photo by Ortega Albert/Sipa Press)

At the NBA All-Star
game, New York City

(Photo by Getty Images)

Madonna at the
Evening Standard Awards,
February 6, 2000, London

*(Photo by James Peltekian/
Corbis Sygma)*

Madonna singing "American Pie" for the soundtrack of *The Next Best Thing*

Madonna between costar Rupert Everett and Guy Ritchie at the U.K. charity premiere of *The Next Best Thing*, June 6, 2000

(Photo by Steve Lemere/Sipa Press)

Madonna and Guy Ritchie at the New York premiere of *The Next Best Thing*, February 29, 2000

(Photo by Jean Catuffe/ Sipa Press)

Reacting to fans at a launch party for her *Music* album, September 19, 2000, in Los Angeles

(Photo by Chris Weeks/ Getty Images)

Madonna and Guy Ritchie leaving after the baptism of their
son, Rocco, at Dornoch Cathedral, Scotland, December 21, 2000

(Photo by Bob Foy/Getty Images)

walked onstage, she really shocked me because it was the first time I had ever seen anyone who looked like that. She was dressed in punk—torn T-shirt, hair chopped off in all different lengths all over her head—and with a really rebellious attitude."

Patrick Hernandez remembers the first time he saw Madonna as well. "We chose random pieces from my album, and Madonna was supposed to make up her own combinations, cold, no rehearsal, just free and easy, because my album hadn't come out yet in America so she wasn't familiar with the music." Muriel Van Lieu describes the scene that followed. "When my choreographer asked her to show us how she moved, I must admit, I was knocked out. She was fantastic, and to this day, I'm convinced that with all her videos and stage shows, she holds back, because I never saw anyone with a better dance technique. In fact, my choreographer was bothered. He came running down from the stage and whispered in my ear, 'Listen, Muriel, excuse me, but I don't think I have to bother giving her a combination to follow because she is absolutely elastic, like rubber, and she has already shown us that she can do ten times better than I would ask of her at this audition.'"

All that was left was to hear Madonna sing. But when Muriel Van Lieu asked her to sing something, she had her first glimpse into the star's character. According to Van Lieu, Madonna refused, claiming that she did not do things if she could not do them better than anyone else. "I came here to pass a dance audition," she told the startled woman, "and not to sing. I don't sing. I'm a dancer, and you've seen what I'm capable of doing so that should be enough." Muriel Van Lieu persisted since she was not willing to make an exception, especially in front of the hundreds of other hopefuls who were watching this exchange with alarm and interest. At the same time, she didn't want to antagonize Madonna and take the chance that she might just stomp out. "I told her to sing anything, a tune she sings in the shower, and that my arranger would follow her," Muriel Van Lieu says. Still,

Madonna refused. "Look," she said impatiently, "I don't make a habit of putting myself out there to lose. For me, perfection is primary!"

The argument went on for several long minutes until, finally, Muriel Van Lieu managed to convince Madonna to sing "Happy Birthday." Muriel shrugs. "How hard was that?" she asks rhetorically. "But even when she sang it, it was in this singsong voice without any expression and with an attitude that clearly said, 'I lost this round, but you'll lose the match!' She had a nice, pleasant voice, nothing extraordinary, but at least I was assured that she could carry a tune."

Patrick Hernandez realized something else after that incident that had nothing to do with Madonna's talent or her character. "She seemed sadder and lonelier than the others were," Hernandez says, "and at a much deeper level, not just depressed about not getting a callback after an audition or living in squalor. She had her priorities set from the beginning, and that made her stronger, light-years ahead of the others when it came to her determination to survive and, more than that, to be the best." Years later, he would remember something that Madonna said to him while they were driving in his limousine from the airport in Tunisia to their hotel. "Take advantage of the fact that you're number one, Patrick," she told him, "because today it's you, tomorrow it's me!" Hernandez is still convinced that Madonna didn't say it as an act of aggression, just simply as a fact that she knew absolutely would happen.

On the last day of auditions, when the choice had been narrowed down to fifty people and then again to twenty-five, Jean-Claude Pellerin joined Muriel Van Lieu to make the final choice. "We had each of the twenty-five do a short song-and-dance sequence," Muriel Van Lieu explains, "and when Jean-Claude saw Madonna perform, he decided immediately that she was exceptional and that my husband should see her as well." According to Muriel Van Lieu, she called her husband and insisted that he join them at the audition because there was one dancer who was extraordinary. "My husband came racing downtown and we asked Madonna to perform alone on the stage," Muriel Van Lieu recalls. "When he saw her, he understood why we had been so excited. She was absolutely exceptional. Along with us, he decided that she was too good to waste as part of the chorus. He wanted to bring her over to Paris and make her a star."

At the beginning of her video "Material Girl," in a scene in a screening room, a cigar-smoking movie mogul watches the rushes of a film in which Madonna, playing a new discovery, is performing. "She's fantastic," the mogul raves. "I knew she'd be a star!" One of his lackeys who is with him in the screening room replies, "She could be! She could be great! She could be a major star!" The mogul turns his head and says in a disgusted tone of voice, "She is a star, the biggest star in the universe, right now as we speak."

When Jean Van Lieu and Jean-Claude Pellerin watched Madonna on that final day of auditions, they had almost the same conversation.

The next day, the Van Lieus, Pellerin and his wife, Danièle, and Patrick Hernandez invited Madonna to the Pierre Hotel for lunch in their suite. They told her that they were prepared to bring her over to Paris, support her, pay for dancing and singing lessons, and sign her to an exclusive contract until, eventually, they would manage her career. "We told her," Muriel Van Lieu says, "that we were convinced that she could be a big star in her own right." Without any hesitation, Madonna agreed. Within two months, while Patrick Hernandez stayed behind to finish his American tour, Madonna left for Paris with Jean-Claude and Danièle Pellerin.

chapter twenty-one
....

*P*arc Monceau is an oasis of manicured green lawns, flowers, and sculpted trees in the center of Paris surrounded by an elaborate black iron fence trimmed in gold leaf. The area itself, not far from the Arc de Triomphe, the outdoor flower market at the Place de Wagram, and several pedestrian streets filled with fruit and vegetable stands, begins in the Eighth Arrondissement and continues into the Seventeenth. Along with the Sixteenth, where the fabled Avenue Foch continues up from L'Étoile to the Bois de Boulogne, and the Seventh Arrondissement, where the gold-domed Napoléon's tomb, the Hôtel Matignon, the residence of the prime minister, and other government ministries are located, Parc Monceau is considered one of the most expensive neighborhoods in Paris.

Danièle and Jean-Claude Pellerin rented an entire floor of a four-story building that had once been a *hôtel particulier,* or private home, of one of the leading French aristocratic families, who found that high taxes and heating costs forced them to transform the structure into an apartment house. The architecture of the buildings in that area is Haussmann in style, typical of the nineteenth-century designs built during the Second Empire of Napoleon III, ornate stone buildings with intricately carved sculptures decorating the facades and friezes of acrobats or gargoyles in bas-relief running the width of the structures. Heavy wood-and-iron doors lead to cobblestone courtyards where horses and carriages were once kept, and where now, those residents who

have been there the longest enjoy the privilege of parking
their cars. The elevators still are often the charming turn-of-
the-century, classic glass cages that climb slowly and pre-
cariously, or they have been transformed into metal boxes
the size of a coffin, suitable for one or two slim occupants
who don't suffer from claustrophobia.

The Pellerins' apartment was on the Rue de Courcelles
with views of the park. They had taken the ten-room, three-
hundred-square-meter flat with the intention of making it
their home as well as the Paris base of Patrick Hernandez
when he came back periodically from his European, North
African, and American tours. When Danièle Pellerin arrived
there from New York, along with her two children, maid,
cook, and nurse, she realized that she had been lucky to have
found such a large space, since there would now be another
person living with them indefinitely, a young woman whom
they would come to consider a member of their family.

Madonna was enchanted by the apartment. She had never
seen so many wood-burning fireplaces, one in each bedroom
as well as in the double living room and dining room. There
were parquet floors and high ceilings with moldings of
grapevines and ornate birthday-cake designs made of white
plaster from which chandeliers hung that bathed the rooms
in soft light. The floor-to-ceiling windows were really
French doors, which opened onto a small garden in the back
of the building, and Madonna's room faced a fountain of
cherubs that spewed water into a marble basin.

Jean-Claude and Danièle Pellerin, both born in Tunisia,
had decorated the flat with modern furniture, including
glass-and-chrome tables, leather-and-steel chairs, but had
added colorful rugs, ceramic vases, and native art that they
had brought back from North Africa. The result was a cheer-
ful and sunny apartment that was unlike the usual bourgeois
style, which included heavy velvet draperies, thick wall-to-
wall carpeting, and seventeenth- and eighteenth-century
French provincial furniture that made the atmosphere dreary
and dim. Madonna's room had a wicker dresser, futon bed,

and a floor-to-ceiling mirror, which she danced and exercised in front of every morning from six until eight.

Ironically, she wasn't the only future star who lived in that four-story mansion on the Rue de Courcelles. Professor Hamburger, an eminent research scientist, and his wife, a piano teacher, had lived directly across the hall for more than two decades, along with their son, Michel. Years later, the young musical genius would change his name to Michel Berger and go on to become one of the most famous singer-songwriters in Europe. Along with Jean-Jacques Goldmann, Berger would compose the hit musical *Starmania,* which continues to play to sold-out audiences throughout Europe. In 1992, already married to the popular French singer France Gall and the father of two small children, Michel Berger collapsed and died on the tennis court at their country house near Paris at the age of forty-four.

From the first day that Madonna arrived in Paris, she made it clear to Danièle Pellerin that she wanted to continue her dancing lessons and insisted that Danièle find her a suitable school. The problem was that Jean-Claude Pellerin and Jean Van Lieu had returned to the United States to oversee Patrick Hernandez's American tour, while Muriel Van Lieu, having just given birth, had recently moved into her own apartment and was trying to get settled before her husband returned. Danièle Pellerin assured Madonna that as soon as the others got back to Paris, they would focus their attention on her and organize a definite schedule that would include concrete plans for her career. In the meantime, she suggested that Madonna study French with a young student whom she had arranged to come to the house twice a week, and to acquaint herself with the city.

Madonna was housed in a beautiful apartment, fed, and given enough pocket money for her personal needs. After she exercised for two hours every morning, she found herself with nothing to do. Danièle Pellerin was busy with her children, the others were still in the States, and Madonna, left to her own devices, would head to the flea markets in Montreuil or Montmartre, combing the stands for outrageous outfits and cheap jewelry. Eventually, she discovered the Gare du Nord, one of the six large railroad stations in the city, where bands of Vietnamese and North African boys hung out, trying to make a few dollars a day as porters. Riding around on the back of their motorcycles, tagging along to inexpensive Arab restaurants, staying out all night, hopping from bar to bar in the demimonde district of St.-Denis where drug dealers and prostitutes spent their leisure hours, Madonna amused herself while she waited for her new life to begin. It was not exactly the glamorous existence that she had read about when she envisioned the creative atmosphere that Hemingway, Gertrude Stein, and Zelda and Scott Fitzgerald had lived in Paris as expatriates. In her own limited circle, far from the intellectual salons she had imagined, Madonna was nonetheless considered an exotic bird by her new friends, a woman who came from a country where they still believed the streets were "paved with gold." She had a lot of success, especially with the North African boys. An incident in one of the bars could have been the theme of a French apache dance or an Argentine tango.

Pierre Trenet tended bar at the Zaf Zaf, which was near the St.-Denis arch, the eighteenth-century port of entry to that section of Paris. According to Trenet, Madonna had arrived with her boyfriend of the moment, a recent arrival from Algeria, who was doing odd jobs, painting and refinishing furniture. During the evening, Madonna apparently focused her attention on another young man, an Algerian as well, who suddenly found himself with a knife at his throat. The fight between the two suitors ended when Trenet called the police and they were hauled off to the local precinct. "She had no money to get home, and I lent her the cab fare," Trenet says, "because she was shaken up and it was too late." Trenet admits that he was surprised when Madonna reappeared the following evening with her original Algerian escort. "She was wearing lace gloves without the fingers, and she reached into a beaded evening bag and gave me back the several francs I had lent her."

Several weeks later, Jean-Claude Pellerin, Jean Van Lieu, and Patrick Hernandez finally returned from America and turned their attention on their American protégée whom they hoped to groom as the next Edith Piaf.

From the beginning, things were not easy between Madonna and her French hosts. Patrick Hernandez recalls that living with Madonna under the same roof was amusing, because she was charming and adorable. He also remembers how meticulous she was. "She had a little notebook," he says, "and she would write her thoughts, little poems that became lyrics for song, and pages and pages of her impressions of life in Paris." Trying to persuade her to follow their advice and do what they considered necessary to become a star was another story, and one that her benefactors considered the antithesis of charming and amusing.

"She was very *sauvage*," Hernandez says, "and very American. In the beginning, we tried to humor her and didn't force her to sing or take music lessons, because we believed that if we gave in and let her take dancing lessons, after a while she would do what we wanted her to do and what we brought her over to be, which was a hit singing star."

After Muriel Van Lieu's husband returned, she found Madonna a dance class in a studio at Les Halles, once famous for its slaughterhouses and meat markets. The area had been transformed into a cultural center built around the Pompidou, a monstrosity of a building that has pipes and steel girders painted in primary colors that are exposed on the facade in an attempt to create a new trend in architecture. Wandering around Les Halles, Madonna was more intrigued by the long-haired hippies, beggars, and drug addicts who roamed the grounds than she was with her lessons, which turned out to be an intermediate ballet class. Often, she followed groups of tourists and watched the fire-eaters, acrobats, and mimes, who performed for small change that was dropped into their cups or bowler hats. After several weeks, Madonna got bored with Les Halles and came home early, furious. "Obviously," she told Danièle Pellerin, "there is no one in Paris who can teach me what I need to learn." Later that evening, Hernandez sat Madonna down and asked her exactly what she wanted to do. "I want to be an actress and dancer," Madonna replied, "like Juliet Prowse or Ginger Rogers, and not a singer. I refuse to sing!"

The two French producers were naturally worried since Madonna had signed a management agreement with them in return for their financial and professional support. Their immediate reaction was to threaten Madonna that if she didn't cooperate, they would be forced to stop all support and let her fend for herself. Hernandez tried a different approach. In an effort to convince her to change her mind, he spent several evenings with her at home, listening to music. "I remember once at the apartment," he says, "we were playing a song by Linda and Paul McCartney, and Madonna and I began singing along and she sang really well. Even Linda didn't have a voice like Barbra Streisand, and I told her, 'See, you can sing, you sing as well as Linda, even better.'"

At the time that Madonna was with Patrick Hernandez in Paris, he lived the life of an international star. Every time he went out, limousines were waiting to chauffeur him around, with fans crushing to touch him and get an autograph, boys and girls throwing themselves at him, and crowds of people willing to give him anything he wanted just for the privilege of being in his company. When Madonna saw the attention that Hernandez received and the life of luxury he led because of his one hit record, she began to be less rigid about her refusal to become a singing star. "At the time I was the number one star worldwide," Hernandez explains, "and Madonna realized what it meant to lead the life of a star. She suddenly realized that it wasn't such a stupid idea to become a rock or disco singer. I'm still convinced that because of me and because she was young and talented and had so much going for her, that she decided to grab it all and go as far and as fast as possible." Reluctantly, Madonna agreed to a rigorous schedule of conversational French, music, and singing lessons, but only if she could continue to study dance. This time, her French teacher was an older woman, while her singing coach was a middle-aged man. Eventually, Muriel Van Lieu found her another dancing school that was more advanced and more geared toward musical comedy and jazz. The arrangement between her benefactors and an obedient Madonna lasted only two months.

Despite her commitment to her managers and Patrick Hernandez's sincerity when it came to helping Madonna, the French press predictably assumed that she was his girlfriend rather than the rock star's newest discovery whom he had imported from America. On one occasion, when Hernandez was invited to do a photo spread for a glossy magazine, he brought Madonna along on a press junket to Tunisia, organized by a public relations company. According to Hernandez, not only did he pose for the various photographers, but he insisted that they take pictures of Madonna alone as well as of both of them together in preparation for her future career as a singer. Hernandez, who is surprisingly down-to-earth for someone who has enjoyed such success, recalls that although they were having an affair, he never deluded himself that Madonna was either in love with him or particularly faithful. "Let's just say," he says with a small smile, "that she was very active and had a healthy appetite. But regardless of our personal relationship, everything I did for her when it came to grooming her for stardom was done out of friendship."

Muriel Van Lieu joined the couple in Sidi Bou Said, a pleasure port where the white masts of hundreds of sailboats were docked in the sapphire blue water of the harbor. A rich man's paradise where Europeans and Gulf State Arabs came to sun and sail, and also the headquarters of the Palestinian Liberation Organization, it was a cliff-top monastic fortress that had grown around the tomb of a holy man named Sidi

Bou Said. Muriel Van Lieu, Madonna, and Patrick Hernandez stayed at the Abou Nawas, a luxury hotel built on the beach. There, around the kidney-shaped swimming pool, Van Lieu saw yet another side of the young woman she had met only months before at the audition in New York. "I came down to the pool to help out with the press," Muriel Van Lieu says, "and at one point, Madonna was being ignored while Patrick was the center of attention. I was barely aware of what she was doing when all of a sudden I looked up, and there she was. She had climbed onto the high diving board and, dressed in jeans and a T-shirt, just dove right into the swimming pool. When she came out of the pool, her T-shirt clung to her breasts, which provoked the response that she needed from the photographers. That's just one example of how important it was for Madonna to exist, to be the center of attention."

When Madonna returned to Paris from Tunisia, she began complaining once again that things were moving too slowly. She had been in Europe for nearly a month, and so far, there were no auditions for stage appearances, no record deal, nor any prospect to accompany Patrick on one of his tours. Jean Van Lieu decided that it was too complicated, especially since he was so busy managing Hernandez's career, television appearances, and foreign sales of his record, to devote his time to a girl who refused to follow his advice. According to Muriel Van Lieu, every step was a battle—to persuade Madonna to keep taking her singing lessons, to convince her that disco was the sound that she should concentrate on for her first record, to encourage her to behave properly when she met other singers or record producers who could potentially help her—until finally her husband lost his temper. "There are millions of kids out there," he told Madonna, "who would jump at the opportunity that we're giving you."

Rather than abandoning Madonna, Patrick Hernandez and Danièle and Jean-Claude Pellerin persuaded Jean Van Lieu to let them take over for a while. "The truth was," Muriel Van Lieu explains, "that Madonna was very patient. My husband was too busy to devote the kind of time that was necessary to make her a star."

The relationship between Madonna and Patrick Hernandez was waning, mainly because he was touring the world, traveling to Brazil, New York, Mexico, as well as to other European cities. Away for two or three weeks at a time, he would return to Paris between trips for only several days. There was no doubt that though Madonna appreciated who Hernandez was and what he had accomplished and was always happy to be with him because they had fun together, she began to consider, despite the beautiful surroundings and easy life, that she was wasting her time in Paris. She told Patrick that if she was going to make it the way she knew and felt she could, it was not in Europe but back home in the United States. Still, the Pellerins and even Jean Van Lieu were reluctant to let her go, partly because they had already made a big investment in her, and partly because they still believed that she had the talent and the discipline to become a star.

One evening, in an attempt to make peace among everyone, Patrick Hernandez invited Madonna and the two couples to Brussels, about two hours away by car, for a reconciliation dinner. "We went to a typical four-star restaurant," Hernandez says, "which serves about ten or so courses, and I made her taste everything. She was sitting next to me, and I was acting like her teacher, describing what each course was, and finally we got to the foie gras and I told her, we're going to eat this, and with foie gras, there are several drinks that we have, sauterne, which is a sweet wine, or champagne or a bit of *porto,* which is also sweet but heavier than sauterne. She had never had foie gras in her life and naturally she didn't know which wine to choose, so I told the waiter to bring all three and set the glasses in front of her so she could taste everything. I was acting a little like Professor Henry Higgins to her Liza Doolittle. As the meal progressed, I guess I didn't pay attention to her for a minute or so because apparently, very quietly, she had asked the waiter to bring her a Coke, which she kept at her feet. She would take a bite of the foie gras and, when no one was looking, quickly washed it down with Coke to kill the taste." According to Hernandez, Madonna tasted the champagne, *porto,* and sauterne but didn't like them. "She was never into alcohol or drugs. She exercised, took her dance class, and ate healthy food."

As the Christmas season approached, the chestnut trees that line the Champs-Élysées were decorated with strands of delicate white lights, while the windows of the stores along the grand avenue were surrounded by garlands and glittering displays. In the Parc Monceau, a layer of fine powdered snow covered the grass, and several of the pine trees had been decorated by Madonna along with others from the neighborhood, who actually put empty gift-wrapped packages underneath in the spirit of the season. Parisians know how to celebrate Christmas, and even for those who don't recognize it as a religious holiday, it is an occasion for families and friends to get together for a classic gourmet meal. Madonna was homesick. It wasn't a yearning to be back in New York as much as it was a desire to see her family to spend the holidays with them in Michigan. On the night before Christmas Eve, in another gesture of warmth and friendship, Muriel and Jean Van Lieu invited Madonna along with Patrick Hernandez and the Pellerins to dinner at Fauchon's, a chic Paris restaurant that was as famous for its clientele as it was for its take-out dishes. Madonna seemed sullen and uncomfortable. People came over to Patrick to ask for his autograph, while the maître d'hôtel sent over a complimentary bottle of champagne. Typical of festive dinners during the Christmas season in Paris, the group discussed and dissected the menu and took what seemed to Madonna an eternity before choices were made. Suddenly, just as the first course was being served, Madonna jumped up from the table. "If this is a career, it doesn't interest me. All you do is talk and eat, and I don't like to eat, I have to pay attention to my health and my figure, and you stay out all night, and I don't like that either. Frankly, I'm better off back in New York scrounging around for a meal instead of tasting gastronomic delicacies in Paris or Brussels." And with that, she took a taxi and went back to the apartment.

When the others returned home, she was perfectly calm. She wanted to spend Christmas with her family. Would they give her a round-trip ticket? That way, they would be assured that she would come back to Paris after the holidays. "The truth was that we all felt it was better for Madonna to leave," Muriel Van Lieu admits. "We had been discussing the idea of telling her to go home because we knew that Jean was too involved with Patrick to give her the kind of attention she deserved. Our intention was that when he was free to focus on Madonna, we would contact her in New York and get her back over to Paris."

Madonna took nothing with her when she left France except her diary and the clothes on her back. Whatever the Pellerins and the Van Lieus had bought her while she was there she left in a small valise in her room.

All contact with Madonna ceased after she left Paris and returned to the United States, supposedly just for Christmas, but as it turned out, forever. Even Patrick Hernandez never heard from her again. "People who met her after she was famous, in New York or London, who knew me," Hernandez says, "always mentioned me, and Madonna always sent her best but nothing else."

In 1991, when Madonna was in France on tour, she was invited to be on TF-1, the privately owned television station, to do a talk show to promote the show. The producers suggested that Patrick Hernandez appear on the show as well, not only to sing his hit, "Born to Be Alive," but to evoke memories about Madonna during the time she lived with him in Paris. Word came back to Hernandez that Madonna refused to appear with him.

"In other words," Hernandez says, "at the time, she considered that she didn't need the image of Patrick Hernandez with her. When she finally made it, she was determined to give the impression that her style of music was hers alone, and she didn't particularly want anyone comparing her to me or to anyone else, and certainly she didn't want anyone saying that she was derivative of so-and-so. . . . Then, there is the other possibility that she had no respect for me because, unlike her, I wasn't that ambitious to keep plugging away to have successive number one hits. I think she considered me to be a has-been perhaps. Or maybe she resented me because I was the one who forced her to sing disco music, something she resisted when she was with me in Paris and what she eventually did and got famous for afterwards in New York. What surprised me years later when she was already a star was that she was singing songs exactly like the ones I wanted her to do, the ones that she had vehemently refused to do, which were disco dance music. Her videos and stage shows are much more variety shows than straight videos, and I believe she learned that from me. Anyway, I found that very sad since I'm a sensitive guy, and things like that deeply disturb me, when people forget friendship and loyalty and aren't generous. If she wanted to see me far from the cameras, it would take her about fifteen seconds to get my telephone number here in France. She could have called."

Several months after she left Paris, Madonna mailed a cassette of her first recorded song to Jean and Muriel Van Lieu, who responded instantly. "Fabulous," they wrote, "really great! Go for it!" According to Muriel Van Lieu, her husband had always told her, after Madonna became famous, that he wasn't certain that he could have achieved for her what she did on her own in the United States.

chapter twenty-two

·····················

When Madonna returned from Paris in December 1980, she went directly to her father's house in Rochester Hills, Michigan, to celebrate Christmas. Nothing had changed when it came to the cool reception she got from her stepmother and the berating from her father, who was still angry at her for abandoning her studies. There were changes, however, subtle differences that made Madonna realize that she no longer belonged in the house from which she had been plotting her escape since childhood. Her siblings seemed to keep a wary distance, almost as if they had been warned not to get too close, as if rebellion were a contagious disease.

During the brief visit, Madonna was aware of the coded language the family used, expressions that perhaps she once understood and even spoke when she lived with them under one roof. Now she felt like an intruder, the orphaned child that she had come to believe she had been since her mother died. After two days, she announced that she was going to visit her grandmother in Bay City before returning to New York. The usual perfunctory promises were made to keep in touch. Though everyone hugged and kissed and expressed their sorrow at seeing her leaving, Madonna felt that it was a relief not only for her but for everyone else that she didn't stay as long as planned.

Elsie Fortin hadn't seen her favorite granddaughter for more than two years, since she had left Ann Arbor for New York and Paris. If anyone gave Madonna the feeling that she believed in her, it was Mrs. Fortin. Describing Paris to the woman who had never been farther east than Detroit delighted Madonna, and she embellished the characteristics of the French, imitating their accent when they spoke English, mocking them for the way they took their gastronomical delicacies so seriously.

"Madonna hadn't changed at all," Elsie Fortin said. "She was the same Madonna, full of life and fun except that she seemed thinner and more fragile physically, as if she wasn't getting enough to eat." There was no doubt in her mind that Madonna had the same determination to succeed, and although she was convinced that she would, she detected a sense of loneliness in her granddaughter that she had never seen before.

"She made me laugh when she talked about the French," she says, "but then she said how difficult it was for her to be in a strange country without knowing the language or having any friends. I think she felt cut off from the rest of the world, because she couldn't even pick up the phone to call people."

As Madonna prepared to leave for the airport, Elsie Fortin, aware that Madonna's father had made a point not to give her anything unless she went back to school, offered to give her some money. Madonna refused. "Before she left, I just slipped fifty dollars into her pocket without telling her," Mrs. Fortin says.

Madonna returned to New York before the New Year and, unannounced, went directly to the abandoned synagogue in Queens where Dan and Ed Gilroy lived. When Dan opened the door and saw Madonna standing there, without any bags, holding only a piece of mistletoe over her head, he took her in his arms and kissed her. Her hair was dark and cut short in a gamine style, and she was thin, but other than that, she was the same direct young woman who had left him so abruptly nearly six months before. Before she even took off her denim jacket, she made it clear that she wanted things to be the way they had been when they were lovers and collaborators. She was back for good, and she expected to live with him, at least for a while, until she could learn enough to go out on her own. Admittedly, Dan was pleased to see her, although he knew that her presence presented a problem for his brother, Ed, who thought she would distract Dan and the others in the band. Out of loyalty, and because he still had feelings for Madonna, Dan persuaded his brother to let her stay with them, and to give her a chance to practice the drums and guitar while they were at work during the day, waiting tables. The only promise that Ed Gilroy extracted in return was that he wouldn't let her join the band unless all the members agreed. The arrangement didn't last long.

While Madonna was practicing her music, she was also writing songs. "When I got back to New York, for a year I locked myself away in Dan's studio and taught myself to play drums, guitar, and piano so that I had enough knowledge to write music. And then the songs just started coming like crazy. I didn't want to go in a rock vein back then, which was what ultimately caused the schism between my manager back then [Camille Barbone] and myself. I was really being influenced by the urban radio stuff that was starting to be everywhere, on the streets and in the clubs. I loved to dance in clubs, and I loved all the music they played. It made me really want to dance, because it was so soulful. I thought, why can't I do that? I wanted to make music I would want to dance to when I was out at the clubs."

Along with writing and practicing her music, often at night, when Dan and Ed Gilroy were either sleeping or rehearsing with their band, Madonna went out. Taking the subway into Manhattan, she discovered the downtown club scene. "Up until then," Madonna admits, "I had no idea that downtown even existed." At the time, in 1981, the Latinos who hung around the dance clubs like Danceteria or My Father's Place had a style of their own, which Madonna promptly appropriated as her own. She wore studded bracelets all the way up her arms, Adidas sneakers with different-colored laces, nylon tracksuits in iridescent pinks, greens, and yellows, and leather caps. The trend was also to have a made-up moniker on a belt buckle that served as a calling card. Madonna came up with the name Boy Toy, which has often been misinterpreted to mean that she was the boy toy or the toy that boys played with. In reality, Madonna chose that name to describe how she toyed with men or picked up boys, using them before she discarded them. "Eventually, I invented my own style, which was a combination of the dance ragamuffin and the Puerto Rican street style," Madonna recalls.

It came as no surprise to the Gilroy brothers that Madonna finally launched a one-woman offensive to persuade them to let her join their band. While both brothers realized she had a talent for composing songs, as long as one of them could translate her tunes into real musical notes, and a natural ability to write lyrics that were touching and catchy, and while they admitted that she had become quite proficient on the drums, they were reluctant to include her because of her penchant for taking over and her need to be in control. Eventually, Dan Gilroy convinced his brother to give her a chance. He agreed, and before long, Madonna became the force behind the group, the member who pushed them to rehearse all night and often into the early-morning hours, the one who mocked them when they pleaded exhaustion and wanted to take a break. Appropriately, the band was named the Breakfast Club since everyone usually ended up having breakfast in a local diner after all-night sessions. Acting as the principal singer and drummer, Madonna also became the band's manager. Her perseverance and ability to convince club owners to give them a chance resulted in work for the band on the Lower East Side at such nightspots as UK, My Father's Place, and Botany Talk House. Not surprisingly, the audiences noticed Madonna, who would regularly get up from her seat behind the drums to take the microphone and belt out the songs at the front of the stage. To the dismay of the others, eventually people considered the Breakfast Club to be nothing more than her backup group.

Madonna kept pushing the band to demand more money and better working conditions, and she would often spend her days phoning management agencies and club owners at random to try to get dates and representation. As Norris Burroughs remarked at the time, Dan and Ed Gilroy were "laidback and in no particular rush to become stars." Burroughs says, "They had their own sense of reality when it came to their talent, and they believed they were pretty aware of all the obstacles and competition they'd be facing if they tried to take that extra step forward. Madonna was in a hurry, because she was so sure that she had as much or more than the singers who were doing much better than Dan's group."

Madonna finally realized that the group not only didn't appreciate her aggressive efforts to get proper management but actually resented her for the way she drove them to rehearse. The time had come for her to move on, and she told Dan exactly that without rancor or excuses. She simply felt that she could accomplish more on her own by forming her own band rather than wasting her time and energy trying to convince the Breakfast Club that they were stuck in a rut of their own making. According to Dan Gilroy, who was upset at the time that she was abandoning them to start her own group, he admitted that Madonna was a "demanding collaborator." "There is no one who has worked with her who doesn't agree that she has limitless energy and stamina and little tolerance for musicians, directors, crew, or other performers who insist upon taking the usual breaks. She was absolutely single-minded in her goal, and it was nothing personal against any of us."

Through contacts and new friends she had made in the downtown clubs, Madonna returned to live on the Lower East Side, moving from one abandoned loft to another or borrowing a studio for a night before picking up all her possessions and sleeping at a friend's apartment while he or she was out of town.

Eventually, through aspiring musicians that she had met on the club circuit, Madonna joined up with a drummer,

Mike Monahan, and a bass guitarist, Gary Burke, to form her own band, which she named the Millionaires. Several weeks later, she changed the name to Emanon, or No Name spelled backward, until she finally settled on Emmy, a nickname that would stay with her for the next few years. Her new group also played in abysmal conditions in dreary basement rooms in tenements, not much different from the engagements she had had with Dan Gilroy, and never earned enough to live on. They seemed to be everywhere, and even when they weren't performing, Madonna would be in the middle of things, talking up prospective agents and managers and pitching club owners to give them a chance. Before long Emmy had gathered a limited fan base that would follow them from club to club. Things might have continued like that if Mike Monahan, the drummer, hadn't announced that he was leaving the group to get married. He needed to think about his future, which meant that he had to get a job that would allow him to support himself and a family.

Whether she was born under a lucky star or somewhere in the back of her mind had been planning the change all along, several days before Monahan quit, Madonna called her former boyfriend from the University of Michigan, Steve Bray, in an attempt to keep in touch and to find out how he was doing. To her surprise and delight, he told her that he was tired of playing in small restaurants in Ann Arbor and was thinking about coming to New York. Her response was immediate: "Get your ass here tomorrow because you've got yourself a job as the drummer in my band!"

Within days, Madonna and Steve Bray had resumed their relationship. They were not only working together but living together in an abandoned music studio in the Music Building, a run-down structure on Eighth Avenue and Thirty-eighth Street, where the walls were painted an industrial gray and decorated with album covers in cheap wood frames. The building had eight floors of loft space and was home to several less prestigious recording studios and music managers as well as other down-and-out musicians who lived illegally in hallways and abandoned offices. Though Madonna's life in that Parisian bourgeois apartment near Parc Monceau was a distant memory, Patrick Hernandez's influence was very present.

Determined to make music that people could dance to, she listened to artists like Garry Puckett, Bobby Sherman, and the Turtles until she found what she considered to be her perfect sound. Scrounging around to get the money they needed to make a demo tape of a song that Madonna had written along with Bray for Emmy with Bray also on the drums, they finally got the recording made.

Carrying the tape, she went to the Danceteria at 31 West Twenty-first Street and persuaded Mark Kamins, one of the disc jockeys, to play it repeatedly one night. The crowd went wild. As inexperienced and naive as Madonna was, she instinctively knew how to use subliminal suggestion and even a variation of the Pavlovian theory of conditioning when it came to promoting herself and her music. While the music blasted over the speakers, Madonna danced alone in the middle of the club, moving suggestively to the beat and the sound of her own voice. Not only did she attract attention, but she also made sure that the crowd would identify the music with her uninhibited dance style. Before long, people were requesting the record and even imitating the way she danced.

After all these years without a word from the young girl he had taken to Paris to make her a star, and because her style is so similar to that of Patrick Hernandez, it is to his credit that he is not at all bitter. "I find my reaction interesting," Hernandez muses so long after the fact, "when people tell me how lucky I was to have known Madonna, what an extraordinary chance I had to be with her before she became Madonna. Usually, I look at them and think to myself that I honestly don't consider myself lucky at all. When I knew her, there were certain aspects of her character that were very childish. When she wanted something, she would act capricious or falsely tender to get her own way, like a little girl does with her father."

Adam Alter would say the same thing about Madonna when he recalled her behavior at the time he was supporting her in New York. Back then, Madonna's sense of entitlement ran deeper than her belief that, as a motherless child, the world and God owed her recompense.

When Alter, a self-described "sheep among the wolves" and the head of Gotham Music, the man who had groomed her for stardom, supported her, and fed her, faced financial demise after she left, she shrugged off the blame and chalked it up to choice. "He believed in me," she said, "and he was right. He just wasn't willing to go the limit."

When Camille Barbone, Alter's partner, who had nurtured Madonna during those early days, acting as mommy and manager, got her priorities mixed up and let her personal feelings override her professional duties, the singer made it clear that there was a time to play and a time to work.

chapter twenty-three
....

*A*dam Alter lives in a small, cluttered apartment in a quaint three-story, wood-frame private house in Cornwall, New York, with a parrot and two small dogs. The atmosphere in the three large rooms is similar to that of a graduate student's apartment in which every surface is covered with papers, unopened mail, textbooks, and notepads, while unwashed dishes are piled in the kitchen sink and clothes are strewn on the living-room sofas. The furniture in the apartment is heavy mahogany, vintage 1950s thrift shop or heirlooms that have been taken out of a family garage or attic to fill up a house in which the owner seems to be in transition. Alter, who is forty-nine and bears a striking resemblance to John Malkovich, is currently working in the Westchester County court system in the foster-care section while completing a master's degree at Hunter College in Manhattan.

Adam Alter met Camille Barbone in 1975 when he was twenty-three and she was twenty-six. At the time, he had a truck route and was selling alfalfa sprouts to health food stores throughout the New York City area, not exactly a profession that gave him hard life lessons to go out into the world of rock and roll. Still dressed in army fatigues with his hair pulled back in a ponytail, Alter resembles the "nature boy" that he claims he was when he decided to go into the music business. "I learned about horticulture," Alter says, "because it interested me. At the time I lived at Fourteenth and Third Avenue and felt really like a nature boy trapped in Manhattan."

Adam Alter grew up in the music business. His father, Lewis Alter, was a jazz and popular instrumentalist and composer who wrote, among many other hits, the well-known instrumental "Side Street and Gotham," which was the inspiration for the name that Adam Alter chose for his company, Gotham Music. In his childhood, his family lived in Manhattan, on Riverside Drive, Central Park West, and eventually on Park Avenue, where Henny Youngman and Milton Berle were considered part of the family and even taught Adam how to play pool.

"My childhood could be described as privileged, I guess," Alter says. "My mother was an opera singer, and she had a lot of good times until I was born and then my sister came along, who is a dwarf. We were very stressful on her and she suffered for fifteen years from terminal cancer, so things weren't what you'd call ideal."

Looking back to the exact moment when he first got interested in the music business, Alter admits that it was naturally due to the atmosphere around his house. But he also got involved in the underside of the business through a manager and friend named Keith Allen, who introduced Alter to Camille Barbone.

"When I met Camille," Alter explains, "I was very naive, especially about business. Camille came in with some experience because she had worked at CBS Records, so she felt very sure of herself and high-and-mighty. And me, not having any experience on my own other than my parents and what they had shared with me, I took her word as something like gospel."

It was a bad moment for Adam Alter to consider going into the music business. In 1980 and 1981, the business, which had revolved around rock and roll, hit bottom. People were not investing, mainly because the earnings were not good, and because they sensed a new wave was coming

and that the music would be drastically shifting and changing directions, although no one could really predict what
the new sound would be. Barbone told Alter that before she
could commit to any partnership with him, she needed to
borrow several thousand dollars to get her out of a previous
arrangement she had made with someone else. If Alter was
hesitant about joining up with Barbone, he quickly
changed his mind when she produced the Rolling Stones'
rhythm guitarist, Keith Richards, as a friend and someone
who knew her when she had worked with the group at CBS.

"I gave Camille the money to bail her out of that other
partnership deal and we formed Gotham Music," Alter recalls. Working against incredible odds, with little financial
backing and surrounded by people who were heavily into
drugs, Alter regrets that he didn't pay more attention to his
father's warnings. "At the time," he says, "my father saw
that, and I see now what he saw back then."

Gotham Music took offices in the Music Building, and
there, waiting for the elevator one morning, Adam Alter met
Madonna. Furiously cracking gum, she was dressed in her
usual outfit of torn jeans and a midriff blouse, her hair
sleeked back in a boyish bob, her big green-blue eyes taunting and amused as she approached him.

"I was wearing my John Lennon glasses," he recalls,
"these small, round shades, and she struck up a conversation, telling me how cool my glasses were and how I looked
just like John Lennon." It took only minutes more for
Madonna to explain that she was camping out in one of the
abandoned studios and was looking around for a manager
who would be willing to let her use his studio to rehearse
and to listen to a demo tape that she had made.

"She was very young and very, very seductive, and she
asked me if I knew anyone who could help her make music.
I didn't hesitate for an instant. I told her that maybe I could
help her, or my partner, and I took her right upstairs, which
was basically just one flight up, to meet Camille." With
Madonna in tow, Adam walked into the office and was

about to introduce the two women when Camille and
Madonna, at the same moment, started laughing. "Apparently, Camille had already met her in the lobby and probably just thought she was another 'tobacco row' squatter,
because she had ignored her pleas to help her meet someone
in the music business."

Madonna played her one demo tape for Alter and Barbone, and immediately both knew that there was something special about this young girl. "We both had a good
ear for music," Alter says, "but our ability to convince the
industry about Madonna was our weak point and would
turn out to be our downfall. At that point, with the music
business in such bad shape, we just couldn't do it. The industry just locked up. Two years later, the industry was
shopping, buying, and picking up everyone around and
signing them up."

Years later, Adam Alter still believes that Madonna could
have been their major shot to make their business succeed.
"I don't know if I looked at it that Madonna would stay with
us forever," Alter admits, "but I believed she was our
stepping-stone, and I saw that in her immediately."

When Alter and Barbone formed their partnership, it was
understood that Alter would finance the company. "At the
time," he says, "I was the man who paid the rent, all the expenses, as well as Camille's salary." After they signed
Madonna up as their first client, Alter began paying all of
Madonna's expenses as well, including her rent, food,
pocket money, dental bills, as well as giving her free studio
time during which she could practice on the company synthesizer and the Rhodes piano, which he had brought from
home. Eventually, after Gotham Music went bankrupt, Alter
donated the piano and all the other equipment in the studio
to Staten Island College.

For the two years that Adam Alter was paying the bills,
Barbone was engineering Madonna's career to the exclusion
of any other client they managed to get as well as ignoring
the business. For most of that time, Madonna followed Bar-

bone's advice and created music that was light rock. "Her voice was possibly the least special thing about her," Alter recalls, "although for some reason, she sounded better when we had her. It was her writing ability, her enthusiasm, her zest for working, that was responsible for her stardom. From a strictly professional point of view, she had tremendous drive. She was unwilling to take no for an answer, and if you do something and do it well and keep on doing it, you can't fail."

According to Adam Alter, the problem was that Camille Barbone was not only enchanted by Madonna, but physically attracted to her as well.

Adam Alter believes that Barbone took her professional relationship with their client Madonna to the "brink of impropriety." Alter says, "I don't know if they actually had an affair, but it was close." He himself had an "intense relationship" with both women. "My relationship with Madonna and Camille was brief and chaotic, and in a sense we were like a family. I was like an orphan and Camille felt like an orphan, and Madonna was all alone in a strange city," Alter explains. "We were like a family and spent a lot of time together. We argued. We made up. It was only a year, but it was fast and furious and a lot happened during that time."

In one incident between Madonna and Barbone, the singer made it clear that her rejection had nothing to do with her sexual tastes and everything to do with her freedom. On the way back from a downtown club, Madonna necked in the backseat of Barbone's car with a girlfriend, while the distraught manager was at the wheel, looking in the rearview mirror and cursing her soon-to-be ex-client. According to Barbone, often before Madonna or the girlfriend would go to bed with a man, they would put him to a test. Kissing each other in front of him, they would watch his reaction. If he got flustered or embarrassed, they would leave him. If he seemed open to their relationship, they would give him their seal of approval.

According to Alter, Madonna was flirtatious by nature and always in need of something, either money or free studio time to practice or just someone to comfort her when she felt alone. Although Adam Alter insists that he drew "strict boundaries" with Madonna, Barbone had a penchant for mixing up her personal and professional relationships. "Camille wound up taking an apartment with another client we had," Alter says, "a lady who went to Sarah Lawrence with my ex-wife and who was a very talented keyboard player and songwriter and a much more genuine person than Madonna. Camille had no scruples or ethics about mixing business with pleasure. Eventually that client wanted to sever the personal aspect of their relationship, because it was getting too strained and incestuous." For a brief time Alter and Barbone moved in together after he lent his studio apartment on the Lower East Side to the client, in an effort to keep her and to help her to distance herself from Barbone. "Camille and I just decided we were sick of the city, so we rented a four-story Victorian house on the water in Bayside, Queens, where we each had our own floor. We had a car and we drove in every morning and back out every evening."

Camille Barbone has a different interpretation of events, especially concerning any impropriety that occurred between her and their client. "Is Madonna a lesbian?" she asks rhetorically. "I wouldn't exactly say so. What I will say is that Madonna loves beautiful women, and she is into anyone sexually who she thinks is beautiful."

According to Barbone, for the year and a half that they were together, she functioned not only as a manager and mentor but also as a mother figure. "She confided in me and revealed some of her most intimate hopes and fears, and I even arranged for her to get birth control," Barbone maintains.

Barbone insists that if anyone was the seducer in the relationship, it was Madonna: "She used to taunt me by flaunting her body. She sweats profusely while she's performing, and when she did a show, she used to rip off her clothes and throw me a towel to dry her off."

In August 1981, while Madonna was waiting for her big break in the music business, Camille Barbone suggested that she meet a friend of hers from Queens. Steve Lewicki, a graduate student at the film school at New York University, was making a Godard-type movie that he described as "primitive and fluid," and that its detractors would eventually label pornographic. With a budget of only $20,000 to make the film, Lewicki put an ad in *Back Stage,* describing the woman he wanted as his star for the movie he would call *A Certain Sacrifice:* "a dark, fiery young woman, dominant, with lots of energy, who can dance and is willing to work for no pay." Barbone showed Madonna the ad and suggested that she answer it immediately. Lewicki had already gotten more than three hundred replies from young, would-be actresses, who were willing to work for nothing, when Camille Barbone delivered a three-page letter herself to his office. Madonna had written it in longhand.

"Dear Stephen," the letter began, "I was born and raised in Detroit, Michigan, where I began my career in petulance and precociousness. By the time I was in the fifth grade, I knew I either wanted to be a nun or a movie star. Nine months in a convent cured me of the first disease. During high school I became slightly schizophrenic as I couldn't choose between class virgin or the other kind. Both of them had their values as far as I could see . . ." Signed, "Madonna Ciccone."

Camille Barbone didn't wait around to find out what Lewicki thought. After he read the letter and studied the photograph, he knew without any doubt that Miss Ciccone was perfect for the role. *A Certain Sacrifice* is the story of a young woman named Bruna, who, not unlike Susan in *Des-*

perately Seeking Susan, is a vagabond, street-smart New Yorker. But any similarity between the two characters that Madonna plays ends there. Bruna, a girl with a healthy sexual appetite, lives with three sex slaves, whom she agrees to give up only when she falls in love with the perfect man. Eventually, Bruna's Prince Charming appears, but just as she is about to embark on a new life, she is raped and enlists the help of her three ex–sex slaves to avenge her rape. They agree and track down the rapist, kill him, and drink his blood. Key scenes in the film include a dance orgy with her lovers, her rape in a coffee-shop rest room, and the ritual sacrifice of the rapist.

The film was shot from September 1980 through June 1981. On September 20, 1980, in the middle of production, Madonna signed a release authorizing commercial depiction of her performance at the same time that Lewicki agreed to give her $100 to pay her rent. Several years later, when Madonna was just beginning to be successful with her singing career, she tried to stop Lewicki from selling the film. Madonna's lawyer Paul Schindler accused Lewicki of trying to capitalize on his good luck at having captured Madonna on film while she was an unknown. In an affidavit in which Madonna also sought unspecified punitive and compensatory damages from Stephen Lewicki, she stated, "While I have consented to the use of my voice and pictures of my physical likeness from the movie, I did not consent to the use of my name." Justice Ethel Danzig heard the case and assigned a show-cause order that required Lewicki to show why he should not be barred from distributing the film with Madonna's name attached. In response, Lewicki claimed that the movie was not pornography and Madonna's current image was hardly "saintly." He described the film as "new wave, Lower East Side, postpunk," and insisted that it was "definitely not porn . . . but sexy." In the end, Paul Schindler conceded that any effort to prevent Mr. Lewicki's exploitation of the film could result in publicity that would give it black-market value—which is exactly what happened. In the end, Lewicki released the film on videocassette for $49.95.

By the time A Certain Sacrifice *was finished*, Gotham Music was in financial trouble, and the relationships between Alter and Barbone, and Barbone and Madonna, were also having problems. One of the last times that the two women were together was on August 16, 1981, which was Camille Barbone's thirty-second birthday, and Madonna's twenty-third.

Packing a lobster picnic supper, Camille invited Madonna to a Long Island beach near New York City to celebrate.

"It was a beautiful sunset and we walked along the beach and talked. We were more physically affectionate than we had ever been. I kept telling her what a big star she was going to be, and at that moment, we both felt as if we could do anything. There were no limits." According to Barbone, at one point, Madonna threw her arms around her neck and hugged her for a long time before she said, "Thank you. I love you."

"I told her I've never put anyone before me," Barbone concludes, "She lives before I do, she breathes before I breathe. We drove back to New York hugging."

Despite Madonna's relationships with both men and women, her sexuality remains a matter of speculation. There have been rumors about affairs with such well-known women as Sandra Bernhard and Ingrid Casares. In the case of Casares, Madonna fueled those rumors when she and the nightclub owner briefly lived together in Castille del Largo, Madonna's Hollywood home that once belonged to Bugsy Siegel, the founder of modern Las Vegas. At the time that the affair with Casares was purported to have taken place, in 1990, Madonna had just broken up with a male lover, Tony Ward, and had gone through an abortion. Just as she had done with previous lovers, as a token of her esteem, Madonna featured Ward in her video "Justify My Love," as the erotic object of her affections.

Equally ambiguous was Madonna's relationship with the openly gay comedian Sandra Bernhard, which was made public when the two women appeared on David Letterman's show. The late-night television host held up a magazine article that claimed that the two women's relationship was more than just platonic. "Is there any truth to this nonsense?" Letterman asked. Bernhard answered, "We party, we drink tequila. We get to know each other a little better." Letterman then asked how the couple spent their time, and if he could be a part of it. "Only if you get a sex change," Madonna replied. Bernhard added, "We meet up with Jennifer Grey [the star of *Dirty Dancing*], and sometimes it's just the two of us. You can usually find us at the Canal Bar or at MK." If the audience didn't understand the reference, Letterman explained that these were two gay nightclubs in downtown Manhattan. And, if the audience still didn't get it, Madonna added, "Or at the Cubby—" "Hole," Bernhard interrupted, referring to the city's best-known lesbian bar.

Then, the banter became even more specific as Madonna announced, "She doesn't give a damn about me. She's using me to get to Sean."

"I slept with Sean Penn," Bernhard suddenly confessed, referring to Madonna's estranged husband, "and Madonna is better in bed!"

Madonna has never discussed her less spectacular lesbian relationships that occurred in high school, college, and during those early days in New York. If anything, she always rejected any notion that she was either homosexual or bisexual. As she told Kathy, her high school lover, when she quoted Truman Capote, "A person is either sexed or not . . ."

It is perhaps more logical to assume that loving women, for Madonna, was just taking the loss of her mother to another level. When Carrie Fisher interviewed Madonna on two occasions for *Rolling Stone,* published in the June 13 and June 27, 1991, issues of the magazine, they discussed many subjects, including the loss of her mother. Fisher asked Madonna, "What's your mother complex?" to which Madonna replied, "That I don't have one, so I'm always looking for someone to fill up my hole—no pun intended."

chapter twenty-four

•••••••••••••••••

When the partnership ended, Alter was angrier at Camille than he was at Madonna for allowing her personal feelings to break up their potentially lifelong friendship. "Camille let the allure of Madonna completely blind her to anything else around her that may have had some real value, like friendship. She should have been stronger with Madonna, but apparently she couldn't be. Her feelings for her made her keep pushing me to give her more and more money. Eventually, Madonna walked out because I refused to go bankrupt, and Camille couldn't support Madonna without me. I was the Daddy Warbucks of the group."

When Alter refused to go further into debt to keep funding Gotham Music and supporting their future star, Madonna threatened to leave Camille. "Camille didn't level with me about what she had promised Madonna, which was the reason why she walked out on us. She counted on Camille's guarantees based on what she imagined I had already agreed to. I didn't know the extent of those financial promises."

As the relationship between Madonna and Camille Barbone had gradually become more intimate, Alter felt that his star client never really took the time to get to know him. "I was basically the man with the money," Alter says, "and it was Camille who engineered a lot of that. When she needed some cash, she'd go to Mommy Camille, and Camille would tell her to ask her daddy. And then she'd come to me, very shy and very coy. 'Adam, can I have a little money?' In addition to paying all her bills and giving her fifty dollars a week spending money, she had free run of the studio every day. We never charged her for studio time. So when she needed more money, I'd naturally ask her why and for what, which I suppose made me a kind of daddy. The way I saw it, Camille was the good cop, and I was the bad cop. Basically, Camille was ungracious about everything I did to help her and Madonna. Camille was manipulative and kept Madonna away from me, because she knew that eventually Madonna would break away from me. She really thought that if she created this chasm between us, Madonna would eventually break away and go off with her. Of course, she was wrong."

At one point, shortly before the final rupture, Adam Alter got Madonna a job performing at The Underground, and the response was so overwhelmingly positive, he decided to introduce her to his parents. "We called her Brat or Emmy, and I told my father about her and how she was so completely narcissistic," Alter says. "My father was reassuring because he told me that if you want to be a star, you have to be narcissistic, it was a form of star quality. You had to have a very evident passion for what you do, something that really shines, comes out of you, an energy, so that whatever you do, you'll succeed. There was no doubt that Madonna had that quality."

The meeting took place at the Alter family Park Avenue apartment. Lewis Alter was charmed by his son's young discovery. In return, Madonna was equally impressed by Lewis, a man she was fascinated to learn was a legend in the world of jazz. Several months later, Madonna's father, stepmother, and sister Paula came to New York, and she introduced her family to Adam Alter and Camille Barbone. "She was like a little kid," Alter recalls, "let's do this, let's go here. She was really proud to be able to show her parents that, finally, she had people who believed in her. I remember that they were a very lovely, quaint couple, at least that was my impression. I also remember her sister Paula, who looked a lot like Madonna except she was taller. She struck me as the sister who wanted to be Madonna. She was very interested in auditioning and wanted to know if we were willing to listen to her sing."

By 1982, Gotham Music was bankrupt. Nothing of any value was left except for the furnishings and equipment. "Whatever the studio earned," Alter maintains, "went to supporting Madonna when she should have been helping to support the studio. My problem was that I cared for her like a father. When she needed dental work, I sent her to my dentist and ended up paying the bills. Even years later, when she had money, she made no attempt to pay me back."

More discouraging for both Alter and Barbone was that Madonna, along with Steve Bray, who was still living with her, decided that they did not want to continue singing songs that they described as "pop rock," the type of music that Barbone had insisted that they focus on. "We were on the verge of getting Madonna a record deal with Warner Brothers," Alter explains, "when suddenly money got scarce and they dropped out." According to Alter, he still has one of Madonna's first master tapes, which was never released. "That was the one we thought was good enough to shop," Alter says, "and we would have had a record deal if a man we were dealing with at the time hadn't decided to snort the deal away up his nose."

Leaving emotion and gratitude at the door, Madonna confronted Camille Barbone in the studio and announced that she was no longer interested in continuing the association. Rather than alluding to the reality that there was no more money left in the coffers to support her, she told Barbone that she and Steve Bray had decided that what worked for them was a harder kind of music. In a fit of rage and frustration, Barbone put her fist through the wall.

Immediately following Madonna's departure and the dissolution of Gotham Music, Adam Alter dislocated his knee in a karate accident. A friend of his moved all Adam's equipment from the Gotham space into a smaller studio in the building. While Alter was at home recovering, the friend called to say that Madonna needed some studio time and would he allow her to use it for a while until she got settled. Alter agreed. By the time that he was back on his feet and had returned to the studio, he found that Camille Barbone had stripped it of everything that had anything to do with Madonna. "When you're surrounded by perverts and sleaze," Alter says, "a lot of people become innocent victims. It happened to me when all that craziness was just heaped on me and I didn't know what to do with it." He smiles. "So, that's the reason why I'm working for foster care up in Westchester. I'm trying to salvage the people who are victims. My battle now is the have-nots against the haves."

Those people who expect loyalty are usually prepared to give it. One observer says of Madonna that "if you cross her once, you might as well have never existed as far as she is concerned." Adam Alter wonders about the reverse situation. "She's an opportunist," he says. "What happens to all those people that she crossed on her way to stardom?"

Within days after firing Camille Barbone and Adam Alter, Madonna went back to the Danceteria to see her friend Mark Kamins. She quickly told him the story of her rupture with Gotham Music and asked him to listen to another demo record she had made. Kamins was not only considered the best of the "New Wave DJs," but he also did some scouting for Island Records and had just signed up an obscure Irish rock group called U2. After taking the demo to Island Records, who turned it down, Kamins went directly to Warner Brothers, where he had recently finished work on the new David Byrne album. Through his success with Byrne, he had become friendly with Michael Rosenblatt, who was in charge of an offshoot label at Warner's called Sire. Inviting Rosenblatt to stop by the Danceteria to listen to Madonna's record and to meet the singer, Kamins predicted that he wouldn't have to convince Rosenblatt to do anything more. Rosenblatt invited Kamins and Madonna to his office at Warner Brothers headquarters at Rockefeller Center and played the first song on her tape, "Everybody," before listening to the other three. According to Rosenblatt, the recording was good but nothing spectacular. What kept his interest, however, was Madonna. "She radiated something I had never seen before," he said. "I knew that she was a star!"

They drew up the contract right there. Madonna would receive an initial advance of $5,000 plus royalties and publishing fees of $1,000 for each song that she wrote. But the deal couldn't be signed until Rosenblatt got permission from the president of Sire Records, Seymour Stein, who was in Lenox Hill Hospital recovering from a double bypass. The next day, Rosenblatt, Kamins, and Madonna piled into a taxi and headed for the hospital, where they met Stein in his underwear with an intravenous drip attached to his arm.

Madonna's only problem was that she had promised Steve Bray that he could produce her records, and now she found herself indebted to Mark Kamins, who had every intention of functioning as the producer. In an effort to compromise with Bray but not lose the deal with Sire, Madonna offered him the job of arranger. Bray refused and didn't speak to Madonna for several years.

Sire Records decided to put out Madonna's first single with "Ain't No Big Deal" on the B side and "Everybody" on the A side. When the people at Sire didn't like "Ain't No Big Deal," at the last minute, they made the unheard-of decision to put "Everybody" on both sides of the record, which catapulted the song to the top of the dance charts.

After the success of her first record, Madonna was asked by several journalists if she had used men to get "to the top." "Every one of those men that I supposedly stepped on to get to the top," Madonna answered, "would take me back, because they still love me and I still love them."

It is debatable whether Steve Bray, Mark Kamins, Dan

Gilroy, Adam Alter, or anyone else during those early days would "take Madonna back" because they still "loved her." What is clear is that after the release of "Everybody," immediately followed by "Physical Attraction," Madonna already had another record producer. Reggie Lucas not only produced that second hit, but he also wrote it. After that, Sire Records gave Madonna their support and approval for an album. "Reggie Lucas only knew R&B," Madonna explained, "and he's a good producer, very open and sensitive, but Nile [Rodgers] has worked with so many kinds of musicians, and every record he's made is a great one as far as I'm concerned. He has the pop thing in him really strong, and he's done great dance stuff with Chic and Sister Sledge and all those others, and he's worked with a lot of female vocalists like Diana Ross. I identified with him, too. He's a real street person, and we hung out at the same clubs. Even before I started to interview producers, I thought he was the one I wanted for that second record."

The feelings were apparently mutual. "In my opinion," Nile Rodgers said, "Madonna is an excellent natural singer, a natural musician, a serious artist. It would be real nice if some ostensibly smart people who know about music would get past her image and get into the music. I'm hoping she can just ride out all the crap people are saying about her. I think a lot of the real nasty stuff is coming from men. And all that arrogance bit—she sticks to her guns, that's all."

In the beginning, Madonna's problem was to convince the executives at her record company to take her seriously as a businesswoman and to realize that she was worth their time as a singer. "I think people are intimidated by women who are incredibly ambitious or competitive, because it's easier to deal with girls who aren't," Madonna said. "It's easier to deal with people who aren't. Perhaps the people in my record company would have preferred in the beginning for me to be this demure, sweet, accepting girl or something. I don't know. I think when they finally met me and sat down and had a conversation with me, they were surprised, you know? People tend to expect a certain kind of personality, and then, when they meet me, I think they're surprised. Perhaps they don't perceive me to be as intelligent as I think I am. I do like to have control, but I'm not a tyrant. I don't have to have it plastered on my album that everything is written, arranged, produced, directed, starred in, and so forth by Madonna."

Madonna's first album, entitled simply *Madonna,* was a major success, although less for its music than for her sense of style and instinctive understanding of what would shock. After its release, Madonna inspired a national craze among teenagers and eventually among young adults with her lacy underwear, rosary beads as jewelry, Boy Toy belt buckles, and tousled blond hair with black roots. Only after the release of *Madonna* did the singer, despite her many subsequent transformations, settle on what she felt was the right personal style and rhythm in her music. Even after her debut album for Sire Records garnered attention, it took a year before anybody outside the clubs paid attention to her. Once again, she relied on her instincts when she contacted David Bowie's record producer and convinced him to produce her next album.

Her second album, *Like a Virgin,* made her a star and led to her first video sensation, "Material Girl," which would ultimately change her life.

part four

....

Material Girl

chapter twenty-five

•••••••••••••••••••

Cis Coreman is a movie producer and one of Barbra Streisand's oldest and closest friends as well as her business partner in Barwood Productions. Coreman remembers meeting Madonna before she became famous and has the same impression that most people have of the singer. At the time, Coreman was casting for Warner Brothers in New York and on one occasion, at an open call, she met the future star. "She walked in with a ghetto blaster," Coreman recalls, "and she was wearing torn jeans and a T-shirt and had her hair tied up in a rag, but she looked absolutely gorgeous. I knew from the beginning that she was going to be a star because she was so determined and, in fact, she reminded me of Barbra when she was young and first starting out."

As they began talking, Cis Coreman became intrigued by Madonna's life story, how she had left home and college and traveled to New York without knowing anyone. "It was this kind of determination," Coreman continues, "and her electrifying personality and fabulous looks that convinced me that she was extraordinary. Sometimes, very rarely, you see that, as a casting director, when a young person comes in and you just know that they are going to become something important in the business. I knew Madonna was going to make waves."

Cis Coreman became interested in Madonna enough to consider making a movie about her and her struggle to become a star. "Rusty Lemeron wrote a treatment for us," Coreman explains, "but unfortunately, it never went anywhere. But I sent a tape of Madonna to Jon Peters, Barbra's friend at the time, with a note that said he should meet her because I believed that she had absolute star quality." In fact, she believed it to such an extent that she asked her son, Richard Coreman, a photographer, to go down to Madonna's apartment on the Lower East Side and take some pictures of her. "The neighborhood was so bad that my son was even terrified, which said something about how courageous Madonna was and how willing she was to suffer just to be in New York. Richard couldn't imagine how she could have lived there and not been afraid of being raped or murdered."

Years later, Jon Peters called Cis Coreman, respecting her attempts to develop a movie about Madonna, to ask her if she would mind if he contacted Madonna. At the time, Peters was doing a film entitled *Vision Quest,* starring Matthew Modine as a high school wrestling champion. In the film, released in 1985 by Warner Brothers and directed by Harold Becker, Madonna's character performs two songs, "Crazy for You" and "Gambler," when she appears as a nightclub singer. The videos that Madonna eventually made for those two songs used many shots from the film, although neither the movie nor the videos were a financial success.

In February 1985, despite having made two unimpressive films, *A Certain Sacrifice* and *Vision Quest,* Madonna was selling records at the astonishing rate of seventy-five thousand a day. "Material Girl" was at number 18, and "Crazy," from the sound track of *Vision Quest,* was climbing on the music charts as well. Her videos were constantly on MTV and viewed by critics with curiosity and acclaim.

In Madonna's mind, she had not achieved nearly enough. She had more money than she had ever had in her life, which wasn't too difficult for the girl who had landed in New York a mere six years before with only $35 in her pocket. She was earning more than her father at that point, her reference to financial security, but not nearly her goal.

When she thought about her family, she resisted thinking about them with affection and nostalgia. The trick was not to be crippled by the resentment, but to use every negative moment to its best advantage. Her music came out of her life, and she needed to hang on to all those painful memories to keep making the kind of heartfelt compositions her public craved. Just as she learned how not to separate Madonna the waif from Madonna the star, she taught herself to think about her past as if it belonged to someone else. Only when she was alone did she allow herself the momentary luxury of wallowing in self-pity. Her plan was to convey her suffering to her fans without evoking pity, but instead making every man, woman, and child identify with the waif as if she belonged to them, as if they lived to see her happy and secure. She discovered her voice the way a writer finds the rhythm and beat of his words. She found her style, sexy and tough, which came naturally as it was her very own sexual personality that had attracted so many lovers in the past. On one hand, she offered herself as the hurt little girl from the wrong side of the tracks who grabbed at the romantic heart of anyone who watched her perform. On the other, she was the shrewd businesswoman who knew that any decision she made about her image and sound, any choice of collaborator or manager, would stay with her forever, even if she eventually banned the person from her life. She was on her way to becoming the sex goddess of rock and roll, and she was learning how to act self-assured, rich, and sophisticated. If she was successful at creating a flawless portrait of a woman who was destined for stardom, she was obsessed with belonging in a world that was dangerous and unwelcoming to any newcomer who threatened to upset the status quo. For the first few years of her trip toward fame, it had been nothing but fun. Now that big money was invested in her, she had to perform to perfection. No one had to tell her, because she knew instinctively that one false move and she was out.

Concerning her career, she was certain of only one thing: while it might have its ups and downs and could go from better to best, she was in the public eye forever. Concerning her image, she knew that, deep down, she would never change. She was still the motherless child who felt like an outsider in her own home. It didn't make any difference that she had created an enormous distance between herself and her family, she was in this alone. She needed an ally who didn't take a piece of her earnings. She needed a friend who didn't expect to be carried without pulling his or her own weight. She needed a partner.

She needed a husband, for better or for worse.

While she was on the set of her video "Material Girl," dressed up like Marilyn Monroe, a brooding young actor, dressed all in leather, walked into Madonna's life.

A disciple of the Actors Studio, Sean Penn was already considered one of the most talented and brilliant actors in Hollywood. Born in 1960 to show business parents—the actress Eileen Ryan and the director Leo Penn, best known for his television work on *I Spy* and *Columbo,* Penn grew up in a privileged show business environment. There was never any struggle to break into an industry filled with strangers. The people who ran Hollywood had been his parents' close friends and neighbors all his life, and as he matured, the children of the moguls and stars became Penn's lifelong friends. Two of them lived next door, Emilio Estevez and Charlie Sheen, sons of Martin Sheen, who, like Sean's parents, was another well-established Hollywood personality. In fact, the two Sheen brothers, along with Sean Penn and his own brother, Chris, would eventually become members of the Brat Pack, a group of promising young actors that also included Rob Lowe, Tom Cruise, Timothy Hutton, Matt Dillon, Andrew McCarthy, and the late River Phoenix.

In 1979, Martin Sheen, along with Emilio and Charlie, returned from making *Apocalypse Now* in the Philippines. Sheen, recovering from a heart attack that occurred during the filming, was forced to spend time at home to recuperate. The Sheen boys had brought back a bag of prosthetic hands that had been used as props during the filming of the movie. Along with the Penn brothers, they set about to make a super-8 horror film that had a slim plot but spectacular special effects. Tying firecrackers to stage-blood squibs made of condoms, the budding filmmakers made an unpromising start to what would turn into a successful cinematic future for all four. Though the finished product amused the ailing Martin Sheen as well as Eileen Ryan and Leo Penn, everyone agreed that it was not a particularly gripping or impressive first effort. It was enough, however, to convince Penn that his future was as an actor and director. With the encouragement of his parents, he began an apprenticeship with the Repertory Theatre in Los Angeles and was enrolled in a drama class with Peggy Feury, another family friend. Before long, Penn got small parts in one highly rated television series, *Barnaby Jones,* as well as in *Concrete Cowboys,* a series that lasted only seven weeks, from February 7 to March 21, 1981, before he finally got his first role in a television movie, *The Killing of Randy Webster.*

In 1980, just as his future wife had done, Penn took off for New York to try to make a name for himself in the theater. Unlike Madonna, he had the blessing of his family and solid connections that eventually helped him land an audition with the theater director Art Wolff, who was casting for a new play by Kevin Heelan called *Heartland.* According to Wolff, he knew the instant Penn walked through the door to read that he was physically perfect for the part. His first audition was unimpressive, but Wolff persisted until Penn gave him the kind of performance he would continue to give for the three weeks that the play ran on Broadway. Well trained, dedicated to his craft, and with an instinctive technique that was all his own, Penn won rave notices on Broadway. With his spirits high and with confidence in his talent, Penn returned to Los Angeles, where he landed his first film role in Harold Becker's *Taps,* starring Timothy Hutton. By the time the film was released in 1981, Penn was already working on another movie, *Fast Times at Ridgemont High,* about a group of high school students who are determined to lose their virginity. During the making of *Fast Times,* Sean met Pam Springsteen, Bruce Springsteen's sister. Within weeks, they were engaged, and within months, Penn was already being compared to a young Marlon Brando. Perhaps Springsteen should have been concerned that the comparison was not limited to her fiancé's acting skills.

Single-minded about his career, Penn was more focused on improving his technique than he was on settling down. In a statement he made at the time about love and marriage, he said something that was curiously similar to what Madonna would say years later after the couple had married and were billed in the press as the "Poison Penns." "With the exception of acting, all the other stuff is just part of the experience, you know, as we go along," Penn said when announcing his engagement to Springsteen. "I don't mean I'm getting married for the experience of marriage, it's just like you have to keep breathing."

In reaction to Penn's spitting at two photographers, which he claimed was a "protective act" toward his wife, Madonna defended her husband by saying, "Love is like breathing. You just have to do it."

Sean Penn and Madonna, despite their vastly different backgrounds, had many things in common. Both had taken on the appearance of 1950s icons—Sean as James Dean and Madonna as Marilyn Monroe—and had become two of the most popular figures in a new generation of stars. In the beginning of their careers, Penn and Madonna also wove tales of their poverty-stricken childhood, which in either case was patently exaggerated. Madonna told stories about emotional and financial deprivation, while Penn cultivated a streettough image that ultimately appealed to his future wife's sense of danger and excitement. That Penn actually came from a well-established Hollywood family was an added incentive for Madonna to get involved with the young actor. Just as Tony Ciccone had done years before when he courted Madonna Fortin, considering her his ticket into Middle America, as she became increasingly successful, Madonna considered Penn important to her quest for security and acceptance in the world of established Hollywood stars. She had gained recognition in her chosen profession, but she was alone in a world that was not yet familiar or comfortable to her. Just as she would later move to England in 1998 and insinuate herself into the A-list of rock idols, designers, and movie stars, she was determined in the early 1980s to meet someone who would give her the artistic and social respectability that she craved. Before she met Penn, she had seen him in *Taps* and had remarked that he was James Dean incarnate, exactly the type of raw intellectual actor she admired. "He's a combination of a cowboy poet and a bad boy," she told a friend.

In 1983, Penn appeared in *Bad Boys,* a film in which he played a teenage gang member who ends up in a correctional facility. When the prison psychiatrist informs him that his girlfriend has been beaten and raped by his Puerto Rican counterpart in a rival gang, Penn's instincts were *not* to do "what every other actor in his right mind would have done, which is to go nuts." Instead, the young actor reached deep into himself and decided that if he had heard that news in real life, he would simply break down and cry. The reaction impressed the critics, especially David Ansen, who wrote in *Newsweek,* "He barely raises his voice, but commands the screen as he commands the joint, winning your sympathy without even asking for it." Richard Rosenthal, who directed the film, said Penn was "the most talented young actor in films today."

In 1984, Penn appeared in Louis Malle's *Crackers,* a remake of the Italian film *Big Deal on Madonna Street,* or, in Italian, *I Soliti Ignoti,* a 1956 movie about a bunch of crooks who run a pawnshop. If the title was prophetic, the film was not in regard to Penn's future success as an actor. The reviews were bad, and Penn decided to return to the Broadway stage to improve his acting technique. By the time he appeared in a limited run of Robert Allan Ackerman's *Slab Boys,* his engagement to Pam Springsteen was off. After the run of the play, Penn, with renewed confidence, went back to Los Angeles, where he landed a part in Richard Benjamin's

Racing With the Moon, playing a country boy who, in 1942, is waiting to be called up for the war. The year was 1984, and Sean Penn fell in love with his costar Elizabeth McGovern. During the filming, Penn's penchant for violence and jealousy became a troubling reality, both for his costars and his girlfriend. When Penn learned that a male reporter was sitting with McGovern in her trailer during a break, he began rocking the trailer back and forth and shouting obscenities until a startled McGovern and the photographer finally emerged after they realized what was going on. "It was not a question of Penn being fearful of his fiancée talking to the press," one of the extras remarked, "than he was livid that she was alone in her trailer with another man."

His temper tantrums and uncontrollable rages continued in proportion to his drinking, which was also getting out of hand, and Penn developed a reputation for being "difficult on a set." He had also developed a hatred for the press. During those rare times when he agreed to sit for an interview to promote a film, if he didn't end up stomping off in fury, he affected long silences during conversations, imitating Robert De Niro, another of his cinematic heroes.

In 1984, John Schlesinger directed Penn, along with Timothy Hutton, in *The Falcon and the Snowman,* a film about two friends who sell secrets to the Russians. Though Schlesinger had enormous respect for Penn as an actor, he considered the time spent making the film a veritable nightmare. "No one," Schlesinger said, "is that talented to have to take all that violent crap."

In 1985, Penn's drinking, womanizing, and hostility to the press along with his wild antics when he was roaming Hollywood with his buddies in the Brat Pack gave him a reputation as unreliable. Although he was still getting good reviews, directors were increasingly reluctant to cast him because he got in brawls on the set, showed up late, or turned up so hungover that he was unable to work.

James Foley, who had directed *Reckless* in 1984, starring Aidan Quinn and Daryl Hannah, a movie about a young man who is thrown out of his house by his alcoholic father and goes on to live a reckless life, would also direct one of Penn's least memorable films, *At Close Range,* costarring Christopher Walken and Chris Penn. The film is about a rural family who murder another rural family to get their farm equipment and is filled with gratuitous violence.

James Foley knew Madonna and would eventually direct her in one of her most embarrassing films, *Who's That Girl,* as well as two of her most successful videos, "Papa Don't Preach" and the European version of "True Blue." Also a close friend of Penn's, Foley sensed that Penn was depressed over the breakup with McGovern and despondent that his career had stagnated. He decided that Penn needed a successful and strong-willed woman to calm him and inspire him to get sober and refocus his energy on his talent. He suggested that Penn might want to meet Madonna, although Foley's idea to introduce the pair was in response to a comment that Penn had once made about the singer: "She's me," he said, "my female counterpart."

Mary Lambert is a quiet, small, pale woman who left her hometown of Helena, Arkansas, to study at the Rhode Island School of Design. While she was there, she became friends with David Byrne who was just putting together his group, Talking Heads. Byrne inspired Lambert and marked the beginning of her passion for rock and film. When she left Rhode Island, she had a degree in painting, a taste for Wenders and Herzog, and an ambition to make short, personal films. Her only two features movies were *Siesta* in 1987 and *Pet Sematary* in 1989 before she settled into making rock videos, which included Sting's "We'll Be Together Again Tonight" as well as "Borderline" and "Like a Prayer" for Madonna. A friend of Penn's and of Foley's, Lambert also happened to be directing "Material Girl" when Foley called and asked her to allow the young actor to visit Madonna on the set.

"I was standing at the top of these steps," Madonna recalls, "waiting while people were doing some lighting, and I
looked down and noticed this guy in a leather jacket and
sunglasses, sort of standing in the corner, looking at me. I
came down the steps and walked right by and said, 'Hi,' but
very cold, before I realized it was Sean Penn. Hours went by,
and it had gotten dark, and I saw him poke his head around
the corner again. I was like, 'Are you still here?' "

Instead of getting discouraged by her chilly greeting,
Penn was smitten. He hung around until finally, at the end of
the day's taping, Madonna came downstairs to talk to him.
"There were people everywhere," Madonna continues, "so it
was hard for us to have this conversation, but we were just
kind of throwing questions at each other and being really
protective. Finally, when he was about to leave, I said, 'Wait
a minute, I have something for you.' I had given flowers to
everybody in the cast and the crew of the video, all the guys,
and I had one left so I ran back upstairs, and when I came
back, I handed him a rose."

At that moment, Madonna had a fantasy that they were
going to fall in love and get married.

When Madonna first encountered Sean Penn, she had
been through a series of relationships that had never lasted
long enough to culminate into something serious. In the
spring of 1983, Madonna met John "Jellybean" Benitez, a
talented and ambitious musician from Spanish Harlem who
worked as a master of ceremonies and disc jockey at the Fun
House, the Danceteria's biggest club rival. Madonna knew
that Jellybean had connections in the music business and
was the type of person who knew how to meet the right people and make those contacts work for him. Jellybean used
his first paycheck at the Fun House to hire a publicist to
make sure that he was known around the club scene. Many
people credited Benitez as one of the people who helped
Madonna launch her career. Short, barely standing five feet
six, with black eyes and dark, shoulder-length hair, he was
the typical hot-tempered Spanish lover. Instead of being

frightened by his jealous rages if she even looked at another man, Madonna was excited by the attention. Benitez has the distinction of being one of only three or four men in Madonna's life whom she really loved, or whom she considered a serious partner in a long-term relationship. Unfortunately, the timing was wrong. Neither was willing to sacrifice for the other's career, neither was ready to commit to an exclusive relationship, and neither was prepared to be a parent.

Monogamy was never one of Madonna's greatest attributes. While she was having an affair with Benitez, she was also seeing Futura 2000, the artist who was one of Andy Warhol's protégés, and Mark Kamins, the disc jockey from Danceteria, and Erica Bell, who was running the elevator at Danceteria. Not only were the two women sometime lovers, but they were also good friends and would remain so for many years.

When Sire Records decided to put "Everybody" on both sides of Madonna's first single, eliminating "Ain't No Big Deal," they had a problem replacing it with another song that was a suitable substitute to complete her first album. An even bigger problem was that Seymour Stein and Michael Rosenblatt, the executives at Sire who were in charge of Madonna, were worried that they would be unable to convince the executives at Warner's, their parent company, to put up the additional money to replace the song for the album. Desperate to find a solution, Rosenblatt decided that the best person to "sell" Madonna was Madonna, and he put her on a plane for Los Angeles to convince the financial people at Warner's to increase their budget for her new album to include another song. Ultimately, Madonna was successful, although there was a tense moment when she first walked into the meeting with the Warner executives and they saw her in person for the first time. Visibly shocked, they admitted that they didn't expect to see a pale, blond woman. Based on the sound of her voice and her raw, uninhibited style, they had all assumed that she was black.

After Madonna returned to New York with the financial backing and support to find another song, the people at Sire faced an even more complicated dilemma. Where were they going to find a song quickly that would fit in with the sound and style of the album? Once again, Madonna had the solution. She went directly to her boyfriend Jellybean, who came through with a song that he had written called "Holiday." Initially, Madonna's album was to be called simply *Madonna,* not only to introduce her name to the public but also to avoid putting her image on the cover since her largest audience so far had been on black radio stations. For a while, Seymour Stein was intent on calling the album *Lucky Star,* after one of the songs that Madonna had written for her lover Mark Kamins as a touching way to end their relationship. In the end, under pressure from Rosenblatt and the others at Warner Brothers, Seymour Stein decided to keep *Madonna* as the title to avoid using her image. Madonna dedicated the album to her father.

The album was released in 1983 and was not an immediate success. Reverting to her old ploy of making the rounds of the downtown clubs and dancing suggestively to her music, Madonna was largely responsible for "Holiday" 's slow but steady climb up the charts within six months. By 1984, both "Lucky Star" and "Borderline," two more songs from the album, made it into the Top 10. Even more significant was that the album led to Madonna's appearance on MTV with a video, "Everybody." At the time, Seymour Stein was not convinced that the video would do as well as the records. As he had predicted, Madonna's debut video was not a rousing success since it was too disco in flavor for television. Madonna's next video, "Burning Up," a combination of surreal special effects with a sadomasochistic theme, was her first major success. In the video, Madonna appears with a chain around her neck while she moves seductively down the middle of a highway, aware that a man in a convertible is trying to run her over. The man behind the wheel was another lover, Ken Compton, which did nothing to improve what had become a tempestuous relationship with Jellybean Benitez. Despite the torment that she was going through with Jellybean, her career was finally taking off. Her next video, in 1984, was "Lucky Star," which would be the first of fifteen consecutive Top 5 hits, which gave Madonna the distinction of having surpassed the record previously held by Elvis Presley and the Beatles.

With constant episodes of infidelity, screaming scenes in which Madonna was reduced to hysteria, begging Benitez not to leave her, and after undergoing several abortions, Madonna and Jellybean spent more time separating and making up than they did trying to cement a relationship that was supposed to end in marriage.

On one occasion, when they decided to get back together, Madonna was in Spokane, Washington, shooting *Vision Quest,* the movie in which she made a cameo appearance. Lonely and unhappy, she called her new manager, Freddy DeMann, and begged him to allow Jellybean to come out to Washington to visit her. During that visit, the couple decided to get engaged. Madonna, on an impulse, called her father in Michigan to announce the news and advise him that they would be coming to Rochester Hills to visit.

Her appearance at the family home caused bewilderment and was not a relaxed or happy occasion. On seeing his daughter dressed in what had become her trademark punk attire with her hair uncombed and cut in different lengths, Tony Ciccone asked Madonna if she was, by any chance, wearing "some kind of a costume." According to one of Madonna's siblings, she was a mystery to the family, as well as Jellybean, who was equally bizarre and unkempt. "She looked dirty," the sibling recalls, "and he was a shrimp with long hair and these wild black eyes. No one in the family really understood the chemistry between them, except that they were both in show business and looked really weird."

By the time the couple returned to New York and Madonna was hard at work finishing her *Like a Virgin* album, the relationship with Benitez was over. In Venice to film the "Like a Virgin" video, Madonna was comforted by her director, Mary Lambert. During that trip Madonna and Lambert got to know each other better and discovered that both were deeply moved and influenced by Catholic iconography. As was evident when she directed Madonna's video "Like a Prayer," Lambert designed the special effects so that wounds open and close miraculously, churches and angels abound, and there is a sustained sense of mysticism and transcendence throughout Madonna's performance. Though Lambert was barely ten years older than Madonna, once again the singer had found a substitute mother figure to help her through the sadness of another broken love affair.

The most popular song from the album was "Material Girl," which Mary Lambert directed as a video. It would mark the beginning of Madonna's ascent into superstardom.

After their first meeting on the set of "Material Girl," Sean, still carrying the rose that Madonna had given him, headed over to James Foley's house. Sitting around the living room and talking about Madonna, Penn picked up a book of quotations. Opening it, he turned to a page at random and read a passage to himself: "She has the innocence of a child and the wit of a man." Reading it over again to himself, he finally read it out loud. Foley looked at him and said, "It's Madonna. Go get her."

For a while, the relationship between the bad girl of rock and the bad boy of film was romantic, both of them believing that just possibly they had each found the person they had been searching for all their lives. Too many times the violence and drunken and jealous rages strained them to the breaking point, but what kept them together until the end was the intense sexual attraction they had for each other. Madonna had become accustomed to making love in some abstract middle distance, remote from her emotions. When she found Penn, for the first time in years she felt no separation between the current of their sex and the depth of her feelings. As Paul Freeman would recall when he worked with them on their ill-fated film, *Shanghai Surprise,* whenever they weren't required on the set, they would retire to one of their trailers. "The one thing they were doing whenever they could, which was normal for a young couple who had just gotten married, was making love. By contract, they had separate trailers, but they would usually use Madonna's and the trailer would rock between takes."

While each seemed to have found an ideal sexual mate, during the filming of *Shanghai Surprise* Penn realized how different he was from his wife when it came to promoting their respective careers. Penn was perceived as an actor who embraced his art without concern for the commercial aspect of Hollywood. Madonna was the epitome of what was considered marketable. Penn hated publicity. Madonna lived for it. And yet, because they were both adolescent iconoclasts of their generation, fragile in their emotional development, Madonna profoundly believed that they were perfect together. At one point during the filming of *Shanghai Surprise,* she told Paul Freeman, "We have so much in common that Sean is almost like my brother. His temperament is so similar to mine."

chapter twenty-six

· · · · · · · · · · · · · · · · · ·

*I*n 1984, during her courtship with Sean Penn, Madonna made her third film. Her work in *Desperately Seeking Susan* is still considered, along with that in *Evita,* which appeared in 1996, to be her best cinematic performance. In fact, during the filming, Madonna was offered a role on Broadway in *My One and Only,* which she turned down because the part called for tap dancing, which she had never studied.

Desperately Seeking Susan was an all-woman effort. Susan Seidelman directed, Sarah Pillsbury and Midge Sanford produced, and Lenora Barish wrote the script. The part of Susan had originally been written for Diane Keaton, who, because of other commitments, was forced to turn it down. The character Madonna portrayed was a parody of herself during her early days in New York City when she lived the life of an uninhibited street child, slept in abandoned music studios, and occasionally scoured garbage cans behind the Music Building for untouched and discarded Burger King hamburgers. In fact, Madonna identified so closely with her character that she insisted on doing her own hair and makeup until she completely changed the role to fit her own chemistry and identity. The reviews were good, and the gossip around Hollywood circles was that Madonna was destined to make the transition from singer to actress as Barbra Streisand had done when, by age twenty-eight, she had won an Oscar, an Emmy, and a Grammy. Working with Madonna on the set, the crew was not only impressed with her talent but also with her discipline.

In 1975, Susan Seidelman was a film student at New York University in Washington Square when she joined an organization called AIVF, or the Association of Independent Video and Filmmakers. Founded in 1974 by New York University professor John Culken, and Ed Lynch, a cameraman, AIVF was an outcrop of the Filmmakers Cooperative, which had been started in 1962 by Jonas Mekas with the idea of supporting a more avant-garde generation of film directors. With Culken and Lynch at the helm of AIVF, they changed the focus of the group in keeping with the changing tastes of the public. As a result, AIVF became more conscious of what Hollywood wanted in terms of product and orientation and became more sophisticated when it came to distribution, showcasing the product, and marketing. They also made sure that AIVF functioned almost like a union or an advocate for actors, directors, and writers, while providing its members with information concerning who was available or suitable to work on a project that any of their members was interested in doing. In 1985, AIVF celebrated its tenth anniversary and had thirty-five hundred members, among whom were the Coen brothers, John Sayles, Claudia Weill, and Jim Jarmusch.

The prototype for *Desperately Seeking Susan* was a small-budget film that Seidelman had made for $80,000 called *Smithereens* about a girl who was involved in the East Village punk rock scene. After Seidelman was able to begin production for *Desperately Seeking Susan,* and Diane Keaton dropped out, she heard about Madonna's interest in taking on a movie role through a friend who claimed that the singer had auditioned for a part in another film, which she didn't get. Coincidentally, Seidelman lived on Broome Street, only two blocks away from where Madonna was living. She called her up, and Madonna rode her bicycle over to meet her.

In 1985, the same year that *Desperately Seeking Susan* was released, Madonna began her nationwide, twenty-eight city Virgin tour. During a stop in Michigan where she performed at the Silverdome in front of forty-two thousand spectators, including some of her old friends and relatives, she introduced Sean Penn to her family. This time, Tony Ciccone was pleased. Relieved that his errant daughter was finally getting married and impressed by his prospective son-in-law, whom he admired as an actor, he was optimistic for the first time since Madonna had left home that she was doing something sensible. That Madonna was famous and earning millions of dollars seemed to move Tony less than that she was about to settle down with one man. Elsie Fortin, who also met Sean Penn during that trip, was only concerned about her granddaughter's happiness. As she said years later, "Madonna seemed to be in love, and if she was happy, that's all that mattered. He could have been a factory worker, as long as he was decent and honest and treated her right."

Several weeks later, when the Virgin tour was in Los Angeles, Penn took Madonna home to meet his family. Eileen Ryan and Leo Penn were also pleased that their son was settling down. They viewed Madonna as disciplined and determined to succeed, and they only hoped that she would influence their son and help him to mature. An actor who was a friend and neighbor of the family's recalls their reaction: "If anything impressed Leo and Eileen, it was that Madonna didn't drink or use drugs. Her background, her past, her image, didn't faze them at all. She was a performer, and they understood show business better than anyone. They judged her as an individual, a woman their son loved and wanted to marry. They were one hundred percent in favor and very optimistic."

It seemed as if everything was finally falling into place for Madonna. The engagement to Sean Penn was about to become official and the marriage was imminent.

In June 1985, Penn was in the middle of filming *At Close Range,* directed by his friend James Foley. Given the violence of his part, Penn reverted to his old habits and was belligerent not only on the set but off, getting into violent confrontations with the photographers and reporters who were constantly present. Madonna came to visit on location and stayed with Penn at a small inn in Nashville, Tennessee. According to the singer, one morning when they woke up, Penn had a curious look in his eye. "I read his mind," she said, "and I told him, 'Go ahead and say it. Whatever you're thinking, I'll say yes to.'" Penn proposed and Madonna accepted. To celebrate, they went to a neighborhood 7-Eleven and bought jawbreakers.

When the press heard about the engagement and knew that Madonna was visiting Penn, Foley prevailed upon the couple, for the sake of the movie, to hold a brief press conference during which each made a statement about their impending marriage. "There will be times I will regret having gotten married," Penn predicted, "but it doesn't matter, you know, as long as you've got acting, it doesn't matter." In response, Madonna stated, "Anyway, I think it would be kind of boring if everyone really just loved me a hundred percent."

Privately, Madonna confided in a friend that even if one day she would no longer be Mrs. Sean Penn, she would go on "being whoever it is that I am anyway."

Describing the events leading up to the marriage and the wedding itself, the incidents of violence that followed, the reconciliation and the ultimate divorce, without mentioning the vulgarity, the excess, Penn's reaction to the attention of every trashy tabloid, and the involvement of the dregs of show business, would be like describing World War I without mentioning the horrors of the trenches.

Next to the Penn/Madonna nuptials, Truman Capote's Black and White Ball in honor of Katharine Graham could be deemed the most understated social event of the decade, Archie Bunker could be accused of being liberal, and Elizabeth Taylor's marriage to Larry Fortensky could be considered a heartfelt and elegant affair.

As the nuptials approached, Nancy Huant, the fiancée of Madonna's record producer Nile Rodgers, threw a bridal shower for the singer at her Upper East Side New York apartment. Some of the women who were invited were the singer Alannah Currie of the Thompson Twins and Mariel Hemingway, as well as six of Madonna's male friends who were dressed in drag. The gifts she received included a sequined telephone, lingerie, a quilt, and some jewelry. Two days later, back in California, the couple seemed to be competing for who could throw the most tasteless bachelor or bachelorette party.

Madonna invited ten friends to the Tropicana, a mud-wrestling club in a run-down section of Hollywood. Wearing no makeup and with her hair in a bun and sunglasses covering her face, Madonna seemed to be having a great time cheering on the women who were wrestling in her honor. On his side, Penn hosted an old-fashioned stag party where a stripper, Kitten Natividad, took everything off to the tune of "Material Girl." According to Miss Natividad, the guests all had a good time although, in her words, they all seemed "a little buzzed." "The wildest moment," Miss Natividad recalled, "was when Sean's friend Harry Dean Stanton arrived a little late." Pushing Stanton's face into Kitten's cleavage, Sean purportedly said, "See what you missed?"

Several weeks later, Madonna lost her engagement ring when it was stolen from a New York hotel. Several weeks after that, a sapphire bracelet that Penn had also bought her was stolen from another New York hotel room. A week before the wedding, while she was driving the 1956 white-and-coral convertible Thunderbird that was a wedding present from Penn and talking on a cell phone, she got into an accident. The car was deemed a total loss by the insurance company.

On August 16, 1985, on Madonna's twenty-seventh birthday and one day before Penn's twenty-fifth, the couple married at the $6.5 million home of Dan Unger, a real estate developer and close family friend of Leo and Eileen Penn's.

As the paparazzi took up their places in the bushes or buzzed overhead in helicopters, Sean Penn's greeting to his wedding guests was appropriate. "Welcome to the remaking of *Apocalypse Now*," he said as people gathered high above the bluffs of Point Dume in Malibu.

Security guards dressed in blue blazers were stationed outside the estate to check the identification of every guest who presented an invitation, cross-checking them with the names on a list. Inside the house, another battery of guards were armed with infrared binoculars to scan the perimeter of the property for intruders. One uninvited guest, an Italian photographer in camouflage gear and blackened face, who had been hiding in the shrubbery since early morning, was discovered and thrown off the property, his camera and film confiscated.

Sean Penn, dressed in a double-breasted Gianni Versace suit, paced frantically up and down the beach in front of the house. At one point, he wrote FUCK YOU in the sand as a message to the press that hovered in helicopters above the gathering. One guest recalls a frantic moment when Madonna came tearing out of the house, her hair in curlers, her silk dressing gown flapping in the summer breeze, when someone told her that Penn had a loaded gun. "I just want to shoot down one helicopter," he told his startled future wife. "I want to watch it burn and see all the bastards inside melt." Madonna pleaded with Penn to put the gun away and ignore the press.

"She was beside herself," the guest says. "When Sean threatened to shoot down one of the helicopters, Madonna, more than anyone else, took him seriously. I remember how she took his face between her hands and talked very quietly to him, almost like he was a kid and she was his parent. At one point, he tried to twist out of her grasp and she just pulled his face closer to hers and kissed him on the forehead, the nose, the cheeks, the chin. After a couple of minutes, he seemed to calm down, and Madonna, without talking to anyone who had watched the scene, ran back into the house to get dressed. She was carrying the gun."

The wedding gown that Madonna wore was designed by

Marlene Stewart, the woman who also created her costumes
for her Like a Virgin tour. It was a strapless, cream-colored
antique tulle with a bustle that Madonna described as having
a "1950s feeling and something that Grace Kelly might have
worn at her wedding." Madonna's hair was wrapped in a
French twist that was tucked underneath a black bowler hat
with a cream-colored tulle veil that matched her dress and
covered her face. The only accessories she wore were one
long earring and an antique pearl bracelet that belonged to
her grandmother.

There were 220 close friends, family, and professional associates. Madonna's father, stepmother, seven siblings, and
grandmother were there, along with Andy Warhol, who had
suddenly become an admirer of Madonna's after having ignored her when she was starting out in New York. Cher was
there as well, along with Rosanna Arquette, Madonna's
costar in *Desperately Seeking Susan,* and Carrie Fisher, who
would marry Paul Simon, who had coincidentally been married to Shelley Duvall, the future companion of Dan Gilroy,
Madonna's musician boyfriend with whom she had lived for
a while in the abandoned synagogue in Queens. Christopher
Walken was another guest, Sean Penn's costar in *At Close
Range,* who would play Madonna's guardian angel in her
video "Bad Girl" years after she and Penn were divorced.
Diane Keaton was present as well. At the end of Madonna's
marriage to Sean Penn, Keaton would be the only person on
the cooperative board at the San Remo apartment building
on Central Park West in New York City to vote in favor of
Madonna buying an apartment there. Ultimately, on January
23, 1988, Madonna would buy another apartment for
$850,000 that was several blocks away on Central Park
West.

Tom Cruise was there as well, along with the Sheen family and the other members of the Brat Pack, while James Foley, the man who had introduced the couple, was Penn's best
man. Paula Ciccone, the sister who looked most like

Madonna and who resented her success, served as her maid of honor.

The ceremony was not unlike one of Madonna's videos or, more aptly, as Penn had said, like *Apocalypse Now*. As Madonna walked down the grassy aisle on her father's arm with the Pacific Ocean in the distance and the guests standing on the lawn facing the beach, the helicopters continued to buzz overhead. There was a brief exchange between father and daughter as they walked. "This is it, Madonna," Tony said, "the one and only time." "Cross my heart," Madonna answered, making the sign of the cross on her chest with her left hand. As she reached Sean, who stood between James Foley and Paula, Madonna kissed her father's cheek and said, "Bye, Dad."

The ceremony took five minutes and was conducted by Judge John Merrick, who incorporated words that had been written by the couple. Because of the noise from the aircraft, the judge, along with Madonna and Penn, were forced to shout their vows to be heard. "Although there will be times that your moods may falter," the judge read from a small white card, "and you'll question each other's motives, the faith and love that you share will help to show that your inconsistency is only for the moment."

After the couple were pronounced man and wife, Penn lifted Madonna's veil and kissed her to the theme from *Chariots of Fire*.

Unfortunately, those momentary inconsistencies would last for more than two years before the marriage was irretrievably and definitively over.

The wedding dinner, catered by the Spago restaurant in Hollywood, consisted of lobster ravioli, rack of lamb, swordfish, and baked potatoes stuffed with sour cream and caviar and served with an Acacia pinot noir from California's Madonna Vineyard. Michael Ochs, a friend of Madonna's, who had a vast archive of music, helped her choose a combination of operatic and classic romantic tunes. The result was Michael McLaren's *Madame Butterfly* and standards by Bing Crosby, Ella Fitzgerald, Cole Porter, and Sarah Vaughan. At the end of the sit-down dinner, as Madonna prepared to cut the cake, she turned to Cher, who was standing directly behind her. "Hey, you've done this before. Do you just cut one piece or do you have to slice up the whole thing?"

Following the meal and family photographs, the guests were invited to move to the tennis courts, which had been transformed into a parquet dance floor with pink floodlights and small tables surrounding it. Terence Toy, the disc jockey, played some of Motown's biggest hits along with Madonna's songs while the crowd danced until the early hours of the morning.

Shortly before midnight, Madonna and Sean left their guests and slipped quietly away, to spend their wedding night at the groom's parents' house. Midnight, August 17, was Sean's twenty-fifth birthday, and a group of the couple's most intimate friends came over to celebrate. Later that day, Mr. and Mrs. Sean Penn left for Antigua in the West Indies for a brief honeymoon.

Several weeks after they returned from that idyllic island, Madonna sought psychiatric help to learn how to cope with Penn's drinking and violent outbursts.

One close girlfriend recalls how shocked she was at the way Sean would verbally abuse Madonna and how Madonna would tolerate it without fighting back. Six weeks after she married Sean Penn, Madonna confided in that same girlfriend that she was beginning to wonder if she fell in love with Penn or with the image that she had created of him. "All the questions she began asking herself," the friend relates, "was the result of her therapy. She wasn't sure anymore if she really knew who he was or if she had projected onto him the characteristics she needed to make her feel secure. All of a sudden Madonna began questioning her own motives, if her marriage to Sean was based on illusion and not love."

Madonna tried to persuade her husband to come to one of her therapy sessions. When he refused, she urged him to go into therapy on his own. Again, Penn refused, and not until several months later when he had his first brush with the law after assaulting a photographer would he be ordered by the court to undergo psychiatric counseling.

chapter twenty-seven
....

On October 31, almost three months after they were married, Madonna, under the influence of her husband, agreed to star with him in an adventure film set in China in the 1930s. *Shanghai Surprise,* based on a novel by Tony Kenrick and a script by John Kohn, was directed by Jim Goddard, who was primarily a television director and best known for his British television series *Reilly, Ace of Spies.* George Harrison, through his company Handmade Films, was the executive producer, composed the musical score, and appeared in the film in a cameo role as a cabaret singer. Christopher Ciccone, Madonna's brother, was part of the crew. In addition to functioning as his sister's assistant, he helped design some of the sets as well as looking after Madonna's costumes and hair. According to several of the other crew members, "Chris was around a lot, very accessible, and very nice. Their relationship was always very affectionate and very, very caring."

With no experience making movies, Jim Goddard took on the project with the intention of generating as much advance press and publicity as possible, since he was convinced that it made no difference whether the movie was good but rather that it would be an assured success because Madonna and Sean Penn were the stars. From a commercial and artistic point of view, it was a hypocritical way to approach his job because he obviously concentrated more on benefiting from his stars than assuming the responsibility of giving them solid direction. Curiously, after the pair signed on for the picture, Penn made a comment that clearly substantiated Goddard's philosophy: "People will go to see this film because we're in it and not because of the script or the direction or the sets."

Paul Freeman, a well-known British television actor most famous for his roles in *Dark Room* and *Devil's Arithmetic* for the BBC, who also appeared with Juliette Binoche in the 1995 French film *Hussard sur le toit,* or *Horseman on the Roof,* maintains that the film was not as bad as everyone was prepared to believe. "The publicity had been so adverse and the producers quite cynically allowed the press as much leeway as they could possibly get," Freeman says, "that it almost seemed as if the producers started off trying to make a serious film and were looking for the right actors and actresses when suddenly Sean Penn and Madonna arrived in their laps. That's when they thought they had hit pay dirt and dropped all their ideas about making a serious film."

Before Penn and Madonna arrived in Hong Kong to begin shooting, they decided to stop in Macao to look around and get acclimated to the time change. What they didn't know was that Jim Goddard and John Curran, one of the producers, had leaked their whereabouts to the press in an effort to generate advance publicity for the film. Upon their arrival, the couple were greeted by the paparazzi, who hounded them for the duration of their stay. It was only a matter of time before Penn would explode, which he did at the end of their visit when he attacked Leonel Borralho, a photographer. Borralho was only one of the hordes of paparazzi who followed the couple everywhere they went, setting up telephoto lenses that were trained on their hotel suite and terrace in an effort to catch them in compromising positions. Borralho promptly filed a million-dollar lawsuit against the actor.

Their visit to Macao would mark the beginning of what observers claim was a plot by the press to goad Penn into reacting violently. At the time, Penn was insecure about his career and unsure about his relationship with Madonna. Every time she appeared on his arm, the press would shout obscenities at her to provoke him. Given Penn's temperament and the unrelenting presence of the paparazzi determined to incite him into uncontrollable and violent rages, Madonna knew that she not only had to control her own temper when she heard the insults hurled at her, but more importantly, her husband's. It was a full-time job. The abuse and harassment went on every day for the entire two months that they were shooting the film. Putting aside her own feelings, Madonna understood that her husband's masculinity was being threatened since he believed that it was his duty to protect and defend his wife. Ever sensitive to her husband's needs and the problems he had controlling himself, Madonna never corrected him in front of anyone, nor did she criticize him for reacting violently when photographers called her foul names. Instead, she would gently guide him off to a corner and, much the same as she had done on the day of their marriage, would huddle with him, discussing alternatives to his violent reactions. "They know where his soft points are," Madonna told the cast and crew. "They call me obscene names just to get him to react. How would you react if someone said that about your wife?"

Everyone asked at the time why Jim Goddard had been chosen to direct the film, and why, when he proved obviously not experienced nor equipped to control the set, he wasn't replaced. Paul Freeman believes that the answer is that the British film industry is extremely racist, sexist, and class-conscious, something that is not found anywhere else in the world. Those people who work on a film set consider it a "closed shop," available to certain cockney families who have been in the business for generations. "This man, our director," Paul Freeman maintains, "pretended to be more cockney than the cockney crew, one of the lads, a good old boy in American parlance."

After two months on location in China, with such trials as rats in the trailers, fistfights with the press, coupled with a bad script, abysmal direction, and universal pans, promising a commercial and critical failure, the only surprise about *Shanghai Surprise* was that it was ever completed and released.

Long after the film disappeared, when asked why she had agreed to take on the part, Madonna said, "I thought it was a great script and the idea of going to China was exciting to me and the idea of working with my husband was exciting to me, because he's a great actor. But sometimes everything goes wrong." That statement was one of the rare examples when Madonna understated a problem, since nothing went right with the film from the very beginning.

Madonna was drawn to the project for another reason. She had always admired Marlene Dietrich, emulating her onstage style in several of her most successful videos, "Vogue" and "Open Your Heart," and in her offstage electric personal life, with lovers of both genders. Always sensitive to signs, parallelism, and coincidences, it is likely that one of the factors that led Madonna to agree to make *Shanghai Surprise* was that Dietrich had starred in 1932 in *Shanghai Express,* produced and directed by her mentor, Josef von Sternberg. *Shanghai Express* takes place on the Shanghai Express, a train traveling through China, and carrying passengers who have already appeared in one another's lives. In a juxtaposition of roles, Dietrich plays a notorious "coaster," or prostitute, Madeleine, or as she has become known, Shanghai Lily, to Madonna's prim missionary, Gloria Tatlock, in *Shanghai Surprise,* while Clive Brook portrays Captain Donald Harvey, a British army surgeon, to Sean Penn's alcoholic drifter. Years before the meeting on the ship, Madeleine had been Doc Harvey's mistress. They eventually broke up over the question of belief. He thought she had another lover and didn't believe her denial. Also on board is Hui Fei, another "coaster," who is traveling to China to marry a respectable businessman, Chang, who is actually a warlord in disguise. When the Chinese army stops the train and captures one of Chang's men, who is also traveling incognito, Chang holds the passengers hostage. At the same time, he suggests that Madeleine/Shanghai Lily become his mistress and threatens to blind Doc Harvey if she doesn't comply. She agrees. In the end, all the hostages escape, but before leaving, Doc Harvey asks Madeleine why she agreed to Chang's demands. She refuses to tell him, only saying that she had her reasons. . . . Which leaves Doc with the same problem as the last time—should be believe her? This time, he does.

Shanghai Express, like *Shanghai Surprise,* hinges on the question of belief. Madonna, in *Shanghai Surprise,* saw the basic lesson as a question of religious belief, as well as belief in the character that Penn played, the alcoholic drifter, when it is implied that he has decided to change his ways.

In the end, when *Shanghai Surprise* was so badly panned, Madonna was understated when she was asked why someone like Sean Penn, who had always gotten such good critical reviews, had agreed to work under such conditions. Contrary to opinion, she replied, her husband was not at all "blinded by love." "We had just gotten married," she said simply, "and Sean didn't really want to do the film, but at the same time he didn't want to spend four months away from me."

Madonna was cast against type as Gloria Tatlock, the starched and proper missionary, who hires an alcoholic drifter, played by Sean Penn, to recover a cache of stolen opium to be used for medical purposes. Before leaving on location to begin shooting, Madonna gave several interviews in which she claimed that she could "relate" to Gloria Tatlock when it came to the religious and pious aspects of the movie role's character. "Like me," Madonna said, "she falls in love with someone as different from her as Sean is from me, and that's how I explain Gloria's attraction for the character my husband plays."

From the beginning, Madonna and Penn were both miscast. Penn's part had initially been offered to Harrison Ford and Tom Selleck, because the director rightly felt that it called for an older actor to play the part of the used and cynical drifter.

When both actors turned it down, the idea of getting the newly married couple took form. Madonna, who brought an innocence to the role, did not have the kind of experience or weight needed to play a determined, courageous, and headstrong missionary, which, if done right, might have been compared to the role that Katharine Hepburn played in *The African Queen*. Another disappointment was that though the couple spent every free moment in a trailer making love, on-screen there was no chemistry between them.

Paul Freeman, who played Walter Faraday, the villain in the picture, arrived in Hong Kong after the others had already starting shooting as he had been called in to replace another actor who had initially been hired to play Faraday.

"Interestingly, I tested against the actor Bernard Hill, and I lost out to him on the first round," Freeman explains. "Jim Goddard, the director, had already worked with Hill, and he wanted him. As it turned out, Bernard Hill didn't get on with Sean, because Sean observed that Hill had nothing of the 'boy' in him which he judged was essential for the part. He was quite right. There are men who are dour and that's perfect if you want that sort of character, but that was not how Sean perceived Walter Faraday. Sean and I got on fine, there was never any problem."

From Paul Freeman's point of view as an actor, the movie was a challenge. "Most of my part was played in a disguise, and it's essential that the audience doesn't know that it's me since I get killed after the first five minutes. In the next frame, Madonna is working around the front of what is meant to be Shanghai, but what is actually Hong Kong, and a Scottish missionary comes up and talks to her and ends up accompanying her throughout the film. The missionary is me, but the audience doesn't know that the villain has come back until the very end when I whip off the disguise."

When Freeman arrived to take over the part, Goddard had not yet worked out how his character was going to change appearance and costume. "For me," Freeman says, "it was a big challenge to take control of that stuff because I had to reveal who I was on-camera just as I had gone into disguise on-camera."

On his own, Freeman decided that he was going to wear contact lenses, false teeth, and padding, which, according to him, was "a lovely thing to do as an actor." Freeman continues, "The director was out of his depth and had no clue. Goddard was a good social-realist television director, but this film required someone who knew how to do fantasy and who also knew how to deal with big stars."

In one scene in the film, Freeman reverts back into being the villain and locks Penn and Madonna in packing cases before kicking them down a flight of stairs. "They were both good fun," he says, "about getting into the cases, and they never complained. I was amazed by Sean's acting ability, and there was a problem on the set only once." The problem scene was when Penn was supposed to be suffering from a hangover. "He plunged right into the part and actually stayed out the night before and got very, very drunk," Freeman says, "so he really did have a major hangover during the shoot and couldn't work. It was ludicrous. We carried on and eventually got it."

Along with his crew, Goddard would behave badly toward Madonna. "There was a lot of sexist banter and innuendo going on when Madonna was around and which she didn't like at all and stamped on pretty firmly," Freeman recalls. "I think Goddard was intimidated by both Sean and Madonna, and his general method of coping with that was with dirty jokes and put-downs. I was amazed by it, and I was amazed that Madonna never slagged him off or punched him. She reacted badly, but she was always quietly furious and fuming. Sometimes she would simply say that she didn't want to hear that kind of talk and walk away."

A source who worked for George Harrison at the time at Handmade Films claims that Sean Penn tried to get rid of Jim Goddard. However, the film was already too far over schedule and budget to change directors.

Madonna described the time spent working on *Shanghai*

Surprise as both a "hellish nightmare" and a "great learning experience." While she was already a superstar in the world of pop music, she was a novice when it came to acting, as well as the wife of a star who was considered a superb actor. When Penn would stop the action in the middle of a scene to coach his wife and give her a five-minute acting lesson, she always seemed grateful and happy to learn from him. The other members of the cast thought that those breaks did nothing to help the flow and continuity of the plot.

The only time that Madonna seemed completely relaxed on the set was when Paul Freeman's wife and five-year-old daughter, Lucy, came to visit. "My family came to Hong Kong very briefly," Freeman explains, "and Lucy and Madonna would sit on the studio floor and just play together, kids' games, building bricks. Lucy had her little 'pony' with her, a Barbie-doll replica that came with a brush and a long ponytail, and the two of them would spend hours combing the long mane. I had the impression that Madonna was relieved to get away from all the hype that was going on. It was the only time she could finally relax with this little child, who had no idea who she was."

In midwinter, the cast and crew left Hong Kong to film the last sequences of the film in London. With snow on the ground and freezing temperatures, Madonna and Penn rented a house in Holland Park. Nothing had changed. The property was constantly surrounded by reporters, which made it impossible for them to open the blinds. If they did, photographers would take pictures with telephoto lenses.

At one point, they were filming in a hospital on the outskirts of London. When the cast and crew arrived at six o'-clock in the morning to start the day, the paparazzi were already there, standing on the hospital walls, ready to pounce and take pictures. The producer stopped the action and walked calmly over to Penn to show him the *Daily Mirror,* the *Daily World,* and several other sleazy British tabloids. "Look what they're saying about you and Madonna now," the producer said.

Penn's reaction was predictable. Swearing and screaming so that the paparazzi got their daily quota of photographs, Penn eventually stormed off to his trailer, where he remained sequestered for several hours while the director was forced to stop the shooting. Madonna sat with him and tried to calm him down. When she reappeared, she was furious. Confronting the producer, she told him quite clearly that he had provoked the incident by behaving in the most cynical and premeditated way to get media coverage for the film.

Throughout the entire experience of making *Shanghai Surprise,* everyone, crew and cast, agreed that Madonna was an unassuming, straightforward woman, extremely professional, who worked harder than anyone else. "You sort of anticipate something with stars, that you're going to be knocked over by their beauty or their size or their power," Paul Freeman says. "With Madonna, I was surprised by the fact that she was small and quite ordinary-looking, just a clear and simple person. Another thing about her that surprised me was that she and Sean were always together, they were in every shot and in every scene, and there was never any bad behavior. No Marilyn Monroe stories. She was always on time, always knew her lines, and at the same time, she was very protective of Sean. They were actually very sweet together."

In early 1986, at the time that Madonna was in London finishing *Shanghai Surprise,* Robert Stigwood was set to direct *Evita.* Madonna had several phone conversations with Stigwood to explore the possibility of taking on the starring role. She backed away from the project when she learned that the director was intent on making the movie as an operetta, exactly as the theater productions had been staged. "For me," Madonna said, "the only way I would be interested in doing it was if it were done as a straight drama. I'd love to do a movie someday where I sing, but it would be hard to make a transition if I decided to do a movie about a singer."

By March 6, *Shanghai Surprise* was finished, and George Harrison called a press conference, which he hoped would improve the bad feelings that existed between his stars and Fleet Street. As Paul Freeman remarked at the time, "It was too little too late." Recently, Freeman reiterated his opinion about that press conference: "My personal feeling was that the producers should have done an enormous press interview in the beginning and defused the problem. Instead, because they obviously wanted as much bad publicity and attention as they could get, by the time they did the press conference at the end, it was simply irrelevant."

As he stood up and faced the roomful of journalists and photographers, Harrison chewed gum. It was the first news conference that the former Beatle had given since 1974, and surprisingly, he did most of the talking, answering the hostile questions that were hurled at Madonna and Penn. Harrison began by admonishing the press for the treatment of his stars, which, in his opinion, was worse than he had ever experienced during the Beatlemania in England. "This is easy for me," he said to the audience, "because I was young then, like Sean Penn is now, and because now I know who I am and how I feel and you can't get me. I've learned how to deal with it." When Madonna was asked if she fought with Penn, Harrison interrupted before she could respond. "What kind of question is that?" he asked the journalist. "Do you have fights with your wife?"

Madonna's parting remark as she left the press conference was "We're not such a bad bunch of people, are we?"

On March 6, Sean Penn appeared on the cover of *Vanity Fair* magazine. During an interview with the writer David Wolcott, Penn said, "I prefer the bar to the gym any day. I like to drink and I like to brawl." Asked to comment on his wife, Penn replied, "No whale, no nuclear war, no starving country is more important."

From rocking trailers to a breaking marriage, things did not improve between the couple after they returned to California. In April 1986, in a Los Angeles nightclub, the Grammy Award–winning songwriter David Wolinski, who also happened to be a close friend of Madonna's, kissed her cheek in greeting. Once again, Penn's reaction was irrational. He began beating Wolinski with his fists, kicking him with his feet, and finally, he hit him over the head with a chair. If Madonna had not really grasped the seriousness of her husband's lack of control, she realized it when he turned on Wolinski. There was no excuse, since her old friend was neither a journalist nor a photographer. Penn was arrested, fined $1,000 for disorderly conduct, and put on probation. A friend of Madonna's who had witnessed the fight commented, "The marriage has been undergoing stress for some time, but this was the first really traumatic episode for her. Wolinski was someone she knew, and it really shook her up."

One month later, on Memorial Day, Penn's probation was revoked when he was arrested for drunken driving and running a red light, charges that were eventually reduced to reckless driving. By August, Madonna denied rumors of a divorce by making a statement for the press: "I love Sean, and I'm feeling hopeful."

In reality, Madonna was trying desperately to keep up her spirits, for herself and for them as a couple. But after each incident, it got harder and harder for her to ignore the storm of anxiety that plagued her. Her hands shook. She was pale. She had lost weight. She remembered loving Sean, and now she felt as if she had been in love with a person she no longer recognized. She turned to her grandmother as she had always done when she felt completely hopeless and distraught. To Elsie Fortin, she confided that her husband had a problem with alcohol; and that often, she was the target of his drunken tirades. Mrs. Fortin advised her granddaughter to separate, not to prolong the agony of a bad marriage.

To her credit, the more unfavorable the reviews she received for *Shanghai Surprise,* the more determined Madonna was to prove herself as an actress. The only difference was that she intended to try to find movie projects that would not include her husband. Still, it was difficult for her to focus on her career. She felt completely depleted emotionally. Penn's violence did not abate.

In another episode, Nick Kamen, a singer and former model who was rumored to have been Madonna's lover during the final stages of her marriage to Penn, asked Madonna to write a song for his new album. She agreed and wrote "Each Time You Break My Heart" and also ended up producing the album as well. Refusing to believe that his wife and Kamen were working together, Penn accused them of having an affair and would burst into the recording studio and have confrontations with Madonna and Kamen. Even when the couple returned to New York, the violence continued. In August 1986, Penn and Madonna were accosted by paparazzi outside her Central Park West apartment. Penn spit at one photographer, Anthony Savignano, and in response, Savignano shoved Penn. Once again, Penn's reaction was predictable when he slugged Savignano along with another photographer, Vinnie Zuffante, who had come to his aid.

It is debatable if Madonna decided to star with her husband in David Rabe's play *Goose and Tom-Tom* to learn more acting techniques from him, to gain the experience of performing onstage in front of an audience, or to try to keep the marriage together. People who were close to Madonna back then claim that it was Penn who wanted to perform with his wife, and in another attempt to save the marriage, she agreed.

Goose and Tom-Tom played a limited engagement, as planned, in repertory at Lincoln Center. Madonna played a moll to Penn's gangster, and some would say that Rabe's play was good experience for her eventual role as Breathless Mahoney in Warren Beatty's *Dick Tracy*.

chapter twenty-eight
····················

*D*uring the fall of 1986, shortly after *Goose and Tom-Tom* closed, the couple returned to California, where Madonna committed herself to a film called *Blind Date.* When the studio went back on its word and hired Bruce Willis as her costar, after having promised her approval of the male lead, she withdrew. Eventually, the role went to Kim Basinger. Through her own development company, Siren Films, Madonna became involved in an adaptation of French writer/director Agnès Varda's 1962 melodrama, *Cléo de 5 à 7.* At the same time, Diane Keaton and Joe Kelly, a producer at Fox, were trying to commission a script for a remake of the 1930 Josef von Sternberg classic *Blue Angel,* which had starred Marlene Dietrich, for Madonna. When *Cléo de 5 à 7* and *Blue Angel* stalled, Madonna went to work writing the lyrics for a song for her husband's movie *At Close Range,* with Patrick Leonard, who was writing the music.

In what was considered to be the only positive moment in a film that bombed at the box office, Madonna's song, "Live to Tell," had a moderate success. Since the film was about a rural family, Madonna's video, directed by James Foley, shows her more in keeping with the rural setting of the film. Sitting on a chair on a blacked-out set, wearing a housedress, her eyes less blue and more gray to fit in with the dreariness of her character, and with only a single spotlight on her, she sings "Live to Tell." Immediately afterward, Madonna had another success with her record and video "Papa Don't Preach."

*   *   *

Griffin Dunne had seen Madonna in *Goose and Tom-Tom* and decided that he wanted to work with her in a movie. "She seemed to be very inside herself," Dunne said. "When she came out with a cigarette that needed to be lit, all you were concerned about was who was going to light it."

In 1987, Dunne finally got his wish when he was cast with Madonna in *Who's That Girl,* directed once again by James Foley. From the beginning of their collaboration, Dunne had difficulty adapting the way he worked with the way Madonna approached acting on a set. "We work very differently," Dunne said. "She likes her first take best. I think my best is around the fourth. She drove me crazy because she kept telling me, 'You got it,' just the way her character would. I mean she's a very noisy girl. If you're having lunch or something, she's not at all like that, but on the set she'd use this talent she has for grating on my character's nerves—talking nonstop between takes—and I'd look at her and really would go, 'Who *is* this girl?' "

After *Shanghai Surprise* failed so abysmally, *Who's That Girl* was supposed to be Madonna's comeback film. Foley brought the script, originally called *Slammer,* to Madonna as a draft and found her to be instinctively cautious. "I told him that I liked the script," Madonna said, "but I could see where it needed a lot of work." This time around, not only did she exhibit prudence about accepting a role without questioning the director's, writer's, and producer's intentions, but she also had much more control. As a result, the script was rewritten several times by several different writers until Madonna finally approved it, judging it to be the way "we wanted it."

Who's That Girl is a romantic comedy, based loosely on Howard Hawks's movie classic *Bringing Up Baby,* which starred Katharine Hepburn as a zany heiress and Cary Grant as a serious paleontologist. In *Who's That Girl,* Griffin Dunne plays a humorless young lawyer who is about to marry a debutante whose father frames Nikki Finn, played by Madonna, for a murder that he has committed. In what turns out to be a fatefully wrong decision, on the day before the wedding, the father instructs his future son-in-law to drive the newly paroled Nikki Finn to the train station, from which she will speed out of his life. Finn ends up wrecking Dunne's car, getting them chased by gangsters, and going through a host of other mayhem, which predictably makes the prudish lawyer fall madly in love with her.

One of the main problems with Madonna's performance was that, unlike Mia Farrow in *Broadway Danny Rose,* her adenoidal accent, little-girl demeanor, coy facial expressions, and shrewish tantrums did not charm the audience. Another problem was that Madonna played the role as she portrays the characters in most of her videos: as a girl who gets her revenge on the bad man who is out to use her and abuse her. In this case, it was clearly art imitating life.

After the movie was finished, James Foley claimed that while it had been extremely difficult to shoot from a technical viewpoint, Madonna was "absolutely perfect." He said, "She is precociously talented. She's very instinctual; what comes out is unencumbered by analysis. We shot a lot on the streets of New York and on the streets in Los Angeles, and she helped. Everyone on the crew observes the tone the star sets, and she emanated such a sense of ease and dignity that it filtered clear down to the caterer. She's curious as hell, about lights, scripts, people's names."

Madonna's good behavior on the set unfortunately did nothing to change the miserable reviews that she got, although one generous critic compared her to Jean Harlow, even calling her the "Harlow of the 1990s." Madonna's analysis of the role was similar to what she would say about all the characters she has portrayed on the screen. "I could identify with Nikki," Madonna maintained, "as if I was born to play her because I was inspired by her message. A woman can get away with murder if her weapon is laughter, which makes the audience fall in love with her."

Every year in the United States, about fifty movies are released without press screenings. When that happens, it is usually considered an admission by the distributors that the film is bad, and they want to get it out before advance negative press kills whatever chance they have to get back some of their investment. Warner Brothers, in association with Peter Gruber, Jon Peters, and Roger Birnbaum, decided not to do any prepublicity for *Who's That Girl* or arrange for any screenings.

According to a list that was published in the *Los Angeles Times* in 1987, thirty-eight films had been released without press. Topping the list was *Who's That Girl.*

Undeterred by the impending failure of the movie, on July 17, 1987, almost three weeks before the August 7 release date of *Who's That Girl,* Madonna embarked upon a world tour. Freddy DeMann, her manager and the man who was known throughout the music business to defer to his client's every whim, came up with a desperate but brilliant idea to save the film from total disaster. He suggested that Madonna's upcoming tour should be named after the movie, Who's That Girl. In keeping with the title, he also thought up a $50,000 marketing campaign that included three-page ads of Madonna's eyes only with the teasing question "Who's that girl?"

Though DeMann's brilliant idea did little to help the movie's box-office success, when it came to the tour, Madonna had the distinction of selling out the more than fifty-one thousand tickets at New York Giants Stadium in less than six hours. In fact, since her last tour in 1985, she had never played to a seating capacity of less than twenty thousand. Madonna was at the height of her popularity.

The tour was choreographed by Jeffrey Hornaday, whose work on *Flashdance* had put the movie on a caliber with a successful Broadway musical. At one point during her performance, Madonna stood motionless under a single spotlight—exactly what Patrick Hernandez and the others had wanted her to do in Paris—and sang "Live to Tell" with heartfelt emotion. In fact, one of her stops on the tour was in France, where she performed in front of one hundred thousand people in a stadium in Sceaux, a suburb not far from Paris. Jacques Chirac, who in 1987 was prime minister as well as the mayor of Paris, was besieged with requests from residents of Sceaux, as well as political figures, to cancel the concert as they were concerned about crowds, vandalism, and damage to the stadium. Chirac's daughter, Claude, who is one of his most important political advisers and has helped shape her father's image to appeal to young French voters, was twenty-four years old at the time and a big fan of Madonna's. In a recent interview with Claude Chirac, she recalled that she had been responsible for changing her father's mind and allowing the show to go on over the objections of some of his constituents. "I made my father sit down and listen to Madonna's music," Claude Chirac says, "and when he saw how much I loved it, and when he realized that she really had enormous talent, he relented." In appreciation, after the concert ended, Madonna presented Jacques Chirac with a check for half a million French francs, which at the time equaled approximately $83,000, to be given to a foundation to fight AIDS.

At the time the Who's That Girl tour was launched in America, John Scher, a concert tour promoter, called the summer of '87 the "busiest stadium summer in the eighteen years I've been in this business." Barry Bell, a booking agent with Premier Talent, also called the summer of '87 "the summer of the stadium tours, which had a positive effect on the promoter's business."

In the summer of '87, Madonna and David Bowie went out on tour separately, both of them performing on separate occasions to sold-out audiences at Giants Stadium in New Jersey.

Madonna has often been compared and has compared herself to David Bowie. While Madonna has never had as many critical successes as Bowie, she has had more consecutive hits. Both have changed style into substance by transforming their images as well as by predicting the trends and tastes of their audiences. Madonna and David Bowie have also both pursued film careers. Though Bowie has always been cast to type, appearing in films as the androgynous, evil oddity, Madonna has taken on roles that demand more range and dramatic ability than she is able to deliver. Perhaps the most marked difference between the two singing stars is the reaction they evoke from the so-called moral majority or those who make themselves experts in what might be damaging to the young viewer.

Certain of Madonna's videos have been banned from MTV, including her most recent, which appeared in March 2001, "What It Feels Like for a Girl" from her album *Music,* directed by her husband, Guy Ritchie. MTV executives said that the video had gratuitous violence, with images of Madonna stealing cars, torching a gas station, robbing an ATM customer, and running over street-hockey players before she commits suicide by crashing her car into a utility pole. Concerning censorship of her music, Madonna has always claimed that the reason she has been targeted by the moral majority is less because of her music or videos than because of her gender. "When David Bowie has violent images in his videos, there seems to be no problem," Madonna stated. "Or, when Prince has blatant sexual images, there isn't a problem. There's a problem with me and my so-called image which has resulted in the censorship of several of my videos."

The nationally syndicated gossip columnist Liz Smith wrote about the censorship of "What It Feels Like for a Girl" by MTV in the *New York Post* on March 21, 2001. "I have seen Madonna's video," she said, " 'What It Feels Like for a Girl.' This is the one that has been absurdly banned from VH1 and MTV. (So when will MTV cancel *Jackass* completely?) Am *I* shocked? You bet. Not because of the vid's violent content. It's nothing you don't see on prime-time network programs. No, what is shocking is the misdirection of the clip itself. The song, one of Madonna's most plaintive, powerful, and well-written efforts, has here been speeded up in a frantic dance remix. The 'irony' that Madonna and her director/hubby Guy Ritchie say they intended doesn't come across."

In response to what Madonna calls the "moralists" who object to her on the basis of her image and her gender, she has quoted from the I Ching: "So, too, music has power to ease tension within the heart and to loosen the grip of obscure emotions. The enthusiasm of the heart expresses itself involuntarily in a burst of song, in dance and rhythmic movement of the body. From immemorial times the inspiring effect of the invisible sound that moves all hearts and draws them together has mystified mankind. Rulers have made use of this natural taste for music. Music was looked upon as something serious and holy, designed to purify the feelings of men; it fell to music to glorify the virtue of heroes and thus to construct a bridge to the world of the unseen."

Perhaps more to the point would be Madonna's admission that she allows herself to be influenced by her husbands. Penn did it when it came to her movies, both directly and through his friend James Foley. Apparently, Guy Ritchie has been permitted to interfere in the one medium where Madonna has few peers.

In May 1988, as her marriage to Sean Penn was coming apart, and her movie career had proved to be less encouraging than she had hoped, and with her quest to play *Evita* obviously stalled as well, Madonna took a starring role in David Mamet's play *Speed-the-Plow,* a title that proved to be as bewildering as Madonna's performance. Curiously, Madonna researched the title and, once again, found parallels between it and the character, while inferring religious undertones in it that she took as a sign that she was "destined to play the role."

"Speed the plough" is a phrase found in the Anglican, Church of England, service for those concerned with agriculture. During the service the plough is brought up to the center of the church, and members of the farming community gather around to ask God to "speed the plough and the ploughman, the farm, and the farmer." Not only did the religious connotation move Madonna, but also that *Speed the Plough* was a play written by Thomas Morton in 1798. Morton's work introduced the name and character of Mrs. Grundy, and the concept of Grundyism as the extreme of moral rigidity. Once Madonna found those biblical links, she felt that she understood the moral message of David Mamet's play.

When it was announced that Madonna had signed with Mamet, ticket requests were so unexpectedly tremendous that the small theater at Lincoln Center where it had been scheduled to open could not accommodate the enormous demand for tickets. Since the Royale Theatre in Times Square was available, a lease was signed, which meant that the play was upgraded before it even went into previews. The public had difficulty separating Madonna from any character she was slated to perform, proving what Andrew Lloyd Webber feared when Alan Parker was persuading him to give Madonna the role of *Evita,* that she would eclipse the character with her own. Before the announcement was made that *Speed-the-Plow* would be moving from Lincoln Center to a larger Broadway theater, and before Madonna even uttered a word onstage, a feud began between two actresses who had something very significant in common.

Patti LuPone, who had played *Evita* on both the Broadway and London stage, was starring in a revival of Cole Porter's *Anything Goes* at the Vivian Beaumont Theater at Lincoln Center. LuPone was aware that, in 1988, Oliver Stone, now at the helm of the project, wanted Madonna and not LuPone to re-create the role on film. As soon as LuPone learned that

Madonna was scheduled to perform under the same roof with her at Lincoln Center in Mamet's new play, she tacked up a notice on the theater's bulletin board. "Ms. LuPone," the note read, "wishes to inform the management that only one Sicilian diva at a time is allowed in this theater."

Madonna's interest in David Mamet's new play had begun two years earlier, in August 1986, when she was performing in repertory at Lincoln Center in *Goose and Tom-Tom.* The artistic director of Lincoln Center and the director of Mamet's play was Gregory Mosher, who had been associated with Mamet in thirteen of his previous works. Madonna approached Mosher and asked him if she could have the part of Karen, the office temp, who plays opposite Joe Mantegna and Ron Silver, two seasoned actors, the former having starred in Mamet's first movie, *House of Games.* Mosher refused to commit himself, although he promised Madonna that when the time came, she could read for the part.

When the casting began, Joe Mantegna and Ron Silver were assured of the leads and were made to understand that the office temporary whose presence is meant to be unsettling to both men was probably going to be portrayed by Elizabeth Perkins. Though most of David Mamet's plays have had macho undertones, as seen in *American Buffalo, Sexual Perversity in Chicago,* and *Glengarry Glen Ross,* the role of Karen in *Speed-the-Plow* is not large but is important since she acts as a catalyst between the two men, who have been close friends and business associates for years. Karen, who pretends to know nothing about the movie business in order to get a major film studio interested in a movie project, is hired by Ron Silver's character, a cynical film executive. Throughout the play, Karen forces the partners, Silver and Mantegna, to take a close look at the morals and ethics of the film business. After she sleeps with the boss (Mantegna), which tests the men's friendship and loyalty, Karen suddenly demonstrates surprising knowledge about how to leverage a deal in return for her sexual favors.

After Madonna auditioned for Mosher, who was impressed by her performance, she read for David Mamet, who was also convinced that she was perfect for the part. In fact, during the run of the play on Broadway, Gregory Mosher reiterated his opinion of Madonna as the consummate professional. "She's a rock," he said. "She rehearses the changes we make during the day and the play's on every night. It's working fine."

Madonna, cast against type for the role, believed that she would earn the critics' respect as Cher had done, another singer turned actress. Cher had won an Oscar for her role in *Moonstruck,* playing the spinsterish Italian girl who leaves her comfortable Italian suitor, Danny Aiello, to embark on a secret love affair. In the end, Cher falls madly in love with a baker, Nicolas Cage, an unlikely suitor and an odd young man, and Cher makes more of an emotional transformation than she does a physical one when she blossoms into a woman obviously consumed by passion.

On opening night, in an act of generosity and gratitude for what she said had been "everyone's patience and understanding with a novice like me on Broadway," Madonna had thirty bouquets of flowers delivered to the theater for the cast, crew, and even the backstage doormen. As thoughtful and kind as she has been on numerous occasions to those people she has worked with, according to Patrick Leonard— her constant collaborator, the director of her first tour, her cowriter and coproducer on her third album, *True Blue*—and many others, she has been "burned so many times" that she believes it is better "to act like a tyrant than be treated like a wimp and have people walk all over you."

Her love of children is the one area in her life where she has always been sincere. Her friends claim that she "melts" whenever a child approaches her, whether it is a stranger or the offspring of a friend. "Those are the only people whose motives she doesn't question," one friend says. Her detractors believe that her weakness for children is yet another manifestation of her narcissism since, in their view, she relates only in the context of her own memories of vulnerability when she had been so deeply hurt after her mother died.

On Madonna's thirtieth birthday, August 16, 1988, a group of her teenage fans had bought tickets for the evening performance of *Speed-the-Plow.* They had also arranged for flowers to be delivered backstage to Madonna as an expression of their loyalty and love and in recognition of her turning thirty. However, Madonna, while she was performing on Broadway, had made the transition into actress, forgoing her usual image as rock star and teenage idol. Even if she had made a statement to the press, in an attempt to explain to her fans that their presence would upset her concentration or would be considered inappropriate by the usual theatergoing audience, it is doubtful that they would have understood her sudden denial of what she meant to them. They expected loyalty. Madonna expected unconditional love on her own terms.

When Madonna heard that the theater would be filled with her groupies, she instructed the box office to refund their money and prevent them from entering. According to one of the people who worked at the Royale Theatre, Madonna sent word that she didn't want "a bunch of screaming kids upsetting her during the performance." Her fans were crushed, but even more insulting was that, fifteen minutes before curtain, the flowers that had been delivered to her backstage were thrown out her dressing-room window. A ticket-taker at the Royale remembers the scene. "It was pathetic. The kids were picking up all the flowers, some crying, others cursing her. It was not a pretty sight."

Throughout the three acts of *Speed-the-Plow,* Madonna is dressed in dowdy skirts and simple blouses, her hair dyed a nondescript brown, glasses perched on her nose, the antithesis of her usual image and the opposite of a cover she did at the time for *Harper's Bazaar,* where she wore a Christian Lacroix polka-dot halter dress. In the article in *Harper's,* Madonna talked about her character and about Mamet's play. "She's a sympathetic, misunderstood heroine who speaks the truth at any risk," Madonna said. "Fate brought me to this play. I don't take the characters home with me, but I'm incredibly affected by whatever role I'm playing." Following that statement, Madonna seemed to contradict herself when she added, "I felt the girl was defeated, and I felt defeated all summer. I didn't feel she had a lot of focus or ultimately knew what she wanted to do with herself. And I felt that she lost in the end; she didn't have whatever tools she needed to get herself out of the situation she was in."

During the run of the play Madonna claimed that she had lost some of her confidence. "I didn't feel my usual ballsy self," she said. "I just felt really defeated, is the best word to use. And that actually influenced everything I did, because it made me very sad."

She went on to explain that in the beginning of her career, she believed that acting was about being someone else. Based on what she described as several "miserable experiences," she now believed that acting was really about being herself. "It's about being true to yourself and about being honest," she said, "which is what my music is about."

During the run of the play Madonna began writing her album *Like a Prayer.* She claimed that the mood of the music was a direct result of the feelings of defeat she had experienced as she immersed herself in the role of Karen. According to Madonna, the inspiration for her songs and lyrics on the album was her ability to deal with the tragedies in her life that up until then she had buried in her subconscious. "I began to deal with the death of my mother," she claimed, "and the demise of certain relationships. Not only when I was writing the album, but every night when I performed onstage, I would find myself exploring everything that had traumatized me as a child and even as an adult."

In the last scene in *Speed-the-Plow,* Madonna is supposed to walk onstage and convey how deeply upset and frightened she is. "I would sit in my dressing room," she recalled, "with all the lights off, waiting for that scene, and I would force myself to think of something really painful. I did it every night, and I purged myself that way. It was like a goal I set. I would say, 'Tonight I'm going to work this problem out. I need to think about this or the possibility of this terrible thing happening.' They were little psychological exercises that forced me to face my fears."

At the end of the run, Madonna would sum up her experiences after having worked with two consummate actors in terms that were more familiar to her public. Typical of her obsession with the physical and the sexual, Madonna commented that playing opposite Mantegna and Silver was "like having great sex."

As seriously as she claimed to take her debut on Broadway, there was one performance in which Madonna broke up laughing. As she was reading from a book in an effort to persuade her boss, Joe Mantegna, that it would make a good movie, she began to giggle. She laughed for several minutes as the audience wondered if they had missed a joke or a line that the actress was supposed to have found funny. Regaining control, Madonna simply said, "As I was saying," and continued from the script.

David Mamet's dialogue, which has a particular rhythm and almost a musical beat, requires a special sense of timing for any actor if he or she delivers it properly, so that the words don't lose any of their impact or drama. Both Joe Mantegna and Ron Silver were able to perform the lines to perfection, guarding their own rhythm and sense of timing that complemented the writer's prose. Despite all the energy that Madonna displays during her concert tours, she was unable to re-create that energy onstage, and the critics were almost all unanimously vicious in their reviews. Had George S. Kaufman, the eminent playwright of the last century, been alive and sitting on the aisle to review *Speed-the-Plow,* he might have used one of his most acerbic quotes. "I saw the play at a disadvantage," Kaufman once wrote. "The curtain was up." Clive Barnes wrote, "She is not ready to light up the lamps of Broadway," and John Simon reported, "She can afford to pay for a few acting lessons."

Dennis Cunningham recently retired as the WCBS-TV drama critic after reviewing more than five hundred plays during a career in television that spanned more than twenty-five years. He is a shy man by nature, retiring and loath to be confrontational, especially with his colleagues who share his profession and all the opening nights when they have the fate of so many actors, writers, directors, and producers in their hands. As sensitive and intellectual as he is, with a doctorate in theater from Carnegie-Mellon, a vast experience teaching theater to university and postgraduate students, and a genuine respect and love for the art, when Frank Rich came out as the sole positive voice for Madonna's performance in *Speed-the-Plow*, Cunningham exploded. In Rich's review of the play, which appeared in the *New York Times*, he wrote that he found Madonna's performance "intelligent, scrupulously disciplined comic acting."

"This woman cannot move onstage," Dennis Cunningham proclaimed. "She moves . . . as if she were operated by a remote control unit several cities away. She cannot give meaning to the words she is saying. It's not a matter of opinion, it's unconscionable. Frank has taken leave of his senses, and he should apologize to every actor he ever gave a bad review for a performance after this. I'm in a righteous rage, like John Brown at Harper's Ferry. Just think of the hundreds of New York actresses who should have gotten this role. We could have gotten one of the audience who could have read it better than she did."

Dennis Cunningham also made no secret that he was profoundly offended by Mamet's agreement and Mosher's choice of Madonna to star in the play. As far as he was concerned, it was nothing more than a cynical decision that the writer and director hoped would guarantee ticket sales. "Her ineptitude is scandalously thorough," Cunningham fumed, "and I intend to sit down with Gregory Mosher and David Mamet to discuss their casting decision. The theater is being sold like Veg-O-Matics. I have never seen on a Broadway stage someone who didn't have the basic elements of Acting 101."

The reality was that Madonna, despite the opprobrium that the critics heaped on her, was nonetheless performing on the Broadway stage every night at the Royale Theatre, which drew not only fans and curious spectators but also stars like Katharine Hepburn, Sylvester Stallone, and Sigourney Weaver, although Hepburn seemed bewildered by the star's performance. Later that evening Jeffrey Lyons, the drama critic and the son of Leonard Lyons, the creator of the celebrated column from the 1950s "The Lyons Den," ran into Miss Hepburn and asked her what play she had seen. "Mamet's new play with Madonna playing a would-be actress who can't act. She was absolutely convincing!"

Madonna's friends also came to see the play to lend their support, like Jennifer Grey, who would costar with Madonna in her next film, *Bloodhounds of Broadway,* Lindsay Law, the executive producer of *Bloodhounds of Broadway,* as well as John McEnroe and Tatum O'Neal, and the star's brothers, Anthony and Christopher Ciccone. Also a frequent member of the audience was Sandra Bernhard, who was spending a great deal of time with Madonna.

This was a particularly sad moment in Madonna's personal life. Things were not going well in her marriage, and for Madonna, the perfectionist and the woman who believed she could control her destiny, she considered it her failure. It didn't make things any easier that the press seemed intent on linking Madonna with every man she happened to be seen with. Some were merely friends, trainers, business associates, or jogging partners, while others were used to assuage her loneliness. Freddy DeMann, her manager, introduced her to another client of his, a British rocker, Simon F. For a while, Madonna took him along to make the rounds of her old haunts on the Lower East Side. The relationship that the press focused on, however, was with Sandra Bernhard, who often came to the theater to pick her up and take her to a late supper. Often, Bernhard would stay overnight at Madonna's apartment, and when she would leave in the morning, paparazzi would taunt her with their cameras.

The two women met when Madonna went backstage after watching Bernhard's one-woman comedy show, and they became friends almost immediately. Six months into their friendship, Sean Penn accused Madonna of having an affair with Bernhard. Madonna claims he beat her, presumably in a jealous rage, and left her tied to a chair in her Malibu beach house. In May 1989, shortly after Madonna brought charges against Penn, filed for divorce, and subsequently withdrew the charges as well as the divorce petition, she appeared onstage with Sandra Bernhard at the Brooklyn Academy of Music. At a benefit to raise money to save the rain forests, Madonna and Bernhard, dressed in identical sequined bras and knee-length cutoffs decorated with graffiti, sang "I Got You, Babe" as the grand finale. At one point during their routine, with their arms wrapped around each other, Madonna told the audience, "Don't believe those stories," to which Bernhard retorted, "Believe those stories!"

Madonna's attraction to Bernhard was perhaps more a reaction against men in general than it was a physical and sexual attraction to the comedian. Perhaps her boyfriends were less sympathetic about her problems with her husband's drinking and violence, which may be why Madonna confided more in Bernhard. Despite Madonna's claim that her former boyfriends—the ones she had loved and left during her early days in New York, including Jellybean Benitez, Dan Gilroy, Mark Kamins, and Tony Ward—"would all take her back," they were secretly pleased that not everything in her life was going smoothly. Theater critics, all men as well, had destroyed her belief in her acting potential, and she felt that her business associates, also mostly men, were only interested in her as a lucrative product.

Her relationship with Bernhard could have been Madonna's

way of showing the world that she practiced what she preached in her songs and videos. She didn't need a man to exist or feel fulfilled. And, she had no intention of being the victim of men, who naturally took each other's side when there was a problem with their wives or girlfriends.

Madonna was so deeply hurt and disappointed by her husband, angry at her father, distrustful of men in general for having dominated her, used her, and abused her that she intended to send out a clear message to the world. Perhaps only a woman could offer her the kind of tender and serene relationship she had always wanted. After all, how many times has a woman, at a low point in her life, taken a lover just for the comfort of having someone there, to be intimate, close, and understanding when she was terrified of being alone?

chapter twenty-nine

....

On the evening before Thanksgiving 1988, Sean appeared at Madonna's New York apartment. He had stormed out three days before during another argument. For the entire time he was gone, Madonna was frantic that something terrible had happened to him. When he finally showed up, her fury took precedence over her relief that he was alive, and she threw him out.

On Thanksgiving Day, Penn, furious and humiliated, flew back to Los Angeles, only to besiege Madonna with phone calls, which she refused to take. On December 4, Madonna filed for divorce, although she confided in several close friends that she was doing it only in a final attempt to "scare him into changing and to get help with his drinking and uncontrollable fits of violence."

When Penn was informed of the divorce, he was shocked, hurt, and eventually depressed. He stopped calling Madonna, which she took as a sign that he had no intention of talking her out of her decision. After two days, Madonna began to panic. She told the same close friends that she was afraid that her husband was actually going to let her go through with the divorce.

On the third day, Madonna picked up the phone and called Penn in California, but this time he wouldn't take her phone calls. Ignoring her messages, he sent a different kind of message when he began being seen around Hollywood with his friends, drinking, dancing, and making brief appearances at parties. Worried about his mental and physical state, Timothy Hutton, Jan Michael Vincent, and Dennis Hopper began pressuring him to talk to Madonna to try to work things out. On December 8, Penn finally phoned Madonna in New York, but then she was the one who refused to take his calls. Only when James Foley prevailed upon her to reconsider did she eventually agree to speak to him.

On December 11 the couple had their first conversation in almost two weeks, during which Madonna berated her husband for his behavior. After several more days, the calls became warmer and longer, and eventually Penn was sending her balloons, flowers, presents, and even a singing telegram. The singing telegram was delivered by a male singer who not only serenaded her but also delivered the message that "Sean Penn loves his wife very much."

By the following day, they were setting down conditions to resume their marriage. Penn promised to see a marriage counselor, while Madonna promised to start a family within a year. On December 16, she officially dropped the divorce petition "without prejudice," which meant that she could refile at any time within the state of California. One week later, Madonna bought Diane Keaton's house on Roxbury Drive in Los Angeles for $3 million and signed a $10 million deal with Pepsi.

Madonna's house in Malibu was designed by her brother Christopher and, similar to her apartment in New York, was white, stark, and airy with marble floors and furniture and draperies in earth colors with an eclectic mixture of antiques that ranged from Chinese to French provincial and from English country to art deco.

All Madonna's homes are filled with art, and her most precious paintings are the ones by the South American artist Frida Kahlo. Madonna not only appreciated her work and sense of color, but she also identified with the artist, especially because of her violent marriage to the more well-known painter Diego Rivera. "I see some parallels," Madonna once explained. "I mean, she was crippled physically and emotionally in ways that I'm not. But she was also married to a very powerful and passionate man and was tormented by him. Although he loved her and was supportive of her as an artist, there was a lot of competition between them. There weren't that many female artists at the time, and the Latin community is a very macho environment. It was very hard for her to survive that and have her own identity. And I can identify to a certain extent with having that awareness of the male point of view of what a woman's role is in a relationship. It's tough to fight it. She was very courageous, which I admire and can relate to."

Under the tortured eye of Frida Kahlo, Sean Penn allegedly beat Madonna up, tied her to a chair, and left her there for nine hours. Only when a member of her staff returned home late that evening and heard her cries for help was Madonna finally untied.

On December 28, 1988, the Malibu sheriff's office received a call regarding a disturbance at the couple's home. Arriving at Madonna's house, they were greeted by the star, who, according to one of the officers present, was "in a state of complete hysteria. Her clothes were torn. Her face was cut and bleeding, and she had bruise marks on her neck, arms, back, and legs." Madonna filed a domestic violence report as well as a formal complaint that her husband had assaulted her. Twelve days later, she met with Deputy District Attorney Lauren Weiss, who would have prosecuted the case had Madonna not decided to drop the charges.

Madonna's change of heart was not particularly different from the behavior of more than 98 percent of abused women who have been beaten by their husbands or lovers and who refuse to prosecute them. Many of these women stay until their injuries prove fatal. According to Elizabeth Peck, a historian, the question of why women stay with their abusers was first asked in the 1920s. Back then, sociologists believed that battered women stayed in abusive relationships because they were of low intelligence or mentally retarded. During the 1940s, sociologists changed their minds and assumed that battered women remained with their battering mates because they were masochistic and enjoyed being beaten. By the 1970s, the victim was thought to stay with her abuser because, as a married woman, she was isolated from her friends, family, and neighbors, had few economic or educational resources, and had been terrorized into a state of "learned helplessness" resulting from repeated beatings.

Lenore Walker, an expert on battered women and the author of *The Battered Woman,* believes that "once the women are operating from a belief of helplessness, the perception becomes reality and they become passive, submissive, and helpless."

On the surface, Madonna did not fit the profile of the typical battered woman. She was financially independent, had no children with Penn, could have fled to any one of her many homes, had access to a battery of lawyers, and had friends who were willing to give her emotional support. By the time that she was the victim of abuse, it was not even a question of love that propelled her to stay with her husband, but rather embarrassment and stubbornness, although Madonna claimed that she had decided to drop the divorce proceedings because she "still considered him to be a soul mate." "All love is lucky," Madonna said, "even when it breaks your heart."

Deeply committed to succeed at everything she tried, she was unwilling to admit that she had made a mistake in picking Sean Penn for a husband. During a conversation that she had with a Catholic priest in Los Angeles who had served as an unofficial spiritual guide for the singer, she was extremely anxious to know if, because she had never married in the Church, she would be excommunicated if she divorced. The priest told her that if she ever decided to remarry in the Church, she would have to get an annulment approved by the Vatican. Privately, the priest told a New York colleague that divorcing a man who "beat her was less offensive to God and the Church than some of her other antics." Only when Madonna became convinced without a doubt that, as powerful as she was perceived and as she had always willed herself to believe, the situation was hopeless, did she finally make the painful decision that the marriage was over.

On January 9, 1989, Penn had another drunken temper tantrum, this time over what he described as his wife's "affair with that dyke." He was referring to Sandra Bernhard, who had been staying with Madonna and Penn in the singer's Malibu home. Once again, the police were called for what they later said was a "peripheral involvement" and politely suggested that Penn might leave and stay at a friend's or with his family until things settled down. Apparently, he agreed and went to his parents' house several minutes away, but sometime during the night, he broke into Madonna's house through a rear door and the drunken tirade continued. This time, Madonna calmed her husband down by asking Bernhard to leave.

The next day, January 10, when Penn went out to do some errands, Madonna called her lawyers and instructed them to file for divorce in the Santa Monica district court. "That's it," she told her staff and friends. "I can't take it anymore. Sandra is gone, and I intend to go through this alone." Changing the locks, she called Eileen Ryan, Penn's mother, and told her what she intended to do.

The papers were filed on January 10, and her staff was deposed by her lawyers about the events that had taken place on December 28 when she had been beaten and tied to a chair. Under California law, which is based on community property, Penn could have demanded and won half of Madonna's assets earned during their marriage. Instead, he refused to take anything. "I'll go," he said, "and I won't take one stinking cent. You can have it all."

After the divorce was final, Madonna admitted that the failure of her marriage to Sean Penn had been one of the "great losses in her life," as he was one of the few men that she respected. "He had balls," she added.

On March 20, 1989, her album *Like a Prayer* was released, which she dedicated to her mother, "who taught me how to pray."

In April 1989, Madonna began shooting a television adaptation of Damon Runyon's *Bloodhounds of Broadway,* starring Tony Longo as Crunch Sweeney, the actor, who would also briefly become her lover. Longo would also benefit from Madonna's generosity when, driving together in Los Angeles, she dropped him off at his house and was shocked to see that he lived in a run-down neighborhood. Without being asked, she insisted on lending him money to buy a decent flat.

In 1990, shortly before *Bloodhounds of Broadway* was released, Howard Brookner, the writer and director, who had also made an appearance in the film, died of AIDS. Madonna was devastated. Brookner was only one of many friends and colleagues she would lose to the disease. When the reviews appeared and they were mediocre, Madonna was more upset for Howard Brookner than she was for herself. For probably one of the few times in her career, she ignored the critics and, instead, forged ahead to find a viable theatrical or cinematic project to get her mind off her troubles. Within weeks, she announced that she would appear as a Holocaust victim in a film entitled *Triumph.* The project never went beyond cursory discussion.

Whether it was a coincidence or a calculated publicity ploy, Madonna began dating Warren Beatty, who, against the advice of his producers, decided to take a chance and cast her as Breathless Mahoney in his production of *Dick Tracy.* She said about Breathless the same thing that she would say about *Evita,* that she had been "preparing for the role for her entire life." "She is a girl," Madonna explained. "She's scared. She's a seductress in a lot of pain."

Warren Beatty and Stephen Sondheim had been friends for about ten years before they began working together in

1990 on *Dick Tracy.* Sondheim had written the music for Beatty's film *Reds,* the story based on the life of John Reed, the American journalist who covered the Russian Revolution and introduced his readers to the burgeoning Communist Party. The collaboration between Beatty and Sondheim on *Reds* had always been symbiotic. Sondheim's compositions and orchestrations were harmonious with Beatty's roles as director and star. Things were not as harmonious when the composer agreed to score *Dick Tracy.*

Madonna found the three songs that Stephen Sondheim wrote for the film to be extremely difficult for her to learn and to sing because, as she explained, "He writes in a kind of chromatic wildness. For instance, one song was written in five sharps. Another was a torch song, kind of slow and sad, that a singer sings at a smoky nightclub at three in the morning when the club is empty, kind of melancholy, just a piano and a voice." The third song was about gluttony and was more up-tempo, funny, and ironic, similar to "Diamonds Are a Girl's Best Friend." Madonna performed "What Can You Lose" as a more modern duet, accompanied by her pianist in the film, Mandy Patinkin, who starred in *Sunday in the Park with George* on Broadway. He also played Che in the New York stage production of *Evita.*

Dick Tracy never achieved the level of success that similar films such as *Batman* or *Superman* did, although Madonna got decent reviews for her performance and as a result was once again optimistic about her film career.

In 1990, Robert Stigwood was still trying to make *Evita,* and during a lunch at Il Pallazzo, a Hollywood bistro, with Sid Bernstein, Alan Grubman, and Freddie Gershon, the former president of Stigwood Productions, Madonna's name was once again mentioned as the "only actress who could make the film a reality." When it came to the music and the format for the movie, her demands were unreasonable. She had her first meeting with the composer, Andrew Lloyd

Webber, and alienated him by demanding that a whole new score be written in keeping with her image as well as to accommodate her limited vocal range. As Webber remarked after the meeting, "Madonna wanted *Evita* revamped to become *Madonna*." Eventually, Madonna backed down when she realized that she had come across someone whose ego was justifiably as large or larger than her own.

Despite her initial unpleasant meeting with Webber, Madonna was still considered the sole contender for the part until Disney Studios decided not to put up the money. According to Alan Grubman, the lawyer on the deal, "Basically, Disney was fearful that the film would never be brought in under budget, and since musicals were not known to be big box-office successes in Hollywood, they were certain that they would never get their money back."

Added to their concern was that neither the film *Dick Tracy* nor Madonna's performance as Breathless Mahoney had impressed Disney enough for them to reconsider financing the project. At the time, those close to the negotiations predicted that if there was to be a solution, it would have to be between Madonna and Disney directly. In other words, Madonna would have to lower her fee substantially and provide other guarantees that would satisfy the financial people. Either she couldn't or she wouldn't, but in the end Disney walked away from the deal.

After Disney dropped out, the project went to Paramount Studios, who also worried about costs. One executive recalls the concerns back then: "If film people really believed that the movie could be brought in for fifteen million dollars, then everyone would have jumped up to make it. Unfortunately, it had the smell of being a difficult film to control. Madonna's a professional, but she's also a big star, and if the director has to please her as well as everyone else, then it's going to become a thirty-million-dollar picture." As it turned out, *Evita* cost $60 million to make.

Robert Stigwood backed out, and Oliver Stone stepped in for the second time. Having been burned once in 1988, the first thing Stone did was to lobby President Carlos Menem of Argentina for permission to bring his cast and crew to Buenos Aires to film on location. The next thing he did was to hire Loretta Crawford, a well-known casting director, and instruct her to offer the title role to Madonna for a fee of $1 million. From that point on, Stone had nothing but problems. President Menem refused to give his permission for *Evita* to be filmed in Argentina, and Andrew Lloyd Webber and Tim Rice were once again against Stone's choice of Madonna for the title role. Stymied by these problems and by production costs, Stone finally dropped the project after early production work was delayed by a screenwriters' strike.

After completing Truth or Dare in 1991, the documentary based on her Blond Ambition tour, and after enjoying a modest success with *Dick Tracy,* Madonna decided to commission two different scripts based on two women whom she greatly admired and with whom she felt a profound kinship: Frida Kahlo and Martha Graham. Rumors at the time also had Madonna in discussions with Jay McInerney to star in a one-woman show based on his novel *The Story of My Life.*

While Madonna was trying to raise development money and was negotiating to option McInerney's book, she was offered a small part in Penny Marshall's movie *A League of Their Own.* The film, starring Tom Hanks and Geena Davis and costarring Rosie O'Donnell, is a charming story set during World War II about a women's baseball league that takes over and plays for ardent baseball fans while the male baseball stars are called up to war. Madonna played the part of an Italian girl, Mae Mordabato, who is fiercely patriotic, hits long drives to the outfield, and spends most of her time chewing gum and dancing the jitterbug at various soldiers' canteens. Yet again, Madonna claimed that she had been "born to play the part." During an interview in 1992 with Simon Banner of the Sunday *Daily Mail* in London, she claimed that because the film is about a women's baseball team, it was clearly a "feminist statement." According to Banner, a minute later, she contradicted herself by saying that it wasn't "much fun being in a film with so many other women, all clamoring for the spotlight." "If you want to know the truth, I'd rather the other two leads were men," Madonna admitted, "and I'm sure the other women feel the same. They just didn't tell you that."

The movie, which grossed $104 million, was the biggest hit of the summer of 1992 and Madonna, cast in a part that was similar to Susan in *Desperately Seeking Susan,* received decent reviews.

It is not difficult to understand why Madonna was so intent in believing that she was born to be a movie star. Onstage, she has imaginative and creative people designing her sets and costumes, with original choreography, and with an infectious style singing songs whose lyrics speak directly to her fans. With her energy and charisma, she has the aura of a star. When it came to making a successful movie career, her mistake was not necessarily in trying to mold herself after such stars as Carole Lombard, Judy Holliday, Marilyn Monroe, or even Marlene Dietrich. Her error was in believing that she could take her talent for making videos, which are minimalist movies, four minutes and twenty-two seconds, and sustain it for feature-length movies, or ninety to one hundred and twenty minutes. One of her most impressionistic videos, "Open Your Heart," showed Madonna as every adolescent boy's fantasy and every man's secret desire. Directed by Jean-Baptiste Mondino and photographed by Pascal Lebege, with Richard Sylbert as her production designer, who had gained an impressive reputation by designing *Carnal Knowledge* among other films, the video depicts Madonna as a world-weary performer in a risqué nightclub. Straddling a chair, and surrounded by sleazy voyeurs, leering perverts, and an assortment from the underbelly of society's sexual misfits, Madonna, once again, emulates Dietrich from the prewar cabaret days in Germany. And yet, typical of Madonna's constant message of female sexual superiority and control, her performance is clearly another example of how women, throughout the ages, have destroyed men by taunting and tempting them with sex. "Open Your Heart" was a four-minute performance that held together as a story with several subplots and messages.

Paul Gambacinni, the London radio personality and rock-and-roll expert, believes that when critics like Vincent Canby from the *New York Times* criticize Madonna for not making good movies, they fail to realize that she has, in fact, made several outstanding films. "If you think about it," Gambacinni says, "most of Walt Disney's Oscars were for short films. There is nothing disgraceful about a great video. It's like a novella or a collection of short stories. It just happens that Madonna is good at impact and not character development. In other words, for five minutes she'll hold your attention with an image and an effect, but don't ask her to show you how she got to that point because she can't."

Unfortunately, in 1992 and 1993, Madonna once again had grander notions of prolonging her five-minute erotic videos into what became a trilogy—a book, a video, and a movie—that had one common theme running in the three different mediums: sadomasochism.

In 1992, Madonna published the book *Sex* at the same time that she released her video and record *Erotica,* which did not do well because of the public's reaction to the book. These two projects were examples of only several times during her career when the "goddess" erred and forgot who she was, or rather, whom her fans perceived her to be.

In *Sex,* the photographer Steven Meisel shot Madonna in a variety of compromising poses with unknown and known partners, both female and male. In response, many of her fans were disturbed not only by the pornographic contents, but because they were disgusted at her having "sold out" when she crossed the boundary from irony into vulgarity. Others were outraged that, for the first time, she had promised to reveal far more than what was actually seen within the pages. They felt taken in by what most considered to be Madonna's ultimate slide into crass commercialism.

If those two efforts were not damaging enough, she went on to make *Body of Evidence,* directed by Uli Edel, which proved to be embarrassing to the point of being funny. During a screening of the film in New York, Madonna was literally driven out of a theater on Columbus Circle. The audience booed and made grunting animal noises and bizarre birdcalls whenever she appeared on the screen in a graphic sex scene, complete with a variety of props, including handcuffs, hot wax, and broken glass. Madonna was at the nadir of her career.

The mystery is why the film never even became a cult classic, although one of the producers claims that what saved it from that distinction was the participation of two respected actors, Joe Mantegna and Willem Dafoe, who, according to the producer, had obviously been seduced into thinking that Madonna's name on the credits would pull in the crowds.

The movie shared the same title with a best-seller by Patricia Cornwell, although the producers promised Ms. Cornwell that the title would be changed to *Deadly Evidence,* which of course was never done. The play on words in *Body of Evidence* was just too good to pass up, since it implied that Madonna used her body as a deadly weapon. In the opinion of some, the film was based on her book, *Sex,* although in the text, even Madonna didn't write such embarrassing dialogue as was heard in the film. One of the most memorable lines was when Madonna asked Willem Dafoe, "Have you ever seen animals make love?"

The real enigma is why, at that point in her career, Madonna decided to embark on a sexual trilogy that was nothing more than pornography. Apparently, there was no one around at the time to talk Madonna out of copying

Sharon Stone, who had already gained critical and box-office success by copying Madonna in *Basic Instinct,* a film that appeared in 1992. Not only did *Basic Instinct* have more texture and plot and an absence of gratuitous sex compared to *Body of Evidence,* but Stone performed the role of the lethal nymphomaniac with a lot more depth and even humor.

In the movie, Madonna plays Rebecca Carlson, an intense woman who lives in a glass house on the water and who preys on cardiac cases, ultimately killing them with her sexual acrobatics. There is no doubt that Madonna believed, after making "Bad Girl," the video that shows her in a role that is familiar to her audience—a woman who uses her body as a sexual weapon—that she could work the same magic in *Body of Evidence.*

Curiously, before making the Edel movie, Madonna said that she preferred passion to violence in films and began to parrot the European criticism that it is difficult for Americans to express sexual desire in their movies. "Something bad always happens," Madonna maintained, "violence or the relationship doesn't last. I will not be attracted to making violent films. I am attracted to roles where women are strong and aren't victimized. Everything I do has to be some kind of a celebration of life."

Apparently, Madonna either forgot what she had said or she made an exception with *Body of Evidence* because she would be working with two actors whom she admired, Dafoe and Mantegna. Mira Rostovo, Madonna's drama coach, was less impressed with Madonna's philosophical reasons for making the film. She offered the simplest explanation for its failure: "This girl will never be an actress. She's too vulgar, and she thinks she knows it all."

Madonna's performance is shamelessly narcissistic, and if she does anything positive in the film, it is to remind the public that good acting should always seem effortless on the part of the actor. In *Body of Evidence,* the viewer can actually see the mental transition that Madonna makes every time she speaks her lines. With two expressions to carry her through the story—sullen or in paroxysms of ecstasy—she faces her costars, either dressed primly or bare-breasted with one hand sliding inside her panties, feigning masturbation. She delivers her dialogue in a stilted and unnatural style and is generally unbelievable, especially when the audience is forced to listen to her thin, tinny, whiny voice in her emotional outbursts. After one watches *Body of Evidence,* the only positive comment that any lucid person could make is that Madonna could have been a devastating actress in silent films. A beautiful dancer, she moves gracefully in every scene where she is vertical and expertly in any scene where she is horizontal.

Following Body of Evidence, *instead* of retiring to a convent for hard-core meditation, Madonna went into serious talks with Abel Ferrara, the director who made *Bad Lieutenant,* a film in which a nun is raped on an altar. That scene alone was obviously the impetus that Madonna needed to seek Ferrara out as someone who could produce a script that would suit her. When the collaboration with Ferrara did not work out, Pedro Almodóvar seemed receptive to putting her in one of his films. This was a logical choice since Almodóvar consistently writes female roles in which his actresses portray exaggerated versions of neurotic or sexually dysfunctional women. The problem, according to those who work with the Spanish director regularly, was that his usual stable of actors and actresses resisted the idea because they were afraid that Madonna's presence in a film would lower its quality and cause the audience and critics not to take it seriously. As one Argentine extra who worked with her in *Evita* and, later, worked with Almodóvar said of her, "She dared to jump in with lightly developed vocal equipment and acting skills while many of us sat at home with Juilliard-trained voices and heavy talent, afraid to make a move. She inspires me as much as a physically handicapped person who beats the odds to live a normal life."

In 1993, Madonna would finally get her wish and work with Abel Ferrara, who directed her in *Dangerous Game*. Again, the result was disappointing. "The way he edited it completely changed the ending," Madonna said after it appeared and disappeared. "When I saw the cut film, I was weeping. It was like someone punched me in the stomach. If I'd known that was the movie I was making, I would never have done it."

At that moment in her life, her wealth and success no longer interested her. She could have bought anyone and anything except the only thing that really mattered to her— credibility as an actress. She was thirty-five years old, child-less, and with no particular romantic interest that could ultimately fulfill her other desire of becoming a mother. There had been too many men in her life, too many mean-ingless dalliances with women, and there were still plenty of volunteers for a one-night stand, but none, in view of her past, who saw her as a reasonable risk for the long term. And she craved the long term. She missed being married. She had to prove to herself that she hadn't spent all those years claw-ing her way to the top, sacrificing friends and family along the way, just to end up as a rich and famous star who was destined to be alone. She had feelings she needed to express, and suddenly there was no one to talk to, learn from, or con-fide in.

In 1994, Madonna Louise Veronica Ciccone, the feline creature who had insinuated herself into the psyche of a gen-eration of her fans, had used up eight of her nine lives.

part five

....

Blond Ambition

chapter thirty

· · · · · · · · · · · · · · · · ·

"*S*he didn't say much," the Che character, played by Antonio Banderas in the film *Evita,* sings about Eva Perón, "but she said it loud." In another song, Che remarks that Eva Perón is the greatest social climber since Cinderella.

Both lines bring up the similarities between Evita and Madonna.

Most of the lyrics sung either by Madonna in the role of Eva Perón or about her by others who observe her climb to power are vintage Madonna. For instance, the first time that Eva Duarte meets Juan Perón, they are at a benefit concert for victims of the famous San Juan earthquake. When she sings "I'd Be Good for You, I'd Be Surprisingly Good for You," the words are a harbinger of what she would tell Guy Ritchie after they met and during the tortuous period when he resisted her advances. At that same benefit concert for earthquake victims, Eva bumps into the hapless Maguldi, the has-been tango singer who drove her out of Junín and into the big city. "You haven't changed," he says, intending to give her a compliment. Looking at him from head to toe, she answers dryly, "Neither have you."

Darius Khondji is a cinematographer whose work in the film *Delicatessen* had so impressed Bernardo Bertolucci that he hired the young Frenchman for his film *Stealing Beauty.* Parker, impressed with Khondji's work on both of those films, hired him to do the cinematography for *Evita.*

Alan Parker considered *Evita* to be a baroque opera rather than a simple musical, so Khondji immediately decided to liken the look of the film to that of Evita's own life. For him, that would be to show the gritty and realistic style that was so typically Buenos Aires. "It's kind of broken like the life she has in the film," he explained, "and she was very broken herself. It has an edge to it . . . so it doesn't look always very polished but rather really harsh and very minimalist in lighting."

Khondji, much the way Madonna had done before shooting began, did extensive research on Eva Perón, not only studying and eventually incorporating actual newsreels into the movie, but watching hours of footage of a 1951 rally of *los descamisados,* or the "shiftless ones," the workers who were Perón's biggest supporters, to see exactly how the rally had been lit. In another example of Khondji's quest for reality, he viewed a film of a demonstration that took place in Buenos Aires after Juan Perón was arrested, when more than a million supporters turned out to persuade Evita to continue her candidacy for vice president. The same meticulous research went into the scene in which Eva renounces her candidacy and appears on the balcony of the Casa Rosada to inform the crowd that she will step down. "For some reason," Khondji explains, "there were searchlights crossing the huge crowd, which I re-created in the film."

Khondji was intent on doing the same kind of minimalist and gritty lighting when it came to his star, although he knew that Parker would have done nothing to stop him from straying from his style to make Madonna look better. Convinced that to make an exception and make Madonna look more beautiful would be "cruel to the director and would have killed his film," Khondji decided to maintain the atmosphere throughout. "The problem," he explained, "was that to light Madonna in the style that best suited her would jar with the technique I had chosen for the film." Standing firm, Khondji went directly to Madonna to discuss the lighting, warning her that she would not look as good as she always had on her videos or in the film's promos. To her credit, without any hesitation or argument, Madonna agreed,

not only because she respected Khondji professionally, but
because she had worked with him before and liked him. According to what she wrote in her *Vanity Fair* diary, of all the
people on the film, she felt closest to Khondji, who bright-
ened her mood each time she saw him on the set and on
every occasion when they went out together after a day's
work.

The most popular and recognizable song on the *Evita* album, "Don't Cry for Me Argentina," had been a hit for Julie
Covington in 1977, who took it to number one on the charts
in England. Two years later in 1979, the Shadows recorded
an instrumental version of the song with strings and harp.
When Madonna sang it, the words became even more meaningful to the millions who heard it again. Several lyrics could
have described Madonna's as well as Evita's justification for
her ambition: "*And as for fortune and as for fame, I never invited them in . . .*" Another song, "You Must Love Me,"
which Evita sings to the people when her motives are found
to be more self-serving than altruistic, became a hit single
for Madonna in 1996. Since the song makes no specific reference to Evita or to the political situation in Argentina, it
stood on its own. When Maguldi sings "Beware of the City"
to a young Eva Duarte, the audience is aware that it could
have been the same warning given to Madonna when she left
her hometown and set off for New York in search of stardom.
In the same vein, "Another Suitcase in Another Hall," also a
hit single for Madonna, in 1997, describes not only Evita's
nomadic existence once she arrived in Buenos Aires, but also
Madonna's itinerant life in New York when she lived in
abandoned buildings or in a rat-infested tenement.

"High Flying Adored" is sung by Che to Evita to remind
her that she is "*a fantasy of the bedroom, a saint, and a back
street girl.*" When Madonna answers him, "*And I did it all at
twenty-six,*" it draws the clear comparison between the two
women, since Madonna "did it all" at twenty-five—five
years after she'd arrived in New York in 1978—when she
had her first hit single.

* * *

After three exhausting months on location in England, Argentina, and Hungary, Madonna was back in London to shoot the final scene for *Evita*. The action was taking place in St. John the Baptist Church, on a quiet, tree-lined street in a shabby section of the city, not far from where two major city highways merge near heaps of concrete. A handful of curious spectators, bundled up against the chilling London wind, lingered outside along with several members of the technical team, who warmed their hands on steaming paper cups of coffee. Inside the church, twenty women dressed as Argentine peasants, wearing colorful smocks with kerchiefs tied around their heads, were on their knees, their hands clasped together in silent prayer. Set high above the main altar and trimmed in gold leaf and surrounded by a semicircle of votive candles, a statue of the Virgin Mary on an ornate wood platform gazed down on the congregation of extras.

Madonna, her face pale and passive beneath a smart pillbox hat, was dressed in a gray suit trimmed in black velvet, the jacket nipped at the waist. When Alan Parker called, "Action," the cameras rolled, turned on the star as she led a small procession up the aisle toward the altar. The only sound came from her stiletto heels, which clicked against the white marble floor. Approaching the flickering red candles at the base of the Virgin Mary, she suddenly fainted. On cue, a collective gasp resounded within the small church.

It took thirty-two takes before Alan Parker finally had what he considered a perfect scene. As a result, Madonna was forced to fall repeatedly, her body hitting the floor of the church with a resounding thump and resulting in black-and-blue marks over her left hip and shoulder. Each time she fell, she was careful not to drop the tiny carved African fertility god she clutched in her hand, the same icon that President Carlos Menem had given her so many months before, at the beginning of the long cinematic journey.

It was a torturous scene for Madonna to play, and one that

touched her profoundly. While she was elated that the film was finally finished, she was also sad that she would be leaving the cast and crew, people whom she had come to consider a family throughout the course of the project. Perhaps even more significant was that the scene she had just completed represented the moment in the story when the audience realizes that Eva Perón is desperately ill. After immersing herself so totally in the body and soul of Evita, Madonna wondered if the physical symptoms she had been feeling were psychosomatic, just another example of her cosmic connection to the character. When she thought about it, she realized that she had felt weak and drained long before she had arrived in London to film this particular scene. In fact, almost from the moment she had set foot in Argentina, she had had bouts of nausea and dizziness. On one occasion in Buenos Aires, when she was standing on the balcony of the Casa Rosada, about to lip-synch the words to "Don't Cry for Me Argentina," she had almost fainted. Clutching the ornate brass rail, she had attributed her malaise to Evita, or at least to her spirit, which she claimed had "entered my body like a heat missile, starting with my feet, traveling up my spine, and flying out of my fingertips, into the air, out to the people, and back up to heaven."

Madonna said at the time, "I couldn't speak, I was so happy, and yet I felt a great sadness, too, because she was haunting me, pushing me to feel things."

When the cast and crew were preparing to move on to Hungary, where the filming would continue in a winter climate, Madonna's symptoms became even more acute. The sporadic nausea and dizziness suddenly plagued her every day. "I felt a bit seasick," she explained, "but it was very hot, and we were working out of doors, the food was bad, and everyone was complaining of upset stomachs. I imagined that I was feeling the same thing as the rest of the team."

Taking advantage of the several days' break between Buenos Aires and Budapest, Madonna decided to make a quick trip to New York to see her doctor. The results of the tests revealed that she had never been in better or more glowing health. Her symptoms simply reflected that she was eleven weeks pregnant.

Her first reaction was shock. She had often missed her period when she was traveling and working under stress, so the possibility that she was pregnant had never really occurred to her. Later on, she admitted that she had made no particular effort to prevent it, although she never acknowledged her attempts to be artifically inseminated by Carlos Leon's sperm.

"You could have knocked me down with a feather," she said. "I certainly wasn't planning for it to happen when it did. I had more than enough things to worry about, just getting through the movie. I didn't want to do anything that could sabotage the film. On top of all that, to take on board the reality of motherhood . . . it was like, 'Oh, God, this is the last thing I need.' But I had wanted to have a baby for some time and I was exhilarated and worried about the remaining tango sequences hurting the baby. But everyone involved was so supportive of me, and I was so prepared for what I was doing in my work that, in the end, I settled down."

With six more weeks left to film, Madonna decided to tell Alan Parker. Extremely happy for his leading lady, he immediately assured her that he would do everything to accommodate her. The most pressing problem was to make sure that the wardrobe could be altered to conceal her condition when she began to show. Parker also agreed with Madonna that the news should be kept secret for as long as possible to avoid the press's storming the set as they had done in Buenos Aires for much less spectacular reasons. Obviously, the people in wardrobe had to be told, as well as some of the crew, since the shooting schedule would have to change.

It was a miracle that the news was kept secret for two weeks before Liz Smith, with Madonna's permission, broke the story on April 7, 1996, in her syndicated gossip column. But not until ten days later, on April 17, did Madonna confirm what the British press had been printing for several weeks. Alan Parker issued a statement, saying that "we are doing everything possible to accommodate her condition and to keep to the schedule," adding, "she has been splendid throughout, utterly professional and giving the performance of her life. I'm very happy for her."

When Madonna learned that she was pregnant, her relationship with Carlos Leon had been going on for a year and a half and appeared, at least on the surface, to be an ongoing affair. He had not only visited Madonna on weekends when she had first arrived in London to record the *Evita* score, but he had also made several brief trips down to Buenos Aires. Throughout the months when they were separated, they talked almost daily by telephone. There was no doubt in Carlos Leon's mind that the baby was his.

Friends of the former fitness trainer recall that when Madonna announced the pregnancy, he was "over the top with joy." Cuban by birth and extremely close to his parents and older brother, his life had always revolved around family. The idea of becoming a father was exhilarating, especially since he was having a baby with the woman he loved.

Madonna had always said that she "liked to do things to take power away from men." In the beginning of their relationship, in the gym or in the workout room of her Central Park West apartment, Carlos had pushed her to the limit of her physical ability. For a woman who was used to being in charge, their daily encounters seemed an unlikely place to begin an affair, but Carlos was dealing with a different Madonna from the one that her fans or business associates knew. During the two hours they spent together every day, she was focused, disciplined, obedient, and completely reliant on his expertise. She allowed him to be in command, and never for a moment did she act like the demanding, powerful, impatient, predatory star. Carlos had dedicated his life to physical fitness, not only to keeping his own body in shape but also those of his clients. It didn't seem to matter that he was far from being her equal in fame or financial success. He was the ideal lover for a woman who had an insatiable desire for self-improvement and an unquenchable thirst to be the fittest, most taut, and limber. Admittedly, Madonna was happiest when she was exercising. "I'm always running around like a chicken without a head," she has said. "The only place where I can focus and relax is while I'm doing my workout. If I had nothing to do all day, I would stay in the gym and exercise." Those who have worked with Madonna on movie sets can attest that regardless of how early the morning call is, she is not only on time but has already spent two hours either running or working out on a stationary bike. Those friends closest to the star at the time thought that she had possibly found the perfect mate.

Carlos Leon had come to New York from Cuba as a toddler with his parents, Armando and Maria Leon, and his older brother, Armando Jr. Tall, muscular, and strikingly good-looking, Carlos was the son that his mother believed could become "another Arnold Schwarzenegger." Both parents had aspirations for their children to achieve fame and fortune in America. When Armando Sr. finally mastered English, he got a job at a check-cashing business and, after a few years, worked his way up to supervisor. As the family gradually settled into a financially secure lower-middle-class existence, Maria encouraged both her sons to excel in sports. Neither son was particularly inclined toward studying. Armando Jr., concerned about a safe job and benefits, joined the doormen's union in New York City. He considered himself fortunate when he finally got a job in an elegant Upper East Side apartment house. Carlos, on the other hand, with his good looks and natural athletic abilities, was more inclined to follow his mother's advice. After he finished high school, he went to work in a gym and, before long, was singled out by several clients who offered him jobs as their personal trainer. By the time that Madonna met Carlos Leon in 1994, he was earning a decent salary and had no trouble finding girlfriends, and was often pursued by some of the older women and models whom he trained. Carlos Leon was happy and even believed that if he could make it in the competitive world of physical fitness, why not as a movie star?

With a long list of lovers of both genders, and a sensational marriage and divorce to Sean Penn, at thirty-five years old Madonna seemed to have accomplished more than she had ever imagined. Yet, the one thing that she didn't have was a child of her own. "I need something that's mine," she once said, "something that I can be proud of."

When she was married to Sean Penn, there were constant reports that she was pregnant. Much to her dismay, she never was. After the divorce, articles began appearing alluding to her "biological clock" and the possibility that the girl who had everything simply could not manage to conceive. The articles wounded her deeply. She was aware that as she approached her midthirties, she did not have a stable relationship, and time was running out for her to become a mother. "I thought people used it against me," she explained. " 'Oh, she can't even have the baby that she wants.' In answer to that question in interviews, I would say, 'Well, of course I want to, sometime soon.' . . . So it seemed that there was this huge time that I was wishing for it, but actually I was just responding to everybody's nosy inquiries." In a rare interview that Madonna gave Norman Mailer, during which she seemed more sincere than ever before, she explained, "As an unbelievably famous person, you are only allowed to operate with everyone's approval for a limited amount of time. Then you need to disappear, run out of steam, run out of ideas, get fat or something." For Madonna, having a child was forever, something that no one could take away from her. And yet, she had always maintained that she did not want to raise a child without a father, for, in her words, she would be "raising a cripple." Once again, underneath the rebellious woman who lived to shock, emerged the middle-class girl with good Catholic values. Madonna believed that, ideally, a child needed both parents to be assured of a good beginning for a successful life. Madonna was determined that her child would have everything she had lacked.

In 1986, when she was starring with Sean Penn in the play *Goose and Tom-Tom* in repertory at Lincoln Center, Oliver Stone was trying to bring *Evita* to the screen. Stone, with the consent of Webber and Rice, offered the role to Meryl Streep, who passed a vocal audition. Only weeks before shooting was scheduled to begin, Streep pulled out, citing exhaustion. Stone then offered the part to Michelle Pfeiffer, who also passed the vocal audition, but also dropped out when she discovered that she was pregnant. In 1989, when Madonna's marriage to Sean Penn was officially over, and after the affair with Tony Ward ended, Madonna was involved with a variety of other men, including the basketball star Dennis Rodman. Rodman wrote in his autobiography, *Bad As I Wanna Be,* that Madonna inundated him with faxes, saying, "In three weeks time, you have to be in this hotel in Vegas to make me pregnant."

Years later when Madonna was finally chosen to play *Evita,* she attributed her luck in landing the role partly to Michelle Pfeiffer's pregnancy. What intrigued Madonna was that Pfeiffer had adopted, as a single mother, a little girl whom she named Claudia Rose, only a year before she married television creator and producer David Kelley and got pregnant. Inspired by Pfeiffer's own story, Madonna decided that she, too, would adopt a child. According to sources close to the star, she hired a New York lawyer who specialized in adoptions and, through him, placed advertisements in newspapers in Europe and Latin America, asking for a mother who was willing to give up her baby for adoption to an internationally famous star who was prepared to pay any price that was asked in return for the child. At the time, information about Madonna's ad was allegedly leaked to several American tabloids by America's National Adoption Register.

Though Madonna claimed to be unconcerned about the race of the baby, she wanted a child of her own. For her entire life, she had suffered from a fear of abandonment. It was an odd way for her to view motherhood, based on her relationships with her father and stepmother, and the fact that she had left home at an early age. Another aspect of her complex concerned the men in her life. She had always picked boyfriends and lovers who were dependent financially and a husband who had relied on her for emotional strength. Once she and Carlos Leon became a couple, she assumed that she would make the rules. Imagine her surprise when she asked him to sign away all rights to the child and he refused. He finally agreed that he would never seek either sole or joint custody of the baby.

According to Raoul Felder, a New York lawyer who is an expert on divorce and custody proceedings, any signed agreement by one parent, promising not to challenge custody, is assailable. "If Madonna died or became physically or mentally incapacitated," Felder explains, "so that she couldn't perform her maternal duties, the father has every right to petition the court for custody." In Madonna's situation, Felder agrees that there are always ways around the legalities of such an agreement. "Short of death," he continues, "obviously there would never be a time when Madonna wouldn't have the means to hire nannies or nurses."

Another way around those legalities was a financial deal that would encourage Carlos Leon to function as a good but distant father to the child. According to sources who are close to Madonna and Leon, immediately after Madonna gave birth to Lourdes, delivered by Paul Fleiss, the father of Heidi Fleiss, the Hollywood Madam, she insisted that DNA tests be run on Carlos and her baby daughter. If Madonna lacked discretion when it came to having a variety of lovers, she wanted to be sure that Carlos was the father of her child. When the results came back showing that he was, Madonna reportedly made a deal with Carlos. Numerous press reports indicate that in return for never seeking joint or sole custody, he would get $1 million in a lump sum. In addition, she guaranteed that if he ever wanted to invest in a business, she would put up the money, the total of which was not to exceed $5 million, and under specific conditions that included a possible percentage of the profits if the business succeeded.

In response to media speculation that Carlos Leon was nothing more in Madonna's life than a sperm donor, she said, "It's all part of the view the media likes to have of me, that I'm not a human being. That I don't have any feelings and don't really care for people. That I'm just ambitious, cold, and calculating. It's all just part of the image that unhappy people like to construct for me. I'm not surprised by it. . . . It's just one of the nonsense things that people who don't know anything like to invent. I'm incredibly offended by it. It's nobody's business what sort of relationship I'm having and what I plan to do."

It didn't help to quell the rumors when Madonna gave Alan Jackson an interview that appeared on October 12, 1996, in the *Times Weekend Magazine* in London, during which the reporter was particularly struck by Madonna's total lack of sentiment when she talked about Carlos Leon. When Jackson asked the star if she might marry, she said, "I don't think marriage is a religious thing. It's an economic thing. It's more about money than anything else. It evolved out of women not being able to take care of themselves financially and so having to become a man's possession— promising to love, honor, and obey him. So I don't know what I think of marriage anymore, other than that it's an institution which grew out of a very sexist way of thinking and living." When Jackson pointed out that there obviously hadn't been any financial imperative for her to have married Sean Penn, she answered, "True, but I was also younger, and I hadn't thought things through properly." She smiled and sighed. "I don't know if I believe in it anymore. I don't know what function it could have in my life. If I love someone and want to be with him, there isn't a piece of paper or a ceremony in the world that is going to keep me away from that person. And if I don't want to be with him, the reverse applies. . . . I think marriage is more about what society expects from you than what God does."

Lourdes is deeply attached to her father, her paternal grandparents, as well as to her uncle Armando Jr. As a result, Madonna has done everything to encourage Carlos's presence in her daughter's life. In fact, Lourdes is also extremely close to her two cousins, Anthony, who is six, and Allesandra, who is four. So far, Lourdes has been happy and seems adjusted to living in two very different worlds. When she is with her mother, she lives in total luxury, currently in a large English whitestone with nannies and servants in a chic area of London. When she visits her father at his New York apartment, she spends much of her time with his family, along with her cousins, in their modest apartment on the Upper West Side of Manhattan.

After Madonna moved to London and fell in love with Guy Ritchie, the geographic distance presented an obstacle for Carlos Leon's visits with his daughter. He began complaining that he wasn't able to see Lourdes as often as he wanted. At that point, Madonna offered to buy him a business in London so he could be closer to their daughter. The British press began circulating rumors that Madonna and Ritchie were having problems when the truth was that she was torn between living where her lover wanted and moving back to the States for the sake of her child. According to several members of the Leon family, Madonna had every intention of moving back to New York or at least spending more time there until she discovered that she was pregnant with Ritchie's baby. As of now, Carlos seems to have accepted the situation. When Madonna was obliged to go to New York for the premiere of *The Next Best Thing,* he went to London to stay with Lourdes. When Madonna married Guy Ritchie in Scotland, Carlos Leon was invited to the wedding.

Carlos has also begun acting. While he made his debut on Don Johnson's television series *Nash Bridges,* he has only managed to get insignificant parts in several films, including *The Big Lebowski* and *Wishmaster 2: Evil Never Dies,* directed by Jack Sholder, which went straight to video.

Long after *Evita* made its premiere in theaters throughout the world and Madonna had already given birth to Rocco, her son with Guy Ritchie, she was even more convinced than ever that if she hadn't traveled to Buenos Aires and received that ebony icon of the African god of fertility from President Menem, she would never have had her children. *"Evita* was really challenging," she says, "an emotionally exhausting and soul-searching couple of years for me. It was a real education, the farthest I've ever had to push myself creatively. It was exhausting and intimidating. I've never been so drained by anything. From the beginning I walked into another world—and kissed the world as I knew it good-bye. Even more important, it was an event that profoundly changed my life and gave me enormous joy because, after it was over, I had my two children." Once again, there was no doubt in her mind that everything that had happened to her since she had embarked upon the project had been directly influenced by the spirit of Eva Perón.

chapter thirty-one
·················

*M*adonna won a Golden Globe award for her performance in *Evita,* but was not nominated for an Oscar that year by the Academy of Motion Picture Arts and Sciences, a slight that she has still not forgotten. "The Academy was too scared to nominate me," Madonna says simply. "I wasn't politically correct enough to make a speech about the downtrodden. Unfortunately for me, my concept of winning an Oscar is all about my performance as an actress."

A member of the Academy, a formidable actor and much-loved performer, responds to Madonna's interpretation of events. "She is absolutely right," he says. "Winning an Oscar should be all about her performance as an actress, and there you have it. She just wasn't good enough in that particular film."

Undaunted, Madonna continued to search for roles that mirrored her own life. Soon after she gave birth to Lourdes, Madonna became involved in several film development projects for her company Maverick Films. "I'm interested in unforgettable cinema," she said, "like directors such as Martin Scorsese has made, not the uninteresting products that Hollywood turns out today." Several of the projects she pursued were *Dino,* written by Scorsese; an adaptation of the Oliver Mayor play *Blade to the Heart;* as well as Jennifer Belle's novel, *Going Down*—none of which ever went further than discussions. Following those unsuccessful attempts, Madonna became entranced by the story of Libby Holman, the torch singer from the 1920s and 1930s who had been suspected of murdering her husband, Zachary Smith Reynolds, the heir to the R.J. Reynolds tobacco fortune. Holman was ultimately acquitted of the murder during a sensational trial. Her love affairs, with a series of such well-known women as Tallulah Bankhead, Josephine Baker, and Jeanne Eagels, were constantly exposed in the press long after Holman became a recluse. According to Madonna, she felt a "kinship" with Holman because she, like the torch singer, experienced "ridicule and shame as a result of the unconventional pattern of my life, my sexuality, and the tremendous drama and passion which motivates me."

After the Holman project fell through, Madonna expressed interest in acquiring a novel called *Velocity,* written by Kristin McCloy. The story centered on a young woman whose mother dies and who returns home to repair a strained relationship with her father. "It's my life," Madonna explains. "In the midst of all the tragedy, the character falls in love with someone who is all wrong for her. I can relate to that especially since, in the end, the girl doesn't get the guy, but she becomes close to her father, which I found especially touching."

If McCloy wasn't confident that the plot would entice Madonna, she made sure that the star knew that while she had been working on her book, she had kept two photographs in sight: one of the Dalai Lama and the other of Madonna. And finally, in July 1999, when Madonna considered optioning the best-seller *Memoirs of a Geisha,* she took on the physical persona of Hatsumomo, the book's protagonist. During the Grammy awards that year, Madonna performed a Kabuki-style dance dressed in a red kimono and subsequently appeared in her video "Nothing Really Matters" dressed as Hatsumomo. In the end, she did not option the book, undoubtedly because Columbia Pictures made it clear that if they financed the project, Madonna would definitely not be under consideration for the part.

* * *

During the filming of The Next Best Thing, Madonna came to view Lynn Redgrave, who played Rupert Everett's proper English mother, as a mother figure as well as an actress whom she greatly admired and was determined to emulate. While Madonna was believable as the character Abbey, a yoga instructor, from a physical viewpoint, since she is an avid student of yoga and is able to put her body into some of the more difficult contortions, she kept slipping in and out of a bizarre English accent, which made Abbey seem affected. According to one of the producers of the film, at one point during the shooting, Madonna told Lynn Redgrave that she looked upon her as a "role model" and was making progress when it came to speaking "proper English." Redgrave was not particularly flattered, especially since she had no idea why Madonna found it necessary to affect a British accent. For the duration of the shooting, Redgrave, not unlike the other actors, had a feeling of impending doom about how the critics would respond to the movie.

"There were just too many problems," the producer maintains, "and Madonna certainly didn't help things by taking on that affected way of speaking. I mean, come on, Abbey was supposed to be an ordinary girl from southern California. The problem with Madonna is that she is often a victim of her own self-confidence. Nothing shakes her. But more than that, she brings her own neurotic baggage with her on the set and ends up screwing herself. Madonna is like a parrot or a monkey. She can take on everyone's particular physical tics and accents." He pauses. "As a nightclub mimic, she'd be great. As an actress, the whole experience was a disaster for everyone."

Some people actually held Madonna responsible for putting John Schlesinger in the hospital when shooting was completed, making him unable to edit the finished product. "His resistance was at rock bottom," the producer maintains.

It is difficult to blame Madonna for John Schlesinger's coronary bypass surgery and prostate cancer, although the whole exercise of making the movie completely exhausted him. Still, Schlesinger remains the consummate gentleman. "While the critics questioned her performance," he explained, weak but recuperating as he sat comfortably on a sofa in his Kensington penthouse in London, "I was the director and therefore responsible for the project. Obviously, I failed, and even my friends in the business began to distance themselves from me and from the movie. Whatever the final result, I felt as if I couldn't win because of Madonna's almost hypnotic belief in herself."

Publicly, Madonna once again blamed the critics for their cynical and relentless determination to destroy any hope of her making the transition from singer to actress. "Music is the good life," she said after the film was so badly panned. "To delve into acting more is a lot more of a risk for me. The good life is to just stay in music where I've already established myself and it's easier. I will continue to write music as long as I'm inspired."

Privately, she was crushed. Her age, her image, her desire to start over in a new country, where she could appropriate new styles, customs, an accent, and make different kinds of friends and find new collaborators, accounted for her decision to move to London. The other motivating force that drove her from America was more negative.

In 1995, before Lourdes was born, Madonna had been terrorized in her Hollywood Hills home by a stalker, Robert Dewey Hoskins, who threatened to slit her throat if she refused to marry him. Hoskins was shot in the leg by Madonna's bodyguard when he was caught on her property. Arrested, tried, convicted, and jailed for stalking, which is a felony in California, Hoskins continued to issue threats from behind bars. After the baby was born in October 1996, Madonna's relationship with Carlos was fraught with separations and jealous arguments. Dan Cortesi, the former advance security guard, claims that the reasons stemmed mostly from Carlos's possessiveness. "By then, Madonna was spending all her free time with Ingrid Casares," Cortesi says, "even though she let Carlos see the baby as much as he wanted. The three of them were in California, in Madonna's house in Los Feliz. When they got back to New York, Madonna was still spending time with Ingrid and with Rosie O'Donnell without Carlos."

Al Pacino is a close friend of Madonna's and someone whom she admires and adores. On several occasions, Madonna and Lourdes would visit Rosie O'Donnell at her home in Rockland County, not far from Pacino's house, and Madonna would spend the afternoons going between the two homes with her baby. While Carlos was acutely aware of the distance that was developing between them and felt sad and dejected, it was his brother, Armando Jr., who tried to turn that sadness into anger and resentment. According to Dan Cortesi, it was Armando Jr., along with Liz Rosenberg, who was responsible for his being fired.

When Madonna and her entourage returned from California, she arranged for Liz Rosenberg to represent Carlos in negotiating an agreement to model for a Versace advertising campaign. According to Cortesi, the deal did not work out as Carlos had hoped, and he got less money than he had antici-pated. Again according to Cortesi, when Carlos complained that things had not worked out as she had promised, Madonna arranged, through her West Coast lawyer, Rob Heraldson, to give Leon several checks drawn on the account of Maverick, her record company. On four occasions, Cortesi says, he brought Leon an envelope containing a check as well as envelopes that he was instructed to give to Prodigy, Alanis Morissette, and Candlebox, all artists who were signed on the Maverick label. "One time, the envelope was open," Cortesi claims, "and I saw the amount of the check made out to Carlos was for eighteen thousand dollars."

Despite the chilliness that had developed between Madonna and Carlos, when the star was obliged to return to Los Angeles several weeks later, she once again invited Car-los to come with her and Lourdes, although on that occa-sion, she was accompanied by not only Ingrid Casares but also her brother Chris Ciccone and his lover. "I was fast asleep in my apartment in the Bronx," Cortesi recalls, "when the phone rang. It was a photographer I know who worked for LGI, a photo agency. He was excited. He told me that he had something really hot for me. Apparently, a photographer he knew had made a deal with Armando Jr., Carlos's older brother, to buy some pictures that he had of the baby and of Madonna in the early days when she was sitting around his mother's kitchen table, staying over at Carlos's, getting in the skashabonga and just hanging out up there at their apartment. He told me that the photographer was going to sell the photos to *OK* or *Hello* and he was set to meet Armando at the apartment building where he worked and give him fifty thousand dollars for the shots."

Cortesi has very mixed emotions even now when he relates the story. On one hand, he admits that his affinity for Carlos, and the fact he can appreciate that fifty thousand dollars is a "score" that only happens once in a lifetime to hard-working people who are struggling to make a living, made him somewhat sympathetic to Armando Jr. On the other hand, at the time he realized that he had his own family to support, which made him come to the conclusion very quickly that he had the moral and practical obligation to report what he had just found out so that the deal didn't go through. "What do I do now?" Cortesi asks rhetorically, remembering his reaction. "My first thought is forget about Liz, and if I went to Caresse, Madonna's manager, it's the same as going to Liz. So I decided to tell Carlos."

Dan Cortesi had a code to contact Carlos Leon on his portable, so if he left a message that merely said "911," Leon would know that it was urgent and to call back promptly. "I could hear the whole scenario in my head," Cortesi recalls. "I was sure that Carlos didn't know anything about it, but if he did, I could hear Armando telling him, take the money and run. She doesn't want to marry you, so what difference does it make?"

After trying to reach Carlos several times on his cell phone, Cortesi finally heard from him. According to Cortesi,

Carlos was shocked when he heard the story and immediately defended his brother, claiming that the photographer had made everything up to cause trouble. He asked Cortesi to at least let him talk to his brother to make sure that he was innocent before he informed the others. Cortesi agreed, and within several hours, Carlos called him back to report that as he had suspected, Armando claimed to know nothing about it. "He assured me that he would take care of it," Cortesi says, "but even then, how could I be sure? My heart was broken because I didn't want to believe that Carlos could do such a thing, but even if he didn't, what guarantee did I have that those photos wouldn't appear? I knew that I couldn't come between two Cuban brothers, so the only thing left for me to do was to go to Caresse."

The palace intrigue that surrounds Madonna is worthy of Shakespeare. The paranoia and competition among the people who are part of her closely guarded inner circle are undoubtedly the same as in any household where a movie star, rock singer, or member of a royal family is the focal point of all that attention. Dan Cortesi profoundly believes that Liz Rosenberg is a staunch and loyal member of that inner circle. "If I needed someone to protect me," Cortesi says, "I'd want that person to be Liz Rosenberg. She knows if a photographer is having an affair with a married woman in Tibet. She knows what a paparazzi is eating for breakfast in Venezuela and with whom. At the same time, she has certain photographers that she favors for whatever reason. When Madonna enters a room or appears at an event, Liz always turns her toward one or two in particular."

The photographs that Armando Leon Jr. was alleged to have sold never appeared in any publication, either in the United States or abroad. Several days after telling the whole story to Caresse Henry-Norman, who recounted it to Liz Rosenberg, Dan Cortesi tried to contact Madonna and found that all her private numbers had been changed. Shortly afterward, Liz Rosenberg informed him that his services were no longer required. In April 1997, Madonna and Carlos Leon separated. Within two weeks of the incident, Madonna decided to leave California for London, announcing that she would live there temporarily. She rented a house in Chelsea with the intention of dividing her time behind the United States and England so that Lourdes could continue to see her father regularly.

These days, Dan Cortesi works as a porter in a building in New York City and does odd assignments with several rock stars when they happen to be in New York.

When she first arrived in London, Madonna began working quietly with the renowned percussionist Talwin Singh, who is considered one of the leaders of the new wave of music and who would do several arrangements on her album Ray of Light. Without fanfare, press, or publicity, Madonna also invested in Anokha, a collective recording studio that Talwin Singh founded that focused on new artists with an innovative sound, a combination of ancient Indian and techno music. In 1997, Madonna also began courting Björk, Iceland's singing sensation who became popular in the 1980s when she headed up a group called the Sugarcubes, in the hope of recording, publishing, and distributing Björk's music on the Maverick label. After the group had broken up and Björk went out on her own, she was often compared to Madonna for her originality and innovative music and lyrics.

As Madonna got settled into the music world in London and began to feel more comfortable in a strange country, she put a bid on the first of what would be many English homes, changing her mind either for reasons of security or because she felt that real estate prices were unrealistically inflated. In one of her first real estate ventures, Madonna put a deposit on Toddingham Manor in the Cotswolds, a thirty-room estate with its own river. After George Harrison was attacked by an intruder in his guarded London home on Hampstead Heath, Madonna withdrew her bid on Toddingham Manor. She still remained committed to several new British film projects, however, as well as spending half the year in London. When her album *Ray of Light* was completed, she went into talks to bring Noël Coward's *Blithe Spirit* to the screen, a project that she claimed she would produce and star in, as well as *Quadrille,* which she announced would begin filming in February 1998 in London and in the south of France, to be directed by Gavin Millar, who directed *DreamChild.* *Quadrille,* also by Noël Coward, which appealed to Madonna in her English phase, is about a philandering English aristocrat who leaves his wife to elope to the south of France with the young wife of an American industrialist. The aristocrat's wife, whom Madonna intended to play, teams up with the industrialist to find their respective spouses and avoid scandal. Along the way, they develop a relationship of their own.

On one of Madonna's trips back to Los Angeles in September 1997, her old friend and producer Alek Keshishian introduced her to Andy Bird, an accountant's son from a middle-class English family who lived in Warwickshire. Bird, tall, slim, with long hair and a good sense of humor, who never touched alcohol or drugs and whose show business experience was limited to singing in the streets in London, had come to Hollywood to make a career acting and writing. At the time Madonna met Bird, he was a male Blanche DuBois, relying on the "kindness of strangers," moving from house to house, staying with friends or housesitting. The attraction seemed to be mutual, and to the surprise of everyone who knew Madonna, within weeks of meeting him she invited Bird to move into her Los Angeles home. When she traveled back to her rented house in London, Bird accompanied her. Madonna, determined to make him presentable as an escort, bought her new lover a new wardrobe so he could accompany her to parties, gallery openings, and charity events. She also put him on a weekly allowance. Acting as a calm, amusing husehusband to supervise the help, watch over the grocery shopping, play with her child, and be available to give her romance and comfort whenever she needed it, much to the distress of Carlos Leon, Bird also became somewhat of a father figure to Lourdes. Unemployed and whimsical by nature, Bird was a good playmate for the toddler when her mother was unavailable.

The relationship between Madonna and Bird would last about a year, during which Madonna met the unemployed actor's parents. Despite periods of separation when the singer was forced to return to America for her work, she felt a sense of relief that she was in a calm and stable relationship. With a small child to raise on her own, Madonna needed someone in her life whose presence was soothing to Lourdes and comfortable for her.

By 1997, when Madonna had returned to Los Angeles to work on the final aspects of her album *Ray of Light,* boredom had set it. After a long conversation with Carlos Leon, who was undoubtedly the one person who could understand his former lover's weariness of supporting someone who seemed no closer to his goals of stardom than he had been when they met, Madonna decided that the affair with Bird was over. In a brief transatlantic telephone conversation, she informed him that she wanted him out of her Chelsea house. Penniless and with no job prospects, Bird gratefully accepted Madonna's offer to pay the first six months' rent on an apartment as well as to give him $25,000 to get himself settled.

As Madonna was about to release *Ray of Light,* she discovered that she was pregnant. In her mind, this was not the time to have another child, and Bird was not the man with whom she wanted to be connected for the rest of her life. Another brief transatlantic telephone conversation ensued between Madonna and Bird, during which she told him that she was two months pregnant and intended to have an abortion. Installed in a modest flat in London and still singing on the streets near Trafalgar Square for small change, Bird could do nothing much to change her mind.

Within days, Madonna had the abortion and was back at work promoting her new album. According to a nurse who no longer works in the doctor's office, but who was there at the time Madonna underwent the procedure, the star was extremely upset and worried. "This is an unpleasant moment for every woman who goes through something like that," the nurse says. "But having an abortion at forty made her extremely concerned about whether or not she could conceive again. There's no doubt that Madonna planned on eventually having another child."

After Lourdes was born, Madonna openly discussed the abortions that she had undergone when she lived in New York. At the time, her words were surprisingly honest: "You always have regrets when you make those kind of decisions, but you have to look at your lifestyle and ask yourself, 'Am I at a place in my life where I can devote a lot of time to being the really good parent I want to be?' None of us wants to make mistakes in that role, and I imagine a lot of women look at the way our parents raised us and say, 'I definitely wouldn't want to do it quite that way.' I think you have to be mentally prepared for it. If you're not, you're only doing the world a disservice by bringing up a child you don't really want."

With all the pragmatism that Madonna exhibited, she still admitted that she had a deep sense of regret and sadness whenever she thought about what she had done: "I think about it when I think that I could have a child right now who is five or even ten years old. Things happen when they're meant to happen, and if it comes along again, the chance of parenthood, and I'm ready, I'll do it. And that's all there is to that."

If there was ever any doubt about the message that Madonna had sent in her controversial video "Papa Don't Preach," it should have been apparent to everyone who still wondered what her position was that she was definitely pro-choice. And if there was any confusion about her feelings toward her own father now that she was a mother herself, she cleared that up as well after Lourdes came into her life: "He [my father] could be narrow-minded and stubborn, but he was a wonderful father. I really love that man!"

If the feeling was mutual, Tony Ciccone was still too upset to return the compliment. Though he adores Lourdes, he was not particularly pleased that his daughter had once again defied tradition when she had the baby out of wedlock and dissolved the relationship with the child's father. Not only was it a difficult time in Madonna's love life, but it was a disturbing and chaotic moment in her relationship with her father.

chapter thirty-two
....

*I*n the spring of 1998, twelve years after her marriage to Sean Penn, Madonna was invited to lunch at the Wiltshire country home of Sting and his wife, Trudie Styler. Guy Ritchie, a young British director, who had recently directed *Lock, Stock and Two Smoking Barrels,* a movie that pioneered a new style of British gangster movies and that reputedly made British films once again hip, was a friend of Sting and Styler's. Trudie Styler considered Ritchie the English version of Quentin Tarantino and, because of her faith in his talent, had invested £2 million in SKA Films, Ritchie's company along with his partner, Mathew Vaughn, the son of Robert Vaughn, the star of the television series *The Man from U.N.C.L.E.* When Ritchie's first film effort went on to earn more than £18 million at British box offices, Styler's faith in the director seemed justified as she more than recouped her investment.

Madonna, who had known Sting for many years and shared one of his video directors, Mary Lambert, had become close friends with his wife since she'd moved to London. She made it clear that she would not be averse to Styler's introducing her to an eligible man. Though Styler claimed that she really didn't intend to "fix up Madonna and Guy," she realized in her dining room that day the obvious curiosity on Ritchie's side and the attraction on Madonna's. Over lobster bisque soup and cold rack of lamb, Guy Ritchie had no idea that the petite blond woman whom he had heard of since he was a child would launch a tenacious campaign to captivate him. Before the lunch was over, Madonna told Trudie Styler that the chemistry was instant. Much the way she had had a premonition about Sean Penn, she told Styler, "I saw my life in fast-forward. He's my future husband and the father of my second child." As Madonna later described her feelings to a British magazine, she said that when she first saw Ritchie, she felt "all wobblybonkers." According to Ritchie's girlfriend at the time, Tania Strecker, a television personality, Ritchie's ignoring of Madonna during the lunch piqued her interest. "His upper-crust background gave him an aura of indifference," Strecker claimed, "which obviously incited her. Madonna is not someone accustomed to people ignoring her or being indifferent."

Strecker wasn't wrong.

One reason for Madonna's attraction to Ritchie was that he was British, which fit in with her plans to make a new life for herself and her daughter in England. What made him even more appealing was that Ritchie, unlike most of her other lovers, who had been passing affairs, displayed an unexpected and surprisingly stubborn immunity to Madonna's appeal, advances, and ardor.

Still, she persisted and made it her business to research his life much the way she had studied newsreels and interviewed people when she wanted to find out about Eva Perón.

Ritchie covered up his upper-class British background and presented himself as a tough cockney—a man who came from London's East End—who had mingled with many unsavory characters and been involved in several illegal incidents. The feeling around London was that Ritchie promoted that image to coincide with his gangster movie and to fit in.

"I've lived in the East End for thirty years," Ritchie claimed, "and let's just say I've been in loads of mess-ups, and I've lost lots of money on cards." Ritchie also claimed that the scar he has on his right cheek was the result of a row in a pub where he was slashed with a knife. Others claim that he was attacked because of an unpaid £1,000 gambling debt.

In reality, Guy Stuart Ritchie, who was born in 1968 in Herefordshire, two years after his sister, Tabitha, was raised in a smart West London suburb. He is named after two officers in the Seaforth Highlanders who had died in action during World War II. His father, John, was a military man who had trained at Sandhurst, and his paternal grandfather, Major Stewart "Jack" Ritchie, had won the Military Cross for bravery during World War I. When John Ritchie abandoned the military and went into the advertising business, he became highly successful for his Hamlet cigar commercials, which were popular in the 1970s. His wife, Guy's mother, Amber, is a beautiful woman who had been a model before her marriage.

When Guy Ritchie was five, the same age as Madonna when her mother died, his parents divorced and his childhood became disjointed as he moved around a lot and mixed with a variety of different people. Shortly after the divorce, Amber married Sir Michael Leighton, a fisherman and wildlife photographer who functioned more as a father for Guy than his own biological father did. Ritchie lived in Sir Michael's grand Shrewsbury estate, in an atmosphere that was loving and calm. For the first time in many years, Guy Ritchie felt as if he had a secure home. The idyllic family life ended, however, when Guy was twelve and Sir Michael and Lady Amber Leighton divorced. Any stability he had known from that union crumbled, and Ritchie blamed his mother for depriving him of that happy English country family life he had loved so much. From then on, his relationship with his mother became strained.

Immediately after the divorce, Guy, who suffered from dyslexia, was sent off to the exclusive £4,725-a-term Standbridge Earls school in Hampshire, which specialized in students with learning disorders. A behavior problem, Guy was eventually expelled for drugs, although his father believes that the real reason was that Guy was caught in a girl's room and cutting classes. Long after the divorce and right before Guy Ritchie and Madonna announced their intention to marry, Sir Michael Leighton talked for the first time about his former wife and stepson. "Amber was a beautiful woman," Sir Michael said, "much prettier than Madonna, but our marriage didn't work out, and I haven't seen her since she left. But in my opinion, what attracted Madonna to Guy is that she sensed a neediness in him. He suffered from a learning disorder. His parents were divorced, and he was younger than she was."

The relationship with Guy was not progressing, and Madonna, desperate to see him again, asked Trudie Styler to arrange another meeting. The occasion was Guy Fawkes Day, a holiday in England on which Sting has always opened his estate to neighbors and other local residents of Wiltshire, for a barbecue and an extravagant fireworks display. Styler complied and invited Ritchie, who accepted, although she warned Madonna that the young director was still involved with Tania Strecker. Whether he was or whether the affair was not an exclusive relationship, Madonna and Guy were inseparable for the entire evening. Instead of staying over as planned at the estate, Madonna left Lourdes with the couple and went back to London with Ritchie.

If Madonna expected a radical change in her new lover, she was mistaken. When the affair was only weeks old and Ritchie had obviously not turned over his life and fate to Madonna, nor given any indication that he was willing to settle down, to change his style of clothes or his habits, or to accept her lavish gifts and eventually be referred to as Mr. Madonna, the star became even more determined to land him. It was an agonizing few months for Madonna, who was aware that while they were having an affair, Guy was still seeing other women, including Strecker. According to a friend, she even asked Guy for a part in his next movie. "He turned her down," the friend says. "She was too brassy for him." Another English friend says, "By then, Madonna was into her I-want-to-get-Guy-Ritchie mode. She took up this simple, natural look because she didn't want to look like a man-eater."

Her British incarnation had begun, and Madonna embarked upon a quest to turn herself into an upper-class Englishwoman, softening her looks by styling her hair in Pre-Raphaelite waves that fell to her shoulders, wearing loose-fitting clothes carefully chosen to be chic and not vulgar, and finally, softening her Midwestern vowels and assuming a Harrods store-bought English accent as well as many English expressions.

Patsy Rodenburg is the most respected vocal coach in England, who has worked with the Royal Shakespeare Company and the Royal National Theatre, where she is currently the head of the voice department. Rodenburg has taught such British stars as Judi Dench, Maggie Smith, Sir Ian McKellen, and Ian Holm how to speak and project their voices. One of Trudie Styler's close friends claims that Madonna engaged Rodenburg to help her perfect an upper-class British accent. According to the source, the lessons took place in the privacy of Madonna's London home once a week. According to Rodenburg, she never coached Madonna.

In yet another attempt to become the ideal woman for Guy Ritchie, when Madonna learned that one of his greatest pleasures was to wander down to the local pub and drink a couple of beers, Madonna, a teetotaler for most of her life, suddenly developed a taste for Guinness stout. As that same Styler friend says, "By doing all those things, Madonna thought it would be easy to get control and get him."

Ritchie's mother, Lady Amber, was not particularly enamored of or impressed by the American star who seemed determined to snare her son. A friend of hers claims that she was convinced that her son was unprepared for this campaign and too naive to defend himself. "Amber told me that

Guy got sucked up so quickly into Madonna's fantasy world," the friend says, "that he didn't even know what hit him. And Amber feared that things would get even more sticky."

Another friend of Lady Amber's, a titled English gentleman who has known Guy Ritchie since he was a small boy, remarked that it was nothing more than an infatuation. "Guy got entangled with the glitter of her life," he maintains, "as if he was a child who was mesmerized by a circus performer."

All of Guy Ritchie's friends as well as those people who have worked with him professionally claim that, despite his youth, he is a straightforward man who has a healthy ambition to succeed as a director. "Everything he does he takes his time and makes sure that he will do it right," an old friend says. "Whether it comes to shooting ducks or drinking at the neighborhood pub with his buddies, Guy is a man's man, an honest bloke who is exactly what he seems to be. There are no hidden agendas or double meanings in his personality."

The more that Guy Ritchie resisted, the more obsessed Madonna became. To her mortification, he showed little interest in her except for the "occasional date on a timetable of his choosing." He continued to see other women openly, and often when Madonna would reach him on his mobile phone, he would tell her that he was with someone else and couldn't talk. What drove her even more crazy was that while they were dating, he not only refused to move into her house but refused to spend the night. "Guy really didn't want to be in a position to see Lourdes in the morning," another friend explains, "as long as he was completely unsure of his intentions toward Madonna. But the other thing was that he refused to give up his single life at that point. He still intended to go off with his friends without telling her. If Madonna found out, he would hear about it afterwards."

After a while, Ritchie couldn't stand Madonna's aggressive and controlling behavior, and he stopped calling her altogether. Madonna found herself without even that small part of him that he had once been willing to give her.

In March 1999, Ritchie sent a message through Trudie Styler that he wasn't seeing Tania Strecker anymore. Madonna took that to mean that he was finally ready to settle down. She rang Ritchie and told him that she had to go to Italy to do some publicity for the Italian release of *Ray of Light* and had decided to stay several days longer to go on a yoga retreat. While in Italy, Ritchie called her and arranged to meet her. Instead of staying on for several days, they stayed for two weeks, and when they returned to England, they were a couple, a couple, however, who had frequent arguments. They were still the same two people who were used to getting their own way, two strong-willed individuals, each of whom had a temper.

Arguments would erupt from reasons as simple as Guy's forgetting a dinner date to his canceling at the last minute because he had to stay late in an edit room, making cuts on his movie, from Madonna's criticism of the way he chewed his food to Ritchie's making fun of his future wife's hairpieces and extensions.

People who know the couple maintain that it was because of his strong character that Madonna fell in love with him, while still others argue that Madonna chose him because she desperately wanted someone who would guarantee her a sense of belonging in a foreign country. Those close to Madonna hold the cynical belief that she desperately wanted to have another child and considered Guy Ritchie the perfect partner. Even long before she met Ritchie, she had often said that Lourdes, or Lola as she calls her, needed "some competition." "I don't want her growing up to be a spoiled brat," she said.

All the reasons given for the attraction between the couple were undoubtedly accurate. Madonna wanted a secure and guaranteed place among the rich and famous in England. She wanted Guy Ritchie. She wanted another child. In essence, she wanted all of the above and not necessarily in that order.

In September 1999, their relationship had once again reached an impasse because Madonna and Ritchie couldn't agree on where they would live, or at least, if they would divide their time between England and the United States. Madonna had made a commitment to Carlos Leon that she would be spending a good portion of the year in America so that he and Lourdes could see each other. Guy, in the meantime, refused even to consider spending months away from London, where he had his film company, his future, his financial backers, and his friends. It was then, in the middle of these ongoing disputes, that Madonna offered to move Leon over to London and buy him a business. Leon refused, claiming that his life was in New York or in Los Angeles since he was still trying to establish himself as an actor.

In an effort to give her ex-lover and their daughter some time together alone, when Madonna went to New York, accompanied by Ritchie, for the opening of *The Next Best Thing,* Carlos Leon went to England to stay with Lourdes in the couple's London house. After Madonna returned and presumably after Carlos Leon realized that her living in England was not at all "temporary," when he saw that Lourdes had friends and seemed happy in her new school, he confronted Madonna. "What about our arrangement?" he asked her. "Do you intend to keep your word?" In confidence, she told Leon that she intended absolutely to keep her word about dividing her time, and she was certain that she would ultimately convince Guy Ritchie that this was the only way things could work out between them.

One of Ritchie's friends at the time commented that this "geographic problem" was the basis for a potential rift or breakup in their relationship and eventually in their marriage, if it ever got to that point. "He is too young and too headstrong to be controlled," the friend said. "And he doesn't want to be bought or paid for or use Madonna's connections to further his career. He has his own ambitions and confidence in his own talent. Hollywood simply doesn't interest him."

chapter thirty-three

....

*R*eal estate reveals a great deal about people. The houses that Madonna has bought, sold, and rented in Los Angeles, Miami, and most recently in London show that she is not only quixotic in her tastes but also unconventional, daring, original, and has a need to change homes every few years. It is a metaphor for her restlessness, and not for her wealth. Most people, even movie stars, regardless of how much money they have, don't move or renovate houses every few years. It is as if Madonna can't stay put in a house just as she can't stay in one place in her career, which is what has kept her so successful, the endless reinvention. Her need to move from house to house reflects, in her private life, the restlessness that has served her so well in her public life.

In Los Angeles, during the years before Guy Ritchie, and then briefly after they were together, Madonna has moved at least six times, ending up in such strange neighborhoods as Los Feliz and most recently in Beverly Hills, which in some ways is even stranger for Madonna than Los Feliz.

Before Madonna met Guy Ritchie, and in the beginning of their relationship, she had the reputation around London real estate circles as a "nightmare client." For the first eighteen months that she lived in London, from 1999 until the middle of 2000, she looked at property, put deposits down on homes, and even went to contract on several, from Bermondsey to Highgate. One of Madonna's problems was that a shortage of houses on the market sent the prices soaring. At one point, Madonna bought a four-story house in

Chelsea, not far from Rod Stewart, Nicola Horlick, and Adnan Khashoggi. Prior to that, she had been renting a home in Kensington in an area known as Millionaire's Row, for approximately $6,000 a week. When she finally settled on the idea of buying a house, it was surprisingly in a busy neighborhood of London, in the heart of the West End, not far from some of the city's most luxurious and trendy stores.

The Georgian mansion cost Madonna $10 million and was bought through her company Chelsea Girl LLC and her London lawyer, Mishcon de Reya, only a week before her wedding to Guy Ritchie. Madonna bought the house from a London property developer, Robert Wallace, who is married to the heiress to the Yates Wine Lodge fortune. Wallace, who only owned the property for six months, had bought it from James Kirkman, a millionaire art dealer, who had a long and lucrative professional relationship with the British artist Lucien Freud.

The property is an interesting choice for Madonna, as it sits directly on the sidewalk of a busy road, close to the crowds and tourists who wander around Oxford Street. Inside, the house is a world apart from the popular neighborhood in which it is located. Eighteenth-century, with an old-fashioned elevator and mahogany staircase, it is completely restored to its original condition, with five living rooms, a wood-paneled library, study, and a twenty-eight-foot salon. Each room has a fireplace and high, sculptured ceilings; the dining room opens up onto a back courtyard and garden, and there are two large kitchens. In addition, there are eight bedrooms, including a master suite with its own dressing room and bathroom. In the rear of the house, over a large garage, are two maid's rooms, as well as two more servants' quarters in the basement of the main house.

While Madonna was looking for a permanent residence in London, she was also making real estate transactions in the United States. In February 1999, she put her Biscayne Bay property, in Miami, up for sale, for $8.9 million. The house, which was next door to Viscaya, an Italian palace that had been turned into a museum and gardens, had approximately 7,128 square feet, and according to Alan Jacobson, whose firm, Wimbish-Riteway, Inc., handled the sale, "Madonna started a selling trend among celebrities in the South Beach area. Michael Caine sold his house, Cher renovated hers and sold it, and Sylvester Stallone eventually sold his for $16.2 million."

In June 2000, Madonna's Miami home sold for $7.5 million. The owners remain a mystery. At first, rumor had it that a German shepherd named Gunther and his anonymous master had been interested in Stallone's house, but eventually found the price too high. Dennis Bedard, the vice president of the Gunther Corporation and a lawyer, confirmed that Gunther had bought Madonna's Miami property. "The money comes from Europe," Dennis said. "The corporation has one hundred and fifty million dollars at its disposal." Larry Schatz, Madonna's New York attorney, whose firm represented her in the sale, also claimed not to know who the actual owners were. "The sale has been completed," Schatz said. "It's a done deal. I have no knowledge of who the buyers are, or what they intend to do with it." By then, more rumors began to spread about the prospective residents, and in response, Dindy Yokel, a publicist, claimed that four "young, blond people, two women and two men in their early twenties," had moved into the house, along with Gunther, the German shepherd. Still other neighbors in the area claim that the occupants are a rock group called the Burgundians, a boy band backed by an unnamed investor. In European society, the truth seems far more complicated.

Maurizio Mian has claimed that he represents the Gunther Group, which, he explains, has assets from a trust left to Gunther, the German shepherd, by the Countess Karlotta Leibenstein, who died in 1992. Checking the records of trusts throughout Western Europe, the Gunther Group doesn't exist, nor does the countess. When confronted with the facts, Mian retracted his original statements and said that the new owners of Madonna's house are a multimedia quartet called the Burgundians: Barbie K., Gene X., Charlotte R., and G.G. According to Mian, "These are four physically beautiful people who are intelligent and educated. Not just people who can sing and dance, but who are interested in business. In fact, they happen to be marketing and advertising students." It is a story that is undoubtedly even too far-fetched and complicated for Madonna to option for a video or a feature-length film. The only concern Madonna had was that the deal to sell her house in Miami not fall through.

In the middle of her problems with Guy Ritchie, Madonna went ahead, without informing Ritchie, and bought the house on Roxbury Drive in Beverly Hills that Diane Keaton had restored and renovated. The property, situated just below the foothills of Beverly Hills, in an area north of Sunset Boulevard known as "the flats," was designed by the architect Walter Neff. When Keaton sold Madonna the house, it was surprisingly almost in its original condition, although when it had been on the market before Keaton bought it, it was advertised as a "tear-down." Neighbors were surprised when Keaton restored the four-thousand-square-foot property, modest and considered "cramped" for Beverly Hills, bringing back both the interior and exterior to their most simple and unadorned architectural purity. Many people found not only Madonna's choice of the house but also the neighborhood curious and inappropriate for a star who craves privacy. The area was not considered chic or trendy, and the house presented security problems. Because the surrounding grounds are relatively small, the house is exposed to the street on all sides, including from a back alley. Even the proximity of the neighbors' windows on either side was a significant security risk, since, according to a real estate agent, shortly after Madonna bought the house, a neighbor rented out his living room window to a tabloid photographer. But Madonna was into her unpretentious mode, and the house in Beverly Hills was just offbeat and old-world enough by American standards to be what she thought Guy Ritchie would want. Expecting that he would at most be momentarily annoyed when she told him what she had done, she was shocked that he considered it the breaking point in their affair.

In October 1999, Trudie Styler gave a dinner at Chez Es Saada, a bistro on New York's Lower East Side, to celebrate the New York performance of her husband's American tour. Guy Ritchie was in London doing the postproduction for his second film, *Snatch,* and Madonna, dressed modestly and described as extremely tense, was one of the twelve close friends who were invited to share the occasion with the couple. During most of the dinner, Madonna was on her cell phone, trying desperately to reach Ritchie on his cell phone in London. Either there was no answer or she got his message machine. Every five minutes she would redial the number, until one of the guests felt incredibly sorry for Madonna. Putting her hand on her arm, she said in a low voice, "Let him be for a while. Don't smother him or he'll run away. Men don't like to be hounded. Give him some space."

Madonna looked startled for a moment, and according to the woman, she seemed so vulnerable, so fragile, so innocent, that "my heart went out to her." She says, "She was behaving like any average woman who was madly in love and insecure. She kept saying over and over, 'But I love him and I'm so frightened that he's going to dump me.' Finally, she agreed not to touch the phone, and it became a kind of game. She would look up like a child and say, 'Now can I try him? It's been fifteen minutes.' I would shake my head and say, 'Not yet, you've waited fifteen minutes, let's try for twenty.'"

Eventually, Madonna gave in to Ritchie's demands to live in London for most of the year because she realized that, unless she did, there would be no happily ever after to their story. But she kept the house in Beverly Hills, and after their son was born, they would indeed spend more time there than Ritchie had ever dreamed.

When she returned to London, gossip and rumors reported in the press about Madonna and Guy's relationship and comments made by friends and the Ritchie family about her propelled her to make a statement about her new life. Once again, she explained that she had changed, that her previous rebellious behavior was because of the trauma she had suffered after the death of her mother. Falling in love with Guy Ritchie had made her the woman she had always known she could be. Explaining away her many romantic liaisons, she added, "All my excesses were in my youth. When I married my first husband, I was in love and truly believed the marriage would last. When I had my daughter with Carlos Leon, it was a real relationship, which I also thought would last."

During those tumultuous months, when Madonna was telling friends that she wanted another child, Ritchie, according to members of his family, did not really pay attention or take her seriously. When she finally announced that she was pregnant, during a quiet moment after dinner in her rented house in Kensington in front of the fire in the den, Ritchie was shocked. He slammed out of the house and went to a pub for a few drinks. "Then he went to see his father," a friend relates. "Apparently, the old man said, 'Look, if it's yours, and you're sure about it, then you have to stand by her.'" Later that night, Ritchie returned to the Kensington house and told Madonna, "Okay, if you really want this baby, it's great. I love you."

Privately, both John Ritchie and Lady Amber Leighton were crushed. They had expected that their son would concentrate on his career before he settled down to marriage and fatherhood and that, when he did, he would choose a more refined Englishwoman. One of Amber Leighton's friends says, "They believed that Madonna deliberately got pregnant. This was not some teenage girl who didn't know how to use birth control. His father told him that right out. No one in the family was happy about it, although they are decent people and told him that he had to do the decent thing." But even then, Ritchie did not commit to marriage.

Once again, Madonna was living out one of her most popular songs and videos, "Papa Don't Preach," when she made it clear to Guy Ritchie and to his family that she was going to "keep her baby." If it wasn't clear in the song to which "baby" she was referring, in real life, there was no doubt that Madonna intended to keep them both, her unborn child and Ritchie.

Throughout the pregnancy, there were rumors that Madonna had refused to marry Ritchie. Friends and spokespeople for the singer assured the press that it was her choice to remain independent. Friends of Ritchie's maintain that it was the director who was reluctant to make a legal commitment to the mother of his child.

When Tony Ciccone was told that Madonna was pregnant without any firm date for getting married, he made no secret that he considered it damaging to the unborn child. He also criticized Madonna for making it so geographically difficult for Lourdes to see her father. Tony undoubtedly adored his granddaughter and would love his unborn grandchild as well, but he was furious at his daughter for her apparent refusal to "settle down." The pregnancy would cause an even greater rift between Tony and Madonna, which would only heal when she finally told him that she intended to get married. Curiously, it was Joan Ciccone who leaked the result of a sonogram to the press when she was quoted as saying, "We're so glad Lourdes will have a little brother to play with."

What finally persuaded Ritchie to propose was the difficulty of Rocco's premature birth and Madonna's heroism.

* * *

On Thursday night, August 10, 2000, Madonna was at home alone in her Beverly Hills house, while Ritchie was at Brad Pitt's house, only ten minutes away by car. Pitt, who was starring in Ritchie's new film, *Snatch,* had organized a poker game along with the Welsh actor Vinnie Jones. Both Madonna and Ritchie had no reason to worry about the baby's impending birth, which was, according to doctors, a month away. In fact, only three days before, Madonna had gone for a complete checkup at St. Joseph's Good Samaritan Hospital and had been assured that all was perfectly normal. Suddenly, at nearly midnight, Madonna began to hemorrhage. Her first call was to her doctor, who, suspecting that she had what is called placenta previa, or a detached placenta, promptly arranged for an ambulance to take her to Cedars-Sinai Medical Center, which has the best postnatal care in the country. Ironically, just a month before Madonna, Lourdes, and Guy Ritchie had left for California in preparation for the birth, Madonna had caused a scandal in England when she had told the British press that she felt more comfortable having her baby in the United States. In several interviews she gave at the time, she stated that American hospital facilities are cleaner and more advanced than in Britain. One hospital source at Cedars-Sinai believes that her decision might have saved her life as well as the baby's, since the California hospital has the most advanced technology for neonatal care.

Madonna's second call on that harrowing night was to Ritchie's cell phone to tell him what was happening. Within minutes, the ambulance arrived, almost at the same time as the distraught father-to-be. Paramedics rushed Madonna onto a stretcher, and Ritchie followed her to the hospital in his car. Still wearing her blood-soaked nightclothes and clutching her stomach, she was rushed into the emergency room, where her private physician was waiting along with a team of specialists who would tend to both mother and child. Ritchie checked Madonna into the hospital under the name of Tabitha Leighton (Tabitha is Guy Ritchie's sister and Leighton is the last name of his mother's second husband). The telephone diagnosis was correct. The placenta, or spongelike tissue that carries oxygen and other nutrients from mother to child, had detached itself from Madonna's womb. The decision was made instantly. Madonna would have an emergency cesarean section. Seconds counted in getting the baby out of the womb and breathing, since the risk was great that he could die from oxygen deprivation and that Madonna could bleed to death. As she was being wheeled into the operating room, Ritchie, pale and shaking, ran beside the gurney, holding her hand. "Save my baby," Madonna kept repeating, "just save my baby." Ritchie never left her side, standing next to her as the doctors performed the lifesaving surgery.

Two teams of doctors worked on Madonna, one to deliver the baby and the other to stanch the flow of blood. An hour after the ordeal began, at 12:54 A.M., August 11, 2000, Rocco John Ritchie was born, weighing six pounds three ounces. Still, Madonna's only thought was for her child. She kept asking the doctors, "He's going to be okay, isn't he? Tell me he's going to be okay."

By the time she was wheeled into the recovery room, Madonna's condition was stable, although she had lost a great deal of blood. Rocco was placed in an incubator under an ultraviolet light in the neonatal intensive care unit. He was suffering from jaundice and was having difficulty breathing. Twelve hours later, Madonna was allowed to see her son. Holding him in her arms, she kissed his head and said tearfully, "This little guy is my little miracle."

Later that day, Lourdes, accompanied by Ingrid Casares, also pregnant at the time by a German male model, visited her mother and spent time with Guy Ritchie.

On August 25, Eric Berg, a film producer and close friend of Guy Ritchie's, told the press that Madonna and Ritchie would be getting married before Christmas. He also said that the couple planned to divide their time between London and Los Angeles. "Guy plans to keep a house in London with Madonna," Berg reported, "but they are going to set up home in Los Angeles. He just wants them to be a family. . . . He has been over the moon since the birth of his son. The man is gushing."

chapter thirty-four

·················

Newspapers and magazines throughout the world carried the story of Rocco Ritchie's birth and the imminent marriage of Madonna to her baby's father. What Madonna neglected to share with the press was that as soon as Lourdes was told that her mother and Guy Ritchie were going to get married, she began asking questions like "Why didn't you ever marry my father?" or "When am I going to see my daddy?" Because of Lourdes and her obvious confusion about her father's place in her mother's life, Madonna invited Carlos Leon to the wedding.

In September, Tony and Joan Ciccone flew from Detroit to Los Angeles to see the baby for the first time. Despite the announcement of the marriage, there was still a coolness between Madonna and her father. Several weeks later, after he had returned home, Tony Ciccone expressed his feelings about his new grandson, who had been named after one of Tony's brothers, and about his daughter's marital plans. "He's adorable," Tony said. "We're very happy and very relieved that everyone is well. As for Madonna's wedding plans, I couldn't be happier. I just hope everything works out."

By October 2000, Tony and Joan Ciccone were already making plans to go to London for Madonna's wedding in December. They had also decided to go to a château in the Bordeaux region of France while they were overseas to learn as much as they could about French techniques for growing grapes for wine.

As the British press began inundating the public with stories, speculating on where and when the marriage would take place, the chemistry between Madonna and her British lover mystified many observers who had known the pair both as a couple and individually. The question that everybody seemed to be asking was how could a relatively sheltered thirty-one-year-old man, who was just starting out in a career, who had been virtually unknown, find happiness with a forty-two-year-old superstar who had always picked up the bills for all of her men, with the exception of Warren Beatty?

The question was unanswerable when it came to the emotional and physical dynamic between the couple. If Guy Ritchie had begun the affair as an unwilling object of pursuit and had turned into an ideal husband, his family, more than Madonna's, was not at all happy with the way things had turned out. In Amber Leighton's camp, people were pessimistic. "At the moment," one friend said, "I think Guy is somewhat caught up in the excitement of the wedding and doesn't quite realize what's hit him." Another friend agreed: "Once he realizes how manipulated he has been by Madonna's fantasies about becoming the perfect English wife and mother, I am afraid this will have a dismal end."

An actress friend of Madonna's who lives in New York was also not particularly optimistic: "While she was trying to catch him, she was sweet and endearing, but there are already signs that the sweetness won't last." Yet another friend of the singer's, who was a guest at the wedding, said, "I have no doubt that this marriage won't last. As a matter of fact, shortly after Rocco was born, Madonna began making noises about getting bored. She jokingly asked me on the phone from Los Angeles, 'When are we going to raise a little hell?' "

Behind the scenes, in the days leading up to the ceremony, there were signs that the relationship was in trouble, and several observers predicted that if the marriage happened at all, it wouldn't last two years. London bookmakers gave the marriage a one-in-three chance of lasting five years.

"The atmosphere in their house can be cut with a knife," a friend said. "For the first time Madonna is impatient with Lourdes and yelling at her, and Guy is just getting out as much as he can, finding every excuse not to be there. They are bickering over the most benign things. It could be the pressure of the relatives arriving for the wedding or simply prenuptial nerves, but let's face it, these are not two wide-eyed kids."

Several of Madonna's friends believe that this turmoil is for the good. "The one thing Madonna never could stand is being bored. Huge rows have been a pattern in her longer relationships, and she really is looking forward to the wedding. It will be her biggest show in years!" Yet another friend said, "One of the major problems that the couple have had throughout their relationship is that Ritchie, unlike Madonna's other lovers, who have enjoyed basking in her wealth and reflected fame, is uneasy with the prospect of the lavish life that she envisages for them."

In the weeks leading up to the wedding, there was speculation that the couple would marry in Scotland. The guessing game was ended by the appearance of a simple set of typed paper displayed at the Register Office in Dornoch. Miss Lesley Connor, registrar in Dornoch in Sutherland, revealed that among a list of four forthcoming weddings was that of Guy Stuart Ritchie and Madonna Louise Ciccone, set for Friday, December 22, 2000. Just as Madonna and Sean Penn had chosen to marry on her birthday, the Madonna–Guy Ritchie wedding was to be held on Ritchie's thirty-second birthday. In another sentimental tribute, the couple chose the castle for their wedding in honor of Ritchie's grandfather Major Stewart "Jack" Ritchie, who served with the Seaforth Highlanders and was killed near Dunkirk in World War II.

Several weeks before the baby's baptism and the wedding, Madonna went to Skibo Castle, where the nuptials would take place, to go over details with the Reverend Susan Brown, who would marry them, Stuart Anderson, the cathedral organist, as well as with the staff at Skibo. The Reverend Susan Brown, forty-two, is the United Kingdom's first female minister in charge of a cathedral and the woman who would guide the couple through the Church of Scotland's nine-part wedding sequence. With a reputation for being down-to-earth, she explained that she had been chosen to marry the couple because the bride is divorced and has children, and there is no Free Church minister in Scotland who would agree to do it, while the Anglican priest was not full-time. "During the day, he's a pharmacist here," Reverend Brown added, "so he's incredibly busy with a massive area to cover."

Skibo is a nineteenth-century castle that sits on seventy-five hundred acres in the Scottish Highlands, in the town of Dornoch, an area that is surrounded by grouse moors, deer forests, and lochs. It is forty-five miles north of Inverness with a population of just over twelve hundred people. The main castle, bought by Andrew Carnegie in 1898, has twenty-one bedrooms with an additional twenty-six more bedrooms in eleven lodges that are scattered around the grounds. The name Skibo comes from Schyberbolle, which means "fairyland of peace," and it is a favorite resort for the rich and famous. Carnegie, who bought the crumbling original Skibo Castle after he returned from America to settle permanently in Scotland, replaced the structure with a completely new castle with towers and turrets, stained-glass windows, an enormous ballroom, a staircase of Sicilian marble, and an indoor swimming pool. After Carnegie's death in 1919, Skibo stayed with his descendants until it was bought in 1990 for £6.5 million by Peter de Savary, a businessman, who intended to renovate it for commercial use. At the time de Savary bought it, it was in abysmal ill-repair, and he spent approximately £17 million and devoted four years to restoring it to the condition that it is in now. There are oak-paneled walls, marble pillars, chandeliers, and chintz-upholstered chairs and sofas, and the forty-seven bedrooms all have four-poster beds, giving the castle an air of old-world luxury. There is also a championship golf course. While the price of a room starts at $750 per night, the wedding cost Madonna, who paid for everything, approximately $1.7 million. Her wedding gown alone, designed by Stella McCartney, Paul McCartney's daughter, who is the chief designer for Chloé, cost more than $30,000, and the flowers, red roses and white lilies, cost $75,000.

The wedding ceremony was described by one friend as a "religious potpourri: Catholicism for Madonna, Protestantism for Guy, and Buddhism for God knows what reason."

Four days before the actual ceremony, the couple left their Kensington house in a silver Mercedes, accompanied by Lourdes, Rocco, and two nannies. A second car followed filled with luggage and the rest of the entourage, including bodyguards, hairdresser, and an armed guard who carried the borrowed diamonds from Harry Winston. Arriving in a Falcon 2000 jet from RAF Northolt in Middlesex, the wedding party was welcomed by a lone piper, Clum Spud Fraser, who played "Scotland the Brave" plus his own version of "Like a Virgin." Lourdes tripped delightedly off the aircraft, while Rocco was carried in a carry-cot by one of the nannies. Superintendent Jim Heddle was in charge of the police security operation, although he made it clear that Madonna had her own personal security. "We are only responsible for the safety of the public," he said. "But since she is a massive star, we have got to cater for anything that might happen."

Only close friends and family members stayed at the castle. The first guests to arrive were Sting, Trudie Styler, and their children: Mickey, sixteen, Jake, fifteen, Coco, nine, and Giacomo, four. Other celebrities, including Stella McCartney and Gwyneth Paltrow, also stayed there and on the ride from the airport shared a black Range Rover with tinted windows, which was only one of a fleet of cars that was sent by Skibo to pick up the guests at the small airport and bring them to the castle. Donatella Versace and Mathew Vaughn also stayed at Skibo, as did Madonna's sister Melanie and her husband, Joe Henry, along with Madonna's brother Christopher and their parents, Tony and Joan. Guy Ritchie's family was housed at the castle as well.

In the film Evita, Madonna is at her best when, as Eva Perón, she stands before a crowd of her adoring fans, whether they are weeping women or sexually aroused men who are clearly seduced by the image of Evita as much as they are by the political agenda of her husband. In the crowd below the balcony of the Casa Rosada are also the Evita wanna-bes, who cry out to the Argentine first lady. "Please, Santa Eva, make me your favorite, smile at me and choose me as the one you love the most."

At the christening, Madonna stood next to Guy Ritchie, who held the baby, Rocco, in his arms, swathed in a $15,000 cream silk christening gown, designed by Donatella Versace. Over the gown, Rocco wore a warm furry suit that covered him and a matching white bunny hat that shielded him from the paparazzi with their telephoto lenses and the damp Scottish wind.

Kay McDonald, a receptionist who works in Dornoch, remarked how startling the resemblance was to Eva Perón. "I remember the film," McDonald said, "and Madonna was Evita, just as today she is Evita once again." Wearing a long, loose-fitting, off-white silk coat, with a black veil covering her hair, pulled back in an neat twist, a pair of antique crystal earrings dangling from her ears, Madonna raised her hand in a measured wave, smiling slightly to the crowd of local residents who stood before the Dornoch Cathedral and cheered.

Casa Rosada, the official residence of the Argentine president, is named the Pink House after the pink stones that cover the facade, and the Dornoch Cathedral, where the baby was baptised on December 20, is a thirteenth-century, pink-tinged stone building with a steeple and clock tower that ascends into the swirling mists that float in from the surrounding hillside. "It was a simple ceremony," said Father Benedict Seed, who attended the service but did not officiate. "The baby was well behaved and didn't cry. His father, however, overcome with emotion, did."

Apparently, Tony Ciccone cried as well, although some speculate that they were tears of relief because of the marriage that was to take place two days later, and because the rift between him and Madonna had finally healed. John Ritchie, Guy's seventy-two-year-old father, wept as he stood between his second wife, Shireen, and her son, Oliver, twenty-one. Gwyneth Paltrow was visibly moved.

"It was very emotional," said Jean-Baptiste Mondino, Madonna's friend, the director of so many of her videos, who was to take the wedding pictures.

Trudie Styler, Rocco's godmother, read the lengthy Lorica hymn. Sting sang "Ave Maria," and Guy Oseary, Madonna's Israeli-born partner in Mad Guy Films and Mad Guy Television, her film and television companies, as well as in Maverick Records, took his place as the baby's godfather. Madonna, Guy Ritchie, Guy Oseary, and Trudie Styler, who carried the baby, stepped up to the font at the appropriate moment to participate in the baptism.

The ceremony lasted thirty minutes and was conducted by the Reverend Susan Brown. Rupert Everett rushed in at the end of the ceremony, wearing jeans and a leather jacket. His plane was late on the way from Inverness due to heavy fog over Dornoch. The next day, he said, "The only sad moment for Madonna, as usual, was when she thought about her mother and wished that she could have lived to see this."

As she always does during christenings, after the service was over, Reverend Susan Brown carried Rocco John Ritchie in her arms, walking all around the church to welcome him into the house of God.

On December 22, the afternoon of the wedding, Guy

Ritchie went duck shooting with his two best men, while Madonna went clay-pigeon shooting and strolled the grounds, did yoga, and watched displays of falconry with Gwyneth Paltrow, Stella McCartney, and Trudie Styler from the castle windows.

The girl from Bay City had come a long way to Dornoch, Scotland.

On December 22, at six-thirty in the evening, surrounded by hundreds of candles, Madonna Louise Veronica Ciccone and Guy Ritchie were married in the Great Hall of the castle. Accompanied by one lone bagpiper and the music of French pianist Katia Labèque along with the cathedral organist, Lourdes, four years old, shoeless and draped in a long ivory dress with short sleeves and a high neck, also designed by Stella McCartney, led the procession down the aisle, tossing handfuls of red rose petals from a basket. The groom wore a vibrant teal blazer, a Hunting Mackintosh plaid kilt of navy and green that had been made by Britain's Scotch House with a sash that incorporated Guy's family tartan, and antique diamond cuff links, which were a gift from his bride. Rocco John Ritchie, in the arms of his nanny, wore a matching kilt. Ritchie's two best men were Mathew Vaughn, his partner and the producer of his two films, and Piers Adam, a London nightclub owner. Madonna's maid of honor was Stella McCartney, who wore a gray-and-beige pants outfit of her own design.

As Madonna walked down the aisle on her father's arm, and as Lourdes, Gwyneth, and Donatella Versace walked toward her, instead of the wedding march, a Scottish air called "Highland Cathedral," often played at the Edinburgh Tattoo, swelled around them. During the wedding service, "Nessun Dorma" and Bach's Toccata and Fugue in D Minor played.

Madonna and Ritchie had written part of the vows, which included "cherish, honor, and delight in family." Reverend Susan Brown added that the "challenges of life should be superseded by their love for one another and their children, and that any obstacle is a challenge to be met." At the end of the ceremony, Brown presented Madonna and Guy Ritchie with a twin pack of Andrex toilet paper, to symbolize a soft, long, and durable marriage.

For her previous wedding to Sean Penn, Madonna had assumed a fifties look. For this wedding, her strapless, ivory silk gown was nineteenth-century and had a fitted corset bodice and long train with an antique veil embroidered with nineteenth-century lace that covered her face and cascaded down to her Jimmy Choo shoes. She wore a diamond tiara loaned by Asprey & Garrard of London, several pearl and diamond bracelets courtesy of Adler of London, and around her neck was a twenty-seven-carat, two-and-a-half-inch diamond cross designed by Ronald Winston of the House of Harry Winston in New York. Madonna's wedding band was platinum with several small diamonds, while Guy's was plain platinum, both designed by Stephen Webster.

For her wedding with Sean Penn, Madonna had said that she wanted to wear "Something that had a 1950s feeling and something that Grace Kelly might have worn at her wedding." For this wedding, she actually wore the diamond tiara, designed by Cartier, that Princess Grace had worn to her daughter Caroline's first marriage, to Philippe Junot.

Unlike *Apocalypse Now,* the theme of her last wedding, this time Madonna was hermetically sealed off from the press, television cameras, sound trucks, and scores of photographers as well as fans and local residents who waited outside in the freezing temperatures for more than ten hours in an effort to catch a glimpse of the star and of her famous guests. A security force of more than seventy men as well as Madonna's private force of fifteen wandered the grounds or were positioned in front of the castle.

During the ceremony, Madonna couldn't stop smiling, and one friend of Ritchie's thought that he looked "proud." After the ceremony, Madonna tossed her bouquet of flowers into the crowd. Lourdes caught it.

Family and friends gathered in Skibo's drawing room for champagne and toasts before going into the oak-paneled dining room for a sit-down dinner. Madonna was gone for several minutes, and when she returned, she had changed into a Jean-Paul Gaultier outfit. Fires blazed in the stone hearths as the guests ate haggis, a Scottish dish that is a combination of lamb, oatmeal, and spices, along with langoustines, salmon, mussels, Aberdeen Angus beef, roast potatoes, and red cabbage, accompanied by champagne and Beaujolais. Throughout the meal, a traditional four-piece Scottish band played, and some of the musicians even serenaded the guests with spoons. Dessert was a caramelized profiterole cake baked by a London chef flown in for the occasion, and the wedding cake was a gift from Sting and Trudie Styler, a customized cake in the shape of a piano, with Austrian chocolate and marzipan, which sat on wooden legs made by a joiner, designed by Harry Gow of Culloden, who had also made a white-iced christening cake for Rocco with his name spelled out in lemon icing.

The affair had the feeling of a family dinner, and Lourdes, along with several of Sting and Styler's children, ran around the dining room. In the middle of the dinner, Mathew Vaughn read telegrams from guests who had not been able to come, including Luciano Pavarotti, Rosie O'Donnell, Elton John, the Dalai Lama—whose invitation had prompted the rumors that the wedding would be a Buddhist ceremony—and Brad Pitt and Jennifer Aniston.

After dinner, the group retired to a disco in the basement, and Madonna appeared in yet another outfit, an ivory pantsuit that had been designed by Donatella Versace. The disc jockey, Tracy Young, was from Miami, a friend of Ingrid Casares's, and played a mixture of Madonna and Sting tunes.

At dawn, Madonna and Guy Ritchie left the party and spent their wedding night in the bridal suite, the room that Andrew Carnegie had used as his own bedroom. Later that day, surrounded by Tony and Joan Ciccone, John and

Shireen Ritchie, and Lady Amber Leighton, the couple planted a baby oak tree on the grounds, promising to return every year to watch as it grew.

Even Madonna couldn't persuade the staff at Skibo to let them stay on through Christmas. The castle was reserved and guests were arriving from as far away as Abu Dhabi. Madonna, Guy, Lourdes, and Rocco and their nannies spent Christmas at Sting and Trudie's country estate in Wiltshire. During the visit, the two couples dropped in at a local pub for beer and sang carols with other local residents during the midnight mass at the town's church.

It was another circle. Madonna and Ritchie ended their wedding week and the baptism of their son where it had all begun for them, a mere two years earlier, in Wiltshire, in England, Madonna's new country.

chapter thirty-five
••••••••••••••••••

*O*nce again, Madonna is a pioneer in the new definition of publicity in the twenty-first century. Instinctively she realized that selling nuptials to tabloid magazines is no longer considered acceptable for celebrities or appreciated by their fans. On her own, even after Catherine Zeta-Jones and Michael Douglas included the world in their affair, the birth of their son, and their wedding, Madonna understood that the only way to control the kind of press that she wanted this time around was to cloak the event in secrecy. Only then could she be assured of a dignified result. The international media would recount every detail with respect and awe, and the paparazzi would be censored by the mainstream photographers. Just as she once made sex her most potent image, she now uses dignity as the most effective way to get attention.

What is fascinating and a tribute to her sense of timing is that Madonna garnered as much attention by eluding the media during her wedding to Guy Ritchie as she did during her wedding to Sean Penn, when she allowed the press to turn the event into a garish circus.

In 1985, Madonna was a different woman. She was not only willing but determined to get all the publicity that she could get, even if most of it did not depict her as a stunning actress or a refined young bride. In 1998, when she met Guy Ritchie, he was still bent on shedding his aristocratic background, and Madonna, newly arrived in England, was determined to acquire a touch of class. Almost immediately, she understood that her husband did not really come from the rough East End, was not an authentic cockney, did not scrounge around for meals or owe money to nasty underworld characters, but rather was a wellborn, privately educated son of a successful businessman and his beautiful former wife, who eventually remarried and got herself a title.

By the time Madonna was pregnant with their child, she put an end to his fantasy by convincing him in her own inimitable way that luxury and excess, extravagance and success, were attributes that made it possible to have what she most craved, personal freedom, and what her new husband was working so hard to achieve—artistic recognition. She also understood that accepting his beginnings was as difficult for him as it was for her when it came to going back to Bay City as the beloved granddaughter of one of the oldest families in town. In some perverse way, Guy Ritchie accepted his wife's demands, because marrying Madonna, according to British standards, was marrying down, since money was nothing compared to title and lands and family history, not unlike the Fortin family in Bay City, who considered anyone who had moved there after World War II to be a newcomer and not part of the old guard.

Ironically, both of Madonna's husbands tried to pretend that they were low-class boys who had passed a misspent youth getting into fights and committing petty crimes. The difference is that when Penn grew up, he dreamed of shooting paparazzi in helicopters, while Ritchie, following family tradition, went about shooting ducks in Dornoch. There is something similar about Madonna, Sean Penn, and Guy Ritchie. Just as Madonna picked the bad boys who came from good families, she tried to do the same when she changed the reality of her own background and family to satisfy what she believed her fans needed to hear.

What is odd is that several weeks after the wedding, close friends of Guy Ritchie suddenly began saying that the thirty-two-year-old director was actually thirty-eight years old. One close friend of Lady Amber Leighton's denies the age

discrepancy. "It is absolutely untrue. Madonna decided that
it was plausible to say that Guy, as some people in show
business have done, lied about his age when he first began
directing, to make him more of a wonder boy. What this tells
us is that Madonna is extremely sensitive about the age difference and, as she has done in the past concerning her own
life, is determined to rewrite history when it comes to Guy.
Lady Amber is a very down-to-earth, realistic woman. She
didn't care about her own age as much as she was appalled
at the fabrication for the sake of Madonna's ego."

How different is this Madonna who wandered around the
Scottish grounds of Skibo Castle before her wedding,
gamely shooting clay pigeons and standing on her balcony,
with her new best friends, Gwyneth and Trudie, watching
the Scottish mist roll in over the hills, from the Madonna
who fell madly in love with the violent and drunk Sean
Penn, the woman who made her fame making bad movies
and seducing her audience onstage, wearing chains and
black leather bustiers?

Was it maturity that changed her, or was it love, or was it
simply that she had gone from one extreme to the other?

If Frida Kahlo, the tortured artist and abused wife, was
once her heroine, and Eva Perón, the woman who accomplished all her dreams against all odds, was her idol, at forty-
two Madonna has a new idea of the ideal woman. She is Mia
Farrow, the earth mother and actress, or Trudie Styler, the
adored wife of the rock idol who has her own career, four
loving children, and the good sense to know that money is
not the root of all evil but rather the root of all goods, the
best way to buy freedom and a guarantee of living happily
ever after.

As Madonna enters her fifth decade, she has decided that
stability, common sense, religious values, and a life filled
with a husband's love and adorable children are all she
needs to make her feel alive. And yet, shortly after her mar-

riage to Guy Ritchie, someone asked her if her transformations are over, if her public should never again expect the same shocking images and shows that she has given them throughout her career.

"You never know," she replied, echoing a line that has been her mantra through so many of her transformations. "Never say never."

Epilogue

....

*I*n April 2001 the French magazine *Madame Figaro* once again asked me to do an article on Madonna, this time on her Drowned World tour that was scheduled to arrive in Europe at the beginning of the summer. The request was made and several months passed without any reply as to whether I could have an interview with the singer alone or if I would be part of a group if she decided to have one press conference for the print media.

On June 26, 2001, Madonna appeared in Paris for the first of four concerts at Bercy, a stadium that regularly hosts rock stars, political meetings, and sporting events. My request to interview Madonna was denied by her French handlers and, in fact, Madonna refused all press and radio interviews as well as all television appearances in the City of Light. French journalists made the trip to Barcelona, the city that preceded Paris on the tour, to see the show and join their Spanish colleagues in a welcoming press conference there.

By the time Madonna arrived in the French capital, local newspapers and magazines were filled with reviews of her Drowned World tour. Some of the articles concentrated on the star's efficiency and organization that resulted in one hundred tons of equipment being safely transported overseas in two Boeing 747s, while other journalists respectfully cited the songs that she performed and offered a review of each costume and every set. Still others focused their attention and accolades on Mirwais, the French musician and arranger, a guitarist who was once a member of the new wave group Taxi Girl, who is credited with the success of the star's latest album, *Music*. A few reporters wrote about Madonna's trip to Sachsenhausen, the Nazi concentration camp, while she was performing in Berlin, quoting from *Bild*, a German tabloid, which photographed the star, dressed all in black, posing under the sign at the entrance, which reads, *"Arbeit macht frei,"* or "Work makes you free."

When the concert began in Paris, an elevated platform lowers Madonna onto the stage. She is wearing black boots with chains, a tartan plaid skirt—a nod to her new husband—and a black T-shirt with *mother* written on the front and *fucker* on the back, a nod to her fans lest they believe that the once-provocative star has become only a staid wife and mother. The muscles in her arms bulged, her medium-length blond hair with a hint of black roots moved loosely around her face, a white bandage was wrapped around her right arm that had a diamond cuff at the wrist, while on the fourth finger of her left hand, there was a wide gold wedding band.

Sitting in the audience on opening night at Bercy and watching the frenzy of the fans who came from all over Europe to see her, stomping and swaying, singing and screaming, in their seats and in the aisles, I suddenly realized how easy it is to be crushed during an event of that size, as has happened all too many times during soccer matches throughout Europe. The heat inside Bercy was oppressive, something that Madonna would comment on during her show. "Don't you fine French people believe in air-conditioning?" she drawled in an ersatz Southern accent that dripped with irony. At one point during the show, she looked frighteningly frail, and sitting close enough to the stage to see her face, I noticed that her expression was contorted into one of complete and total exhaustion from the heat. At forty-two years old, Madonna nonetheless displayed incredible stamina, since dozens of young people fainted during the show and were pulled out of the pit, a small area reserved for a standing-room-only crowd, by burly security guards. The enthusiasm of the audience continued when the one-hour-and-forty-minute spectacle ended. As I sat in my car in the middle of an impossible traffic jam trying to leave the stadium, surrounded by a cacophony of sound blaring from car radios, different clips of Madonna's music, I realized that despite an eight-year hiatus from the tour circuit and a somewhat minimalist performance that seemed to be calculated down to the last millisecond, Madonna had by no means relinquished her place in the hearts of her fans.

On June 25, accompanied by her husband, Guy Ritchie, and her two children, Lourdes and Rocco, Madonna arrived at the Crillon in Paris, one of the most magnificent hotels in the city, overlooking the Place de la Concorde. A friend who works at the Crillon told me that Lourdes is an articulate and poised little girl who is wise beyond her years. Excited to be back in Paris, already an old haunt for a six-year-old who had made several visits there alone with her mother before they became a family of four, she announced that she wanted to return to the Louvre to see the *Mona Lisa* and to shop along the Faubourg St.-Honoré, where the summer sales had just begun. At ten months, it was Rocco's first trip, and as he was carried through the cavernous marble lobby by his father, according to my friend, he appeared to be a happy and complacent baby, smiling readily and oblivious to the curious crowds and hordes of paparazzi who had gathered to welcome his mother. Guy Ritchie also seemed to be taking all the chaos in his stride as he dutifully followed his petite wife to their $10,000-a-night suite. Several other staff members who were also waiting to welcome the group remarked that "Monsieur Madonna," as they called him, was completely consumed by his new role as father. Holding Rocco as they got off the elevator, he reached for Lourdes's hand to walk the long corridor that led to their corner suite. Observers had the distinct impression that there was an unspoken understanding between the couple, that while Madonna was proud and happy to have her family with her, her first priority was the show. She was all business. She questioned the staff about the double-paned windows, black-out shades, and the security guards who were on twenty-four-hour duty throughout the hotel. Above all, she wanted the management's assurance that she would be able to sleep without being disturbed by the noise in the street and that she was protected from overzealous fans who might try to penetrate the family's living quarters.

This tour was a pivotal moment in Madonna's career and there was no doubt that critics and fans were waiting to see how married life and motherhood had either inspired her to new heights of creativity or had tamed her once-unquenchable ambition to seduce the world. As it turned out, and as she has always done in the past, Madonna didn't disappoint them. She provided enough material so that her fans would remember—as if it were possible to forget—what had made her a star in the first place. And she even gave them a bit more. Typical of Madonna's innate talent to communicate with the millions who hang on her every word and gesture, she made us all understand that she had gone beyond what we might have expected of her, only to emerge as a consummate performer who could finally separate the private person from the public personality.

Ask two people their opinion of Madonna and you'll get five different answers. As the hour approached for her appearance on stage and with an absence of Madonna on the popular television and radio talk shows, on-air personalities began speculating on who was the real Madonna, encouraging debate from the audience. Some ardent fans addressed the issue of Madonna's sexuality, insisting that she is gay and that it is only her Catholicism that forces her to go through the motions of love affairs with men and her two forays into matrimony. Others argued that she is exactly as she presents herself to her public, an uninhibited and liberated woman who has always done what she pleased at the moment it pleased her, while the more cynical responded that her sexuality is less important than her determination and her extraordinary discipline that has allowed her to achieve the financial and professional success that she enjoys. A couple of fans observed that still, no one has ever seen a photograph of the wedding gown she wore on December 22, 2000, when she married Guy Ritchie at Skibo Castle in Scotland.

What struck me after I saw her show was that after twenty years in the public consciousness, with Madonna keeping her longings a well-guarded secret from her fans, and her true personality a mystery from the press, with this latest offensive on the international stage, she has finally provided, if not an answer, then at least a substantial clue as to who she is and what she values above everything else at this point in her life.

There is not one haphazard moment in the entire show. Drowned World, by omission, is the most autobiographical and revealing of all Madonna's performances, clean and clear in its meaning and message of who she is or perhaps who she wants us to believe she has become. And yet, several things haven't changed, specifically the anguish she harbors over her mother's death and the ambiguity she feels for her father. In one instance, a video clip portraying Madonna's face, rotting and bloody, her eyes rimmed in ghoulish black and red, reminiscent of a corpse, appeared behind her as she sang "Frozen." In another, a ditty she composed to the tune of "Davy Crockett," she talked about her daddy and cannibalism, after which she asked the audience rhetorically, "Who doesn't come from a dysfunctional family?"

The demons and phantoms may still be there but they have been tamed and controlled. She makes it clear that all she is willing to do now to keep our attention is to remind us, by video clips, subtle allusions of costume and dance, and a brief musical retrospective, why we turned her into a goddess in the first place. She expects us now more than ever before to be satisfied with Madonna, the consummate performer who is only willing to give us a show, our money's worth, the price of admission, one hour and forty minutes of energy, without having to make us believe that she is granting us access into the deepest recesses of her mind, or to make us privy to the innermost secrets of her sexual and emotional life.

Beginning with the dark sets that take Fritz Lang's *Metropolis* one step further into a sexually twisted subculture to the members of the chorus dressed in cutting-edge wet suits and gas masks, giving the impression of extraterrestrial insects, Madonna confirms her maturity, sophistication, and growth as she moves from the blatant to the subtle. In the past her appeal was in her ability to connect with her public, to draw them in by convincing them that her performance was a privileged glimpse into her private world. Today she gives us just the right amount of the sordid and the tawdry, with several *fuck you*s and a couple of *motherfuckers* thrown in for good measure. Even the sadomasochistic theme and allusions to religion are more subtle. Rather than focusing on the crucifix that has been her most familiar trademark prop, there are videos of born-again Christian babies being baptized in rural Southern American rivers, Indian rituals, and Hasidic Jews praying at the Wailing Wall. She assures us that her life is still fraught with cross-connections between pain and pleasure when several dancers swig from bottles and spit into the audience, or when naked dancers hang upside down from their heels, or when a scrawny girl dressed as a bug is squashed and choked by another dancer disguised as a larger insect, her legs and arms flailing in a macabre dance of death, or when Madonna herself is menaced by a Japanese wrestler wielding a sword over her head.

Sex remains a violent and capricious act to Madonna. And yet, somehow she projects a sense of objectivity and distance that forces us to realize that she is doing it only for *us*, rather than to satisfy her own prurient tastes. Madonna, the eclectic pop icon, has apparently settled her internal debate on God and the Church that raged within her for the first eighteen years of her career. When she dresses as a geisha, or as a superwoman, with sexually explicit cartoons projected on the screen behind her, as she kicks and jabs at hapless male and female dancers, or when we see her briefly in her "American Pie" T-shirt or hear several bars of "Don't Cry for Me Argentina" from her film *Evita*, she makes sure that we recall her previous works without actually bothering to perform them for us in their totality. She gives us every transition in her career in shorthand, acknowledging her search for an image that in the past was her guarantee to keep us interested, yet making it clear that after all these years, she has decided that changing images is no longer necessary to hold our attention. She is here to stay. She has made it. She is secure in our adulation. It is no longer imperative for her to work constantly, putting in twenty-hour days, seven days a week. Her career has been put into perspective and what she owes her fans has been redefined so that the performer has been surgically separated from the individual. Curiously, had she presented herself to the public as a mere artist when she first started out, giving only one hour and forty minutes of music and dance, sets, and costumes, she might never have endured. Even with this latest transformation, however, we are still part of her world. After all, she is allowing us in, inviting us to share in her nostalgia, to reminisce about her career, even if we are no longer crucial to her survival, no longer necessary to validate her existence, no longer required to function as the substitute mommies who give her unconditional love and approval. We should be happy for her. She has her children now and a new husband.

It is no coincidence that Madonna took an eight-year hiatus from the stage to tend to her personal life and even less coincidental that when she did return, she presented herself in an abbreviated version of all that she once was. The difference between Madonna today and Madonna yesterday is that she has created a distance between herself and her audience. With complete confidence, she has no doubt that this new technique will work because she gives her fans enormous credit. She counts on them to understand that she has earned that privilege of distance and repose. How can she err? This is a woman who survives and thrives on her instincts.

At the end of the show, on that June night in Paris in 2001, the house lights suddenly went dark and the stage bare. There were no bows or encores, no curtain calls or speeches. Madonna was gone but not forgotten. . . .

source notes

The abbreviation N/A stands for nonattributable. An asterisk denotes a pseudonym.

AUTHOR'S NOTE
Vanity Fair, March 1998.
Author's meeting with Madonna in Buenos Aires.
Author's interview with lapsed Catholic priest in L.A.
Author's N/A interview with friend of Madonna in New York.
Eva Perón's biography, *Razón de mi vida*.

PART ONE: DON'T CRY FOR ME ARGENTINA

Chapter One
Premiere magazine, September 1996.
Film Review, February 1997.
Vanity Fair, November 1996.
Daily Mail, November 1, 1995.

Chapter Two
Author's N/A interviews with government officials in Buenos Aires.
Vanity Fair, "Diaries," November 1996.
Author's N/A interviews in Buenos Aires.

Chapter Three
Author's N/A interview in Buenos Aires.
Author's interview with Marikena Monti.
Author's interview with Andres di Tella.
Author's N/A interview with José Camaro.*
Vanity Fair, "Diaries," November 1996.

Author's N/A interview with Consuela Stamos.*

Chapter Four
Vanity Fair, "Diaries," November 1996.
Author's interview with President Carlos Menem.
Author's N/A interview with entourage of President Menem.

PART TWO: WHO'S THAT GIRL?

Chapter Five
Author's N/A interview with Lionel Bishop.*
Bay City Times, August 8, 1987.
Author's interview in Bay City with Timothy Sullivan.
Author's N/A interviews with Bay City residents.

Chapter Six
Author's interview with Michelle Campau.
Author's interview with Elsie Fortin.
Bay City Times, November 29, 1984.
Author's interview with Tracey Horne.
Author's N/A interview with Bay City residents.
Author's interview with Roy "Jay" Crete.
Author's N/A interview with friends of Madonna Fortin Ciccone.

Chapter Seven
Mail on Sunday, January 3, 1988.
Unauthorized Madonna, Christopher Andersen, Signet, 1991.
Author's interview with Tony and Joan Ciccone in Sutters Bay Vineyard.
Time, May 27, 1985.
Author's interviews with Elsie Fortin, neighbors, and friends of Ciccone
    family in Bay City, Rochester Hills.
Author's N/A interviews with Fortin family.
Author's N/A interviews with relatives in Bay City.

Chapter Eight
Cosmopolitan, October 1985.
Unauthorized Madonna, Christopher Andersen, Signet, 1991.
Author's N/A interviews with Madonna's teachers.
Rolling Stone, Spring/Summer 1989.
Psychoanalysis of Children, Melanie Klein, The Free Press, 1984.

Chapter Nine
Psychoanalysis of Children, Melanie Klein, The Free Press, 1984.
Author's interview with Claude Delay Tubiana.
Author's interview with John Schlesinger.
"Confession of a Catholic Girl," Betsey Johnston, *Interview,* May 1989.
Author's interview with Rupert Everett.
Author's interview with Elsie Fortin.
Author's N/A interviews with guests at Sting's party.
Vanity Fair, April 1991.
Record, March 1985.
Author's N/A interviews with Fortin family.
Author's interview with Elsie Fortin.
Author's interview with Don Davis.
Don't Let Death Ruin Your Life, Jill Brook, Dutton, 2001.

Chapter Ten
Author's interview with Pat McPherson.
Author's N/A interview with former Ciccone neighbors in Pontiac and Bay
    City, Michigan.
Author's interview with Anita Harris.
Author's interview with Michelle Fine.
New York Times, March 3, 2001.
Show and Tell, John Lahr, Overlook Press, 2001.
Unauthorized Madonna, Christopher Andersen, Signet, 1991.
Madonna, Robert Mathew-Walker, Sidgwick & Jackson, 1989.
Psychoanalysis of Children, Melanie Klein, The Free Press, 1984.
OK Magazine, January 5, 2000.

Chapter Eleven
Truth or Dare (video).
Author's interview with Joan Ciccone.
Author's N/A interviews with Ciccone neighbors.
Interview, May 1989.
Author's N/A interviews with Ciccone neighbors and Ciccone siblings.
Bay City Times, April 3, 1998.

Chapter Twelve
Author's N/A interviews with Ciccone neighbors.
New York Post, December 2, 2000.
Unauthorized Madonna, Christopher Andersen, Signet, 1991.

The Advocate, February 15, 2000.
Author's N/A interviews with Ciccone neighbors.
Rolling Stone, June 13, 1991.
Author's N/A interview with teacher.
Author's N/A interview with Ciccone neighbors.

Chapter Thirteen
Unauthorized Madonna, Christopher Andersen, Signet, 1991.
Author's N/A interviews with Ciccone friends.
Author's N/A interview with a Ciccone sibling.
Author's N/A interview with Ciccone neighbors.
"Confession of a Catholic Girl," Betsey Johnston, *Interview,* May 1989.
The Sun, November 3, 1986.
Author's N/A interview with sister at St. Andrew's.

Chapter Fourteen
Author's interview with Mother Dolores, Mother Placid.
Author's interview with Father Gary Siebert.
Author's interview with Paul Gambacinni.

Chapter Fifteen
Author's N/A interviews with siblings and friends.
Madonna Companion, Allan Metz and Carol Benson, editors, Schirmer
    Books, 1999.
Time, May 25, 1985.
Author's interview with Cal Townsend.*
Author's N/A source with Madonna's friend and coworker.
Author's N/A interview with Kathy.*

Chapter Sixteen
Author's N/A with Kathy.*
Madonna in Her Own Words, Mich St. Michael, editor, Omnibus Press,
    1999.
Unauthorized Madonna, Christopher Andersen, Signet, 1991.

Chapter Seventeen
Author's interview with Pearl Lang.
Unauthorized Madonna, Christopher Andersen, Signet, 1991.
Cosmopolitan, July 1987.

PART THREE: LUCKY STAR

Chapter Eighteen
Author interview with Norris Burroughs.

Chapter Nineteen
Unauthorized Madonna, Christopher Andersen, Signet, 1991.
USA Today, July 9, 1985.
Daily News, July 10, 1985.
Daily News, July 9, 1985.
Penthouse, September 1987.
Rolling Stone, September 10, 1987.
New York Post, March 30, 1985.
Madonna in Her Own Words, Mich St. Michael, editor, Omnibus Press,
    1999.
Author's N/A interview with Kitty Romano.*
Vanity Fair, October 1992.
Empire Magazine, 1990.

Chapter Twenty
Author's interview with Norris Burroughs.
Author's interview with Patrick Hernandez.
Author's interview with Muriel Van Lieu.

Chapter Twenty-one
Author's interview with Patrick Hernandez and Muriel Van Lieu.
Author's interview with Pierre Trenet.

Chapter Twenty-two
Author's N/A interview with Madonna relatives.
Unauthorized Madonna, Christopher Andersen, Signet, 1991.
Madonna, Robert Mathew-Walker, Sidgwick & Jackson, 1989.
Author's interview with Adam Alter.

Chapter Twenty-three
Author's interview with Adam Alter.
The Sun, July 14, 1988.
Daily News Magazine, September 29, 1985.
Daily Mirror, January 19, 1989.

Sunday Mirror, February 11, 2001.

Chapter Twenty-four
Author's interview with Adam Alter.
Spin, May 1985.
Record, March 1985.

PART FOUR: MATERIAL GIRL

Chapter Twenty-five
Author's interview with Cis Coreman.
Cosmopolitan, September 1987.
Madonna, Robert Mathew-Walker, Sidgwick & Jackson, 1989.
Cosmopolitan, September 1987.
Unauthorized Madonna, Christopher Andersen, Signet, 1991.

Chapter Twenty-six
Madonna, Robert Mathew-Walker, Sidgwick & Jackson, 1989.
Unauthorized Madonna, Christopher Andersen, Signet, 1991.
Author's N/A interview with a wedding guest.
Author's N/A interview with friend.

Chapter Twenty-seven
Author's interview with Paul Freeman.
USA Today, March 7, 1986.
People, December 14, 1987.

Chapter Twenty-eight
American Film, July 1987.
Author's interview with Claude Chirac.
Interview, December 1985.
Daily News, April 24, 1988.
Harper's Bazaar, May 1988.
"Confession of a Catholic Girl," Betsey Johnston, *Interview,* May 1989.

Chapter Twenty-nine
People, December 14, 1987.
Unauthorized Madonna, Christopher Andersen, Signet, 1991.
Rolling Stone, March 23, 1989.
"Confession of a Catholic Girl," Betsey Johnston, *Interview,* May 1989.

Today, June 11, 1990.
Daily Mail, May 21, 1991.
Mail on Sunday, June 14, 1992.
Author's interview with Paul Gambacinni.
Daily Mail, December 15, 1992.

PART FIVE: BLOND AMBITION

Chapter Thirty
Eye, October/November 1996.
Vanity Fair, "Diaries," November 1996.
Author's interview with Dan Cortesi.
The Guardian, May 17, 1996.
Vanity Fair, March 1998.
Vanity Fair, April 1991.
Daily Mail, May 13, 1993.
Author's interview with Raoul Felder
Madonna: The Style Book, Debbi Voller, Chris Charlesworth, editor, Omnibus Press, 1999.
Daily News, February 5, 2000.
Film Review, February 1997.

Chapter Thirty-one
Author's interview with John Schlesinger.
Sunday Mirror, February 11, 2000.

Chapter Thirty-two
Author's N/A interviews with friends of Lady Amber Leighton, Guy Ritchie, John Ritchie, and Madonna, as well as friends of Sting and Trudie Styler.
The Globe, January 2, 2001.
OK Magazine, January 5, 2000.

Chapter Thirty-three
The Star, June 27, 2000.
The Globe, May 16, 2000.
Author's N/A interview with several guests.
The National Enquirer, May 16, 2000.
Author's N/A interviews with friends of Leighton and Ritchie families.
The Toronto Sun, August 25, 2000.

Chapter Thirty-four
Author's N/A interviews in London and New York.
OK Magazine, January 5, 2000.
Daily Standard, December 14, 2000.

Chapter Thirty-five
Daily News, "Showtime," February 27, 2000.

index